ALTRUISM AND REALITY

Studies in the Philosophy of the Bodhicaryāvatāra

CURZON CRITICAL STUDIES
IN BUDDHISM

General Editors:

The Curzon Critical Studies in Buddhism Series is a comprehensive study of the Buddhist tradition. The series explores this complex and extensive tradition from a variety of perspectives, using a range of different methodologies.

The Series is diverse in its focus, including historical studies, textual translations and commentaries, sociological investigations, bibliographic studies, and considerations of religious practice as an expression of Buddhism's integral religiosity. It also presents materials on modern intellectual historical studies, including the role of Buddhist thought and scholarship in a contemporary, critical context and in the light of current social issues. The series is expansive and imaginative in scope, spanning more than two and a half millennia of Buddhist history. It is receptive to all research works that inform and advance our knowledge and understanding of the Buddhist tradition. The series maintains the highest standards of scholarship and promotes the application of innovative methodologies and research methods.

THE REFLEXIVE NATURE OF AWARENESS
A Tibetan Madhyamaka Defence
Paul Williams

BUDDHISM AND HUMAN RIGHTS
Edited by Damien Keown, Charles Prebish, Wayne Husted

WOMEN IN THE FOOTSTEPS OF THE BUDDHA
Struggle for Liberation in the Therigatha
Kathryn R. Blackstone

ALTRUISM AND REALITY

Studies in the Philosophy of the Bodhicaryāvatāra

Paul Williams

Routledge
Taylor & Francis Group
LONDON AND NEW YORK

First Published in 1998
by Routledge

Published 2014 by Routledge

2 Park Square, Milton Park, Abingdon, Oxfordshire OX14 4RN

711 Third Avenue, New York, NY 10017

First issued in paperback 2014

Routledge is an imprint of the Taylor & Francis Group, an informa business

British Library Cataloguing in Publication Data
A catalogue record of this book is available from the British Library

Library of Congress Cataloguing in Publication Data
A catalog record for this book has been requested

ISBN 978-0-700-71031-7 (hbk)
ISBN 978-1-138-87887-7 (pbk)

For Richard Gombrich,
with gratitude and affection

Contents

Preface

This book consists of five essays on aspects of the philosophy of the eighth century Indian Buddhist thinker, spiritual practitioner, and poet Śāntideva. As far as I recall they were all written between 1990 and 1996, and three of the essays have been published elsewhere. Somewhat over half the material is new, at least in the form in which it appears here. These essays are independent studies, and no attempt has been made to bring them into line with each other in style, approach, translation or content. I wanted to reprint together the three essays (1–3) which have appeared before in a form which is more or less unchanged from their previous and perhaps inaccessible published versions. Occasionally, however, I have had some second thoughts which I have inserted into footnotes and indicated at the relevant points. Alongside the present collection and very much part of the same series is my monograph *The Reflexive Nature of Awareness* (*Rang Rig*), which will appear with Curzon Press in 1997. That book originally started as a further paper for the present volume, and stands in the series printed here between papers 4 and 5. It was written in 1994, and occasioned the second thoughts indicated in footnotes with references to that year. The present papers are given I think in the order in which they were written.

My interest in the *Bodhicaryāvatāra* reflected in these studies has two principal concerns. The first is the sheer range of interpretations, shifting patterns of interpretation, and integration of interpretations into a wider systematic doctrinal and practical framework found among Indian and particularly Tibetan commentators. I have long been interested in what happened when Indian Madhyamaka ideas reached Tibet and were presented in a different milieu and language, and also in the best way to approach the extensive Tibetan Madhyamaka material, given that it is not possible at the moment even for a team of scholars to read all the available material and come up with anything like an overall understanding of the history of Tibetan Madhyamaka. A good deal of study has taken place on certain dGe lugs interpretations, but rather less on the approaches of other Tibetan traditions and very little indeed on the historical development within and between traditions. The problem is that without a wider understanding of doctrinal differences and developments it becomes difficult to appreciate very precisely the specific aspects. Still, in the short term, I decided that there might be some value in turning attention from a range of textual material found within one tradition, perhaps at one phase in its development, towards looking at some very specific material – individual verses from just one text, chosen for their appeal and interest to me, and perhaps also their neglect – in the light of a wide range of Indian and Tibetan commentaries from all the major traditions and from different historical periods. I chose the *Bodhicaryāvatāra* because I like it, and because along with all the commentaries in the bsTan 'gyur – many more than on the *Madhyamakāvatāra*, for example – I also had a number of Tibetan commentaries which fitted my requirements, from all the major schools.

One result of this approach has been to highlight the range of Tibetan interpretations of even one verse, with very little evidence indeed for clear lineages of interpretation going back to Indian sources, and also the astonishing innovative inventiveness of dGe lugs commentators like Tsong kha pa and rGyal tshab rje who, in subordinating the text to their overall innovative system-building, also sometimes showed philosophical good sense. But then sometimes they did not. One corollary of all of this is to underline the problems involved in any translation or interpretation of an Indian text with reference to (in this instance) a dGe lugs commentary in isolation. It should be obvious that such a translation gives nothing more than (and nothing less than) a dGe lugs interpretation, and like all interpretations dGe lugs interpretations are often at variance with those of others, Indian and Tibetan.

My interest in these essays therefore, and in the *Rang rig* book, has been in the doctrinal interpretation of the commentaries. I have not been concerned with textual questions of whether Śāntideva actually was or was not the author of a verse which interested me.[1] The commentators thought he was, and that has been enough for my purposes here. My other concern has been with critical philosophical analysis. This interest will be found reflected mainly in the two papers on the development of altruism in *Bodhicaryāvatāra* Ch. 8 (papers 2 and 5), particularly in the last paper. It seems clear to me that Śāntideva is here offering us arguments which are intended to lead to certain conclusions, and I have been concerned with what those arguments are, and whether they will work or not. In this approach I believe I take seriously Śāntideva's invitation to us to engage with him in the meditation. Readers may notice, I think, that my philosophical interests in the last and most recent essay have really taken over from my concerns with the range of Indian and Tibetan commentarial interpretations, and in unravelling Śāntideva's argument and its presuppositions here I have found myself engaging critically and at length with a number of central issues in Buddhist philosophy, particularly the position of no independent and unchanging Self as the stable monadic referent for the indexical 'I'.

In studies written years apart there should not be expected necessary consistency. During the period I have been writing these essays I have found my philosophical interests and understanding undergoing some revision and evolution.[2] I do not know if change is an intrinsic good, but for the moment I am happy to keep exploring and to keep changing.

Paul Williams
Centre for Buddhist Studies
University of Bristol

Acknowledgements

I am grateful to the following for permission to reprint papers in this collection:

Peter Lang AG Verlag, Bern: 'On *prakṛtinirvāṇa/prakṛtinirvṛta* in the *Bodhicaryāvatāra*: A study in the Indo-Tibetan commentarial tradition', *Asiatische Studien/Études Asiatiques* 1992, XLVI:I: 516–550.

Tadeusz Skorupski, Ulrich Pagel, and the School of Oriental and African Studies, University of London: 'On altruism and rebirth: philosophical comments on *Bodhicaryāvatāra* 8:97–8', Tadeusz Skorupski and Ulrich Pagel ed., 1994. *The Buddhist Forum Volume 3: Papers in honour and appreciation of Professor David Seyfort Ruegg's contribution to Indological, Buddhist and Tibetan Studies.* School of Oriental and African Studies, University of London. 307–32.

Per Kvaerne: 'An argument for cittamātra: reflections on *Bodhicaryāvatāra* 9:28 (Tib. 27) cd', Per Kvaerne ed., 1994. *Tibetan Studies: Proceedings of the Sixth Conference of the International Association for Tibetan Studies.* Oslo: Instituttet for Sammenlignende Kulturforskning. 965–80.

In addition, a short version of paper 4 can be found in: 'Identifying the object of negation: on *Bodhicaryāvatāra* 9:140 (Tib. 139)', *Asiatische Studien/Études Asiatiques* 1995, XLIX 4, 969–85; and a short version of paper 5 will appear in a Felicitation Volume for Professor G.M. Bongard-Levin, to be published in India by Ajanta Publishing.

It gives me very great pleasure indeed to dedicate this collection to my friend Richard Gombrich. It is mere coincidence that 1997 will mark twenty-five years of our acquaintance, but a fortuitous coincidence nevertheless and a chance for me to express publicly my appreciation of his challenging, sharp, witty scholarship and presence, and his unstinting generosity and kindness.

One

On *Prakṛtinirvāṇa/Prakṛtinirvṛta* in the *Bodhicaryāvatāra*

A Study in the Indo-Tibetan Commentarial Tradition

According to Tsong kha pa, writing in his early *Legs bshad gser phreng* commentary to the *Abhisamayālaṃkāra*, in general texts speak of four types of *nirvāṇa*: the *prakṛti* or 'natural' *nirvāṇa*, the nonabiding (*apratiṣṭhita*) *nirvāṇa* of bodhisattvas and Buddhas, and the *nirvāṇas* with and without remainders familiar – although not necessarily with the same meaning – from both Mahāyāna and non-Mahāyāna Buddhism. The first of these, the *prakṛtinirvāṇa* (*rang bzhin gyis mya ngan las 'das*) is defined by Tsong kha pa as 'the nature of *dharmas* which is free from extremes of verbal differentiation'.[1] It is clear therefore that for Tsong kha pa the *prakṛtinirvāṇa* is a type of *nirvāṇa*, although why it should be called this remains to be seen. It is a *rang bzhin*, a (fundamental) nature, the nature of *dharmas*. The Tibetan *rang bzhin* translates *prakṛti* here, but of course it is more familiar as the Tibetan translation for *svabhāva*, inherent existence. The equivalence of *prakṛti* and *svabhāva* in the expressions *prakṛtinirvāṇa* and *prakṛtinirvṛta* is attested from Sanskrit sources. Prajñākaramati, commenting on *Bodhicaryāvatāra* 9:104cd (=Tib. 103cd) glosses the verse's *prakṛtyā parinivṛtāḥ* with *prakṛtyā svabhāvena parinirvṛtāḥ*. Interestingly, the Tibetan here uses only one expression, unusually in this context *rang gi ngo bo nyid kyis mya ngan las 'das pa*. *Rang bzhin* had been used for *prakṛtyā* in the verse, so the use of *rang gi ngo bo nyid* in the commentary preserves some sort of distinction although it lacks the clarity of the Sanskrit. For Prajñākaramati the equivalence of *prakṛtyā* or *svabhāvena parinirvṛta* with *prakṛtinirvāṇa* is attested from his subsequent comment – enormously important from the point of view of Tsong kha pa and the dGe lugs interpretation – that living beings have the nature of liberation 'because of the continued existence in the continuums of all sentient beings of the *prakṛtinirvāṇa* which is defined as absence of inherent existence'. This time the Tibetan for *prakṛtinirvāṇa* is the usual *rang bzhin gyis mya ngan las 'das pa.*[2] Much earlier the *Samādhirājasūtra* had spoken of all *dharmas* by nature (*svabhāvena*) conforming to an identity with *nirvāṇa*, 'in all *dharmas nirvāṇa* is set forth'.[3] The idea that all *dharmas* are by nature 'nirvanated' is of course familiar from the *Prajñāpāramitāsūtras* and works in the same genre. It is clear that for Tsong kha pa, presumably following Prajñākaramati, the *prakṛtinirvāṇa* is another name for emptiness found in all *dharmas* without exception but particularly with reference to the mental continuum of sentient beings. It is the *nirvāṇa* which is the *rang bzhin* of *dharmas*. For a Tibetan there immediately resonates two references here. The *prakṛtinirvāṇa* as an unchanging nature within the continuum of sentient beings, a *nirvāṇa*, carries with it a flavour of the *tathāgatagarbha* theory found in the *Ratnagotravibhāga*. The *prakṛtinirvāṇa* as a nature, a *rang bzhin*, in *dharmas* indicates Candrakīrti's *Madhyamakavāvatārabhāṣya* on 6:181–2 in which Candrakīrti talks about the true nature of things, the *dharmatā* which is the same whether Buddhas occur or not, the true *rang bzhin*, *svabhāva*, of entities which is their emptiness of any *svabhāva*.[4] In dGe lugs thought these two frames of reference come very firmly together. The *prakṛtinirvāṇa* is emptiness, which applies to all *dharmas*. In the mental continuum of sentient beings this emptiness is called the *tathāgatagarbha*, and with it goes other terms perhaps originally not thought of in this vein in the Madhyamaka context of the *Bodhicaryāvatāra* such as 'purified by nature' (*prakṛtipariśuddha*) and 'radiant by nature' (*prakṛtiprabhāsvara*).[5] In Tibetan almost invariably the standard word for *nirvāṇa* – *mya ngan las 'das*, the transcendence of sorrow – is used for *prakṛtinirvāṇa* and *prakṛtinirvṛta*. If all *dharmas* are fundamentally or by nature *nirvṛta*, in Tibetan they have by nature transcended sorrow. There is a psychological and soteriological aspect implicit in the language used which draws together the two dimensions of emptiness and *tathāgatagarbha* in a much stronger way than is necessarily the case with the Sanskrit. In spite of the apparent identity of *prakṛtinirvṛta* and *prakṛtinirvāṇa* for Prajñākaramati, it is the former term which is used more often than not in Sanskrit texts, with its implications of 'by nature, fundamentally, from the point of view of inherent existence, extinguished', that is, empty. As the *sūtras* say, this is the nature of things whether there are Buddhas or not. It does not necessarily carry with it the direct psychological and soteriological overtones of '*nirvāṇa*'. And if we look at the use of these notions in the commentaries to the *Bodhicaryāvatāra* it is striking that there is no employment of what might be called '*tathāgatagarbha* concepts' in Indian commentaries on the relevant verses. These are, however, abundant in Tibetan commentaries, where the notion of the *prakṛtinirvāṇa/prakṛtinirvṛta* – and thus also the *Bodhicaryāvatāra* – become absorbed into the nexus of *tathāgatagarbha* thought.

The concepts of *prakṛtinirvāṇa* and *prakṛtinirvṛta*, and their relationships to the *tathāgatagarbha*, have been dealt with in his usual thorough and lucid way by David Seyfort Ruegg in his monumental *La Théorie du Tathāgatagarbha et du Gotra*. Ruegg has noted some of the relevant verses from the *Bodhicaryāvatāra*, together with Prajñākaramati's commentary. In addition he has particularly devoted some space to a discussion of the *prakṛtinirvāṇa* and the *prakṛtiprabhāsvara* nature of *citta* found in the work of the eighteenth-nineteenth century Tibetan lama Gung thang 'Jam pa'i dbyangs. In common with late dGe lugs writings, Gung thang lama's work is a culmination of much that had gone before and is replete with subtle definitions and distinctions. As I have pointed out elsewhere, however, the contemporary study of Tibetan Madhyamaka is rather like shining a narrow beam at various points in a dark attic.[6] We cannot see the whole picture, we do not yet know much about relationships and rivalries involved, the development of ideas, alternative interpretations of the same text and how these relate to their Indian precedents. In spite of the pioneering work by scholars like David Seyfort Ruegg, we cannot yet write a history of Tibetan Madhyamaka. Ruegg has approached the issue of the *prakṛtinirvāṇa* in Tibet largely through reference to dGe lugs materials. By way of a footnote to his study I would like to take just four verses of the *Bodhicaryāvatāra* which their commentators deem to be particularly relevant to our issue, and see what of interest for understanding the development of Madhyamaka can be derived from looking at a wider range of Indo-Tibetan commentaries.

1 Indian commentaries

a) Śāntideva seems to have lived during the early eighth century. His earliest commentator appears to be Prajñākaramati, who wrote the *Bodhicaryāvatārapañjikā*, which survives in Sanskrit, and was apparently written towards the end of the tenth century.[7] The Cone edition of the Tibetan text can be found in mDo 26, folio 39a ff. (abbreviated as *Praj.*).

b) The *Bodhisattvacaryāvatārasaṃskāra*, by someone whose name was probably Kalyāṇadeva, was composed perhaps in the early eleventh century. The Tibetan alone survives, as with the other commentaries apart from that by Prajñākaramati. It can be found at Cone mDo 27, folio 1 ff. (abbreviated as *Kaly.*).
c) Vairocanarakṣita lived at the same time as Atiśa, and was a monk at the great monastery of Vikramaśīla. His *Bodhisattvacaryāvatārapañjikā*, written in the eleventh century, is at Cone mDo 27, folio 95b ff. (abbreviated as *Vair.*).
d) The *Bodhicaryāvatāratātparyapañjikā Viśeṣadyotanī* was written by Vibhūticandra, from the monastery of Jagaddala, in about 1200. He accompanied Śākyaśrībhadra to Tibet in 1204. The text is Cone mDo 27, folio 192b ff. (abbreviated as *Vibh.*).
e) Finally there is an anonymous commentary to chapters 9 and 10 of the *Bodhicaryāvatāra*, the *Vivṛti*, mDo 27, folio 177b ff. (abbreviated as *Anon.*).

All these commentaries were found to be of interest in looking at the relevant verses from the *Bodhicaryāvatāra*. Others listed in the bsTan 'gyur were not.

2 Tibetan commentaries

a) *Byang chub sems dpa'i spyod pa la 'jug pa'i 'grel pa Legs par bshad pa'i rgya mtsho*, by rGyal sras dNgul chu Thogs med. Twelfth century (abbreviated as *Thogs.* – 1994 note: I have now changed my understanding of the date of this text. See 'An Argument for Cittamātra', note 15).
b) *Byang chub sems dpa'i spyod pa la 'jug pa'i 'grel pa*, by bSod nams rtse mo (1142–82), the second Sa skya hierarch (abbreviated as *bSod.*). According to David Jackson (1985), pp. 22–3 bSod nams rtse mo followed in this commentary Phywa pa Chos kyi seng ge (1109–69) who is known to have been hostile to the Prāsaṅgika approach. The commentary also includes quoted material from rNgog lo tsa ba bLo ldan shes rab (1059–1109).
c) *Byang chub sems dpa'i spyod pa la 'jug pa'i 'grel pa Byang chub kyi sems gsal bar byed pa zla ba'i 'od zer*, by Bu ston Rin chen grub (1290–1364, abbreviated as *Bu.*).
d) *Byang chub sems dpa'i spyod pa la 'jug pa'i rnam bshad gZhung don rab gsal snang ba*, by Sa bzang mati paṇchen 'Jam dbyangs blo gros. Fourteenth century (abbreviated as *Sabzang.*). I do not

know whether this Sa skya pa lama is the same as Sa bzang mati rin chen, who was a pupil of Dol po pa Shes rab rgyal mtshan (1290–1361). The dates are possible, and some of Sa bzang mati paṇchen's comments do suggest a possible *gzhan stong* orientation in his interpretation of Madhyamaka, as we shall see.

e) *Spyod 'jug shes rab le'u'i ṭikkā bLo gsal ba*, rJe Tsong kha pa's (1357–1419) brief commentary on the ninth chapter of the *Bodhicaryāvatāra* (abreviated as *Tsong.*).
f) *Byang chub sems dpa'i spyod pa la 'jug pa'i rnam bshad rGyal sras 'jug ngogs*, by Tsong kha pa's pupil, rGyal tshab rje Dar ma rin chen (1364–1462, abreviated as *rGyal.*).
g) *Byang chub sems dpa'i spyod 'jug rnam bshad Theg chen chos kyi rgya mtsho zab rgyas mtha' yas snying po*, by the great historian dPa' bo gTsug lag phreng ba (d. mid-sixteenth century), a Karma bKa' brgyud scholar and pupil of the eighth Karma pa, Mi bskyod rdo rje. An enormous, rambling commentary (abbreviated as *dPa'.*).
h) *Spyod 'jug gi 'bru 'grel dBu ma'i lam gyi sgron ma*, by the 'Brug pa bKa' brgyud lama Padma dkar po (1527–92, abbreviated as *Padma.*).
i) *Spyod 'jug shes rab kyi le'u'i tshig don go sla bar rnam par bshad pa Nor bu ke ta ka*, by the rNying ma lama 'Jam mgon 'ju Mi pham rgya mtsho (1846–1912, abbreviated as *Mipham.*). This commentary to the *Prajñā* chapter of the *Bodhicaryāvatāra* initiated a fierce written controversy with certain dGe lugs lamas the sources for which survive and would form an interesting and valuable field for further research.[8]

BODHICARYĀVATĀRA 9:13 (=TIB. 13CD/14AB) (AB)

nirvṛtaḥ paramārthena saṃvṛtyā yadi saṃsaret /
[buddho'pi saṃsared evaṃ tataḥ kiṃ bodhicaryayā //]

gal te don dam mya ngan 'das /
'khor ba kun rdzob de lta na /
[sangs rgyas kyang ni 'khor 'gyur bas /
byang chub spyod pas ci zhig bya //]

If from an ultimate point of view there is cessation, from a conventional point of view there would be *saṃsāra* /[8b]
[Then the Buddha too would be in *saṃsāra*. Because of this, what is the point of conduct towards enlightenment? //]

Kalyāṇadeva alone of our commentators gives us a canonical reference. It is said in the *Prajñāpāramitā(sūtras)* that ultimately all *dharmas* are *mya ngan 'das* – here, to parallel the verse, *nirvṛta*, ceased or extinguished (f.69b). The opponent argues against the Mādhyamika that it follows that a Buddha is in *saṃsāra* and the religious life is useless. One interpretation of this is that the opponent confuses *nirvṛta*, ceased, which applies to all *dharmas* from an ultimate point of view precisely because 'from an ultimate point of view' refers to a hypothetical inherent existence which simply does not exist – that is, from an ultimate point of view there is emptiness of inherent existence – with *nirvāṇa*, the attainment of enlightenment by (in this case) a Buddha. Thus for the opponent all are already enlightened (a view held consciously, of course, sometimes in a very strong sense, by some Tibetan and East Asian traditions influenced by the *tathāgatagarbha*). Since all are already enlightened there is no difference between a Buddha and others. Interestingly, the conclusion then is not that others can act like Buddhas – they patently cannot – but that Buddhas are in *saṃsāra*. Such an interpretation of the opponent's position and its confusion is broadly correct, but it has no *consistent* linguistic basis in the Indian tradition, however, since *nirvṛta* and *nirvāṇa*, as we have seen, are sometimes used as equivalents. In Tibetan the distinction is not made at all. Nevertheless the binary opposition between innate cessation and enlightenment does underly the opponent's confusion and the Mādhyamika reply. On a deeper level, however, the real problem behind the opponent's objection here is an identification of *paramārtha* and *nirvāṇa* on the one hand, opposed to *saṃvṛti* and *saṃsāra* on the other. There is a tendency sometimes (not the least in works on Christian-Buddhist dialogue) to think that the word for the ultimate way of things in Buddhism is *nirvāṇa*. Generally this is false, but there is some basis for it in Mādhyamika writings. Nāgārjuna states in his *Yuktiṣaṣṭikā* v.35 that the Buddhas have proclaimed *nirvāṇa* as the sole truth. Āryadeva declares that *nirvāṇa* is emptiness (*Catuḥśataka* 12.23). If *nirvāṇa*=-*paramārthasatya*=*śūnyatā* then since *nirvāṇa* and *paramārthasatya* are in mutually exhaustive and exclusive opposition to *saṃsāra* and *saṃvṛtisatya* respectively it follows that all *saṃvṛtisatya* is *saṃsāra*. Since the Buddha, Śākyamuni as a historical figure, is not identical with *paramārthasatya* – while empty of inherent existence he is not emptiness itself – the Buddha must thus be included under *saṃsāra*. And if the Buddha is in *saṃsāra* then what chance is there for the rest of us! The false identities of *paramārtha*::*saṃvṛti* and *nirvāṇa*::*saṃsāra* implied by the opponent in *Bodhicaryāvatāra* 9:13 are more easily drawn from the Tibetan text which is less straightforward here in its grammatical relationships than the Sanskrit.[8c] It can easily be read as saying that 'If *paramārtha* is *nirvāṇa*, *saṃsāra* is *saṃvṛti*.' This is indeed how it is read by bSod nams rtse mo: 'If the ultimate is *nirvāṇa*, and if *saṃsāra* is the verbal differentiations (*spros pa*) of the conventional . . .' (*gal te don dam pa ni mya ngan las 'das pa yin na 'khor ba ni kun rdzob kyi spros pa yin na . . . : bSod.* p.495:4).

Clearly the opponent has confused an innate cessation (or enlightenment) which applies to all *dharmas* – their emptiness – with *nirvāṇa* as an event in time, the *nirvāṇa* which follows from cultivating the path. In the attainment of this *nirvāṇa* there is a difference between Buddhas and unenlightened sentient beings. Since the Tibetan makes no distinction between *nirvṛta* and *nirvāṇa* the issue of ultimately all being already enlightened – having transcended sorrow – is more glaring in Tibetan. It is not surprising, therefore, that in glossing this verse all our Tibetan commentators apart from dPa' bo gTsug lag phreng ba introduce the concept of the *prakṛtinirvāṇa/ prakṛtinirvṛta* by name. Only Prajñākaramati and Vairocana among the Indians mention it, however, indicating possibly that the expression *don dam mya ngan 'das* – ultimate enlightenment – suggested more immediately to Tibetans the *tathāgatagarbha* which, as we shall see, tended in Tibet to be identified with at least one of the dimensions of the *prakṛtinirvāṇa*. Thus the slide from *don dam mya ngan 'das* to *rang bzhin gyis mya ngan 'das*, a fairly obvious move anyway, was perhaps even more obvious in the Tibetan context. There is no direct association in Indian Prāsaṅgika Madhaymaka texts as far as I know of *prakṛtinirvāṇa/prakṛtinirvṛta* with the *tathāgatagarbha*. It is in commenting on the first part of the verse that the concept of *prakṛtinirvāṇa/-nirvṛta* is introduced, thus underlining the fact that *nirvṛtaḥ paramārthena=prakṛtinirvṛtaḥ*, but rather begging the question on the ultimate answer to the opponent's objection.

Prajñākaramati glosses the word *nirvṛtaḥ* in *Bodhicaryāvatāra* 9:13ab with *svabhāvaśūnyatvād utpādanirodharahitaḥ* – because of emptiness of inherent existence there is freedom from birth and cessation (the Tibetan adds 'etc.'). He explains that *paramārthena= paramārthasatyataḥ*. He then substitutes for *nirvṛtaḥ paramārthena* the expression *prakṛtinirvāṇatayā*. Why is there *prakṛtinirvāṇatā*? *Ādiśāntatvāt* – because of primeval calmness, calmness from the beginning. Translating from the Tibetan: '"*Nirvāṇa*" – because it is empty of inherent existence (or 'inherently empty') there is freedom from birth, cessation etc. "Ultimately" is ultimate truth. "Inherently *nirvāṇa*" – because calm from the very beginning.'[9] The Tibetan *rang bzhin gyis stong pa* parallels *rang bzhin gyis mya ngan las 'das*. It is *nirvāṇa* because it is inherently empty; it is inherently *nirvāṇa* because it is calm from the beginning. Clearly it is *nirvṛta* – ceased – because it is empty. But *because* it is empty it is free of birth and cessation – birth and death (the same point is made by Vibhūticandra (f. 261a)). Freedom from birth and death is, of course, for Buddhism from its origins, *nirvāṇa*. Here, I suggest, lies the easy substitution seen in Prajñākaramati of *nirvāṇa* for *nirvṛta*. It is *nirvāṇa* because it is free from birth and death.[10] And, Prajñākaramati adds, it is *prakṛtinirvāṇa* because of calmness from the beginning. Calmness is of course another old image for *nirvāṇa*. Nāgārjuna speaks of *prapañcopaśama*, the calming of verbal differentiations, and Candrakīrti in his *Prasannapadā* commentary to *Madhyamakakārikā* 25:24 explains *nirvāṇa* from a Madhyamaka point of view using as equivalents terms like *upaśama, śānta* and *upaśānta*. *Nirvāṇa* is the complete calming of all verbal differentiations and distinguishing signs.[11] For Prajñākaramati, therefore, the expression *prakṛti* in *prakṛtinirvāṇatayā* is glossed by the *ādi* in *ādiśāntatvāt*. Things are calm from the beginning because they are fundamentally *nirvāṇa*. The notion of *prakṛti* carries with it the idea of not being adventitiously the case but rather fundamentally, always, in the order of things.[12]

Let us turn now to some of our Tibetan commentaries to *Bodhicaryāvatāra* 9:13ab. The distinction between innate 'enlightenment' and that attained through following the path means that the *prakṛtinirvāṇa* is almost universally employed in Tibet to explain the opponent's objection and its solution. And unlike all the Indian commentaries we have looked at *rang bzhin mya ngan 'das* in our Tibetan commentaries is from the earliest textual material available on the *Bodhicaryāvatāra* used along with such terms as *rang bzhin rnam par dag pa*, fundamental or natural purity (*prakṛtiviśuddhi*), a term known in particular from the tradition of the *Ratnagotravibhāga*, where it refers to a characteristic of the *tathāgatagarbha* on both the level of cause and of fruition, and is contrasted with the *vaimalyaviśuddhi*, the purity from all adventitious taints which characterises what is usually known as *nirvāṇa*. The *prakṛtiviśuddhi* is a sort of primeval 'liberation' which is not disjoined from the the fundamental nature of the mind, which is radiant (clear-light), and is not the result of disconnection from adventitious taints. It is always there, the fundamental purity of the mind which enables us to say that there is a sense in which the mind is always enlightened.[13] The connection of this *tathāgatagarbha* concept with the *prakṛtinirvāṇa* appears obvious, but it appears not to have been made in Indian Prāsaṅgika Madhyamaka, and it brings into the notion of emptiness, even the emptiness of the mental continuum referred to by Prajñākaramati, mentalistic conceptions such as the clear-light nature of the mind which were not present at this point in the original Prāsaṅgika Madhyamaka *Bodhicaryāvatāra* frame of reference. The flavour of the *prakṛtinirvāṇa* is prone to become in Tibet more psychological and less (anti)ontological, more to do with the mind (it is after all *mya ngan 'das*, transcendence of sorrow) and less to do with emptiness.

The earliest Tibetan commentarial material on the *Bodhicaryāvatāra* I have access to are the quotations from rNgog bLo ldan shes rab contained in *bSod.*[14] rNgog was a pupil of Sajjana, the author of the only Indian sub-commentary to the *Ratnagotravibhāga* (See *La Théorie,* p.35), and rNgog lo tsa ba was one of the most important early transmitters of the *Ratnagotra* to Tibet. Commenting on *BCA* 9:13ab rNgog speaks of 'that ultimate *dharmatā* of one's own mind' as the *prakṛtinirvāṇa* (*rang gi sems kyi chos nyid don dam pa de rang bzhin gyis mya ngan las 'das pa yin*). This, of course, is perfectly compatible with the comments by Prajñākaramati, but rNgog goes on to speak of *saṃsāra* and natural purity being without distinction (*'khor ba dang rang bzhin rnam par dag pa'i cha nas khyad med pa'i phyir ro*: *bSod*. p.495:3). From the ultimate point of view, which is to say from the perspective of *prakṛtinirvāṇa* which here equals *prakṛtiviśuddhi*, there is no distinction. It is clear that rNgog is thinking in *Ratnagotravibhāga* terminology. Whether that is compatible with Prāsaṅgika Madhyamaka as an interpretation of the *Bodhicaryāvatāra* depends on how rNgog interprets the *tathāgatagarbha* doctrine of the *Ratnagotravibhāga*, and its relationships to the Madhyamaka conception of emptiness. Leonard van der Kuijp, in his *Contributions to the Development of Tibetan Buddhist Epistemology* (p.43), has pointed out that for the later lama Shākya mchog ldan (1428–1507) a stress on the *prakṛtiviśuddhi* is indeed a characteristic of rNgog's interpretation of the *Ratnagotravibhāga*, but this *prakṛtiviśuddhi*, as with the later dGe lugs pa, is apparently just another name for absence of inherent existence, emptiness. Some other Tibetan writers, however, associated rNgog with the origins of *gzhan stong* absolutism (*ibid*., p.41). It seems that we can see in rNgog's comments here on the *Bodhicaryāvatāra* his assimilation of the *prakṛtiviśuddhi* of the *Ratnagotravibhāga* with the *prakṛtinirvāṇa* of Prajñākaramati, which is of course said by the latter to be the absence of inherent existence in the continuums of sentient beings. According to Shākya mchog ldan this contrasts with the approach of another of Sajjana's Tibetan disciples, bTsan kha bo che, who derived from the *Ratnagotravibhāga* and other works attributed to Maitreya not just a *prakṛtiviśuddhi* but a *prakṛtiviśuddhijñāna (rang bzhin rnam dag gi ye shes*), a fundamentally pure gnosis or awareness which is also the fundamental or natural clear-light (*rang bzhin gyi 'od gsal ba/prakṛtiprabhāsvara*) and the *tathāgatagarbha*. Later, as we shall see, these concepts too are employed in Tibetan exegesis on the *Bodhicaryāvatāra*. For the moment, one must hesitate to suggest with any certainty that a systematic interpretation of the Prāsaṅgika Madhyamaka conception of the *prakṛtinirvāṇa* in Tibet in the light of the *tathāgatagarbha* theory originated with rNgog bLo ldan shes rab, but he undoubtedly provided an early and noteworthy precedent.

The use of *rang bzhin rnam par dag pa* in explaining the *prakṛtinirvāṇa* of *Bodhicaryāvatāra* 9:13ab is continued by a number of our other Tibetan commentators. The dGe lugs tradition is very careful to preserve what it conceives to be a pure form of Prāsaṅgika Madhyamaka. The *Ratnagotravibhāga*, however, was interpreted by dGe lugs writers as a Prāsaṅgika text; the *tathāgatagarbha* is taken as the emptiness of inherent existence in a mental continuum, and is thus equal to the *prakṛtinirvāṇa* when applied as by Prajñākaramati to the mind of sentinent beings. Tsong kha pa comments that 'For the Mādhyamika, because all *dharmas* are ultimately free of all verbal differentiation, there is the *prakṛtiviśuddhi* or *prakṛtinirvāṇa* which is free from birth, old age etc. ultimately' (*dbu ma pas don dam par chos thams cad spros pa thams cad dang bral bas don dam par skye ba dang rga ba sogs dang bral ba'i rang bzhin rnam dag gam / rang bzhin gyi mya ngan las 'das pa yin yang /: Tsong.* folio 6b).[15] For Tsong kha pa, clearly, *prakṛtiviśuddhi* and *prakṛtinirvāṇa* are here synonyms; both refer therefore to the nature of entities as ultimately free of birth, old age and death, i.e. emptiness.[16] rGyal tshab rje makes the dGe lugs view even clearer. There exists a distinction between the *prakṛtinirvāṇa* and the *nirvāṇa* which is purity from adventitious taints (*glo bur rnam dag gi myang 'das*=the *Ratnagotravibhāga's vaimalyaviśuddhinirvāṇa*). The former does not depend on cultivating the path, since it is the true nature (*dharmatā*) of all whether there is cultivation or not. The latter is obtained through cutting *saṃsāra* with its continuum of birth and death (*rGyal.* p.218). The term *vaimalyaviśuddhi* is placed in opposition to *prakṛtiviśuddhi* in the *Ratnagotravibhāga*. Like Tsong kha pa, therefore, rGyal tshab rje is here identifying *prakṛtinirvāṇa* with *prakṛtiviśuddhi* and the *tathāgatagarbha*. The same point is made by Mi pham who shows some evidence of relying on rGyal tshab rje in his commentary to the ninth chapter of the *Bodhicaryāvatāra*, although as we shall see he by no means accepts all rGyal tshab rje's views. Mi pham uses the expression *glo bur dri bral gyi myang 'das* (p.16), the *nirvāṇa* free from adventitious taints. dPa' bo gTsug lag phreng ba, however, (or at least an opponent) shows some interesting differences which may just indicate a move further in the direction of an ontologically stronger interpretation of the *tathāgatagarbha* than that of rGyal tshab rje. Such a stronger interpretation would certainly have been familiar to a Karma bKa' brgyud scholar and pupil of Mi bskyod rdo rje.[17] Alone of our Tibetan commentators dPa' bo does not employ the expression *rang bzhin gyis myan ngan las 'das* at all. He does, however, employ the *rang bzhin gyis dag pa*. dPa' bo's opponent begins by saying that if there does not exist the inherent existence of obscuration then there would be Buddhahood from the beginning (*sgrib pa rang bzhin gyis med na gzod nas sangs rgyas par 'gyur*). *Saṃsāra* would thus not exist. Thus Buddhahood is something which is there when obscurations are removed, but the non-inherent existence of obscurations entails that there is Buddhahood already. For dPa' bo's opponent the non-inherent existence of obscurations must entail their non-existence at all, for otherwise there would be no problem. The issue here is not that all are enlightened already because all *dharmas* are empty of inherent existence. Rather all are enlightened because *obscurations* are empty of inherent existence. The obscurations do not exist, and there is already Buddhahood. It is not impossible that dPa' bo himself may accept these basic premisses of his opponent's position, with their resonances of a *gzhan stong* approach which would maintain the real existence of the Buddha-nature and the non-existence of adventitious defilements. Nevertheless he points out that even though there is no distinction between a Buddha and sentient beings from the point of view of fundamental purity, still conventionally there is a distinction of *saṃsāra* and non-*saṃsāra* depending on whether the conditions for *saṃsāra* such as ignorance and so on have been cut (p.655). Thus ultimately there is no obscuration and the implication appears to be that we are not just empty of inherent existence but in terms of fundamental purity we have never been distinct from Buddhas. Conventionally, however, people obtain Buddhahood. In terms of expression there are only differences of nuance at this point from say, Tsong kha pa, but taken as a whole in the context of a bKa' brgyud tradition of *gzhan stong* thought dPa' bo gTsug lag phreng ba's distinctive discussion of this verse, whether it reflects his own view or not, indicates elements of an alternative perspective on the *prakṛti-nirvāṇa* even in the context of a Prāsaṅgika Madhyamaka work like the *Bodhicaryāvatāra*.[18] Other commentators subsequently manifest clearer moves in the same direction.

BODHICARYĀVATĀRA 9:104CD (=TIB. 103CD)

tan na kiṃcid ataḥ sattvaḥ prakṛtyā parinirvṛtāḥ //

de ni cung zad min de'i phyir /
sems can rang bzhin mya ngan 'das //

That (mind) is nothing at all. Therefore sentient beings are fundamentally (or 'inherently') ceased. //

This is the only point in the *Bodhicaryāvatāra* at which Śāntideva himself uses the expression *prakṛtyā parinirvṛtāḥ*. It occurs in the context of a search for the inherent existence of the mind, and is said with reference to sentient beings. It is in this context, as we have seen, that Prajñākaramati explains the concept of *prakṛtinirvāṇa* with reference to the absence of inherent existence in the continuums of sentient beings. It is possible that Prajñākaramati only glosses *prakṛtyā nirvṛta* with *prakṛtinirvāṇa* when he is specifically thinking of the context of sentient beings and their mindstreams. He appears to gloss *prakṛtyā parinirvṛtāḥ* (in *BCA* 9:104) with *parimuktasvabhāvāḥ* – sentient beings are the nature of liberated (beings). It is *prakṛtinirvāṇa*, defined as the absence of inherent existence, continually existing in the continuums of all sentient beings. If so, this is a point which is completely lost in the Tibetan translation by *rang bzhin gyis mya ngan las 'das* which fails to make any such distinction between *prakṛtyā parinirvṛta* and *prakṛtiparinirvāṇa* and also any distinction here between *prakṛtinirvāṇa* and *prakṛtiparinirvāṇa*.[19]

Among our Tibetan commentators there is a marked distinction in the vocabulary employed to explain the only use of *rang bzhin mya ngan 'das* by Śāntideva. The context of discussing the nature of mind immediately suggests the *tathāgatagarbha* and throws into contrast differing Tibetan approaches to a topic which formed no part of the original *Bodhicaryāvatāra* context. I have already suggested that the dGe lugs approach to the *tathāgatagarbha* may well have been determined to some extent by Prajñākaramati's own comments on this verse. Tsong kha pa explains that there does not exist even the very slightest thing which is truly established. Therefore all sentient beings are fundamentally (by nature) *nirvāṇa* (or 'ceased'), which is free from all verbal differentiations of truth.[20] For Tsong kha pa as always the emphasis is on absence of inherent existence, lacking true establishment. In this respect all sentient beings are no different from anything else. We have seen in the preceding verses of the *Bodhicaryāvatāra* that the mind is not truly established. Because of this sentient beings are *nirvāṇa* by nature, for this *nirvāṇa* is emptiness, freedom from all verbal differentiations of true (i.e. inherently true) existence. Again, rGyal tshab strives to avoid any ambiguity, and in particular any notion that the *prakṛtinirvāṇa* may be some inherently existing nature in the mind: 'There does not exist even the slightest thing established with inherent existence. Therefore the empty nature of inherent existence of the mind is the *prakṛtinirvāṇa*.'[21] For Bu ston, writing rather earlier than Tsong kha pa and rGyal tshab rje, the emphasis however is not on absence of inherent existence in the continuums of sentient beings or otherwise, but on the contrast between an innate enlightenment possessed by all by their very nature, and a state of unenlightenment said to be the case due to being stained by traces of taints due to reification. This is not the case ultimately.[22] The contrast for Bu ston then is between the way things appear to be due to beginningless ignorance, and the way things always have been. In reality (*don dam par*) we have always been enlightened.[23] Bu ston stresses not the *prakṛtinirvāṇa* as another name for emptiness but the *prakṛtinirvāṇa* as a form of *nirvāṇa*. There is no necessary incompatibility with Tsong kha pa and rGyal tshab rje here – it all depends what we mean by 'enlightenment' in this context – but there is significant difference of emphasis and nuance. The same could be said of dPa' bo gTsug lag phreng ba's comment that 'therefore the nature of the mind of sentient beings is from the beginning *nirvāṇa*, not defiled by verbal differentiation' (*de'i phyir sems can gyi sems kyi rang bzhin gdod ma nas mya ngan las 'das pa spros pas ma gos pa nid to /* (p.869)), although the notion of not being defiled (*ma gos*) with verbal differentiations suggests as with dPa' bo's previous comments on *Bodhicaryāvatāra* 9:13ab at least the possibility of some sort of enduring and pure substratum behind verbal differentiation.

It is in the commentary by Sa bzang mati paṇchen to *Bodhicaryāvatāra* 9:103/4cd, however, that we really find ourselves in a terminologically and, I suggest, a conceptually different world from that of Tsong kha pa's commentarial tradition on Prāsaṅgika

Madhyamaka works. Sa bzang states the following in his comment on Śāntideva's critique of the existence of mind and his assertion that 'That (mind) is nothing at all': 'That adventitious conventional mind, if it is examined, is not the slightest bit established. Therefore, because the ultimate *dharmatā* is invariable, sentient beings are established as having the essence (*snying po can*) of enlightenment, the clear-light nature of the mind.' And Sa bzang supports his position with a quote from the *Aṣṭasāhasrikā Prajñāpāramitā:* 'The mind is not mind; the nature of the mind is clear-light'.[24] Clearly for Sa bzang the mind which is not mind is the adventitious conventional mind, and the mind which is not mind is contrasted with the clear-light nature of the mind. For the mind not to be mind is to be not established at all when placed under critical examination. Not to be established because not found under critical examination is the standard Prāsaṅgika formula for lacking inherent existence, that is, emptiness. Sa bzang wishes to draw a contrast between the adventitious conventional mind which is not found and therefore lacks inherent existence, and the ultimate *dharmatā*. He does not *specifically* say that this ultimate *dharmatā* does have inherent existence, but the structure of his comments implies that a contrast is being drawn and the *dharmatā* itself has not been touched by Śāntideva's preceding arguments. Sentient beings are established as having the nature of *nirvāṇa* – the Tibetan expression *mya ngan las 'das pa'i snying po can* immediately suggests the assertion of the *Tathāgatagarbhasūtra* that all sentient beings are posessed of the *tathāgatagarbha* (*de bzhin gshegs pa'i snying po*), and the use of the expression *snying po* rather than *ngo bo* or *rang bzhin* must be meant to refer to the *tathāgatagarbha* itself. All sentient beings are established as having this essence 'because the ultimate *dharmatā* is invariable'. Again, the contrast is with the adventitious conventional mind (and invariablity is one of the requirements for inherent existence). The Tibetan *glo bur* is as we have seen a term significant in the *Ratnagotravibhāga* context where it refers to the adventitious taints which obscure the pure nature which is invariable. Structurally here the reference is clearly to the same pure element, the invariable *snying po* which is here stated to be ultimate in contrast to the adventitious conventional. We have already seen that the *prakṛtinirvāṇa* in Tibet became equated with the *prakṛtiviśuddhi* of the *Ratnagotravibhāga*, and thereby contrasted with the *vaimalyaviśuddhi* referred to in the same text. Here in Sa bzang mati paṇchen we find a further and quite self-conscious stage in the absorption of the *prakṛtinirvāṇa* into the *tathāgatagarbha* and all that is entailed by such an absorption. With this goes the employment of the 'clear-light nature of the mind' as an equivalent for the *tathāgatagarbha*. We are not, I think, very far here from a form of *gzhan stong* absolutism based on the *Ratnagotravibhāga* and employed in a reading of the *Bodhicaryāvatāra*.[25]

BODHICARYĀVATĀRA 9:111 (=TIB. 110)

vicārite vicārye tu vicārasyāsti nāśrayaḥ /
nirāśritatvān nodeti tac ca nirvāṇam ucyate //

dpyad bya rnam par dpyad byas na /
rnam dpyod la ni rten yod min /
rten med phyir na mi skye ste /
de yang mya ngan 'das par brjod //

When the object to be investigated has been investigated, there exists no objective support for the investigating mind /
Because there does not exist an objective support (the mind) does not arise, and that ('also'-Tib.) is called *nirvāṇa* //

Our Tibetan commentaries make it clear there that what is said to be without objective support here is the investigating *mind*.[26] While nearly all the Tibetan commentators and a number of the Indian commentators employ the actual terms *prakṛtinirvāṇa/prakṛtinirvṛta* in commenting on *Bodhicaryāvatāra* 9:13 and 104, on verse 111 not one of our Indian commentators employs the expression, while among Tibetans the actual expression is used by only rGyal tshab rje, bSod nams rtse mo, Sa bzang mati paṇchen and Mi pham. Even where the expression is employed, it is clear from the forgoing that it may well not mean the same to each commentator.

Let us start with rGyal tshab rje's use of the *rang bzhin myang 'das* in glossing *Bodhicaryāvatāra* 9:111. This is particularly significant since, as we have seen, for the dGe lugs tradition the *prakṛtinirvāṇa* is another name for emptiness, and is to be distinguished from the *nirvāṇa* obtained by following the path, what we normally call *nirvāṇa*. rGyal tshab comments:

> Because there does not exist a true subject (*chos can/dharmin*) as support, the object of negation (*dgag bya*) and the negating mind both do not arise with inherent existence. That also is said to be the *prakṛtinirvāṇa*. Having understood directly that referent [i.e. emptiness], once one has familiarisation with it, it is said that one also obtains the *nirvāṇa* which is free of adventitious taints.[27]

For rGyal tshab rje Śāntideva's verse initially involves the interface between logic and Madhyamaka. There is neither object of negation nor negating mind existing *inherently.* For rGyal tshab rje this does not mean, of course, that they do not exist conventionally, which is the level on which logical operations take place. Thus Śāntideva is *not* saying that there should be no activity involving critical reasoning and analysis. The fact that the object of negation and the negating mind do not exist inherently means that they are empty of inherent existence. This is the *prakṛtinirvāṇa*. Hence for rGyal tshab rje it is important to realise that Śāntideva does not mean that when the cognitive object of an investigation and the investigating mind cease that is *nirvāṇa. Nirvāṇa* is not a state of mind involving the calming of subject and object (and it would be even more mistaken to think that it could occur because of making the mind a blank). The *nirvāṇa* referred to by Śāntideva here is just emptiness, the *prakṛtinirvāṇa*, and to indicate the calming of subject and object is simply another means of showing that subject and object are empty of inherent existence. Logical operations are not undermined on the conventional level, and it is emphatically not the case that the real liberating *nirvāṇa* can be obtained simply by calming the critical analytic mind. True, rGyal tshab adds that by familiarisation with emptiness one can obtain the *nirvāṇa* which is freedom from adventitious taints. But this does not help to explain Śāntideva's verse, since by familiarisation with any emptiness (absence of inherent existence), not just emptiness of negandum and negating mind, one can eventually obtain *nirvāṇa*. One possible reason for rGyal tshab's additional reference to the *vaimalyaviśuddhinirvāṇa* here may be that Tsong kha pa in his commentary on this verse makes no mention of the *prakṛtinirvāṇa*. Tsong kha pa simply says that 'the investigating mind does not have a true objective support, and because of the nonexistence of that it does not arise with inherent existence. By familiarisation with that referent, it said that one obtains *nirvāṇa*'(*rnam dpyod la ni rten bden pa yod pa min la / de med pa'i phyir na rang bzhin gyis mi skye ste / don de goms pa las myang 'das 'thob par brjod do*: f.25b). Thus for Tsong kha pa familiarisation with emptiness leads to *nirvāṇa*, and he is able to deal with Śāntideva's apparent association of *nirvāṇa* with the cessation of subject and object by first neutralising it through introducing references to noninherent or non-true existence – which allows existence conventionally – and second by the use of two levels to his commentary whereby the nonexistence of the investigating mind in the absence of its objective support is not *nirvāṇa*, but *nirvāṇa* arises from familiarisation with emptiness, of which absence of subject and object with inherent existence indicates one possible mode of access. So for Tsong kha pa, Śāntideva's reference to *nirvāṇa* is to what can occur eventually through familiarisation with emptiness. For rGyal tshab rje his initial response is to gloss Śāntideva's *nirvāṇa* as *prakṛtinirvāṇa*, in other words Śāntideva is not putting forward at all the actual attainment of *nirvāṇa* here by sentient beings as a result of following the path.

There is a number of reasons why rGyal tshab rje and the dGe lugs tradition want to avoid any implication that Śāntideva is referring directly to the liberating *nirvāṇa* in this verse. Śāntideva's text could be taken to mean that *nirvāṇa* lies precisely in cutting all analytic thought through seeing that the object of investigation and therefore the subject cannot exist. This could be combined with the idea that *nirvāṇa* lies in a clear but blank mind, a mind free of any content, any data involving subject and object. Such a view is, of course, very strongly opposed by Tsong kha pa. Moreover, the suggestion that without object there can be no subject carries with it strong resonances of the Cittamātra tradition, where emptiness comes to mean not absence of inherent existence but precisely absence of subject and object in the truly existing non-dual mind stream.[28] Thus any suggestion that this is *nirvāṇa* might be taken to mean that *nirvāṇa* could be a really-existing non-dual mind stream. Moreover since for the Madhyamaka unlike Cittamātra absence of subject and object is not as such what is meant by emptiness (emptiness for Madhyamaka is *absence of inherent existence*), one might misunderstand Śāntideva to mean that *nirvāṇa* could come through realising the absence of subject and object, without requiring a realisation of emptiness. The result of all of this is that for rGyal tshab rje *Bodhicaryāvatāra* 9:111 is taken to refer to the *prakṛtinirvāṇa*, and not to *nirvāṇa*. *Nirvāṇa* for rGyal tshab rje is not in itself to be taken as the calming of the investigating subject in the absence of its objective support.

Yet the dGe lugs interpretation here is not at all how Śāntideva's verse is taken by some of our other commentators. Indeed the very structure of the verse rather suggests a summary of the stages of meditative practice. In the absence of an investigative object, the investigating mind does not arise. With the calming of both investigative object and investigating mind there is that calm, that cessation of all possible verbal differentiations, which is *nirvāṇa*. This, broadly speaking, *is* the bare structure of Cittamātra meditation practice. Prajñākaramati comments:

> Having negated all reifying superimpositions, because of thoroughly knowing the nature of things, because there has been done that which was to be done, because of the nonexistence of engaging and termination there is nowhere clinging, nor also becoming indifferent. And that is called *nirvāṇa*, since it is the cessation of all the transactional (= conventional). Because of being everywhere without operation, because of complete calming, that indeed is designated as *nirvāṇa*.[29]

Very little needs to be said about this passage. The transcendence of all reifying superimpositions, the cessation of the transactional, complete calming, and the other expressions are all standard equivalents in Madhyamaka for the attainment of *nirvāṇa*. Perhaps most significant is the use of *kṛtakṛtyatvāt* – because there has been done that which was to be done – which has been since earliest times in Buddhism an unambiguous expression for the attainment of enlightenment (Pali: *katakaraṇīya*). There can be no question here that Prajñākaramati is speaking not of the *prakṛtinirvāṇa*, which he does not mention, but of the actual attainment of *nirvāṇa* as a result of following the path.[30] He is not the only one. Vibhūticandra too speaks of absence of diversifying constructions (*rnam rtog med pa*) and freedom from clinging desire (*chags pa dang bral ba*), again standard expressions for the attainment of *nirvāṇa* (f.276b: for *rnam rtog med pa* see the next section on verse 35). None of our other Indian commentators refers to the *prakṛtinirvāṇa*; almost all imply that the refererence in *Bodhicaryāvatāra* 9:111 is to *nirvāṇa* itself.[31]

Among our Tibetan commentators, bSod nams rtse mo does employ by name the *rang bzhin gyis mya ngan las 'das*. It is this, he says, because the obscuration of reality is not ultimate (*de kho na'i sgrib pa don dam pa ma yin pas* (p.507:2)). It may be, however, that bSod nams rtse mo is here referring to the view of rNgog lo tsa ba, who is mentioned on the next line but one, and it is possible that it was rNgog, again influenced by his use of the *Ratnagotravibhāga*, who introduced the *prakṛtinirvāṇa* as a possible gloss on *Bodhicaryāvatāra* 9:111. bSod nams rtse mo's words would certainly fit with rNgog's approach, since in fact they amount to an explanation of the expression 'pure by nature'. It is called 'fundamental *nirvāṇa*' since obscurations, taints, are not ultimate, i.e. they are adventitious and therefore by nature, fundamentally, there is purity. Once more we find the opposition between an innate *nirvāṇa* and adventitious taints. This time, in context, the suggestion is that with the cessation of the investigative object and investigating mind the innate *nirvāṇa* shines forth. Sa bzang mati paṇchen for his part specifically relates the strategy of Śāntideva's verse at *Bodhicaryāvatāra* 9:111 to one of the classic Buddhist statements of *prakṛtinirvṛta* from the Cittamātra tradition, *Mahāyānasūtrālaṃkāra* 11:51. There is a sequence. Inherent existence does not exist. Then there is absence of birth, absence of cessation. Thus calm from the beginning. Thence is established *prakṛtinirvṛta*.[32] Sa bzang explains that since there does not exist a true referential object, the subjective mind also does not arise. That *dharmatā* also, which is the nonarising of object, subject and so on, is called the *prakṛtinirvāṇa* because from the beginning it is completely calm of verbal differentiations.[33] We have already seen that for Sa bzang *dharmatā* occurs in the same context as references to the *tathāgatagarbha* and the clear-light nature of the mind. The *dharmatā* where neither subject nor object arise is from the very beginning completely calm of *prapañcas*. In the attainment of enlightenment there is attained that which has always been the case. Sa bzang's use of a Cittamātra text here at least hints that he would not be unduly worried at rGyal tshab's scruples concerning a remaining substratum to the cessation of subject and object. We shall return to this point later. Mi pham also speaks of the calming of all verbal differentiations. But he adds that when this happens that investigating mind also, like a wave in water, is said to be fundamentally *nirvāṇa* within the nature of the *dharmatā*.[34] The image here is of the investigating mind returning to that from which it came and of which it always is a part – the *dharmatā*. It follows from what Mi pham says that the investigating mind *itself* must be fundamentally, by nature, the *dharmatā*. The conventional is the ultimate, and the actual attainment of *nirvāṇa* through following the path and the primordial natural state of *nirvāṇa* turn out to be not substantially different. In spite of his employment of the expression *rang bzhin gyis mya ngan las 'das* in glossing *Bodhicaryāvatāra* 9:111 the perspective of Mi pham is very different from that of rGyal tshab rje, and it is clear that the *dharmatā* here of which the investigating mind is a part cannot be the same as emptiness as understood by rGyal tshab rje. For the latter, the investigating mind may be empty, but it is not emptiness, and can certainly not be said (apart from the context of specific Tantric practice) to enter into the nature of emptiness.[35] There is perhaps greater ambiguity in dPa' bo gTsug lag phreng ba's discussion of the same verse, although his terminological world has some affinities with that of Sa bzang mati paṇchen and Mi pham. The primordial *nirvāṇa* is said to be the innate or noncontingent nature of *dharmas*, which is to say this mere clear-light and empty absence as regards that which is to be put aside and removed, which is of course the inherent existence of *dharmas*, when the craving of reification and over-negation has been reversed.[36] Is dPa' bo saying that the 'mere clear-light' is the same as absence of inherent existence? Or is he saying that the mere clear-light shines forth in that empty absence? From what we have here it is difficult to tell. One thing anyway is clear. Although dPa' bo does not employ the expression *rang bzhin gyis mya ngan las 'das* his use of *gzod ma nas mya ngan 'das pa nyid* is meant to refer to the same thing.

We have seen that Indian commentators on *Bodhicaryāvatāra* 9:111 seem more or less united in taking it as referring to actual *nirvāṇa* rather than *prakṛtinirvāṇa/prakṛtinirvṛta*. Tibetan commentators often see it as a reference to *prakṛtinirvāṇa*, but their interpretation of *prakṛtinirvāṇa* differs so much so that a reference to *prakṛtinirvāṇa* could also be a reference to actual *nirvāṇa*. Bu ston's terminological world is not that of Mi pham. He speaks simply of the calming of all minds of craving desire and absence of craving desire (*chags pa dang / chags bral gyi blo thams cad nye bar zhi ba*), the transcendence of all the transactional, and complete calming (*tha snyad thams cad las 'das shing rang bzhin gyi zhi ba*: p.560). Bu ston tends to follow in his commentary his Indian predecessors, and some of the language at this point, standard expressions for *nirvāṇa*, is familiar from Prajñākaramati. There is no mention of the *prakṛti-nirvāṇa*, and it seems clear to me that Bu ston is, like Prajñākaramati, thinking here of the actual attainment of *nirvāṇa*. This is even clearer in the earlier commentary by Thogs med. A number of our commentators have used the expression 'calming' in their commentaries, as we have seen an important Madhyamaka term frequently employed to equal *nirvāṇa*. Thogs med, however, initially glosses *nirvāṇa* as 'that calming also' (*zhi ba de yang*), but then explains that 'because of the absence of intentional object there is complete calming, as I have declared before' (*dmigs pa med pas rab tu zhi / zhes sngar brjod pa yin no /*: p.350) There can be no doubt at all that Thogs med's reference here is to his commentary on *Bodhicaryāvatāra* 9:35, where the expression *dmigs pa med par rab tu zhi* is used in the verse. Thus Thogs med specifically wants to link the calming of verse 35 with the calming which he finds in verse 111. This is important because with the possible exception of dPa' bo not a single one of our commentators, including the dGe lugs commentators, take verse 35 as referring to the *prakṛtinirvāṇa*. Nearly all agree that this verse refers to the actual *nirvāṇa*. Clearly verse 111 is taken by Thogs med to refer to actual *nirvāṇa* and not *prakṛtinirvāṇa*. By way of further clarification, therefore, let us look at verse 35.

BODHICARYĀVATĀRA 9:35 (=TIB. 34)

yadā na bhāvo nābhāvo mateḥ saṃtiṣṭhate puraḥ /
tadānyagatyabhāvena nirālambā praśāmyati //

gang tse dngos dang dngos med dag /
blo yi mdun na mi gnas pa /
de tse rnam pa gzhan med pas /
dmigs pa med par rab tu zhi //

When entity and non-entity do not stand before the mind /
Then because there exists no other possibility, without intentional object it is completely calmed //

Prajñākaramati comments that the mind is completely calmed because all diversifying constructions are calmed (*buddhiḥ praśāmyati upaśāmyati / sarvavikalpopaśamāt*). It is like fire without firewood, another old Buddhist image for *nirvāṇa* repeated by a number of our commentators. Vairocanarakṣita also associates *nirvāṇa* here with the complete calming of all diversifying constructions (f.143a), while our anonymous commentary speaks of the calming of all *rtogs pa*, which should probably read *rtog pa*, *kalpanā*, an expression which has much the same meaning as *vikalpa*.[37] Among Tibetans bSod nams rtse mo refers to the arising of wisdom (*prajñā*) which is without appearance, which cuts the continuum of *kalpanās* (*rtog pa rgyun chad pa'i snang ba med pa'i shes rab skye'o /*: p.499:1). Bu ston makes it quite clear that we are talking about the actual attainment of *nirvāṇa* here by stating categorically that it is the *apratiṣṭhitanirvāṇa* which is the complete calming of all diversifying constructions (*rnam rtog thams cad rab tu zhi ba'i mi gnas pa'i myang 'das 'thob bo*: p.524), a point also made by Mi pham (p.29). Earlier Kalyāṇadeva had gone even further, and shown how this verse can be taken to refer to both the *sopādhiśeṣa* and the *nirupādhiśeṣa nirvāṇas* (f.72b).

Bu ston quotes from an unnamed source: 'Thus if there does not exist an object before the mind then, since the mind which apprehends that does not arise, there will be liberation from obscuration'.[38] It follows that for Bu ston the issue in *Bodhicaryāvatāra* 9:35 is the calming of mind in the absence of its intentional objects. When these are both calmed, all diversifying constructions cease. In showing the impossibility of entity and non-entity Śāntideva is showing the impossibility of intentional objects and therefore subjects. Thus for Bu ston, Śāntideva's position on the attainment of *nirvāṇa* in 9:35 is a different version of the same argument in 9:111. There is no subject because there is no object; thus there is *nirvāṇa*. We have therefore additional evidence that for Bu ston Śāntideva's argument in *BCA* 9:111 is intended to set forth actual *nirvāṇa*. Reference to *BCA* 9:35 can also confirm that in spite of his use of the expression *rang bzhin gyis mya ngan las 'das* in his commentary on verse 111, Sa bzang mati paṇchen also sees the cessation of subject and object as the attainment of actual *nirvāṇa*. On verse 35 he says 'if the object has ceased the subjective mind also is completely calmed. Thereby one will attain the supreme *nirvāṇa*' (*yul 'gags na yul can gyi blo yang rab tu zhi ba las / spangs pa mthar phyin pa'i mya ngan las 'das thob par 'gyur te*: p.342). Thus for Sa bzang the attainment of *nirvāṇa* is through calming subject and object, and it is the attainment of a state which has also been the case primevally. He is concerned however that we should not confuse the cessation of the mind which is correlated with the absence of its intentional referent, with the cessation of all awareness altogether. An opponent argues that because the mind has ceased, gnosis (*ye shes/jñāna*: primeval awareness) also does not exist. This is not so, Sa bzang replies, since the *nirvāṇa* which is set forth by way of abandoning the mind which is adventitious consciousness, and the perfect Buddhahood which is set forth by way of approaching the ultimate Gnosis Body (*paramārthajñānakāya*) are synonymous.[39] Just to make sure that we know where these ideas come from, Sa bzang quotes from the *Ratnagotravibhāga*. Thus this gnosis (*jñāna*) which is there when subject and object cease and *nirvāṇa* is attained – abandoning the mind which is adventitious consciousness (*vijñāna*) – is the same as that perfect Buddhahood which is the ultimate Gnosis Body. One is reminded here of Sa bzang's previous reference to the adventitious conventional mind. It seems clear, I think, that for Sa bzang mati paṇchen the adventitious conventional mind equals *vijñāna* which is abandoned when one abandons subject and object. This abandonment is *nirvāṇa*. The attainment of *nirvāṇa* however not only does not entail the cessation of all gnosis, but is actually the same as the ultimate Gnosis Body, which must equal here the ultimate *dharmatā*, the essence of enlightenment (=*tathāgatagarbha*), the clear-light nature of the mind. This *dharmatā* is the *prakṛtinirvāṇa*, which has always been the case. In 9:104 Sa bzang speaks of the adventitious conventional mind (*sems*). Here at 9:35 he refers to the mind (*sems*) which is adventitious consciousness. It is clear that these two *sems* are the same. Thus Sa bzang does not consider that the refutation of mind in 9:111 includes a refutation of all *sems*, of *ye shes*, primordial gnosis, but only of *vijñāna*, (everyday) consciousness (*rnam shes*). For Sa bzang as for Mi pham, the attainment of enlightenment lies in attaining that which one has always been. The ultimate is a *jñāna* which is there primordially and which shines out when subject and object are calmed. Fundamentally there is no distinction, as rGyal tshab rje wants to maintain, between the *prakṛtinirvāṇa* and that *nirvāṇa* which is attained through following the path. *Bodhicaryāvatāra* 9:35 and 9:111 both refer to the same attainment of *nirvāṇa*.

When 9:35, 9:104 and 9:111 are all taken together, Sa bzang mati paṇchen's views as a commentator are I suggest very different from those of Tsong kha pa and rGyal tshab rje, even if all are agreed that 9:35 at least refers to the actual attainment of *nirvāṇa*. Mi pham begins his comments on that verse by what is in effect an unacknowledged quote from rGyal tshab. Since there does not exist the extremes which form the refuge which is the intentional object for grasping as true, so without exception all verbal differentiations are completely calmed.[40] For rGyal tshab rje *Bodhicaryāvatāra* 9:34–5 is particularly concerned with refuting any possibility that emptiness itself is established with inherent existence. There can be no such thing, since with neither entity nor non-entity there can be no objective support for any inherently established entity. There is no third possibility. Thus all verbal differentiations are calmed. And rGyal tshab comments that in the case of a person who cognises emptiness directly even the verbal differentiation of dual appearance is in emptiness calmed. In the case of one who cognises emptiness through the medium of a generic image (i.e. prior to the direct cognition of emptiness at the level of the Path of Insight (*darśana-mārga*)), even though dual appearance has not been stopped, still there has been stopped the verbal differentiation of definitive truth.[41] The implication here is that even those who have understood emptiness through reasoning alone, inasmuch as they have understood emptiness, do not think that anything, including emptiness itself, is truly established. Once more rGyal tshab makes a distinction – this time between the stopping of verbal differentiations (*prapañca*) of definitive truth which while a noble achievement does not in itself equal *nirvāṇa*, and the stopping of verbal differentiations of dual appearance which, in general and in the last analysis can be said here to equal *nirvāṇa*. Thus to speak of calming all verbal differentiations does not necessarily equal *nirvāṇa*. Nevertheless *Bodhicaryāvatāra* 9:35 does indicate the calming which through cultivation eventually issues in *nirvāṇa*. *BCA* 9:111 on the other hand teaches the absence of subject in the absence of object. This, for rGyal tshab rje, is not the actual attainment of *nirvāṇa*. Unlike some other commentators, for rGyal tshab verse 35 indicates not the absence of subject and object but pre-eminently the impossibility of entity or non-entity. The calming which eventually issues from this impossibility is the calm of emptiness and is, therefore, the actual attainment of *nirvāṇa*. Having made his distinctions, rGyal tshab rje follows Tsong kha pa (f.11a) in seeing verse 35 as indicating the calming of verbal differentiations at the time of the Result (*'bras bu'i dus su*) through familiarisation with emptiness, that is, actual *nirvāṇa*.

Mi pham begins by plagiarism – or a homage – to rGyal tshab rje which makes the direction of his subsequent comments all the more pointed. For having calmed without exception all verbal differentiations, he continues to say that this is equality like the circle of the sky, where there does not exist speech, thought or utterance, explained analytically as a mere gnosis which is reflexive awareness (*so so rang rig pa'i ye shes tsam=pratisvasaṃvittijñānamātra*). It is indeed the final mode of being, that is, the ultimate.[42] And Mi pham continues by quoting at rGyal tshab rje Nāgārjuna's *Madhyamakakārikā* 13:8 – emptiness was taught by the Victors for the overcoming of all *dṛṣṭis*, all dogmatically held viewpoints. Whoever takes emptiness as a *dṛṣṭi* cannot be helped. It is, Mi pham says, just like the declaration of sixteen types of emptiness for the purpose of reversing various attachments to entity and non-entity. As regards that unitive (*zung 'jug = yuganaddha*) *dharmadhātu* which is the stopping of extremes of verbal differentiation, there is a distinction in the Mahāyāna of direct cognition and reasoning. Here, Mi pham tells us, people refer to the *dBu ma chen po*, the Great Madhyamaka.[43] What Mi pham is saying here is that when entity and non-entity are not established there is complete calming. This is the cessation of all verbal differentiations. Emptiness, which can be shown through analytic reasoning, has thus fulfilled its function. Emptiness shows absence of inherent existence in the object under analysis. Since we are now on the level of complete freedom from verbal differentiations, to say anything more about emptiness, including any conclusion that with absence of inherent existence that is the end of the matter, is illegitimate. Such would be to cling to emptiness. Anything further is not, cannot be, on the level of words and therefore analytic reasoning. It takes us instead to the level of direct cognition. Since we are here free from verbal differentiations, the sphere of direct cognition is outside the range of refutation through emptiness. We also have no grounds in direct cognition, the only relevant sphere, for concluding with rGyal tshab rje that the direct cognition of emptiness, understood as absence of inherent existence, is all there is to this level. Rather, what we find on the highest level of direct cognition is strictly unutterable (and therefore cannot be said to be simply emptiness), but an appropriate expression for it is 'a mere gnosis which is reflexive awareness'.[44] This is truly the ultimate, known and known to be such directly. It is the unitive *dharmadhātu* spoken of in conventional discourse by reference to the Great Madhyamaka. Mi pham's use of the Great Madhyamaka in *this* context makes it quite clear what he is talking about, and places his views firmly within a tradition in Tibetan thought going back many centuries. It seems possible from what we have seen that one of his predecessors was Sa bzang mati paṇchen. As Leonard van der Kuijp has pointed out, *dBu ma chen po* in this sense is an expression particularly associated with the *gzhan stong* teachings of most notably, although by no means exclusively, the Jo nang tradition. Here the ultimate is thought of as a really existing radiant gnosis, eternal, unchanging, the same in enlightenment and unenlightenment, empty of those adventitious defilements which apparently obscure it in the unenlightened state but not empty of its own inherent existence.[45] Such a view was influenced in particular by the *Ratnagotravibhāga* and its *tathāgatagarbha* theory, and van der Kuijp has suggested that it may have developed originally from a school of meditators, concerned with meditative experiences, which grew up around the *Ratnagotravibhāga* and other works attributed to Maitreya. The Great Madhyamaka was frequently associated with Asaṅga, as the principal student of Maitreya (van der Kuijp (1983) pp.36–46). Thus ideas thought of by dGe lugs writers as characteristically Cittamātra became absorbed into the Madhyamaka. Hence, perhaps, Sa bzang mati paṇchen's use of the *Mahāyānasūtrālaṃkāra*. Mi pham continues with further quotes from Nāgārjuna, who is of course one of rGyal tshab rje's principal sources, but understood in a very different way from rGyal tshab rje. Having mentioned the Great Madhyamaka Mi pham wishes to justify his position from the *Madhyamakakārikā*. Thus *MMK* 15:6: 'Those who see inherent existence, other-existence, entity and non-entity do not see the reality in the teaching of the Buddha' (*svabhāvaṃ parabhāvaṃ ca bhāvaṃ cābhāvam eva ca / ye paśyanti na paśyanti te tattvam buddhaśāsane //*). For Mi pham 'reality' (*tattva*) is Reality, reflexively-aware Gnosis, there beyond entity, non-entity and so on, and beyond the reach of reasoning and any mere emptiness of inherent existence. This is supported by his quote from *Madhyamakakārikā* 18:9: 'Not dependent on another (Mi pham has 'not known from another' (*gzhan las shes min*), calm, not differentiated by verbal differentiations, without diversifying constructions, without multiplicity – this is the characteristic (definition) of reality' (*aparapratyayaṃ śāntaṃ prapañcair aprapañcitam / nirvikalpam anānārtham etat tattvasya lakṣaṇam //*).[46] Reality cannot be touched or undermined by verbal differentiations, and the calm referred too in *MMK* 18:9 immediately suggests *Bodhicaryāvatāra* 9:35 (and 9:111) which for Mi pham also indicates that Reality. The context of Mi pham's quotes from Nāgārjuna shows that for him these references to *tattva* are to be understood in the sense of the Great Madhyamaka. And Mi pham ends with a flourish: 'Therefore, through emptiness [understood] like that, extremes of verbal differentiation having sunk into the *dharmadhātu*, the two obscurations are completely abandoned and there is attained the *apratiṣṭhitanirvāṇa*'.[47] For Mi pham *Bodhicaryāvatāra* 9:35 thus sets forth the attainment of complete Buddhahood when approached through a correct understanding of emptiness (absence of inherent existence) and its function, its possibilities – and limitations.

On this crucial verse, but 9:111 too, we find a marked difference between the approach of the rNying ma pa Mi pham and the Sa skya pa Sa bzang mati paṇchen on the one hand, and dGe lugs tradition on the other. However one should be careful not to create too great a polarisation. Not all Sa skya pas, for example, share the perspectives of Sa bzang and Shākya mchog ldan, while Sa bzang and Shākya themselves do not necessarily agree on all points. It is unclear to me whether our bKa' brgyud commentators Padma dkar po and dPa' bo gTsug lag phreng ba incline towards a perspective on *Bodhicaryāvatāra* 9:35 with some similarities to that of Sa bzang and Mi pham or not. Padma dkar po makes it clear that the concern of 9:35 is with a stage of meditation, not pure intellectual analysis. Entity and non-entity do not stand before the 'mind which is free of taints' (*dri ma med pa'i blo yi mdun na*). At that time, having purified completely the three circles (*'khor gsum*),[48] being without intentional object, there is complete calming. A bodhisattva who has attained a bodhisattva stage (*bhūmi*), at the time of meditative absorption, does not have the appearance of an intentional object. When he has arisen from meditative absorption even appearances arise as mere illusions (*sgyu ma tsam du snang ba yang 'byung bas so*). When there is Buddhahood both the mind and all intentional objects determined by that mind are calmed in the (*dharma*)*dhātu* (*sangs rgyas pa na blo dang des bzhag pa'i dmigs pa thams cad dbyings su nye bar zhi bas*: p.144), which Padma dkar po accepts as an equivalent of the *dharmakāya*. In commenting on *Bodhicaryāvatāra* 9:35 Padma dkar po is certainly thinking of the attainment of meditative stages with Buddhahood at the end, but in treating this Prāsaṅgika Madhyamaka text there is no clear evidence (apart from 'in the *dhātu*') that Padma dkar po wishes to gloss it with any hint of *gzhan stong* absolutism or its associated concepts. dPa' bo is in this respect equally unclear. He tells us that 'even that very stainless wisdom mind (*shes rab dri ma med pa'i blo de nyid yang*) is always calm, having the nature of non-arising and non-cessation from the beginning. It is calm like that in the *dhātu* of reality'.[49] It is interesting that dPa' bo (and Padma dkar po?) includes under the mind to be calmed even the enlightened wisdom mind. This would seem to place him at variance with, say, the positions of Sa bzang and Mi pham.[50] But it may not be quite as radical as it appears since, in *Ratnagotravibhāga* terms, what dPa' bo could be taken as saying is that the *vaimalyaviśuddhinirvāṇa*, that *nirvāṇa* attained through following the path, is dissolvable into the *prakṛtinirvāṇa*, in other words, only the *prakṛtinirvāṇa* is the ultimate way of things and the actual attainment of *nirvāṇa* from an ultimate point of view is lost in that. The implication of this, however, is that dPa' bo gTsug lag phreng ba distinguishes *prakṛtinirvāṇa* from actual *nirvāṇa* and, unlike our other commentators, takes 9:35 as concerned with the *prakṛtinirvāṇa*. Unfortunately in spite of the length of his commentary, dPa' bo leaves the issue unclarified.[51]

I too have written at length, and I fear that I too shall have to leave the issue of dPa' bo gTsug lag phreng ba's own position on pure clear-light gnosis as the *dharmatā*, on the strength of these verses from the *Bodhicaryāvatāra*, undecided. For some of our other commentators, however, the issue is not undecided, and through looking at just a few verses from the *Bodhicaryāvatāra* in the light of a range of commentaries we can see Tibetan developments, and the apparent influence of the *Ratnagotravibhāga* on Tibetan thought in areas where there was originally no sign or need of that influence. We can see that Tibetan commentators do not give us direct access to the 'original' meaning of an Indian Buddhist text – whatever that might be – but bring to bear a whole net of intepretive theories based on their attempts to synthesise a range of Indian material into complete Buddhist systems. The construction of systems differs as criteria and goals differ. Interpretation occurs in the light of a system which gives meaning, and as systems differ both synchronically and through time so interpretation differs. Depending on how the system sees itself and its direction a Tantric text in Tibet may be interpreted in the light of Madhyamaka thought. Or Madhyamaka through Tantric thought, with the *Ratnagotravibhāga* providing a useful bridge. Indeed the *Ratnagotravibhāga*, for example, may itself be interpreted in the light of its ability to serve as a bridge between Tantric thought and Madhyamaka. The result is that a Prāsaṅgika Madhyamaka work like the *Bodhicaryāvatāra* is interpreted in Tibet with reference to ideas which not only did not occur to either Śāntideva or his Indian commentators, but were perhaps unknown to them and if known may well have been considered irrelevant or of marginal interest. Their systems may have been different from those which subsequently developed in Tibet, and we cannot but see Tibetan interpretations of Indian Buddhist ideas as possible interpretations among many others. The point seems obvious, but it is worth remembering. At the present time, when Tibetan interpretations of Indian Mahāyāna ideas show a tendency sometimes to be given precedence over Indian material or taken to have the final say in understanding Indian or even Buddhist concepts, it may be worth underlining the point not only to scholars but also contemporary Western practitioners of Buddhism in general and Tibetan Buddhism in particular. Even more so to the scholars who are practitioners.

Two

On Altruism and Rebirth

Philosophical Comments on *Bodhicaryāvatāra* 8:97–8

It is normal in Indo-Tibetan Madhyamaka to portray analysis as involving the investigation of whether *x* can be found under analysis, in other words – at least for Prāsaṅgika Madhyamaka – whether *x* has inherent existence or not. This investigation is of course central to Madhyamaka, and forms the concern of insight meditation leading eventually to *prajñā*, seeing things the way they really are. However, much of what comes under the range of analytic inquiry in Western philosophy is not simply a matter of the search for putative ultimate reality. Ethical inquiry, for example, is not *in itself* a matter of such ultimates. Clearly in Buddhist meditation and debate also – even in Madhyamaka writing – critical analytic reasoning is not only employed in the area of ultimate investigation, the investigation of whether something can be found under analysis and therefore has ultimate, i.e. inherent, existence. A Madhyamaka meditation manual like Śāntideva's *Bodhicaryāvatāra* shows from the beginning how its author gives arguments, appeals to reason, in order to convince initially himself and then any other reader (see 1:2–3) to adopt a radically new vision and perspective. For Śāntideva, as a follower of Mahāyāna Buddhism, this new vision more often than not moves from his relationship to himself, his own concerns and projects, towards his relationships with other sentient beings. It is a move from self-centered egoism to an anticipated perfect altruism, but nevertheless a move which is accomplished perhaps initially and in part but certainly fundamentally through appeals to reason, the *rationality* of the Buddhist spiritual path and ultimately the complete rationality of altruism.

In *Bodhicaryāvatāra* 8:89ff – the Chapter on Meditative Absorption (*dhyānapāramitāpariccheda*) which occurs immediately prior to his chapter on *prajñā* – Śāntideva develops a meditation which involves an analysis that has become central to the Tibetan vision of how to cultivate the bodhisattva aspiration and path. This meditative analysis is known as 'equalising of self and other' (*bdag gzhan mnyam brje*), and in it Śāntideva starts to touch on some rather interesting issues of practical philosophical ethics.

Śāntideva was no doubt a very nice person, the sort of person who – provided he did not float up into the sky and disappear *too* often – it would be delightful to have as a counsellor and Good Friend.[1] But the fact of niceness does not in itself explain *why* one should be nice. Put more pointedly, why should we care if other people are suffering? What does it matter to us? The point is raised by Śāntideva's opponent, and it might be thought to be the very foundation question for a construction of an ethical system. In attempting to remove the *pūrvapakṣa*'s objection Śāntideva wants to argue that for himself at least the Buddhist vision implies altruism as a necessary consequence and is not (as has sometimes been argued by Western commentators) antithetical to it.

Śāntideva had already urged that suffering is to be removed simply because it is suffering (8:94–6). He appears to want to say that it makes no rational difference, and therefore for Śāntideva no moral difference, who actually experiences the suffering. The fact that the suffering is *mine* does not make it morally more significant. I am neither rationally nor morally justified in removing my own suffering rather than the suffering of another just because it is my own suffering.

BODHICARYĀVATĀRA 8:97:[2]

> Supposing one says that the suffering which happens to that [other] person does no harm to *me*, therefore (s)he should not be protected against [it] /
> Then since future suffering (Skt.: 'the sufferings of future bodies') also is doing no harm [to you now] why is that to be protected against? //

The opponent is putting forward an argument, indicated in the Sanskrit by the conclusion marker *ato*, 'therefore'. Possibly our earliest Tibetan commentary, the *Byang chub sems pa'i spyod pa la 'jug pa'i 'grel pa* by the second Sa skya hierarch bSod nams rtse mo (1142–82), brings out the opponent's argument here very clearly and felicitously. Someone might argue that the grounds (*rgyu mtshan*) by which something is to be protected against is the fact that it causes harm to me. The grounds are not simply that it is not desired by another. Therefore, the opponent continues, because it is another's suffering which is doing no harm to me it is not to be protected against.[3] Śāntideva's reply is in the form of a rhetorical question embodying a *prasaṅga* counter-argument. The opponent's position is inconsistent with his or her own tenet and presumed behaviour. The opponent holds that it is rational to guard oneself against future sufferings and yet, Śāntideva argues, those sufferings are not causing pain to oneself. For bSod nams rtse mo Śāntideva's concern is to refute the suggestion that the grounds for claiming that something is to be protected against are merely that it harms me personally. Rather, the grounds why something is to be protected against are [simply] that it is undesirable, unwanted.[4]

Prajñākaramati, in his commentary, consistent with the Sanskrit reference to future bodies, implies that protection against the suffering of rebirths in the hells and so on after death is strange on his opponent's premisses, since there is not the slightest suffering caused to the body which is here in this lifetime. This is because they are simply other.[5] Prajñākaramati is referring here to the obvious fact that the *body* of the reborn being is different from that of the one who died. But as we shall see in looking at the next verse, there is more to it than this. What Prajñākaramati is saying is that the reborn being and the one who died are other in the same relevant way as myself and contemporary others are other. Thus for Prajñākaramati Śāntideva appeals to an implicit assumption that there is no relevant moral difference here between myself and contemporary others on the one hand, and myself now and my future rebirths on the other. If I protect against suffering in the one case, to be consistent I am obliged to protect against suffering in the other.

In spite of the differences in wording between the Sanskrit and the Tibetan versions of *Bodhicaryāvatāra* 8:97 over whether the argument refers simply to future sufferings, or to the sufferings of future bodies, both Indian and Tibetan commentators seem in the main to take Śāntideva to be referring to future bodies, mentioning explicitly either the hells or unfavourable destinies (*ngan song*). We might speak of this restriction of Śāntideva's argument to future bodies as the narrower application of 'future sufferings'. There is indeed much which can be said for this restriction to the narrower application as an interpretation of Śāntideva. From a textual point of view it must be correct, for it is stated in the Sanskrit version and appears to be confirmed by both Sanskrit and Tibetan of the very next verse. It is moreover quite clear that future bodies will be different from the present body. Thus, as Prajñākaramati develops the argument, Śāntideva can point to a clear-cut case of otherness where everyone with even a rudimentary religious and therefore moral sense does indeed care for the sufferings of others – that is, future lives – sufferings which are not affecting one's present state of being. However, in the Buddhist context it might be possible to develop an interpretation – or perhaps a use – of Śāntideva based on a wider application of 'future sufferings'. If Śāntideva's opponent is saying that there is no need to protect against sufferings which do not affect me, then given mutability why do I need to take precautions now against future sufferings which will come later in *this* life? Myself later in this very life can be seen as other in relationship to myself now, and that otherness is arguably for a Buddhist the very same morally significant otherness as I bear to contemporary others. Clearly this radical wider interpretation would be more difficult to defend than the narrower application, since the otherness of bodies between incarnations gives a sense of 'otherness' not possessed by stages within one life, where there is a bodily continuity which is rather dramatically shattered by death.[6] We might want to argue that it would be consistent to protect myself against future sufferings in this life, while ignoring the sufferings of contemporary others, in a way that would not be consistent if I also protect myself against the sufferings of future lives. Yet Buddhists have had a tendency to diminish if not dissolve the significance of this distinction, arguing that in fact the continuum from one life to another is in no significant way different from the continuum within one life (see *Milindapañha* 2:2:1). In both cases the subsequent stage is said to be neither the same nor different from that which has gone before, by which is clearly meant that the subsequent is not the same as the preceding, but also is not radically separate and intrinsically different from it either. Rather the subsequent exists in causal dependence upon the preceding. As Buddhaghosa puts it in the *Visuddhimagga*, if there were identity curds could not come from milk, for there can be no causal relationship between two things which are numerically identical, but the same unwelcome consequence would also apply for different reasons if there were absolute otherness as well. Absolute otherness involves a denial of all causal relationships (*Visuddhimagga* 17:167). It is clear therefore that the denial of difference here is a denial of complete acausal otherness. It is not a denial of what we usually mean by 'otherness', the sort of otherness which is normally thought to exist in the context of causation, the otherness which in everyday life we all say exists between, for example, seed and sprout. As we have seen, in the case of rebirth otherness is clearly admitted by the Buddhist between the body which died and that (re)born. We shall see subsequently that this otherness is also accepted by at least one commentator between the *person* who dies and the *person* who is reborn. In both cases it is thought to be the otherness of the subsequent to preceding in a causal continuum, but the causal continuum is not thought by Śāntideva and Prajñākaramati to annul the moral significance of – the moral use which can be employed by – the fact of this otherness, an otherness in the same morally significant way as applies to contemporary others. Moreover following the *Milindapañha* the same relationship as occurs between the being who dies and the one who is reborn also applies to stages within the life of one being. From which it would seem to follow that my relationship to myself at future stages in my very own life is also other in the same way that my relationship to my future lives is other, and if I concern myself with my own future stages I am also morally obliged to concern myself with contemporary others. Thus in the Buddhist context it is indeed possible to construct an argument based on the wider application of 'future sufferings'. The fact that this seems to deny a clear phenomenological difference between the otherness possessed by cases of rebirth, and otherness within one life stream where bodily continuity seems to provide a stronger sense of personal continuity (if not identity) may nevertheless itself be taken as an argument against the Buddhist position.

As we shall see, Tsong kha pa's pupil rGyal tshab rje, writing in the fifteenth century, in his *sPyod 'jug rnam bshad rGyal sras 'jug ngogs* clearly and explicitly adopts an understanding of Śāntideva which embraces what we have called the wider application, although there is no evidence that he was aware of the differences between the wider application he espoused and the narrower application of most other commentaries, including those which came from India. The Sanskrit text of Śāntideva's verse makes the narrower application all but inevitable, since it refers to the sufferings of future bodies. In spite of *Bodhicaryāvatāra* 8:98 this inevitability is perhaps less obvious to someone using only the Tibetan. rGyal tshab rje was not however innovating. A wider application of 'future sufferings' is also found in bSod nams rtse mo's commentary. bSod nams rtse mo comments that if it necessarily follows (*khyab* – pervasion) that what does no harm to me is not to be protected against then it would follow absurdly that I should not protect myself against the suffering of a later life (*tshe phyi ma*) and such time as my own old age and so on. This is because it is not doing any harm to my present body, just like the suffering of another.[7] The reference to 'my present body' (*da ltar gyi lus*) is interesting, since if 'present body' is simply being contrasted with 'future body', in other words the body of this present life, then of course the suffering of my old age and so on will indeed occur to my present body, even if it is a future stage of my present body. It will not occur only to the body of a future life. Thus 'my present body' should not be taken here to contrast with the bodies of future lives, but rather with *any* future state – that is, future in relationship to the present moment – of a body identified as mine. In other words, the stress in Śāntideva's argument is taken to be on 'present' rather than 'body'. Future suffering is not present, and is therefore doing no harm *now*. So, on the opponent's premisses, it is not to be guarded against. This understanding of the contrast drawn as one between present and future, rather than present and future lives, contrasts with the use of 'now' (*da lta*) found in the commentaries of Bu ston Rin chen grub (1290–1364) and Sa bzang mati paṇchen 'Jam dbyangs blo gros (fourteenth century), both of whom add 'now' or 'present' (*da ltar*) to their gloss, but clearly imply that the 'now' referred to is the present *body*, the body of this life, rather than the body at the very present moment. Not surprisingly, these commentators also take the narrower application of 'future sufferings', in contrast to bSod nams rtse mo's wider application. Thus Bu ston comments that on the opponent's premisses it absurdly follows that one does not protect the present body (*da ltar gyi lus*) against the suffering (Bu ston uses the Sanskrit *duḥkha* throughout) of the body which, in a later future birth, is born in hell. This is because the harm is not caused to the present body.[8] Bu ston reiterates therefore a point made strongly by Prajñākaramati, that the being who dies and the one who is reborn are different, at least as far as their bodies are concerned. Sa bzang mati paṇchen agrees, and adds the moral implication – that absurdly on the opponent's grounds one would make no effort to give up unskilful acts in order to protect oneself against future sufferings, that is, the sufferings of future unpleasant rebirths.[9] The point is important, since it follows that the opponent's position – the suggestion that I should not concern myself with the sufferings of others because they do not hurt me – has the same negative moral implications as *ucchedavāda*, the teaching that there is no future life, a cardinal wrong view for all Buddhists, and one which is thought to have rather unpleasant consequences in the hellish rebirth which comes no doubt as a considerable surprise to the one who would undergo it. Likewise, of course, Śāntideva wants to argue that the reverse applies. The denial of *ucchedavāda*, the acceptance that there are future lives and our happiness or unhappiness in those lives depends upon deeds done now, has the same moral implications as the suffering of contemporary others. To protect ourselves against future sufferings by giving up unskilful acts is no more rational, and no more morally acceptable, than protecting contemporary others against contemporary sufferings. They have the same rationality and moral acceptability.

Bu ston has nevertheless a problem. He has argued an absurdity would follow on his opponent's premisses, that one would not protect the present body against the suffering of future lives. But, we might reply, actually it is not the present body which is protected against those sufferings, since the present body will not endure the sufferings of future lives. We have seen that commentators seem to agree that the body which dies and the one (re)born are different. This is accepted by Bu ston. While we can speak of the present person protecting him or herself against sufferings in future lives – speaking conventionally and ignoring the issue of what exactly is being protected here – we cannot speak of protecting the present *body* against sufferings in future lives. Thus if Bu ston's addition of 'present' refers to the body he faces problems not faced by bSod nams rtse mo in using 'present' for the present time, the present moment, with reference to the wider application. We can make sense in conventional terms of acting in the present moment to protect oneself from future sufferings, without specifying any particular further reference either as to when in the future the sufferings would be expected or to what will be the subject (body or not) which might otherwise undergo the sufferings, in a way that we cannot make sense of protecting the present body against sufferings in future lives. Let us note moreover that only one of the Indian commentators adds 'now' to his gloss, presumably because the reference to the 'sufferings of future bodies' in the Sanskrit text implicitly but clearly contains a contrast with the body of this present life. The Tibetan, on the other hand, refers simply to 'future' (*ma 'ongs pa*), even though this expression usually is taken to mean future lives. The one Indian exception is the commentary by Vibhūticandra of Jagaddala, whose *Bodhicaryāvatāratātparyapañjikā Viśeṣadyotanī* was written in about 1200. He comments that if the other is not to be protected then, since one is not harmed now by the suffering of a future body in the hells, why is that to be protected against by turning away from unskilful acts? Clearly the contrast he draws is between this life and future lives.[10] Vibhūticandra himself visited Tibet in 1204, and his commentary is later than that of bSod nams rtse mo. Nevertheless he makes no attempt to introduce the wider application which we have found stated in the latter's work. In general it is Tibetan commentators who make explicit the contrast with now/present, but it is left to bSod nams rtse mo and rGyal tshab rje to tease out the apparent absurdity (albeit implicitly) of restricting these terms to the present lifespan or present body alone, and draw a contrast instead between simple present and any other future time.

bSod nams rtse mo sees the issues of future lives and future suffering within this present life as being for Śāntideva's argument exactly the same, and both are here identical in the relevant sense with the suffering of contemporary others. If the opponent wishes to argue that I should protect myself against only whatever is causing harm to me *now*, then there is no difference between referring to suffering in future lives, and suffering which will occur at any time whatsoever in the future. In both cases there are no grounds for protecting myself against those sufferings which are future and therefore not happening now.

In commenting on *Bodhicaryāvatāra* 8:97 rGyal tshab rje seems hardly concerned with future lives at all, and his argument is based solidly on what he sees to be a noncontroversial everyday attitude. From fear of suffering which will arise in old-age, he points out, we accumulate wealth while still young. But it is clear that rGyal tshab precisely wishes gradually to narrow down the gap between precedent and subsequent, that any future related to what has preceded – no matter what the time gap – will serve his purpose in indicating the desired relationship. Thus, he adds, from fear of suffering which will arise tomorrow, or in the late afternoon, we busy ourselves today, or in the early afternoon, in means to overcome that suffering. On the opponent's grounds this must be unreasonable. rGyal tshab rje then generalises and here, perhaps, he makes mention of future lives in passing. Future lives are just a particular example of the general principle: 'It would follow absurdly that if the suffering of later time, or future time (*ma 'ongs pa'i sdug bsngal* presumably equals here future rebirths) does no harm to the former person (*gang zag*) then why is that to be protected against? Such protection would be unreasonable.'[11]

The wider application is philosophically different from the narrower application, although I have argued that in the Buddhist context it is a natural development. It is apparently attractive, for not all believe in future lives, and even those who do profess a nominal belief do not in fact exert themselves to avoid the sufferings of future rebirths. Just about everyone, however, takes pains to avoid future sufferings which will come in this life. On the other hand the wider application has problems in that it portrays as irrelevant the apparent difference between my normal experience of continuous survival in one life, accompanied (although by no means necessarily identical with) bodily continuity, and the sort of survival which is claimed to occur in the case of rebirth, normally with a very different bodily form and some rather radical breaks in continuity. Śāntideva wants a case which he can point to where we all agree it is one of otherness and yet we still have concern. This might be supplied by sufferings in future lives, the narrower application. If we adopt instead the wider application and refer simply to future sufferings whenever they occur it becomes debatable whether any opponent would accept willingly a suggestion that all my future sufferings bear to me now the same relationship as do the sufferings of contemporary others. The bodies of my future lives and their sufferings may be different from my body now, as are contemporary others and the sufferings which occur to them, but it is not obvious that the same applies in exactly the same way to my body tomorrow, and the sufferings which will then beset me.

rGyal tshab rje's comments are noteworthy not only for his explicit adoption of the wider application, but also his employment of the term *gang zag*, person (*pudgala*) in glossing these verses. In this he is alone among our commentaries, for the term is not used either by other Indian or Tibetan sources.[12] For the dGe lugs tradition a *gang zag* is defined as 'an "I" which is conceptualised in dependence upon whatsoever of the five aggregates may be the substratum for conceptualisation',[13] and its emphasis in rGyal tshab rje's commentary reflects the dGe lugs stress on the established status of the conventional world which is found in all dGe lugs writings.[14] A person is a conventional entity, for it is dependently originated, conceptualised in dependence upon one or more of the five aggregates. Although the person in this sense can sometimes be spoken of as a conventional 'self' (*ātman/bdag*), and therefore the *ātman* is not totally negated in dGe lugs Madhyamaka, the term *ātman* has other usages connected with inherent existence, a True Self, which are not accepted in any sense by Madhyamaka.[15] rGyal tshab's use of the term *gang zag* makes it clear that he does not see the opponent's position or Śāntideva's counter-argument as one involving the sufferings of bodies as such, but rather as one between persons, which is much wider in scope than a concern for bodies. Bu ston had argued that the opponent would be unable to protect the present body against the sufferings of future bodies. We have seen that this is problematic, for it seems unlikely that anyone could argue coherently for protecting the present *body* against the sufferings of future bodies. *Prima facie* rGyal tshab could argue much more plausibly for protecting the present person – in other words, say, Archibald – against the sufferings of future persons, that is, the person Archibald will be in his future life/lives. Moreover rGyal tshab rje's use of *gang zag* enables him to develop more clearly Śāntideva's argument, since in removing the sufferings of contemporary others I aim to remove the sufferings of other persons, not only other bodies. Finally, in employing *gang zag* rGyal tshab indicates how his argument is firmly anchored to the level of conventional truth (*saṃvṛtisatya*), there is for him no danger that any of his discussion will be confused with the question of a truly existent Self (*ātman*). But rGyal tshab's apparent innovation in interpreting Śāntideva also leads to some important philosophical differences. For it is one thing to speak of my present body as other in relationship to future bodies in the same significant way that I am other to contemporary others. It is quite another thing to refer to me as a present person as bearing the same relationship to the persons of my future lives as I bear now to contemporary others. The problem would be even more acute were rGyal tshab to apply the notion of personhood across the wider application. For surely my relationship to contemporary other persons could not be the same as my relationship to other persons at any time in the future in my own present-life continuum? Can it make sense to speak of future other *persons* in my own continuum?

The opponent had started by suggesting that there is no need to protect against the sufferings of others, for they do not hurt me. Śāntideva countered by concluding that on the opponent's premisses there should be no actions to protect against sufferings in future lives (or future sufferings), since they too do not hurt me. Of course, the opponent, like anyone with common sense, is going to point out to Śāntideva that my relationship now with my own future psycho-physical states is by no means the same as my relationship with the psycho-physical states of contemporary others. The suffering that is at present happening to someone else is happening to an *other*; the suffering which will come to me tomorrow (on the wider application) or in a future life will happen to *me*. Śāntideva's argument appears to require one of:

(i) The relationship between myself at any time in this life, including the last moment, and myself in future lives, including the first moment of my next life (or the intermediate state for some Buddhist traditions), is the same relationship between myself now and contemporary others (the narrower application);
(ii) The relationship between myself now and contemporary others is the same as the relationship between myself now and myself at any time in the future (the wider application).

The opponent is going to deny both of these. Clearly the relationship between myself in this life and myself in future lives, or myself now and myself in the future is different from that to contemporary others, for in the first two cases we are talking about myself, in the other case my relationship with others. It is rational to protect myself in the one case against sufferings, since they will be experienced by me. In the other case they will be experienced by others, and Śāntideva's argument in *Bodhicaryāvatāra* 8:97 precisely begs the question. The issue is not what is harming me now (or in this life), but what harms me full-stop. Śāntideva has given no grounds for showing that I should concern myself with the sufferings of others. Thus Sa bzang mati paṇchen has his opponent observe with eminent common sense that: 'The cases [of future suffering and the suffering of contemporary others] are dissimilar. The suffering of another is not experienced by someone else, and my suffering is always experienced by only me'.[16] So, rGyal tshab rje points out, it is coherent to act now in order to avert future suffering, since if I do not it is me who will surely experience the recompense.[17] The opponent's position does not collapse into that of an immoralist.

Śāntideva, a Mādhyamika, could scarcely be convinced by common sense:

BODHICARYĀVATĀRA 8:98

> If you consider that 'I will experience that', such conception is false /
>
> Indeed other the one who died; other also is the one who is born /[18]

Note that to say that my future sufferings are to be guarded against because otherwise they will actually happen to me, and naturally I do not want to experience suffering, is not in itself to make any metaphysical or ontological claim about who or what the 'me' is – an enduring Self, for example – to whom these sufferings might happen,[19] and the opponent's argument does not in itself require such a claim. When I tell my children that they should clean their teeth regularly before going to bed because otherwise they will experience toothache I am not *as such* committed in any way to an acceptance of a metaphysical claim about my children's ultimate nature, the existence perhaps of an ultimate and continuing Self. Likewise when I wake up in the morning and claim to be the same person who went to sleep I am not making any claim about an ultimate enduring Self.[20] What it is to be the same person who went to sleep is tied up with the social, psychological, linguistic and perhaps even political construction, the place in the Life World, which is me. Structurally, it is not to wake up and be *someone else*. The psychologist Susan Blackmore has commented that from the point of view of contemporary psychology,

> there is the self-image. We know our names and we attribute personality characteristics to ourselves. We know who we are by all the social and linguistic processes by which people develop ideas about themselves and each other. As we grow throughout our lives we have an ever changing concept of who we are [The self] is a process in flux and dependent upon a functioning brain There is no self, only a process of self-construction.[21]

If I woke up in the morning and I was someone else then I would not be me. If I do not wake up as someone else then it is me. Looked at one way this is of course tautologous, but to state it is not useless. What is to count as being someone else, or not being someone else, depends upon many factors. One of the least relevant candidates however, I suggest, is having the same unchanging absolutely real Self. Looked at another way perhaps we do not have tautology here. To be me is to be the focus of 'me-constructions' from myself and others, and arguably to be the focus of these constructions requires no further explication in this context than *not* being the focus of 'other-constructions'. If I woke up as Archibald I would not be the same person as the Williams who went to sleep. If I do not wake up as Archibald or anyone else then I am the same person as Williams. What more do we need?[22]

So it seems that the opponent is not committed to any notion of an enduring Self in claiming that the one who will get toothache will be me, and therefore I am justified in guarding now against toothache by cleaning my teeth regularly. Why should I care about the toothache of others? Quite clearly when I clean my teeth I am not thinking that I am preventing the toothache of another person. Even if on Buddhist premisses one claims that the I who will experience toothache will actually be different from the I who now cleans the teeth, arguably that 'I' could not be different *in the same way* that contemporary others are different, and speaking of them both as being different in the same way is simply a cause for confusion. It is quite clear that in the one case pain will occur to me, that is, among other things certain brain processes will take place which form part of the continuity which contributes a major part to 'me-contructions', and in the other case the pain sensations will not occur to me but to another.[23]

When we come to the issue of rebirth (the narrower application), however, the opponent begins to face problems. And in spite of bSod nams rtse mo and rGyal tshab rje's treatment of the previous verse it is rebirth and the narrower application which Śāntideva has in mind in *Bodhicaryāvatāra* 8:98. This is clear from the second part of the verse, where Śāntideva specifically refers to death and rebirth. The opponent's problem is serious, although as we shall see it is not clear that Śāntideva's treatment of it will give him the result he wants. What Śāntideva appears to be claiming here is that the relationship between me in this life and 'me' in 'my' future lives is one of complete otherness, like contemporary others. The fact of causal continuity is not relevant to issues of identity and otherness. For Śāntideva the opponent is simply not rationally justified in claiming that '*I* in a future life will experience future sufferings which result from my deeds now.' Whoever will experience the results, it will not be *me*. It looks as though Śāntideva is right. Given the characterisation of self derived from Susan Blackmore, as a fluctuating construct dependent upon bodily, social, psychological factors and so on, it is difficult to see how it could make any sense to speak of the (re)born being – even supposing one accepts the coherence of the process which is usually called one of 'rebirth' – as being me. It will not be the same person as the person who died. rGyal tshab rje makes this point very clearly. That person who has died, he comments, is one thing. The later person who is born is another. It is not at all suitable to see these two as one. Since the two are separate it would be irrational on the opponent's premisses for him or her to argue for the removal of the suffering of the one person by another person.[24] Thus rGyal tshab continues to base his discussion of Śāntideva on the *gang zag*, and what he says is of crucial philosophical importance. It is not just that the body of the reborn being is different from the one that died.

Rather we are dealing with a completely different person. Since the *gang zag* is conceptualised in dependence upon the aggregate(s) rGyal tshab rje is saying that the conceptualisations which enable the construction of a person – Blackmore's self – are different in different lives. We are dealing with a different set of constructions and thus for rGyal tshab rje's interpretation of Śāntideva there is no sense in which I survive death. For the I (the self) in the only way in which it can exist is a conceptual construct for rGyal tshab rje and Blackmore, and that construct does not survive death.

It is doubtful that the I which is me could survive even in the sense of felt psychological continuity. In what is probably the most influential contemporary writing on the philosophy of personal identity, the Oxford philosopher Derek Parfit has attacked the importance of the whole notion of personal identity, arguing that what is important when talking about whether I am the same person is not whether I am *identical* with the person Williams when he was six years old but rather whether I have survived as Williams or not. What makes for survival is a matter of experience, it is precisely not identity but experiences of psychological continuity, and survival, unlike identity, is not a matter of either/or but can rather be a question of degree. Identity, on the other hand, is a matter of all-or-nothing. The Williams who was six has survived, but not as someone who is identical with the six year-old Williams. That Williams has without a doubt changed, and I do not know that there would be any mental or bodily state of the present Williams which still remains from the six year old. Over just one lifetime I can change *completely*, there could in a sense be a series of selves, I might well look back on earlier actions and say that the person who did those is no longer me, but through psychological continuity I could still coherently be spoken of as Williams.[25]

It seems unlikely that any meaningful sense of psychological continuity could be experienced from life to life in most cases of rebirth as it is understood in Buddhism, particularly when conjoined to the radical break of physical continuity which everyone agrees happens at death. What could it mean to speak of psychological continuity between an old man who dies and a foetus? Let alone, say, a beetle.[26] There are problems as to whether the nervous system of a foetus or a beetle could support a form of consciousness which could provide psychological continuity with the person (in this case, a human) who died. Of course it could be claimed that consciousness does not depend upon the structure of the nervous system. But I still find it very difficult to make sense of a meaningful continuity which will enable one to speak of *survival* (in a Parfitian sense) of the old man (or a young man who has died) in the foetus or beetle.[27] The upshot of all of this is to lend support to Śāntideva's contention, as clarified by rGyal tshab rje, that the being who is (re)born is a different person from, albeit causally dependent upon, the one that died.[28]

We should note that for rGyal tshab rje this whole discussion has nothing to do with the (inherently existing, isolated, permanent) Self as such. He makes no mention of there not being a Self, and he states categorically that the refutation taking place here is based on the principle of separation between earlier and later moments (stages of a continuum) and has nothing to do with issues of ultimate truth, which is what is at stake for those who hold to the existence of a Self.[29] Once more rGyal tshab rje is out of line with other commentators, including Indian commentators like Prajñākaramati and Vibhūticandra, all of whom seem to think that the essence of Śāntideva's refutation lies in the Buddhist denial of a Self. rGyal tshab rje does not simply follow his Indian predecessors, and here as elsewhere his apparent innovations are philosophically sophisticated and stimulating, if sometimes problematic. In hinting at the irrelevance of the issue of the Self to Śāntideva's argument at *Bodhicaryāvatāra* 8:97–8 rGyal tshab rje is, I think, making good philosophical sense. Whether I can speak of the (re)born being as in some sense *me*, whether I have survived death, depends on whether there is a psychological continuity of experience which would enable me to live through the death process and still feel that it is me.[30] *One* alternative explanation of why it would still be me is to have recourse to an unchanging Self. But this is just one explanation among others, and rGyal tshab rje's opponent does not appeal to that explanation, nor do rGyal tshab rje's comments require recourse to such an explanation. His point is simply that if the (re)born being is a different person – in whatever way we normally understand the concept of person – from the one who died then the person who died has not survived the death process. And if the person does not survive the death process then it makes no sense to say 'I will experience that in a future life'. The future being whom we seek to protect by our actions now would be no more me than contemporary others. No more me not in the sense of not the same Self as me, but rather not the same person in our ordinary everyday sense of 'person'. The opponent might *now* have recourse to a theory of Self in order to explain why in a future life, although I would not be the same conventional person, still it would be the same identical 'me' who is receiving the results. But rGyal tshab's opponent has not yet done so, and it would not be difficult to show that such a reply is inadequate.[31]

While rGyal tshab rje's use of the wider application in interpreting *Bodhicaryāvatāra* 8:97 was philosophically interesting and stimulating, it was probably not what Śāntideva had in mind. rGyal tshab's complete neglect of the issue of the Self in interpreting 8:98, on the other hand, may well fit Śāntideva's intentions. Śāntideva makes no mention of the *ātman* in his verse. The opponent says simply 'I (*aham*) will experience that'. Neither the opponent's nor Śāntideva's counter argument require any reference to the Self. rGyal tshab rje is not at variance with Śāntideva's verse, and he is here philosophically more sophisticated than his rival commentators. Whether he is at variance with Śāntideva's intention we cannot tell for certain. The latter's use of 'conception' (*parikalpanā/rnam par rtog*), which is an expression often used in the Buddhist context to refer to a wrong view about the nature of things, a philosophically wrong understanding, could provide some evidence for an argument that Śāntideva is thinking here of more than just a misunderstanding concerning the conventional person who dies and the one who is reborn.[32] The only other evidence is that of the commentarial tradition. Tibetan commentators will often follow in broad direction their Indian predecessors. But Indian commentators may well embody a venerable lineage of interpretation which could go back to, in this case, Śāntideva himself.

The evidence of the commentarial lineage for Śāntideva's actual intentions is very far from being conclusive, but should not be lightly dismissed. Thus Prajñākaramati has his opponent objecting that 'the I (*aham/bdag*) is always one, it is not differentiated for [different] bodies'.[33] Bu ston's opponent makes the interesting additional claim that not only is the Self always one, but because of that it's body also is said to be me, so that I can say that 'I experience suffering'.[34] Of course, for a Buddhist there is no such Self. 'If we examine it', Sa bzang mati paṇchen says, '[we will find that] there is not established a single permanent Self. The grounds for this are as follows: The aggregate(s) of the one who has died here are other with reference to the future life, and the aggregate(s) of the subsequent (re)birth are other with reference to the present life.'[35] Sa bzang mati paṇchen may well be quite right. The aggregates of this life are different from the aggregates of the future life. Thus, as rGyal tshab rje points out, we are dealing with different persons, and this is all that matters. But as it stands, Sa bzang mati paṇchen is just making an (unnecessary) assertion against the opponent. He simply states without evidence that there is no Self. Apart from the commentarial tradition he had no need to introduce the Self here at all. Simply mentioning the different sets of aggregates would have been enough. The same applies to other commentators. Vibhūticandra makes the direct assertion that the very five aggregates which die in this life are not what is (re)born later (*phung po lnga gang 'dir 'chi ba de nyid kyi phyis skye ba ma yin no*). This may be true and indeed with rGyal tshab rje sufficient to make Śāntideva's point, but such an assertion will not serve as a counter-argument to one who has (according to Vibhūticandra) just maintained the existence of a Self which is held to ensure identity between the one who dies and the one who is reborn. As an argument, Vibhūticandra's assertion seems to *presuppose* that there is no Self and therefore the one who is reborn is also, because of being a different set of aggregates, not the same person as the one who died.[36]

Both bSod nams rtse mo and dPa' bo gTsug lag phreng ba have interesting additional comments to make here, although in the last analysis they fare little better. The former remarks with reference to the statement that that the one who died is other than the one who is born: 'The mental moment has ceased, and the continuum has [also] ceased' (488b: *sems skad cig 'gags pa dang / rgyun 'gags pa'o*). Without a subcommentary it is difficult to see quite what bSod nams rtse mo means here. Certainly the last mental moment of the preceding life has ceased, but it is not clear in what sense the continuum has also ceased. It would not be normal for a Buddhist to say that the mental continuum has ceased. It is possible that bSod nams rtse mo is thinking here of the *physical* continuum of this present life, which ceases at death. Thus with the cessation of the last mental moment of this life, and the cessation of the physical continuum, it is going to be hard (although not impossible) for the opponent to argue that the reborn being is the same person as the one who died.

dPa' bo gTsug lag phreng ba gives by far the fullest and in many respects the most coherent explanation of Śāntideva's argument from the *anātman* point of view, an explanation unparalleled in any other commentary, an elaboration which it is likely springs directly from his own understanding of Śāntideva's text. dPa' bo seems to want to show his opponent that there can be no Self, rather than simply assert it to him or her. As for the Self, he tells his opponent, the thought that it is true as one in past, future and present is a great perverse conception. At birth we have the (grasping) apprehension 'I am born'. That apprehension of a Self (*bdag 'dzin*) at the time of birth ceases in that very moment, and after that for a long time we have the apprehension 'I am becoming strong'. That apprehension also having ceased we think 'I am old'; that having ceased we think 'I am dying'. Such apprehensions certainly occur in succession. We see that on the cessation of the former apprehensions of a Self later ones arise. Because of this we experience directly (in our very own awareness) that there is not just one apprehension of a Self. Moreover, dPa' bo continues, take the mind or body which are (perhaps) apprehended as a Self. Immediately after birth the mind lacks clarity and the body is feeble. When one is becoming strong the mind is clear and the body is physically hard. In old age both are weak. And at the time of death the power of both collapses. Because of this we see directly in our experience that the former way of existing subsequently ceases. Certainly we see ourselves directly that body and mind are impermanent.[37]

Thus what dPa' bo gTsug lag phreng ba is saying is that we all know from our experience (i) that when we use the word 'I' its meaning and indeed its referent depends upon the context in which it is uttered, and this context will differ from stage to stage in our life – the word 'I' does not have a univocal meaning; and (ii) neither mind nor body which might normally form the referents of the word 'I' are single, inherently existing and unchanging, they do not fit the description for a Self. dPa' bo wants to say to his opponent that we all agree from our own everyday experience that our use of the word 'I' does not in fact refer to the Self which the opponent seems to require. What dPa' bo does not show here however is that there is no such Self. It is open to his opponent to claim that there is indeed a Self which is absolute, unchanging, and *not* that which is referred to (at least directly) in our normal everyday use of the word 'I'. dPa' bo gTsug lag phreng ba has clearly shown to the opponent what the opponent is claiming when he asserts a Self, and he could now of course continue to charge the opponent with introducing an unneccesary metaphysical factor. Since this Self is not what is referred to in our normal use of the word 'I' it is not our *self*, and is completely redundant. But dPa' bo does not go on to say this, and as it stands his refutation of the opponent's Self remains on the level of an appeal to the latter to see it's absurdity, rather than a direct disproof.

Unlike the other commentators, apart from rGyal tshab rje, dPa' bo gTsug lag phreng ba does not simply assert that there is no Self but tries to get his opponent to see that this is in fact the case.

Nevertheless on another level his argument remains with assertion, for he does not show that there is no Self beyond our everyday use of the word 'I'. I have argued, however, that dPa' bo does not need to show that there is no Self, for the opponent's assertion in *Bodhicaryāvatāra* 8:98 need not be taken to rest on an assertion of Self. The opponent simply thinks that I will be the same person in my next life. What is strange, however, is that in commenting on 8:98, which seems clearly to refer to the process of rebirth, dPa' bo gTsug lag phreng ba makes no reference to different lives at all, but rather as did rGyal tshab rje on 8:97 he concentrates on the changing use of 'I', and mind/body continuum, in this one life. Clearly dPa' bo thinks that by showing that there is no Self in this one life, it follows that there also could be no Self to carry on into future lives. But what dPa' bo is adding is that even in this one life it would not be correct to say with the opponent that 'I will experience that', for the uses of 'I' vary depending on context. dPa' bo gTsug lag phreng ba is very close here to rGyal tshab rje's employment in his commentary to *Bodhicaryāvatāra* 8:97 of the wider application. Even within one life my own future states could be other 'I's in relationship to myself now, as with contemporary others.

In actual fact we can separate dPa' bo's discussion from the context of his own treatment of the opponent's putative Self and combine it with the perspective of rGyal tshab rje. dPa' bo shows how in everyday life – within one lifetime – the word 'I' lacks univocal usage, and the conventional person is a construct created for pragmatic purpose out of many different contexts of use. We do not consider in everyday life that our uses of the word 'I' refer to an inherently existing and unchanging Self. rGyal tshab's perspective supplements this. As rGyal tshab states, this conventional person does not continue into future lives, for the constructions will certainly then be different from those which are now occurring. There is no unchanging Self, and moreover there is not even a relatively stable person who survives the death process.

I have argued that Śāntideva's attack on his opponent in *Bodhicaryāvatāra* 8:98 does not logically depend on a denial of the permanent inherently existing Self, the *anātman* doctrine, and this point seems to be appreciated, at least through his treatment of the verse, by rGyal tshab rje. There is also a further way in which rGyal tshab's reading of Śāntideva could be of particular value to Mahāyāna commentators. Śāntideva claims to be writing not only for an opponent but also, and probably primarily, for himself (1:2–3). He is himself following through the meditations he develops. Śāntideva sees his text as a guidebook for the bodhisattva path, and those who do not concern themselves with the sufferings of others are not just worldly hedonists, nor even non-Buddhist teachers. One form of eliminating the suffering of future lives is to attain nirvāṇa, the one-sided nirvāṇa which is simply the cessation of rebirth and is associated by the Mahāyāna with the attainments of arhats and pratyekabuddhas. In aiming for nirvāṇa one on the arhat path aims to destroy forever not just present but also future sufferings, sufferings which are not now being experienced. In the light of this, and in its context in the *Bodhicaryāvatāra* and Śāntideva's vision of the complete spiritual path to Buddhahood, Śāntideva's argument at *Bodhicaryāvatāra* 8:97–8 can be taken as applying not just to Hindu and other thinkers who hold to the existence of an *ātman*, but also to other Buddhists who deny the *ātman* but still follow what Mahāyāna is pleased to call a 'Hīnayāna' and also, in the last analysis, fail to concern themselves with the sufferings of others. This for Śāntideva is at least in part because they do not see that it is as rational to eliminate the sufferings of others as it is to eliminate those of their own future lives. In the light of this, we can imagine Śāntideva asking the person seeking for the goal of arhatship why he or she strives for the elimination of his or her own future sufferings while neglecting to strive at the same time and just as much for the elimination of the sufferings of others? If the 'Hīnayāna' opponent thinks he or she will experience sufferings in future lives if they are not eliminated, this is mistaken (8:98) since the person in a future life is not the same as the person in this life. Rather, the future-life person is other in just the same way as contemporary others are other. 'Thus, O follower of Hīnayāna, it is as rational and therefore morally to be expected to strive for the elimination of the sufferings of all contemporary others as it is to strive for the elimination of your own sufferings by becoming an arhat.' If we take 8:98 as appealing to a Self not only is it philosophically less satisfactory but also an argument which Śāntideva would surely want to make against fellow religionists who have not developed the impartial and altruistic mind of a bodhisattva would be lost.

To sum up. Śāntideva has argued that the person who receives the results of my actions in future lives will not be me, and that person is as much other to me in this present life as contemporary others are other than me. It may even be the case that the one who receives the results of my actions in *this* life is as other to me now as contemporary others. Thus if I strive to eliminate future sufferings I should also strive to eliminate the sufferings of contemporary others. Because survival is a matter of degree Derek Parfit is prepared to accept that even within one lifetime it may be quite possible to speak of a series of different selves. So many changes may have occurred to me and my outlook between now and when I am ninety that from my present perspective the ninety year old me may be no different from one who is for me now a contemporary other. As Jonathan Glover points out, if this it true it may have rather dramatic ethical and even legal consequences. We might argue that it would be unjust to try and punish, say, a Nazi war-criminal some fifty years after the original crimes, for he is no longer the same person (self) as the one who committed the crimes.[38] On the other hand we would have to treat our own future selves in just the same moral way as we might be expected to treat contemporary others. Thus, to use Glover's example, to take up smoking now – which could injure me in thirty years time – may be seen as one self harming another self. The fact that the later self is 'my' self does not make it morally different from harming by inflicting, say, bronchitis, on a contemporary other.[39] If I should have compassion for contemporary others then I should also and equally have compassion for my future selves. Likewise the reverse occurs. I am no more justified in considering my own future than the present (or indeed future) of contemporary others. If – and this is crucial to Śāntideva's argument – I concern myself with my own future (selves) then rationally and therefore morally I am obliged to concern myself equally with contemporary (and future) others. Parfit himself has claimed that 'I find the truth liberating, and consoling. It makes me less concerned about my own future, and my death, and more concerned about others. I welcome this widening in my concern',[40] although Glover has commented that he fails to see why Parfit's work ('one of the finest pieces of work in contemporary philosophy') should be particularly consoling as a way of thinking about death.[41] Parfit himself does not offer much reflection on rebirth, although it would follow from what he says that if there were rebirth the level of 'my' survival would be much more problematic than in this life, where we have bodily continuity and, I would argue, a measure of psychological continuity which I cannot see occurring in most cases of (re)birth as understood by Buddhism. It seems clear that for Parfit as for Śāntideva my relationship now to 'my' future births must be the same as my relationship to contemporary others, and rational moral concern should extend to contemporary others if it extends to my 'own' future lives. On

Parfitian grounds Śāntideva's argument in *Bodhicaryāvatāra* 8:97–8 would appear to be correct.

And yet the Buddhist cannot help feeling a certain unease here. Śāntideva has argued that if it is proper to concern oneself with future lives one should also concern oneself equally with contemporary others. But in arguing that the future person is different from the person who dies rGyal tshab rje (aided by the other commentators) has thrown into very considerable doubt the whole question of whether one should concern oneself with future lives at all. Not only will those lives not be *me*, but I have argued that there is likely to be a break in psychological continuity, and certainly in physical continuity, between me in this life – both now and when I die – and the (re)born being. Thus the sort of factors which ensure a continuity in this life will be lost. 'My' future lives will indeed be others. They will not be me in any sense whatsoever. I will not have survived death. But in that case the opponent of *Bodhicaryāvatāra* 8:97 will ask why we should be concerned with our future lives at all? The problem is not the same as regards future selves within one lifetime, because of physical and psychological continuity. Śāntideva had argued that we should be concerned with contemporary others because we have concern for future lives which are also other. But seeing and truly understanding that future lives are other, with arguably not even psychological continuity at least in most cases, the opponent is likely to conclude that it is no longer rational to concern himself, or herself, with future lives. Thus the result of Śāntideva's argument, as developed by his commentators, particularly rGyal tshab rje, is to stress the otherness between this life and future lives and thereby also create a situation where it would seem to follow that one person does the deed and another gets the result. This is a conclusion much feared by Buddhist thinkers among other things precisely because it will lead to a suggestion that there is no need to concern ourselves with future lives. And that is the dreaded *ucchedavāda*, with the immoral consequences which are thought to flow from ceasing to concern ourselves with our future lives.[42] Rationally Śāntideva, rGyal tshab rje and others are in a dilemma. The more they stress otherness between this life and future lives, the more they open themselves to the reply that there is no need to concern ourselves with future lives. After all, one who argues that we have no need to concern ourselves with contemporary others will not stop at denying the need to concern ourselves with future lives. The more it is argued that there is a need to concern ourselves with future lives because it will be us, the less grounds there can be for arguing a concern with contemporary others.

Of course, it could be suggested that this denies the context of Śāntideva's argument. Śāntideva's opponent already engages in actions in order to ensure favourable future (re)births. Therefore Śāntideva is simply saying (like a good Mādhyamika) that this is incompatible with neglect of contemporary others. Such is undoubtedly true, but Śāntideva's opponent is perfectly free to seek consistency by modifying behaviour through neglecting future (re)births rather than helping contemporary others. What Śāntideva's argument shows is an incompatibility. If the opponent is to be rational and consistent something has to be modified. Śāntideva is caught in a dilemma, and he has given no grounds here in *Bodhicaryāvatāra* 8:97–8 for showing that the opponent should adopt the behavioural modification Śāntideva wishes, rather than unwished-for conclusions. If I am a good and virtuous altruistic person then I will indeed agree with Śāntideva that I should concern myself with contemporary others as much as with 'my own' (re)births. And even 'my own' future (re)births I will treat with exactly the same loving compassion as I treat contemporary others. Moreover because these future lives will be determined by actions done by me at least in part in this life, I have a very direct way of ensuring that those lives at least will be lives of happy beings. And as one who is *already* a bodhisattva, or even aspiring bodhisattva, one should indeed concern oneself with those future lives as well as contemporary others. *If* I am moral then my morality should include 'my own' future lives. But clearly this is by no means the direction of Śāntideva's argument. Why I should concern myself with future lives when they will not be me Śāntideva has left undetermined, and it is a very real problem particularly for Buddhists in the modern world. Alas, without giving good reasons here it is difficult to see how Śāntideva's argument could be taken to support the generation of the bodhisattva's altruistic mind of enlightenment for the benefit of others. If that mind is to be developed Śāntideva needs to convince us with other and rather more effective arguments. I for one profoundly hope that he succeeds.

Three

An Argument for Cittamātra

Reflections on *Bodhicaryāvatāra* 9:28 (Tib. 27) cd

The view that the most appropriate way to approach a Buddhist text is where available through a commentary is one with which I am basically in sympathy. Unfortunately, however, where we can find more than one commentary to a Buddhist writing we will often also find widely differing interpretations of even the same verse, particularly as regards philosophical points where the fact of difference appears not always to be realised by the commentators themselves. That we ourselves are not always fully aware of different interpretations is due partly to the emphasis placed in the past on the primacy of Indian commentaries, where often only one commentary to a key text survives, and perhaps partly also to an insufficient philosophical sensitivity to nuances and differences contained in the words used and their implications. I have attempted to show elsewhere however, in looking at the uses of the terms *prakṛtinirvāṇa/prakṛtinirvṛta* in the ninth chapter of the *Bodhicaryāvatāra*, that not only are there some radically different commentarial interpretations of the relevant verses, but when we turn to Tibetan commentators we find that they bring into their understanding of the *Bodhicaryāvatāra* language from the *tathāgatagarbha* tradition of the *Ratnagotravibhāga* which is entirely missing in Indian commentaries and not implied by the *Bodhicaryāvatāra* itself. Thus the relevant verses of the *Bodhicaryāvatāra* are read by Tibetan commentators with reference to their different understandings of the *tathāgatagarbha* tradition, which latter is not mentioned and presumably not needed by Indian commentators. The source for this way of reading the *Bodhicaryāvatāra* was probably the 11th/12th century lama rNgog bLo ldan shes rab, who was closely associated with the transmission and popularisation of the *Ratnagotravibhāga* in Tibet (see Williams (1992); reprinted above). It is clear that reading the Tibetan commentaries will not necessarily tell us as such what the verse means (at least as regards something like the author's intentions), for Tibetan commentators bring into play their own concerns, and link traditions and ideas which may not always have been linked in India. Tibetan commentators moreover – both ancient and modern – often deeply disagree among themselves, although they are more wary of admitting to disagreeing with their respected Indian commentarial predecessors.

Yet they do disagree, even if perhaps they do not always realise that they have disagreed, or boldly proclaim the fact. By way of illustration I want to look further here at the Indo-Tibetan commentarial tradition to the *Bodhicaryāvatāra*, this time at a half-verse which occurs during Śāntideva's treatment and critique of Cittamātra:

BODHICARYĀVATĀRA 9:28CD (=TIB. 27CD)[1]

vastvāśrayaś cet saṃsāraḥ so'nyathākāśavad bhavet//

gal te 'khor ba dngos rten can /
de ni gzhan du mkha' 'drar 'gyur//

Prajñākaramati is the most well-known Indian commentator, not only because his is the only Indian commentary which survives in Sanskrit – and the earliest – but also because Prajñākaramati's commentary even compared with later Tibetan commentaries is impressive for its comprehensive treatment of Śāntideva's verses, particularly on the ninth chapter which deals with *prajñā*. Prajñākaramati takes this half-verse as part of an ongoing Madhyamaka critique of Cittamātra, where the first part (*vastvāśrayaś cet saṃsāraḥ*) articulates hypothetically the Cittamātra position – 'If *saṃsāra* has a real entity as support' – as a response to the Cittamātra wish to demonstrate that consciousness exists ultimately (*paramārthasadvijñānasādhanāya*). Thus for Prajñākaramati's Cittamātrin, *saṃsāra* requires a real substratum and the implication is that this real substratum must also be *vijñāna*. As a Cittamātra argument such is familiar from several Yogācāra sources. It is found for example in the *Bodhisattvabhūmi*, from where it is taken up by Tsong kha pa in his *Drang nges legs bshad snying po*,[2] but the epistemological version of it is rather neatly expressed in the commentarial literature to the *Dharmadharmatā-vibhāga*, particularly the commentary by the 14th/15th century Sa skya lama Rong ston shes bya kun rig (Smra ba'i seng ge):

The topic is 'The dualistic appearance of object and subject' (*gzung 'dzin*). It is false. This is because the dualistic appearance of object and subject is of that which does not exist in actuality. As, for example, the appearance of two moons. That very dualistic appearance is also a cause of someone being afflicted (*kun nas nyon mongs pa*). This is because in dependence upon dualistic appearance there is born dualistic attachment, and in dependence upon that craving and so on are born. As, for example, in dependence upon the appearance of an illusory elephant, a horse in a dream and so on, craving having taken place there occurs someone being afflicted. Now, as for demonstrating the two causes (*gtan tshigs*) of falsehood: Because there does not appear the absence of Self – which is how it actually is (*yod pa* = exists) – [something] is falsely established. It is like when not apprehending something as a heap of stones – which exists – it is apprehended as a man, which does not exist [there]. Since falsehood is not born from non-existence in actuality or existing as mere appearance separately, in order to show that a combination of both is necessary for falsehood to occur [we can observe that] falsehood does not arise when that which is indeed nothing but a non-existent is apprehended as a non-existent (amending *yod par* to *med par*), since the apprehension of non-existence in the case of the non-existent is not mistaken. Falsehood [also] does not arise when that which is nothing but an existent is apprehended as an existent, since an apprehension of existence in the case of an existent is not falsehood. Therefore it is necessary that there is born the apprehension as existent of that which is non-existent in actuality from the combination of both non-existence in actuality and existing as mere appearance. From among the two of them – non-existence in actuality and mere appearance – if there did not exist anything whatsoever there would not arise a falsehood which apprehends as existent that which does not exist. Therefore, even though there does not exist object and subject if there did not exist the falsehood which is dualistic appearance, arising of affliction also would not be possible since there would be no cause. Without the existence of falsehood, as there would also not exist truth (*ma 'khrul pa* = absence of falsehood) which is the antidote to falsehood, purification which arises from that would also not be possible.[3]

In other words, for the Cittamātrin as for so many other Indian thinkers the paradigm of epistemological error is apprehending a thing as other than it actually is. Thus in order to speak of epistemological error – in order for such language to have any meaning at all – it is necessary to have (i) something which does not exist (ii) seeming to exist. It is clear therefore that in order for an epistemological error – falsehood – to occur there has to be a mental operation in which things are thought to be other than they are. This mental operation is the very *condition* of speaking of epistemological ignorance and therefore conceptually prior to it. As a mental operation it is a consciousness, as a consciousness conceptually prior to speaking of epistemological ignorance it cannot be conditioned by that language and therefore must, it is argued, really exist. As Rong ston pa himself has pointed out, for the Cittamātrin this is the basis for an arising of affliction and therefore the purification which leads to liberation. This epistemological argument for an existent substratum seems to be similar to the old argument for sense-data – that even though I may be able to doubt that I am seeing what I think I am seeing, an actual chair, for example, I cannot doubt that I am having certain sensations of a particular describable type. These, it is claimed are indubitable.

The epistemological argument is however just one of what seems to be three linked but logically separable arguments at play here, arguments which are however often confused in the commentarial literature. The second argument is largely a matter of logic, arising as it does out of the nature of negation. The very act of negation requires a substratum, something which is not negated, for negation is the denial of *x* ascribed to *y*, where *y* is the undenied substratum. Thus an attempt to deny everything is incoherent, quite meaningless, and in fact actually affirms in the very act of denial something which cannot be denied which thereby forms some sort of substratum to that denial.[4] It is not necessary for the success of this argument to delineate what the nature of that substratum might be, as it is with the epistemological argument, where the substratum must in some sense be linked to mind or consciousness. It is enough to show that denial must entail a substratum for denial which cannot therefore be embraced in a universal denial.

The third argument is closely linked to the second but the emphasis here is with ontology. It is impossible to deny everything, for if everything were denied there would be quite literally nothing – not even the *illusion* of anything. Even illusion is grounded in something, and that thing could not itself be illusory for fear of infinite regress. If there were to be an infinite regress then the initial illusion would not be established even as illusion. Thus if there is an illusion there must be something which is not illusory. Absence of illusion is entailed by putative universal illusion itself: If *x* then not-*x*, then not-*x*. It is this argument, I suggest, which the Cittamātrin actually appeals to in *Bodhicaryāvatāra* 9:28cd:

> [Cittamātra hypothesis]: *Saṃsāra* has a real entity as support /
> Otherwise that would be like space //

The urgent assertion that *saṃsāra* must have a real substratum – whatever that substratum might be – would have been felt not only through our ontological argument but also derived from the Abhidharma Buddhist inheritance. As is well known, in the Vaibhāṣika Abhidharma one way of dividing all things is into *dharmas*, which bear substantial primary existence (*dravyasat*), and constructs which bear secondary conceptual existence (*prajñaptisat*). Secondary existents exist precisely as conceptual constructs out of primary existents. There can be no secondary existents – which in Vaibhāṣika Abhidharma are thought to actually exist, albeit through conceptual derivation – without the possibility of explanatory reduction to primary existents. If there were no primary existents then there could be no secondary existents at all. To speak of everything being *prajñaptisat* in Vaibhāṣika terms would be not just a disagreeable hypothesis but a self-evident absurdity, a meaninglessly incorrect use of the term *prajñaptisat*.[5] It should come as no surprise to find that the same could be said in Cittamātra, and this appears to be the very direction of the Cittamātrin argument here in the *Bodhicaryāvatāra* and elsewhere. Thus in the *Bodhisattvabhūmi* it is stated that 'if the real entity (*vastu*) for conceptual designation (*prajñapti*) does not exist, being without substratum conceptual designation also would not exist'.[6] This parallels exactly *Bodhicaryāvatāra* 9:28cd – the term *vastu* used for the existent substratum is identical – and it is totally understandable within what we have seen of the Vaibhāṣika framework. The real entity as support of *Bodhicaryāvatāra* 9:28cd plays the same structural role as the real entity for conceptual designation in the *Bodhisattvabhūmi*. The alternative of *saṃsāra* being like space in the former is structurally identical to absence of conceptual designation without an existent substratum in the latter. Without primary *dravyasat* reality there could not be secondary *prajñaptisat* existence. Unless there is something substantially existing nothing would exist at all. The author of the *Bodhisattvabhūmi* subsequently makes this point even more precisely:

> Some speak thus: 'All is mere conceptual designation, and this is the final reality (*tattva*). Who sees in this way sees correctly.' Because of the non-existence for those of a mere reality (*vastumātra*) which is the substratum for conceptual designation, that very conceptual designation also is completely nonexistent.[7]

The author continues by pointing out that these people destroy both final reality (*tattva*) and conceptual designation (*prajñapti*).

It is manifestly obvious therefore that for the author of the *Bodhisattvabhūmi*, as we have seen with the *Dharmadharmatāvibhāga* commentary, the Cittamātra position like that of the Vaibhāṣika requires that if conceptual designation and the sort of existence it bestows is to be coherent there must also be a reality on which it is based. As Rong ston shes bya kun rig points out – following Sthiramati – in his commentary to the *Madhyāntavibhāga*, an admitted Cittamātra denial of subject consciousness in the negation of its objects does not mean complete denial in the way meant by the Mādhyamika. The consciousness which is appearance itself exists *dravyasat* (*rdzas su grub pa yin*), primarily, that is not as merely a conceptual existent, and therefore in terms which interest the Mādhyamika that consciousness is not lacking inherent existence. Although it is not the case that things exist dualistically, as they appear, it is not the case also that there does not exist the substratum for appearance. Otherwise there would be no falsehood and no liberation from falsehood.[8] From a Madhyamaka point of view the arguments we have been examining give the reason for a substratum, in other words reason purports to show that there must be a substratum. Thus a substratum is found under analysis and must therefore really, substantially exist. It would be incoherent to claim that the putative substratum found through these arguments has only *prajñaptisat*, that is, it exists only conceptually or is lacking inherent existence. The Cittamātrin will say to the Mādhyamika that it is not sufficient for him to reply, as he will if he can, that he does not deny everything but only denies inherent existence. The Mādhyamika has to either accept that it is impossible to deny everything, in which case he must also accept that something *has* been found under analysis since he accepts the reasoning, or if he affirms that it is possible to deny everything he contradicts his assertion that all he is denying is inherent existence. What the Mādhyamika cannot do, the Cittamātrin wants to say, is accept that not everything is denied but try and maintain that the substratum to denial, what is not denied, is *prajñaptisat*, i.e. non-inherently existent. In other words it is not possible to deny only – but all – inherent existence. That is contradictory.

For Cittamātra there has to be two ontological levels. We can note the reference in the *Bodhisattvabhūmi* above to final reality and conceptual designation *both* being destroyed by the claim that all is conceptual designation. This structural opposition between *prajñapti-* and *dravyasat* is at the very heart of Cittamātra. It would be as incoherent in Cittamātra terms to claim that all is *prajñaptimātra* as it would be to claim that all is final reality. The view that all is *prajñaptimātra*, which equals in Abhidharma terms *niḥsvabhāva* – opposed in the *Bodhisattvabhūmi* and elsewhere – is however a perspective of Madhyamaka and it therefore seems quite clear to me that these Cittamātra sources are opposing Madhyamaka with a view that something has greater reality than *prajñapti* status, in other words something has primary existential status (*dravyasat*), which is to say exists with inherent existence (*sasvabhāva*). I state this sensitive to a contemporary view sometimes expressed that there is finally no fundamental ontological opposition between Cittamātra Yogācāra and Madhyamaka, and Yogācāra does not in the last analysis hold to the fundamental inherent existence of anything. This seems to me to be patently quite wrong and, I think, strikes at a central and possibly quite sensible pillar of Cittamātra thought. Of course, if the Cittamātrin claims that something really inherently exists because it can be found under analysis as the substratum to denial, the Mādhyamika will show as soon as that is mentioned that it cannot be found, and thus does not have inherent existence. But one way of being found under analysis is to be demonstrably a presupposition of any analysis. The Cittamātrin will reply that the very Mādhyamika analysis presupposes a substratum, and this argument shows that the substratum can be found. The Mādhyamika will now turn to this; the Cittamātrin will reply – and so on, potentially *ad infinitum*. It is not clear whether one should stop this regress at the Cittamātra or Madhyamaka. One can see arguments in favour of either, and neither is patently absurd. But there is without doubt a disagreement.[9]

I have suggested that the most obvious way to take *Bodhicaryāvatāra* 9:28cd is as a clear statement of the ontological argument for a substratum:

> [Cittamātra hypothesis]: *Saṃsāra* has a real entity as support /
> Otherwise that would be like space //

This argument is linked to but not identical with the logical argument and more clearly separable conceptually from the epistemological argument. Thus the whole of the half-verse states a hypothetical objection by the Cittamātrin. Such a way of reading *Bodhicaryāvatāra* 9:28cd is adopted by Tsong kha pa and subsequently rGyal tshab rje, who indicate a rare philosophical sensitivity in freeing their commentaries from any reference to psychology thereby separating the ontological from the epistemological arguments. Indeed Tsong kha pa's main concern seems to be with drawing-out the ontology of the Cittamātra position. The verse's real entity (*vastu*) is explained as 'truly established'(*bden grub*); the support (*āśraya*) is a 'substratum' (*gzhi*). Thus for Cittamātra 'all falsehood has a true substratum.That *saṃsāra* rests on a true substratum. Otherwise, if there is no support, like space it would become completely unreal.'[10] The expression 'completely unreal' here, in Tibetan *dngos po med pa*, is the negation of *dngos (po)* which translates *vastu*, the 'real entity'of the *Bodhicaryāvatāra* verse. Tsong kha pa is of course quite aware of the standard definitions for *dngos po* and *dngos med* derived from the tradition of Dharmakīrti. As Tsong kha pa himself puts it in his *Don gnyer yid kyi mun sel*, a *dngos po* is able to generate its object (*don byed nus pa*), whereas a *dngos med* is void of such ability (*don byed nus stong*). In other words, a *dngos med* does not enter into any causal nexus.The example given is that of space.[11]

Tsong kha pa's commentary on *Bodhicaryāvatāra* 9:28cd differs notably from that of Prajñākaramati, which is strange since Tsong kha pa is usually keen to follow those whom he sees as his great Indian Prāsaṅgika predecessors. Prajñākaramati takes the whole of 28cd to be an onrunning Madhyamaka objection to Cittamātra, and reads *anyathā* not as 'otherwise' but closer to 'other'. Thus Prajñākaramati reads the verse as:

> If *saṃsāra* had a real entity as support/
> That would be other [than a real entity], like space //

What the Mādhyamika is saying is that granted the Cittamātra position '*saṃsāra* would be other than mind (*citta*), and being other than a real entity it would be an unreal entity. This is because it is indeed mind which has the quality of reality'. The example offered is that of space.[12] For Prajñākaramati *Bodhicaryāvatāra* 9:28cd is not given as an argument *for* the Cittamātra position at all. It is the Mādhyamika who is speaking. He continues with his own argument intended to demonstrate that *saṃsāra* must indeed be a non-reality on Cittamātra premisses, and this argument is I think one of the features of Prajñākaramati's comments here which enables us to trace their influence on subsequent commentators. Is *saṃsāra* a real entity or a non-real entity? If it is a real entity, is it mind or other than mind? If it is a real entity and mind then it is not other than mind, and also that very mind which is *saṃsāra* is the support for *saṃsāra*. That mind is clear-light by nature and for this reason, because it has also the nature of purity, it follows that such a *saṃsāra* is not to be abandoned – which is an obvious absurdity. But if *saṃsāra* is other than mind then, being separate from mind, this would undermine Cittamātra tenets. The only alternative therefore is that *saṃsāra* is a non-reality. Then, however, *saṃsāra* becomes simply non-existent, like the proverbial hare's horn. Which is to say, Prajñākaramati adds, like space and therefore lacking in causal efficacy.[13] Thus Prajñākaramati sees *Bodhicaryāvatāra* 28cd as an attack on the Cittamātrin. He was possibly influenced by the fact that the Mādhyamika in the subsequent verses 29-30 does indeed play on a purported absence of reality for the Cittamātra *saṃsāra*, and the problems this gives in relating *saṃsāra* to a putative existent substratum. Nevertheless the interpretation offered by Prajñākaramati is not an obvious interpretation and is indeed rather clumsy. It is not followed by Tsong kha pa, although it is followed by many other Tibetan commentators. It is possible that Tsong kha pa's approach was influenced in this respect by the short comments of Kalyāṇadeva, who in his commentary to the *Bodhicaryāvatāra* clearly attributes 9:28cd to the Cittamātrin.[14] It seems likely also that Tsong kha pa was impressed by the linkage in 28cd of a *dngos po* in opposition to an alternative of being like space. The opposition of *dngos po* and *dngos med*, and the claim that there must be a *dngos po* in order for causal operations to take place, would have seemed an obvious argument for Tsong kha pa and an obvious way to take the verse given Tsong kha pa's learning in the tradition of Dharmakīrti and his intended integration of all the Buddhist traditions into a unified whole. This holistic approach to the Buddhist traditions, and a thorough background in Dharmakīrti, may well have not been so influential on an Indian like Prajñākaramati. Or perhaps Prajñākaramati simply took advantage of developing another argument to attack Cittamātra.

Prior to Tsong kha pa we find both bSod nams rtse mo in the twelfth and dNgul chu Thogs med in the earlier half of the fourteenth century simlarly taking the whole of *Bodhicaryāvatāra* 9:28cd as the position of the Cittamātrin. Neither commentator shows any sign here of the influence of Prajñākaramati although their commentaries are somewhat less adequate philosophically than those of Tsong kha pa and rGyal tshab rje in that their explanations employ the psychological terminology of the epistemological argument (for example *gnyis med rang rig* in bSod nams rtse mo; *gnyis med kyi shes pa* in Thogs med). Indeed Thogs med expresses the epistemological argument rather clearly: 'There exists a real entity as support for that dual appearance because otherwise, like space, there would not exist even the realistic appearance (*dngos por snang ba*) of object and subject'.[15]

By way of contrast we find Bu ston following Prajñākaramati very closely indeed. Like the latter, Bu ston takes the whole of *Bodhicaryāvatāra* 9:28cd as an argument by the Madhyamaka against Cittamātra.[16] A variation however is found in the commentary by the fourteenth century lama Sa bzang mati paṇchen 'Jam dbyangs blo gros. This teacher seems to have been a pupil of Dol po pa Shes rab rgyal mtshan, and I argued in my paper on *Prakṛtinirvāṇa/prakṛtinirvṛta* that Sa bzang mati paṇchen's commentary to the *Bodhicaryāvatāra* shows certain signs of a *gzhan stong tathāgatagarbha* orientation. Noteworthy about his commentary on 9:28cd, apart from a stress on the need of the Cittamātrin to show that consciousness (*rnam shes*) is ultimately, truly established, is the way in which Sa bzang mati paṇchen splits the half verse, so that the first part (*vastvāśrayaś cet saṃsāraḥ*) is taken to be a hypothesis put forward by the Cittamātrin, while the second part (*so'nyathākāśavad bhavet*) is, with Prajñākaramati, the Madhyamaka reply. Thus far from being able to understand a verse by referring to the commentaries, we find as regards *Bodhicaryāvatāra* 9:28cd at least three variations on so basic a point as who is actually speaking. This is not moreover simply the case in Tibet, as all these variations probably go back to Indian sources, for a predecessor of Sa bzang mati paṇchen's division can be found in the commentary by Vairocanarakṣita.[17]

I want finally to look briefly at two other Tibetan commentaries to *Bodhicaryāvatāra* 9:28cd, the one by Mi pham and the other that of Padma dkar po. Mi pham's nineteenth century commentary provides a wonderful example of synthesis, for he in fact integrates both principal ways of reading the half-verse in what must be the proper *ris med* approach. I have shown elsewhere that Mi pham, who although a rNying ma pa studied at dGe lugs monasteries, had among the works before him while writing his commentary on the ninth chapter of the *Bodhicaryāvatāra* the commentary by rGyal tshab rje.[18] It seems likely that Mi pham also initially followed dGe lugs exegesis on 9:28cd, since although he shows signs of confusing the epistemological and ontological versions of the argument he does indeed take the whole half-verse as indicating the Cittamātra perspective. Thus:

> Someone thinks: This *saṃsāra* has a support which is established as a real entity – the mind which is the dependent nature (*gzhan dbang/ paratantra*). Otherwise, like space, there would be nothing at all, and the arising of this appearance which is *saṃsāra* would be absurd. Were there no substratum as support it would be like a pot without clay, or cloth without threads.[19]

Immediately after this passage, however, Mi pham gives the argument from Prajñākaramati for showing that *saṃsāra* must be a non-real entity, an argument which seems to be characteristic of Prajñākaramati's approach to the half-verse. Mi pham links this argument with the next verse, which does indeed embody a Madhyamaka argument against Cittamātra resting on the problems involved in relating an unreal *saṃsāra* to a real substratum. Mi pham's strategy – which I strongly suspect originated with him – is wonderfully neat and absolutely masterful. He is able both to treat 9:28cd in the obvious way as an argument by the Cittamātrin for a real substratum, while at the same time using Prajñākaramati's clever piece of dialectic in order to show *saṃsāra* as a non-real entity. Mi pham's strategy is so neat one wonders why it was not thought of before, and there is a faint suspicion that it was Mi pham who first realised the difference in the commentators' treatment of *Bodhicaryāvatāra* 9:28cd, and what the nature of that difference was.[20]

There remains the strange case of the 'Brug pa bKa' brgyud teacher Padma dkar po, who offers an interpretation of our half-verse which bears little relationship to any other Indian or Tibetan commentary I have examined. While Padma dkar po like Tsong kha pa and Mi pham takes the whole of 9:28cd to be an argument of Śāntideva's opponent, his understanding of the contrast between the first and second parts of our half-verse lies not in an argument for a real substratum and what would happen if there were no such substratum, but rather the contrast between not engaging in critical investigation and subsequently undertaking such investigation. It stands as a statement of a particular vision of Cittamātra with echoes of certain interpretations of the *tathāgatagarbha*, but in Padma dkar po's version it appears not to be offered as an actual argument for a really existing substratum. Thus Padma dkar po has his opponent suggesting that even though *saṃsāra* is, like an illusion, untrue nevertheless it should be seen from the perspective of the non-critical mode, since it does indeed appear to the mind. To that extent, Padma dkar po explains, like a cloud obscuring the real nature (*vastu/dngos po*) of the mind *saṃsāra* has a support. Thereby deeds of *saṃsāra* take place. Alternatively (*anyathā/gzhan du*), if that is critically examined, having cleansed it away, because the mind's very own nature would be pure like space, deeds of *saṃsāra* do not occur and thus there is enlightenment.[21]

It would be almost impossible to see Padma dkar po's interpretation as a natural reading of the Sanskrit, and it also seems forced as a gloss on the Tibetan. As an interpretation it shows perhaps a preoccupation on the part of Padma dkar po with the innate purity of consciousness and a contrast between critical investigation and non-investigation which reflects certain disputed Tibetan interpretations of Madhyamaka. Our present state of knowledge of Tibetan thought is so extremely fragmentary that it is difficult to know whether or not Padma dkar po derived his interpretation from any previous source. It cannot be found even hinted in any surviving Indian commentary to the *Bodhicaryāvatāra*. Perhaps he was innovating. In spite of what is sometimes thought Tibetans are in general far from slavishly following their Indian predecessors (although we should note that on 9:28cd it is Bu ston who follows very closely the commentary of Prajñākaramati).

One thing anyway is clear. It is not possible to talk of *the* commentarial interpretation of this text, and any attempt to read or translate an Indian text with reference to just one commentary, ancient or modern, and a claim that this commentary gives us the text's meaning is fraught with hermeneutical problems. I have suggested in the case of *Bodhicaryāvatāra* 9:28cd which interpretation seems to me is likely to be closest to Śāntideva's intentions, and is also philosophically the most sophisticated. But even if we can be sure what we are looking for when we talk of closeness to the original intention – or philosophical sophistication – and be sure we have found it, still these are only two criteria for adequacy in a commentary. I have not said which commentary is best. Nor do I intend to do so.

Four

Identifying the Object of Negation

Bodhicaryāvatāra 9:140 (Tib. 139) in Context[1]

Introduction

It is possible, as is suggested by the controversial fifteenth-century lama Shākya mchog ldan, that the requirement of first identifying what exactly is being denied when one puts forward emptiness, and then following through a series of detailed and precise inferences in order to show that the negandum can indeed be denied, in other words that *x* is empty of the negandum, was first made explicit by Kamalaśīla.[2] Whether this is the case or not, such an approach to emptiness is a central feature of the dGe lugs perspective. It rests on an understanding of the logic and epistemology of emptiness as a *negation* or absence, a particular sort of *abhāva*. In order for negation to be coherent it is necessary to know what is being negated. In order for a negation to be seen to be true, it is necessary to have grounds – inferential, perceptual and so on – leading to a conclusion that the negandum is not the case. A negation not understood as negating anything, an absence which is not the absence of anything – a thing which could and at some point should be mentioned – is meaningless. A negation without grounds is pure surmise, and as such cannot be the object of any type of claim to knowledge. Thus if emptiness is a type of negation or absence a statement that *x* is empty must always be capable of explanatory clarification through answering the question 'Empty of what?' Moreover if emptiness is a type of negation then in order to claim to *know* that *x* is empty it must be possible to state satisfactorily the grounds for that claim. A claim to knowledge is also a claim to have grounds. In other words, in the Indo-Tibetan context, it must be possible to show the inferences and so on, to show how emptiness can be demonstrated by one or more of the means of valid – that is, verifying – cognition (*pramāṇa*).

These points concern the logic of negation, and the epistemology of making true negation-claims. They follow from the assertion that emptiness is a type of negation. What also seems to follow is that if there is another mode of access to justifiably claiming knowledge of emptiness in opposition to identifying the object of negation and providing intellectually (rationally) satisfactory grounds (largely inferential) for the assertion of its negation – perhaps what Shākya mchog ldan speaks of as 'an experiential Madhyamaka, based on nonconceptual meditation'[3] – then the emptiness known through that means could not be what we normally mean by a negation, and therefore would have to be a different emptiness, not the emptiness we have spoken of so far and not the emptiness referred to by dGe lugs writers and traced by them to the great Indian Madhyamaka sources.

Whether the need to identify the object of negation and proceed through inferential means can indeed be derived from Kamalaśīla or not, for dGe lugs writers ever since the time of Tsong kha pa the *locus classicus* for the need to identify the object of negation in meditating on emptiness has always been Śāntideva's *Bodhicaryāvatāra* 9:140 (Tib.: 139) ab:

BODHICARYĀVATĀRA 9:140 (TIB. 139) AB

kalpitaṃ bhāvam aspṛṣṭvā tadabhāvo na gṛhyate /

brtags pa'i dngos la ma reg par /
de yi dngos med 'dzin ma yin /

Not having contacted a conceptually-constructed entity (*bhāva*) /
The negation (absence – *abhāva*) of that is not apprehended /[4]

Given the centrality of analytic investigation in the dGe lugs perspective, the fact that analytic investigation is absolutely essential in order to be able to obtain an inferential and eventually a direct non-conceptual appreciation of emptiness, and the centrality of understanding the particular negation which is emptiness for the entire dGe lugs vision of what Buddhism is all about, it is arguable that this half-verse from Śāntideva provides *the* authoritative Indian source – in essence – for much of the dGe lugs perspective. It is quoted by Tsong kha pa near the beginning of the *lhag mthong* section of his *Lam rim chen mo*, where he begins to introduce the procedure for developing an understanding of the actual true way of things (*de kho na gtan la dbab pa dngos*). Tsong kha pa makes it quite clear that inasmuch as it is a negation, absence of Self (*bdag med*) or absence of inherent existence (*rang bzhin med pa*), i.e. emptiness, is understood on the model of any other negation: 'In order to ascertain a person is not present, it is necessary to know that person who is not existing [here]'. On this model it is necessary to identify well the Self and inherent existence which do not exist. If there does not arise well a generic impression (*spyi*) of the negandum (*dgag bya*) then the negation (*bkag pa*) of that could not occur accurately.[5] For Tsong kha pa this is crucially important since, as he goes on to explain, if one does not identify the object to be negated properly then one may fall into one or the other of the two cardinal errors of over- or under-negating, and neither is conducive to liberation. That emptiness *is* a negation may be known from its being the equivalent of absence of inherent existence (*niḥsvabhāvatā*).[6] As a negation, it follows from *BCA* 9:140 ab that for emptiness to be apprehended it is necessary to 'make contact with' the negandum, and what could the negandum be but inherent existence itself? Thus for Tsong kha pa this half-verse from Śāntideva is central in his understanding that what emptiness negates is not existence as such but the *inherent existence* of entities. If entities as such are negated one will fall into the fault of nihilistic over-negation. If some inherent existence is not negated, i.e. only some types of inherent existence are negated and an absolute reality is left, then there is the fault of under-negation and thus the complete cessation of grasping (which regularly takes as its object inherently-existing entities) becomes impossible. The whole dGe lugs reading of Madhyamaka is based on seeing that it is only and entirely inherent existence which is negated by emptiness. Hence the importance of Śāntideva's half-verse. One of the clearest statements of the dGe lugs reading of *BCA* 9:140 ab in the context of a need to identify the object of negation is its citation in the edition of Tsong kha pa's *Lam rim chen mo* which is accompanied by annotations by four later commentators. The annotations are in italics:

> Not having contacted *and ascertained by way of its aspect arising before the mind true establishment,* the entity which is *the negandum and is superimposed* (conceptually-constructed) – *erroneously superimposed through grasping after true [existence]* – one is not *able* to apprehend, *by way of cognising with the mind the absence of truth,* the negation of, *i.e. the nonexistence of,* that *true establishment.*[7]

Let us note however an ambiguity in the logic of the dGe lugs perspective here. It is indeed true that in order to negate I must know that which is being negated. This is tautologous. I cannot say that *x* is not, if I do not (implicitly or explicitly) mention *x*. This is to do with the meaningful employment of concepts. I need to be able to employ the concept *x* properly in order to meaningfully negate *x*.[8] But it does not follow for me to meaningfully employ the concept *x* that I need to know very much about *x*. I may not even be able to define it, and I may certainly have a very mistaken idea about it in many crucial respects. Or I may never think about it again as long as I live. Nevertheless I do have the concept *x* if I can use the term '*x*' correctly. Such is all that is necessary in order also to be able to negate *x*, and this is all that is implied by Śāntideva's half-verse.[9] Thus for Tsong kha pa's point concerning negation to be applied to his understanding of emptiness, i.e. absence of inherent existence, all that is necessary is that I have the *concept* of inherent existence, that is, I can meaningfully use the expression 'inherent existence'. That is all. Clearly, however, there is much more in the use of Śāntideva's authoritative source in the dGe lugs gloss quoted above than a simple point concerning the logic of negation. Tsong kha pa's mention of *BCA* 9:140 ab is to state an undeniable general principle about negation; his use of it, however, is in a context which goes well beyond that general principle. In order to understand emptiness as the negation of inherent existence dGe lugs discussions show that we need to know certain things *about* inherent existence and our normal apprehension of it, and this sense of 'contacting' or knowing the conceptually-constructed entity appears to be much more than is contained in Śāntideva's half-verse. That is, there is at least a *prima-facie* difference between 'knowing' in the sense of 'having the concept of' and 'knowing' in the sense of 'being well-acquainted with', or 'acquainted with in all respects which are relevant to some wider context or purpose'. What we find in dGe lugs writings at this point is a slide from being able to employ the concept *x* in order to negate *x*'s – a point which as a tautology could scarcely be denied by anyone – to the need to know certain additional crucial features of *x* and to apprehend *x* (inherent existence) in particular ways in order to understand its negation (emptiness). In other words, a slide from a general point about negation to a specific point concerning emptiness and its apprehension. What follows from this is a very real need to *concern* oneself with *x*'s. This is reflected in Tsong kha pa's emphasis on the need to identify *well* (*legs par*) the object of negation. That this slide can take place here on the basis of a fairly uncontroversial comment by Śāntideva reflects in origin the well-known dGe lugs stress on distinguishing between *what is and what is not negated* in emptiness, and a particular reading of Śāntideva's verse in this light. So, in order to begin to appreciate this reading and its creativity let us now examine more closely Śāntideva's half-verse both in its context within the *Bodhicaryāvatāra* and also within some wider strands of the Indo-Tibetan commentarial tradition.

The pūrvapakṣa – Bodhicaryāvatāra 9:139 (Tib. 138)

The fact that *BCA* 9:140 occurs within a context of the refutation of the Sāṃkhya theory of causation seems to me to be all but completely irrelevant. Such provides the occasion for what is a general criticism of Madhyamaka launched by an opponent, together with Śāntideva's reply, but not the meaning of it.[10] The opponent's – any opponent's – criticisms concern the inapplicability of the means of valid verifying cognition (*pramāṇas*) for the Mādhyamika, and therefore their inability to establish emptiness:[11]

BODHICARYĀVATĀRA 9:139 (TIB. 138)

pramāṇam apramāṇaṃ cen nanu tatpramitaṃ mṛṣā /
tattvataḥ śūnyatā tasmād bhāvānāṃ nopapadyate //

gal te tshad ma tshad min na/
des gzhal brdzun par mi 'gyur ram /
de nyid du ni stong pa nyid /
sgom pa de phyir mi 'thad 'gyur //

If a means of valid cognition (*pramāṇa*) is not a means of valid cognition /
Then would not that which is determined by it be delusory (*mṛṣā*)? /
In reality, therefore, the emptiness of entities (or, with the Tibetan, 'the meditative cultivation of emptiness') will not [then] be acceptable. //

In comparison with the Sanskrit, the Tibetan version of *BCA* 9:139 contains a significant but understandable variant. The reading *stong pa nyid / sgom pa* suggests a Sanskrit model *śūnyatā bhāvanā* rather than, as at present, *śūnyatā bhāvānāṃ*, while on the basis of the Indian commentaries a Tibetan version of the *Bodhicaryāvatāra* half-verse 9:139 cd should read something like:

de nyid du dngos po rnams kyi /
stong nyid de phyir mi 'thad 'gyur //

In addition to Prajñākaramati, all the other significant Indian commentaries (Kalyāṇadeva, Vairocanarakṣita, and Vibhūticandra) confirm the Sanskrit version *śūnyatā bhāvānāṃ*, while all the Tibetan commentaries use *stong pa nyid / sgom pa*. The translation of the *Bodhicaryāvatāra* verses contained in the bsTan 'gyur, however, reads *stong pa nyid / sgom pa*. Interestingly, the only Tibetan commentator to notice the discrepancy between the verse in its Tibetan translation and the Indian commentaries is Bu ston. He observes that the *'grel pa*, i.e. the *Pañjikā (dka' 'grel)* of Prajñākaramati, reads *bhāva* (*dngos po*) and, following an equivalent of *dharma* for *bhāva* stated by Prajñākaramati, Bu ston glosses the second part of *BCA* 9:139 with 'the ascertainment by a means of valid cognition of emptiness, which is the absence of inherent existence of all *dharmas*, also will not be acceptable'. On the other hand, he says, if we follow the Tibetan text (*dpe*), then we can gloss the text with 'it is not acceptable to cultivate through meditation emptiness, because [it is] delusory'.[12] Bu ston appears to have had available a copy of the Sanskrit text of these verses from the *Bodhicaryāvatāra*, since in commenting on the next verse he refers to the Sanskrit particle *hi,* which occurs in the verse itself and is not given in Sanskrit in any of the Tibetan translations. It may be the availability of a Sanskrit text which alerted Bu ston to the difference between the Sanskrit versions and the Tibetan translation. This is not unlikely, as we know for example that Shākya mchog ldan in the next century saw a Sanskrit manuscript of the *Bodhicaryāvatāra* in gLo bo smon thang.[13] Nevertheless even if they did not read Sanskrit this does not explain why other Tibetan commentators took no notice of the discrepancy between the two versions of *BCA* 9:139 cd. The Tibetan translations of Indian commentaries make no mention of *sgom pa*, which should have alerted commentators who are thought to have been sensitive to the Indian commentarial tradition, like rGyal tshab rje. Bu ston's commentary must also have been fairly widely available.[14] One answer may be that Tibetan commentators learnt the root-text by heart, and would therefore have been inclined to favour a version which they had already internalised. They would anyway be inclined to favour what they would see as the original root-text, even if in Tibetan translation. That said, the general conclusion must be that Tibetan commentators did not think the discrepancy very significant, or it suited them to continue reading *stong pa nyid / sgom pa*, a reading which stresses a practical problem alleged for the Mādhyamika, a problem in relating an absence of the means of valid cognition to the path of meditative cultivation and insight. Certainly, for dGe lugs commentators the need to identify the object of negation, a need which forms for them the subject of the

Mādhyamika rejoinder, is directly relevant to the *practice* of meditation on emptiness, since that meditation (*pace* some rival Tibetan traditions) requires analytic engagement starting from a clear recognition of the negandum. Thus Śāntideva's reply stressing the need to identify the object of negation, interpreted by Tsong kha pa and others as related to the need to identify the negandum in setting-forth emptiness, becomes through the reading *stong pa nyid / sgom pa* a reply directly related to the path of practice – meditation on emptiness – and thus the task of showing that direct insight into emptiness requires identifying the object of negation, and all that goes with it, becomes that much easier. In other words, for dGe lugs commentators at least, it suited their purposes to ignore the difference between the Sanskrit and the Tibetan versions of *BCA* 9:139 cd.

According to the comprehensive Indian commentary by Prajñākaramati, the *pūrvapakṣa*'s point in *Bodhicaryāvatāra* 9:139 can be summarised as follows: The Mādhyamika claims that ultimately (*paramārthataḥ*) a means of valid cognition (or, following Diṅnāga/Dharmakīrti, a valid cognition itself) simply is not a (means of) valid cognition at all. Thus is it not the case that whatever is determined by that means of valid cognition is delusory? What is positively determined (*paricchinnaṃ/yongs su bcad pa*) by that means of valid cognition is delusory and false. And if this is the case then in reality, which is to say ultimately (on an ultimate level), the emptiness of entities, *dharmas*, which is the absence of inherent existence of all *dharmas* and is ascertained by such a means of valid cognition, also could not be acceptable, i.e. would be irrational. Or in other words, because the objects which are set forth by all the means of valid cognition are delusory, the same reasoning can be applied to the absence of inherent existence of all *dharmas,* which is spoken of as 'set forth by the means of valid cognition which investigates it (*tadvicārakapramāṇopadarśita*)'.[15]

Actually it is not completely clear from what Prajñākaramati says whether he thinks the opponent's view is that:

(i) the means of valid cognition can set forth emptiness, but the emptiness thus set forth must be delusory; in other words, the means of valid cognition are means of cognition but not (finally, ultimately) *valid* cognition. As Vibhūticandra puts it, ultimately that emptiness – absence of inherent existence – as ascertained by a means of valid cognition, would be non-existent.[16] Or alternatively:

(ii) the means of valid cognition cannot set forth emptiness at all, simply because they *never* establish their conclusions. As regards the ultimate way of things they thus fail to show emptiness and therefore in the case of emptiness they are not only not means of *valid* cognition but they are not means of *cognition* at all.

For position (i) the means of valid cognition occur, and set forth emptiness, but the emptiness they set forth is delusory (or, for Vibhūticandra, ultimately non-existent) and therefore cannot be the liberating final, ultimate truth. For position (ii) there is a contradiction involved in the very concept of a means of valid cognition, and therefore there is a contradiction in the idea of a means of valid cognition setting forth emptiness. For (i) there exist in terms of conventional transaction what appear to be means of valid cognition, and all the inferences etc. can indeed take place, but the conclusion of emptiness is vitiated by the final problem that on the ultimate level the means of valid cognition are held by Madhyamaka not to be means of valid cognition at all and therefore finally emptiness is not acceptable. Emptiness turns out to be a conventionality, and therefore not the ultimate truth. For (ii) there are no means of valid cognition; all the inferences which set forth emptiness are thus permeated with contradiction. Emptiness cannot be set forth at all, so unlike interpretation (i) emptiness could not turn out on Mādhyamika premisses to be merely conventional. For (i) emptiness is found to be delusory; for (ii) there is an inherent contradiction in the very reasoning which purports to set forth emptiness.

The eventual result of these two interpretations may be much the same – there is no ultimate truth called emptiness – but how they relate to issues like whether for Madhyamaka anyone can employ means of valid cognition at all, whether and how Madhyamaka itself sets out to demonstrate something, and the role of reasoning from a Madhyamaka point of view are complex and different.[17] For (i) there are means of valid cognition conventionally, and the opponent's view is that the Mādhyamika's mistake lies in not realising that on Mādhyamika premisses conventional means of valid cognition cannot set forth an ultimate truth. For (ii) there are no means of valid cognition, they are delusory conventionally and ultimately, and the opponent's view is that on Mādhyamika premisses one cannot employ means of valid cognition at all. Madhyamaka is akin to a form of complete epistemological scepticism.

I suspect that Prajñākaramati would favour some version of interpretation (i), for he introduces his comments (as does Vibhūticandra) by a reference to the means of valid cognition not being means of valid cognition *ultimately* (*paramārthataḥ*).[18] Against this might be urged his observation that the referents which are set forth by all the means of valid cognition are delusory (*sarvapramāṇopadarśitasya mṛṣārthatvāt*), in other words all means of valid cognition are delusory. 'Delusory' (*mṛṣā*) is glossed as '*alīka*', for which the Tibetan translation is *bden pa ma yin*, not true. However since this section of Prajñākaramati's commentary is preceded by the expression *tattvataḥ*, 'in reality', explained by Prajñākaramati as 'ultimately', or 'on an ultimate level', and on this level just as objects set forth by all the means of valid cognition are delusory so emptiness too is delusory, we find thus that there is no contradiction with interpretation (i).[19] When Prajñākaramati's opponent objects that 'in reality, which is to say ultimately, the emptiness of entities, *dharmas*, which is the absence of inherent existence of all *dharmas* and is ascertained by such means of valid cognition, also could not be acceptable, i.e. would be irrational', the objection here is to the contradiction of an ultimate truth established through the means of valid cognition when from the perspective of the ultimate truth itself those are not means of valid cognition and thus all the referents of those means can be only delusory. As Vairocanarakṣita's *pūrvapakṣa* says, in such a case for you the Mādhyamika what confidence could there be in even emptiness?[20]

One of the most interesting Tibetan discussions of *Bodhicaryāvatāra* 9:139–41, which brings in a number of dimensions not explicitly stated in our Indian commentaries, is found in the commentary by the 12th century Sa skya lama bSod nams rtse mo.[21] According to bSod nams rtse mo, the opponent in *BCA* 9:139 is setting-forth two *prasaṅga* arguments against the Mādhyamika. Firstly, he wants to argue that given Mādhyamika premisses the inferential means of valid cognition which is supposed to cut all verbal differentiations (*spros*/*prapañca*) turns out to be mistaken (*'khrul pa*). Secondly, the meditative cultivation of emptiness appears to be pointless (or 'to have no referent' – *don med pa*).

(a) bSod nams rtse mo has his opponent link the first argument specifically to Śāntideva's controversial point in *Bodhicaryāvatāra* 9:2, that 'the conventional is [the referential range of] the mind'.[22] If Śāntideva's comment is true, then since the mind is asserted to be mistaken, then it follows absurdly (first *prasaṅga*) that the inferential means of valid cognition which is supposed to cut all verbal differentiations is also mistaken. In other words, if all mental activity comes within the conventional (*saṃvṛti*), and all conventional is mistaken, then all mental activity must be mistaken and the inferential mental activity which sets forth emptiness, i.e. the cutting of all *prapañcas,* must also be mistaken.[23] Moreover, bSod nams rtse mo's opponent would want to say, if all mental activity comes within the conventional then it cannot reach beyond that conventional to the ultimate which is said to be beyond the range of mental activity. This first argument should be taken as a gloss on the first part (ab) of *BCA* 9:139. The opponent's argument rests on the principle that what applies to all means of valid cognition – they are mistaken – also applies to the means of valid cognition which sets forth emptiness. There is no difference. bSod nams rtse mo makes no mention of 'from an ultimate point of view' (*don dam par*) in glossing the opponent's objection.[24] This first *prasaṅga* is not as such about emptiness. Nor is it as such about the status of the means of valid cognition from an ultimate point of view with reference to their ability to set forth the ultimate truth. It is primarily about the inadequacy of all means of valid cognition in the light of their coming within the range of mental activity, a point which Mādhyamikas such as Śāntideva and Candakīrti themselves hold makes those means of valid cognition conventional and mistaken. Thus there would appear to be a *prima-facie* difference underlying the opponent's objection in Prajñākaramati's (and Vibhūticandra's) commentary, and that of bSod nams rtse mo. Prajñākaramati wanted to say that because ultimately the means of valid cognition are not means of valid cognition then emptiness is not acceptable. bSod nams rtse mo is saying that there are two separate arguments. Firstly, the means of valid cognition (all means) are mistaken, and therefore the inference which sets forth emptiness is mistaken and cannot reach beyond the range of the conventional. Secondly the meditative cultivation of emptiness has no point. This is the result of a separate argument, a second *prasaṅga*, which corresponds to *BCA* 9:139 cd.[25]

(b) bSod nams rtse mo's second *prasaṅga* is an argument based on the ontology of negation which links directly to Śāntideva's reply in *Bodhicaryāvatāra* 9:140. The Mādhyamika maintains against a follower of Sāṃkhya that elements of the latter's system such as cosmic matter (*prakṛti; pradhāna/gtso bo*) are untrue. But, the opponent responds, negation depends upon its negandum (*dgag bya*). Thus if the negandum is untrue the emptiness which is the negation of it must also be untrue. And if that is accepted by the Mādhyamika then in reality (*de nyid du*) the meditative cultivation of emptiness becomes pointless (*don med*).[26] There is a temptation to read this objection by the opponent as a reference to a version of what the logician W.V.O. Quine has called 'Plato's beard'. The negandum which in the case of a true negation is a non-entity, must in some sense *be*, otherwise the negation would not be *of* anything.[27] I do not think, however, that bSod nams rtse mo's opponent wants to make this general point about negation here, arguing that what emptiness negates must in some sense be in order to be able to be negated. Rather this is a *prasaṅga*, a *reductio* for the benefit of the Mādhyamika. Negation originates in dependence upon a negandum. When the Mādhyamika portrays emptiness as a negation, emptiness must be the case in dependence upon a negandum. Granted that the negandum is not true, in other words that there is indeed an emptiness of that negandum, had there not been a negandum there could have been no emptiness. Thus emptiness arises in dependence upon the negandum. But as Nāgārjuna says in the *Madhyamakakārikā*, 'it is what is dependent origination that we speak of as emptiness'.[28] Thus if emptiness itself is dependently-originated it must be empty. Therefore, the opponent wants to argue, emptiness is on exactly the same footing as everything else, no more true than entities which are said to be empty. The Mādhyamika is clear of course that all *dharmas* are empty. bSod nams rtse mo's opponent is saying that it is not just that emptiness cannot be set forth. Rather emptiness is shown to be positively untrue, just like all *dharmas*. And if that is the case, then it makes no more sense to cultivate through meditation an awareness of emptiness any more than an awareness of anything else. In other words, emptiness is not the liberating ultimate truth.

These two arguments of bSod nams rtse mo's opponent are different arguments which seek to make the same general point, that on Mādhyamika premisses he or she cannot treat conventional and ultimate in different ways. Argument (a) purports to show that the means of valid cognition which sets forth emptiness is for the Mādhyamika no different from the means of valid cognition which set forth anything else. Argument (b) tries to show that emptiness itself is no different from anything else and therefore meditative cultivation of emptiness is 'not acceptable', that it is pointless. The assumption underlying argument (a) is that if something is conventional then it is mistaken, and if it is mistaken then it is not true. If it is not true, then it cannot lead to truth, and therefore cannot lead to the ultimate truth. The assumption underlying argument (b) is that if emptiness is dependently-originated it is not the ultimate truth. Thus both assumptions amount to the same general assumption – that on Mādhyamika premisses there can be no move from conventional to ultimate. Both, in a sense, therefore, entail that there is no valid means of cognition which marks that move.

Bodhicaryāvatāra 9:140 – (i) Prajñākaramati's response

BODHICARYĀVATĀRA 9:140 (TIB. 139)

kalpitaṃ bhāvam aspṛṣṭvā tadabhāvo na gṛhyate /
tasmād bhāvo mṛṣā yo hi tasyābhāvaḥ sphuṭaṃ mṛṣā //

brtags pa'i dngos la ma reg par /
de yi dngos med 'dzin ma yin /
de phyir brdzun pa'i dngos gang yin /
de yi dngos med gsal bar brdzun //

Not having contacted a conceptually-constructed entity /
The negation of that is not apprehended /
Therefore, in the case of a delusory entity /
The negation of that is clearly delusory //

According to Prajñākaramati, commenting on the first half of this verse, to be a conceptually-constructed entity (also a *dharma* according to the Tibetan version) is to be superimposed (*samāropita*), the result of *kalpanā*, an act of constructive reification.[29] Having not contacted that, which is to say having not apprehended it by way of a mental act of constructive reification, the negation of it is not apprehended, not perceptually appropriated. [30] Prajñākaramati does not wish to portray this as some complex epistemological theory. His appeal is to our normal understanding of negation. It is just like when we conceive or mentally construct a pot, which then has a form which has been superimposed (on a situation where it is not actually present), and then with reference to that superimposed form we are able to perceive the negation (or absence) of the pot. Thus Prajñākaramati makes a general point about how negation occurs, and the need for implicit or explicit reference in negation to the negandum.[31] We find a similar reference to the everyday negation of a pot in Vibhūticandra's commentary (who may well have been following Prajñākaramati). Vibhūticandra points out that one conceives of the negation (or absence) of a pot by means of having conceptually-constructed (superimposed) the pot at a particular spatial location and then, by means of an everyday type of inspection (*'jig rten la grags pa'i dpyad pas*) one comes to the conclusion that in fact there does not exist at that place any form of a pot at all.[32]

The next stage of Prajñākaramati's argument, however, involves a shift of the concern of his analysis. When the pot is subjected to analytic investigation (*vicāra*), even that analytic investigation which is of the ordinary everyday worldly sort, when no intrinsic form (*svarūpa*) abides then this applies still more to its negation, which has the form of its inversion. This is why Śāntideva states in *Bodhicaryāvatāra* 9:140 cd that 'therefore in the case of a delusory entity, the negation of that is clearly delusory'. [33] In other words, everyone will admit that if there simply does not exist any negandum then also the negation cannot exist. The conceptual shift is important. From an initial half-verse in which Śāntideva puts forward a positive point about the nature of negation, in the second half-verse there is a switch to applying that very same point to the negation of both entity (negandum) and its negation (absence). If Prajñākaramati is right, then Śāntideva as a good Mādhyamika put forward the need of negation for a negandum as a point which would be accepted by everyone – as we have seen earlier, it can indeed be accepted by anyone since it is a tautology – in order then to derive the *modus tollendo tollens* inference that if there is no negandum at all then also there cannot be any negation either. And it is argued that this is all good common-sense. Since, Prajñākaramati continues, by discriminating an entity which has been conceptually-constructed a negation is apprehended, then in the case of an entity which is delusory, the inherent existence of which does not exist, its negation is also clearly delusory.[34] We can see here a further subtle shift in the frame of analysis. Prajñākaramati has moved from:

(i) If there is a negation there must be a conceptually-constructed negandum (a true premise); to
(ii) If a conceptually-constructed negandum has absolutely no existence at all then there can be no negation (a correct inference *modus tollendo tollens*, assuming 'absolutely no existence at all' excludes all forms of conceptualisation); to
(iii) Because a negation is apprehended by discriminating a conceptually-constructed entity, then that entity is delusory and lacks inherent existence as a conceptually-constructed entity; to
(iv) Therefore the negation of that entity is clearly delusory.

The next stage is to argue that the negation also lacks inherent existence. Prajñākaramati explains that a separate negation, of an entity which lacks inherent existence is clearly, certainly, delusory, which is to say untrue. The reason, he explains, is because that negation too has a form which is constructed (*parikalpita*). Thus, he summarises, since both entity and its negation have forms which are constructed there abides (remains) the absence of inherent existence of all *dharmas*.[35] In subtly bringing into play the concept of inherent existence, Prajñākaramati is gradually moving the concern of his analysis from issues relating to negation in general to the specific issue of concern to the Mādhyamika, absence of inherent existence as applied to all *dharmas*. The impetus behind this move is provided by the notion of conceptual construction, since for all Buddhists if something is conceptually-constructed (it is, in Abhidharma terms, *prajñaptisat*) then it lacks inherent existence. Thus if in negation the negandum (*bhāva*) is conceptually-constructed, and its negation (*abhāva*) is conceptually-constructed, then the Mādhyamika requires only one further move – which we have seen Prajñākaramati makes above – to argue that *all* entities and also non-entities, negations, are lacking in inherent existence. That move is a generalisation from the absence of inherent existence of negandum and negation to a claim that all things (positive and negative) lack inherent existence. Then, as Śāntideva points out in *Bodhicaryāvatāra* 9:35:

> When entity (*bhāva*) and negation (*abhāva*)
> Do not stand before the mind /
> Then because there exists no other possibility /
> Without intentional object it is calmed //[36]

But why, we might ask, should negation be said to be delusory or conceptually-constructed – even supposing we accept that what is conceptually-constructed is in *some* sense delusory in that it lacks inherent existence – just because the negandum is conceptually-constructed? In an everyday context we would not normally be prepared to admit that just because it was necessary to operate with a concept of the teapot (rather than a real teapot) in order to say that the teapot is not on the table, the situation of absence of the teapot from the table expressed by the negation is also only conceptual and not real. If a negation *does* occur then in its very occurrence the negandum must be conceptually-constructed. But the negation, the situation of absence, is surely not conceptually-constructed. It appears to be completely real. In reply to this objection it is probable that Prajñākaramati would want to appeal to what Jacques May has called 'le principe de solidarité des contraires ... si A n'existe pas, son contraire n'existera pas non plus'.[37] If the negandum does not exist then the negation also does not exist. What applies to the one applies to the other.[38] The principle underlying this is that of dependent origination. Negation arises in dependence upon the negandum. Since to be dependently-originated is to lack inherent existence, negation must also lack inherent existence, that is, in Mādhyamika terms it must be conceptually-constructed (*prajñaptisat*) and delusory.

That Prajñākaramati does want to appeal to the dependence of negation on negandum is suggested by his reference to the incoherence of a *separate* negation (*abhāvo virahaḥ*), but this dependence is made even clearer by Kalyāṇadeva: 'Because conceptually-constructed entities are delusory, the negation of those is very clearly false. This is because non-existence depends on existence, and if an entity is not established the non-existence also of that is not established'.[39] In general I am inclined to find the principle unconvincing however. Even supposing that negation depends on negandum, the situation expressed by a true negation would still appear to be a actual feature of the world.

Yet it might be possible to argue for another way of looking at it. It is possible to argue that negations are not a feature of the world at all. Negation is the result of a conceptual act, a comparison of some sort between what might be and what is. In a hypothetical world bereft of consciousness there would be no negations. The world would be just what it would be. It is not merely that my *awareness* of an absence of the teapot from the table is the result of mental activity. The very absence of the teapot is also a result of that activity, for in itself there is not a table without a teapot but just a table. The absence of the teapot is a conceptual-construct depending on the postulation that there might be a teapot there. Of course, the causes for there being just a table present, and not a table with a teapot on it, are legion and apparently (*pace* Madhyamaka) by no means all only conceptual. They are causes for a table pure and simple, rather than a table with a teapot, but they are not causes for the negation 'absence of a teapot'. That negation is *only* the result of mental activity – it is purely conceptual.[40] There is an infinite number of things not on the table, but only because there is an infinite number of things which someone might postulate as being on the table. Actually there is just a table, and all those absences *themselves* are the result of mental activity. Not in the sense that were there no mental activity that infinity would suddenly appear on the table, but rather were there no mental activity there would still be what there always was – the table.[41] A negation *qua* negation is as much the result of conceptual activity as is the concept of the negandum which is necessary for negation to take place. Only minds negate, and the situation of absence itself inasmuch as it is delimited from all other situations of absence – and therefore inasmuch as it is a situation of the absence of *x* – is the result of the mind.[42] Thus we can begin to make some sense of Prajñākaramati's claim that negandum and negation are mutually-dependent, conceptually-constructed, and in Mādhyamika terms lacking in inherent existence. Where Prajñākaramati appears to me to be mistaken, however, is in his slide from the absence of inherent existence of *bhāva* and *abhāva* in a situation of negation to a general conclusion that *bhāva* and *abhāva*, entity and negation, in other words all things positive and negative – table as well as teapot and its absence – lack inherent existence. For this he appears to give here no grounds.

Let us conclude our examination of Prajñākaramati's response to the *pūrvapakṣa* of *BCA* 9:139 by noting the salient points of his approach inasmuch as it reflects on his interpretation of *BCA* 9:140 ab. The opponent had argued that since the means of valid cognition are not ultimately means of valid cognition they cannot set forth emptiness. Neither Śāntideva nor Prajñākaramati address *directly* the opponent's points concerning the means of valid cognition or the status of emptiness as delusory. Prajñākaramati puts forward the need for a conceptually-constructed negandum not in order to stress a need to be aware of the negandum in order to understand the negation (a stress on the 'not having contacted'), but rather in order to move *away* from the negandum which is delusory (a stress on 'conceptually-constructed') towards the delusory status of negation and therefore *bhāva* and *abhāva*. This point must be emphasised, particularly in view of what we have seen already concerning the use of Śāntideva's text by dGe lugs sources. In the light of Prajñākaramati's comments (and this is confirmed, or at least not denied, by the other Indian commentaries), Śāntideva's reference to the need for contacting a conceptually-constructed negandum in order to have negation was in order to direct attention away from the negandum through employing the old Mādhyamika strategy of denying the inherent existence of binary opposites. He thus affirms, through accepting the opponent's premisses, universal emptiness, absence of inherent existence. Prajñākaramati's (and, I think, Śāntideva's) interest in the principle that without a negandum there is no negation is solely in order to show that there is no negandum and no negation.[43] It is to move beyond concern with negandum and negation to emptiness, which is affirmed in that very move.[44] Moreover the entity (*bhāva*) referred to in *BCA* 9:140 is *any* entity inasmuch as it is occurring within a context of negation. The verse is not, in Prajñākaramati's discussion, about inherent existence and emptiness as such. Here there is reference to the negandum lacking inherent existence, but not to the negandum in this verse *being* inherent existence, with the negation its lack, i.e. emptiness. Of course, inasmuch as *bhāva* and *abhāva* refer to any entity and its negation the same basic principles could be applied to inherent existence and emptiness (its negation), and there is no doubt that Śāntideva and Prajñākaramati want this conclusion to be drawn. In such a case not only is inherent existence said to be delusory, but also emptiness. It is an implication of emptiness that it must be delusory (i.e. empty), and therefore its delusory nature does not negate emptiness. Thus on that level also it is implicit in Prajñākaramati's discussion that he accepts most of what is contained in the opponent's argument.[45] He accepts that emptiness is delusory, he accepts that ultimately the conclusion of the means of valid cognition is delusory, but he holds that these are not problems – for in that very acceptance emptiness is affirmed. If the opponent is right, and negandum and negation are both delusory on Mādhyamika grounds, then both are empty and thus emptiness is set forth.[46] In the very attempt by the opponent to deny emptiness, emptiness is affirmed. It is affirmed as emptiness, the ultimate truth concerning things. It is not affirmed as an ultimately existent reality, for it is a negation, an *abhāva*, and is therefore correlated to a negandum and is thus naturally conceptually-constructed, empty and delusory. But this does not make it anything other than emptiness, the ultimate truth of things, absence of inherent existence, and it simply does not follow therefore (as we shall see) that to contemplate it through meditative cultivation will not lead to cutting egoistic grasping and thus liberation.[47]

Bodhicaryāvatāra 9:140 – (ii) Some Tibetan comments

bSod nams rtse mo makes explicit a number of the points already drawn from Śāntideva in the light of Prajñākaramati's response.[48] He sees the whole of *BCA* 9:140 as a response by the Mādhyamika to the first *prasaṅga* of the opponent, and bSod nams rtse mo makes it quite clear that Śāntideva accepts that *prasaṅga* in its entirety. The reply, he says, is that we accept that a means of valid cognition which is positively determining is not a means of valid cognition (*thal 'gyur dang po'i lan yongs gcod tshad ma ma yin pa 'dod pa*). In more detail:

> It is accepted [by us] that : Because of having refuted all mentation [the means of valid cognition is] not a means of valid cognition. Or, because the negandum is not established, that emptiness which is a positively determining (*yongs gcod*) emptiness which will negate that [negandum] – because its referent (*gzhal bya*) is not true – [is] not a means of valid cognition.[49]

bSod nams rtse mo's whole strategy in commenting on *Bodhicaryāvatāra* 9:140 is to make the negative point that both negandum and negation are delusory, 'if the son of a barren woman is delusory, his death is also delusory' (*mo gsham gyi bu brdzun na shi ba yang brdzun no*). This is clear from his opponent's appeal to *BCA* 9:2. If *BCA* 9:2 is accepted literally, then everything which occurs within the range of the mind is conventional and delusory. For bSod nams rtse mo the point of Śāntideva's argument in *Bodhicaryāvatāra* 9:140 is to show that all negation – and therefore by implication the negation which is emptiness – must occur in terms of mental operations, and therefore must be conventional and delusory. That is all there is to it, as regards *BCA* 9:140. Apprehending the negation (*bkag pa*) of a negandum (*dgag bya*) is delusory. Why? Because whatever is a delusory entity makes a delusory negandum. Why? Not having contacted with the mind a negandum which is a conceptually-constructed entity – which is to say, not having made the negandum a cognitive referent (*blos yul du ma byas par*) – there is no apprehension of the negation (*dngos med*) of it. There does not arise a cognition (*blo*) which perceptually appropriates the negation.[50] The repeated use of the term *blo* (*buddhi*, mind, intellect or cognitive faculty) here is significant, for bSod nams rtse mo's *pūrvapakṣa* had reminded the reader of *Bodhicaryāvatāra* 9:2, where the conventional is identified with the range of the intellect (*blo*). Everytime the term *blo* is used – here with reference to both negandum and negation – there is reinforced the contention that we are concerned only with the conventional which is delusory. The model, bSod nams rtse mo states, is that of 'Who is not present?', 'This [person] is not present' (*su med ce na 'di med ces*). If there is no negandum then the same in general can be said of the negation. If the negandum is delusory, then the negation also is delusory.[51] It is clearer in bSod nams rtse mo even more than in Prajñākaramati that Śāntideva introduced the reference to contacting a conceptually-constructed entity in *BCA* 9:140 ab as an indisputable point about negation which would lead to a demonstration of negation and negandum as delusory, accepting the *pūrvapakṣa*.

For bSod nams rtse mo as for Prajñākaramati, one precisely should *not* concern oneself with the conceptually-constructed negandum. The whole direction of the verse is towards moving away from the negandum, and in *BCA* 9:140, which responds to the first *prasaṅga* of the opponent, there is not intended to be any argument for *how* one should contemplate emptiness, nor for *why* one should do it. There is only an argument for negandum and negation as delusory, and it is perhaps significant that the example given is that of the son of a barren woman (an example not used in any of the Indian sources examined). The direction of bSod nams rtse mo's text here is entirely negative in the sense of confirming a move away from the conventional, which appears to be given as little existential status as possible.

Which brings us to Tsong kha pa. What we notice from Tsong kha pa's short comments on *BCA* 9:140 is that his entire concern is ontology (and implicitly, of course, what might be called the 'moral and soteriological implications' of getting the ontology wrong – of over- or under-negating). The subject, Tsong kha pa tells us, is the delusory entity. It is delusory because it is established as lacking inherent existence (*chos can rdzun pa'i dngos po rang bzhin med par grub pa'i phyir* – p. 28a). In other words Tsong kha pa immediately distinguishes between being delusory in the sense of simply not existing or being an hallucination, and being delusory in this technical sense. Thus the 'entity' of Śāntideva's verse is not just any entity but a 'non-inherently existing' entity. Unlike many other Tibetans (including rGyal tshab rje – see below) Tsong kha pa does not mention in this context the example of the son of a barren woman. If, without qualification, the relationship between negandum and negation is said to be like that of a son of a barren woman and his death, there is a dangerous implication that negandum and negation, mutually dependent and lacking in inherent existence as they are, have no greater ontological status than that of the son of a barren woman – in other words, lack of inherent existence cannot be differentiated from the complete nonexistence of what is in this case not just an unexampled possible but a complete logical impossibility, a contradiction.[52]

So Tsong kha pa begins by telling us that a delusory entity is established as lacking in inherent existence. This appears to be a gloss on what it is to be a delusory entity, and it is not as such specific to the interpretation of *BCA* 9:140. Tsong kha pa continues to observe that the negation (absence) which depends on that entity, that is, that absence of truth-status (*bden med*), is also clearly delusory because it follows that it [too] is established as lacking in inherent existence.[53] The phrasing of this clearly arises from Śāntideva's text in the *Bodhicaryāvatāra*, but Tsong kha pa has not yet related it to the specific issue of the dependence of *negation* (rather than anything else) on a conceptually-constructed entity. While all delusory entities lack inherent existence, and all entities which depend on delusory entities also lack inherent existence, some delusory entities (e.g. those the conceptualisations of which are what occur as referents in cases of negation) are *only* concepts while others (the table, for example, on which the teapot is not occurring) are what we hold to be normal present everyday objects.

Tsong kha pa initially gives the impression that his main concern in glossing *BCA* 9:140 is that of avoiding a misunderstanding about the ontological implications of 'delusory'. But he has another major concern, and that is to relate this verse from the *Bodhicaryāvatāra* to the specific issue of inherent existence as negandum and emptiness its negation, thus showing that this verse is not about *accepting* the opponent's argument and using it in order to reaffirm emptiness, a move away from conceptually-constructed objects like pots and their negation, but rather the verse is about the need to apprehend inherent existence in order to apprehend emptiness. It also shows that in Śāntideva's eyes emptiness itself is not an ultimate truth in the sense of an entity which is anything other than lacking in inherent existence, as are all things. Tsong kha pa seems to want to avoid any suggestion that this verse is about conceptually-constructed entities like pots. He mentions the expression 'conceptually-contructed' (*btags pa*) only in quoting Śāntideva, and glosses the conceptually-constructed entity as 'the negandum' (*dgag bya btags pa'i dngos po la ma reg ste*). We expect 'the entity' (*dngos po*) here to be the same entity introduced earlier as delusory, lacking in inherent existence (i.e. a pot), particularly as the negation of that was introduced by Tsong kha pa in terms which reflect *BCA* 9:140. But Tsong kha pa continues by telling us that the negation of that [conceptually-constructed entity], *which is to say, emptiness*, is not apprehended as true (*dgag bya btags pa'i dngos po la ma reg pa ste ma bzung bar de'i dngos med de stong nyid bden par mi 'dzin pas so*). Emptiness is not the negation of entities, however, but the negation of inherent existence. Thus the negandum (*dgag bya*) here – the entity – must equal inherent existence, and Tsong kha pa has slid in a way which would have seemed to previous commentators counter-intuitive from a delusory entity as lacking inherent existence to referring to the very inherent existence itself as an entity. Thus the conceptually-constructed entity of *BCA* 9:140 is not for Tsong kha pa something like a pot, for the negation of a pot is not emptiness.[54] The conceptually-constructed entity is the inherent existence of the pot. That this is scarcely the natural way to take 'conceptually-constructed entity' in this verse, which is glossed by other commentators as 'a pot and so on', is what necessitated the gradual slide in Tsong kha pa's commentary from the delusory entity (*brdzun pa'i dngos po*) which is said to lack inherent existence; to the negation which depends on it (*de la brten pa'i dngos po med*), which also lacks inherent existence and is said to be absence of truth (*bden med*); to the conceptually-constructed entity (which we all know therefore lacks inherent existence) which is the negandum (*dgag bya btags pa'i dngos po*); to the negation of that, which turns out to be emptiness and also is not apprehended as true (*de'i dngos med de stong nyid bden par mi 'dzin pas*). Tsong kha pa could have made his points about the term 'delusory' equalling 'lacking inherent existence', and emptiness as itself lacking in inherent existence, without implying a gloss on the 'conceptually-constructed entity' and its negation of *Bodhicaryāvatāra* 9:140 as 'inherent existence' and 'emptiness' respectively. One can only speculate that Tsong kha pa's reading of this verse was a reflection of the requirement elsewhere in his system (seen in the *Lam rim chen mo*) to use this verse from Śāntideva in order to facilitate a stress on the need to know the negandum – true establishment (*bden grub*) – in order to understand the meaning of emptiness, both as a point of philosophy but also (and are they here very different?) a point on the spiritual path of direct insight into emptiness (cf. v. 139: *stong pa nyid / sgom pa*).

As we might expect, Tsong kha pa's approach is elaborated in the work of his pupil rGyal tshab Dar ma rin chen.[55] rGyal tshab rje begins by specifically relating the discussion to the means of valid cognition which set forth emptiness, and the emptiness set forth by those. For the Mādhyamika both are certainly delusory. This is because the ascertainment which is a negation which negates an entity [which is conceived of as] true through an act of constructive reification (*rtog pa*) is dependent upon the arising of the negandum.[56] rGyal tshab rje is the only commentator examined (prior to later dGe lugs writers) specifically to introduce in this context in a commentary on the *Bodhicaryāvatāra* the concept of the 'arising (*rnam par shar ba*) of the negandum', and his usage certainly stems from Tsong kha pa's discussion of *BCA* 9:140 ab in the *Lam rim chen mo* (see above, note 5). This idea of the arising of the negandum is a technical one in dGe lugs writings and appears to signify, as we have seen, more than just having the concept of x in order to negate x. In negating inherent existence, for example, it is necessary to know what inherent existence would be like if it did exist, and the generic impression (*spyi*) of the negandum has to appear as a mental object.[57] In meditating on emptiness in the dGe lugs tradition some concentrated effort has to be put in to 'identifying the object of negation', causing to arise before the mind an accurate image of inherent existence (the *dgag bya*, the negandum) as related to the substratum for meditation (the *dgag gzhi*, for example the pot which is being analysed to see if it exists inherently) in order to know what it is that is to be negated by the processes of reasoning which set forth lack of inherent existence. Thus in terms of the analytic meditative path causing the object of negation to arise (supported by this interpretation of *Bodhicaryāvatāra* 9:140 ab) is a definite identifiable and important step, and the move is at this stage *towards* this identification as a prequisite to the proper understanding of emptiness, not *away* from the object of negation as we saw in other commentaries such as those of Prajñākaramati and bSod nams rtse mo. The difference is encapsulated in a comment by the Fifth Dalai Lama, introducing his own quote from *BCA* 9:140 ab in his *'Jam pa'i dbyangs kyi zhal lung*: 'if both the self [that is the validly existent person] and the self that is the non-existent object negated are not intimately identified, it is like dispatching an army without knowing where the enemy is and like shooting an arrow without having sought the target.'[58] It follows, rGyal tshab rje comments, that not having contacted with an act of constructive reification true establishment (i.e. inherent existence), which is the entity conceptually-constructed, that is to say, an aspect of true establishment not having arisen [in the mind], there is not apprehended by constructive reification that [situation of] actual absence of truth, i.e. emptiness (empty) of truth, of that.[59]

This completes rGyal tshab rje's commentary on *BCA* 9:140 ab. The second part of this verse he sees as directed at showing that emptiness too must lack inherent existence, it cannot be taken as an inherently existing absolute reality in the way that some rival Tibetans and also modern interpreters have done. For Tsong kha pa and rGyal tshab rje it is not that Śāntideva is making a general point about, for example, the absence of a pot being delusory if the conceptually-constructed pot in a situation of negation is delusory. Rather Śāntideva's point is a specific one about emptiness being delusory (lacking inherent existence) if the negandum, inherent existence itself, is delusory.[60] Like some other commentators, rGyal tshab rje employs the example of the son of a barren woman, but in order to point out that if there does not arise the aspect (*rnam pa*) of a son of a barren woman to constructive reification, similarly there could not arise the aspect of his death. In context it is clear that 'the son of a barren woman' here is equivalent to 'inherent existence', which is indeed completely non-existent, and the point to be made concerns the nonoccurrence of x in the absence of y.[61]

If the emptiness of truth which negates the negandum were to be truly established, rGyal tshab rje comments, then the appearance of emptiness of truth (*bden stong snang ba*) for an inferential cognition (*rig shes rjes dpag*) would necessarily be [of a] truly established [thing].[62] In other words, emptiness would be found when searched for through an ultimate analysis which seeks to see if emptiness can be found to exist under analysis and therefore as an inherently existing thing.That being the case, there would be no possibility of a series of negations [of the inherent existence of one thing, then another, for example] (*de lta na ya gyal bkag pa'i tshogs pa mi srid*). rGyal tshab rje's text here is terse to the point of obscurity (not surprising if he is simply repeating his notes from Tsong kha pa's lectures) but if I understand the argument correctly, the point is that if emptiness were inherently existent then it would make no sense to speak of the emptiness of this thing and the emptiness of that thing. There would be just one immutable emptiness, not dependent and therefore not relative to anything. Thus emptiness might be *a* negation, but not *the* negation of this and that specific inherent existence related to this or that specific entity. Moreover, rGyal tshab rje continues, because the negandum [now] truly appears there (or to that inferential cognition), true appearance also would necessarily be truly established (*cing de la dgag bya bden par snang bas bden snang yang bden par (p. 270) grub dgos la*). That is, since emptiness is no longer the emptiness of inherent existence of this or that, this or that which appear to unenlightened beings as true would indeed be truly established. That being the case, there necessarily would be truly-established existence (*de lta na bden grub yod dgos na*). But, rGyal tshab rje observes, that is not truly established (*de med pa'i phyir* – this much is granted by the opponent who is urging that nevertheless emptiness inherently exists)! Therefore (*modus tollendo tollens*) the emptiness of truth which negates that [inherent existence] also is delusory, which is to say it is not truly established (*de bkag pa'i bden stong yang rdzun pa yin gyi bden par ma grub bo*). And rGyal tshab rje completes his refutation through reasoning with an appeal to authority – Nāgārjuna's *Madhyamakakārikā* 13:7:

> If there existed the slightest thing not empty /
> There would also exist the slightest thing empty /
> When there does not exist the slightest thing not empty /
> How will there exist empty? //[63]

rGyal tshab rje has indeed shown on his own premisses (emptiness as equivalent to dependent origination, emptiness as the absence of inherent existence applied to that basis which lacks inherent existence) that since everything is empty, so emptiness itself which must be relative to each empty thing cannot be inherently existent. Emptiness as it is understood in this vision of Prāsaṅgika Madhyamaka is something about each thing, no matter what it is. It is because it is true *of each thing* – and only of each thing – that emptiness cannot be an absolute inherently existing reality.[64] And rGyal tshab rje completes his commentary to *BCA* 9:140 with a satisfied summing-up which I suggest indicates a profound and impressive, yet marked, change of direction from pre-dGe lugs commentaries (including the Indian commentaries) which we have examined: 'Since one cannot ascertain well emptiness of truth (*bden stong*) if there does not arise the generic impression of true establishment, [in order to] ascertain emptiness it is necessary for the wise to apprehend the measure of the negandum (*bden grub kyi spyi ma shar bar bden stong legs par mi nges pas stong nyid nges pa dgag bya'i tshad 'dzin la mkhas dgos pa yin no* p. 270)'.

Let us look now at an interpretation of *Bodhicaryāvatāra* 9:140 found in the commentary by Tsong kha pa's contemporary, the Sa skya pa lama Sa bzang mati paṇchen, in the light of what we have seen of Tsong kha pa's own approach. Sa bzang takes very seriously the claim of the opponent in *BCA* 9:139 – reading with the Tibetan version *stong pa nyid / sgom pa* that as regards the true way of things (*de kho na nyid du na*) even the meditative cultivation of emptiness, which is the antidote [to *saṃsāra*], lacks truth and will therefore not be acceptable.[65] Sa bzang mati paṇchen's only concern appears to be to show why it is nevertheless worth practising meditation on emptiness, a direct reply to the negative conclusion of the *pūrvapakṣa* (bSod nams rtse mo's second *prasaṅga*). He comments that if we examine it critically, we will see that even though it is delusory there is no contradiction in something acting as an antidote. And, in contrast to Tsong kha pa and rGyal tshab rje but in harmony with earlier commentators, Sa bzang takes as his example of a negandum 'a pot and so on', but supplements 'not having contacted' in *BCA* 9:140 with 'and not having critically examined' (*cing ma dpyad par*), thus showing a move towards the negandum in a context of justifying meditation on emptiness which has itself the flavour of Tsong kha pa (although there is no suggestion here of any need to cause a generic impression to arise before the mind). Without this contacting and critically examining the negandum – a *pot* – there is no possibility of the apprehension of the absence (*dngos med*) which will negate (*bkag pa*) that.[66] Thus Sa bzang mati paṇchen on the one hand talks of the pot and its negation – an example of a general principle of everyday negation – and on the other he makes it quite clear that his concern is with emptiness, the apprehension of which results from a particular sort of critical examination of the pot. But, Tsong kha pa would say, for that examination and that very particular sort of negation the negandum is not the pot but the inherent existence of the pot. The unclarity (for Tsong kha pa) of Sa bzang mati paṇchen's approach is illustrated by the latter's subsequent comment, that:

> the negandum, a true entity, is not established (*dgag bya bden pa'i dngos po ma grub pa*), and therefore in the case of a delusory entity, emptiness also – which is the absence which will negate that – is without a doubt clearly delusory. Nevertheless, the meditative cultivation of that [emptiness] is acceptable because it can act as an antidote to truth-grasping (*bden 'dzin*).[67]

Thus the negandum is now said to be 'a true entity', which for Tsong kha pa would suggest in this case and context an inherently existent pot, although the negandum is not as with rGyal tshab rje true establishment (*bden grub*) – absence of inherent existence itself – for which the pot merely happens to be the substratum in this particular example. It is in fact unclear whether Sa bzang mati paṇchen does want to say here (as would Tsong kha pa) that the negandum as a true entity equals an inherently existent entity contrasted with mere existence which is not here being denied, since Sa bzang had earlier glossed the negandum as simply 'pots and so on' and he could therefore be read as implying that there is not established a true pot, in the sense of any pot at all. Through not being quite clear and specific about the object of negation, Sa bzang mati paṇchen appears to have been left open to an accusation by Tsong kha pa of over-negation.[68]

Another example of a tendency towards Tsong kha pa's over-negation can be seen in the large commentary to the *Bodhicaryāvatāra* by the sixteenth-century Karma bKa' brgyud historian dPa' bo gTsug lag phreng ba. dPa' bo refers to the conceptually-constructed entity of *BCA* 9:140 ab as 'merely' a conceptually-contructed entity (*btags pa'i dngos po tsam*), and he gives as an example to illustrate the need to contact a conceptually-constructed entity in order to understand negation that of space *(nam mkha')*, which is defined in standard Tibetan sources as an 'absence of obstructive contact' (see Hopkins (1983), p. 217). Without relying on the transactional convention (*tha snyad*) of space, dPa' bo tells us, one is not able to engage also in space as an absence (*dngos med*).[69] The example is a strange one, since this is not at all an example of conceptually-contructing an entity in order to be able to negate it. The parallel there would be conceptually-constructing space in order to speak of the absence of space. Rather dPa' bo gives us an example of a particular sort of negation which, as a pure absence, has to be conceptually-posited as if it were an entity in order to engage with it as an absence. Or in other words, for pragmatic purposes non-entities have to be treated as if they are quasi-entities. It is tempting to suggest that in using this example dPa' bo gTsug la phreng ba has simply missed the point, but I suspect that he is in fact operating with a much stronger sense of the negation of conventional entities than we have seen in sources like Tsong kha pa. dPa' bo chose this particular example because it allows him to imply of conventional entities that without relying on a transactional convention one is not able to engage in conventional entities as absences, in other words as empty. As with space, entities are actually empty (i.e. non-entities, pure negations) but are treated *as if* they are entities – quasi-entities – in order to be able to engage with what they are, which is empty. In order to be realised as what they are, they have to be posited in conventional transactional terms as precisely what they are not. This interpretation of the direction of dPa' bo's choice of example is also suggested I think by his following comments:

> Therefore, because sentient beings crave as true that delusory entity which is mere appearance, they fall into *saṃsāra*. If one knows that very thing as not true, mere illusion, then even though certainly it would act as an antidote to that, that emptiness – which is conceptually-constructed as the negation of that delusory appearance as an entity – also is clearly delusory.[70]

dPa' bo makes no mention of the negandum being simply inherent existence, and he makes no mention of entities being *like* illusions rather than actual illusions. Entites are stated to be mere appearance, not true, illusions, and while it would be possible for Tsong kha pa (emanating from his Pure Land) to give a reading of even this passage in a way which would dissolve its tendency to complete negation, nevertheless when it is combined with dPa' bo's choice of the example of space there does look like a strong implication here that not only is dPa' bo agreeing with the *pūrvapakṣa* that the means of valid cognition are not means of valid cognition, and emptiness itself is delusory, but also that he would want to go as far as possible in minimising the ontological implications of the conventional everyday realm. dPa' bo concludes by telling us that one engages in that apprehension of an entity known as emptiness as an antidote to apprehending an entity which is constructively reified as true, just as an illusory lion kills an illusory elephant.[71]

dPa' bo gTsug lag phreng ba was a follower of the Karma bKa' brgyud tradition, and he was also a pupil of the Eighth Karma pa, Mi bskyod rdo rje. In his great commentary to Candrakīrti's *Madhyamakāvatāra* Mi bskyod rdo rje stridently attacked any interpretation of Madhyamaka which would see the conventional as in any way to be given an established status (*pace* Tsong kha pa). On the other hand he also attacked those such as the Jo nang tradition and Shākya mchog ldan who would adhere to a form of *tathāgatagarbha* absolutism which would maintain that the conventional is ultimately quite other than a truly established emptiness, and the conventional really does not exist at all.[72] We know however that Mi bskyod rdo rje in his youth wrote in support of this 'other emptiness' (*gzhan stong*) – which is commonly interpreted as teaching a truly-established ultimate and a conventional reality which is in the light of that not established at all – based on the *Ratnagotravibhāga* and *tathāgatagarbha* teaching, and also the Third Karma pa Rang byung rdo rje and many other Karma bKa' brgyud masters have been associated with such teachings, which form a framework for certain interpretations of Mahāmudrā meditation which are central to bKa' brgyud practice. It is possible that Mi bskyod rdo rje simply wished to avoid the confusion of thinking that these absolutist teachings can be found as an accurate interpretation of Prāsaṅgika Madhyamaka sources.[73] Prāsaṅgika texts have a value only as far as they go. It is not impossible that dPa' bo gTsug lag phreng ba too wished to be associated with such a perspective and as such wished to minimise any suggestion that Madhyamaka accepts the conventional realm as established.

These 'other emptiness' teachings are also known in Tibet as 'the Great Madhyamaka' (*dBu ma chen po*), and I have shown elsewhere that the notion of the Great Madhyamaka is explicitly employed in interpreting the *Bodhicaryāvatāra* 9:35 – the verse which portrays *nirvāna* as related to the calming which occurs when neither entity nor non-entity (its negation) stand before the mind – by the great nineteenth-century rNying ma lama Mi pham.[74] We have seen already that Prajñākaramati's reading of *BCA* 9:140 introduces the idea of that emptiness which is set forth when entity and non-entity are seen to be delusory. It is not surprising therefore that *BCA* 9:139–41 should also suggest to Mi pham once more the Great Madhyamaka, and in his comments on *Bodhicaryāvatāra* 9:140 Mi pham prepares the way for the introduction of the Great Madhyamaka which he in fact introduces in his commentary on the very next verse. His language is very carefully chosen in order to lead to a perspective where a distinction is made between (i) a relative emptiness, which is a negation correllated to a negandum, and as such is delusory although for all that valuable as a means of cutting attachment; distinguished from but revealing (ii) the Great Madhyamaka, which is freedom from all assertions, and occurs when one abides in a gnosis (*ye shes*) which is the calming of all verbal differentiations (*spros pa thams cad zhi ba'i ye shes la gnas pa;* p. 86), in other words beyond all dualistic differentiations such as subject and object.

Thus Mi pham begins by stating quite clearly that we do not put forward at all as a tenet a truly established referential object (*dmigs gtad kyi yul*) called 'emptiness', which would be a referent established by a means of valid cognition. Rather, not having contacted, or not having relied on, something like a pot or such like, which is an entity conceptually-constructed, there is never apprehended all by itself the negation of that entity. For Mi pham this is clearly a general point about negation – hence the illustration of a pot – which he then applies to the case of emptiness.[75] Therefore we accept, Mi pham states, that in the case of verbal entities (*rnam grangs pa*) such as 'absence of a pot' and 'empty of a pot', or moreover the relative empty (emptiness – *nyi tshe ba'i stong pa*) – because they are the sorts of things which dispel or negate some other entity – [when they occur] in the case of an entity which is delusory by nature, such a negation of that also would be clearly, certainly delusory.[76] In other words, since negations are relative to that which is negated it follows, as we have seen previously, that according to this way of thinking if the negandum is delusory the negation will certainly be delusory.

What is so important in Mi pham's discussion here however is his introduction of a reference to the *nyi tshe ba'i stong pa [nyid]*. I have discussed this concept at some length elsewhere.[77] To summarise: The expression *nyi tshe ba'i stong pa nyid* is used by certain Tibetan writers such as Mi bskyod rdo rje to refer to what is known in the *Laṅkāvatārasūtra* as the *itaretaraśūnyatā*, the sort of emptiness which occurs when we speak of a locus being empty of something – 'The pot is empty of water'. It is mutual absence. In the *sūtra* it is made quite clear that this is not the sort of emptiness referred to as the ultimate in Mahāyāna Buddhism. In the *Samādhirājasūtra* the Tīrthakas, non-Buddhist teachers, are said to have a *nyi tshe'i stong pa* which Mi bskyod rdo rje associates with certain Sāṃkhya and Vaiśeṣika doctrines. Thus a *nyi tshe ba'i stong pa nyid* is a 'limited emptiness', limited in the sense of relative to a context where *x* lacks *y*, but also it is implied in the polemic of Mi bskyod rdo rje that it is limited to what is in origin the unenlightened perspective of non-Buddhist thinkers. It is to this emptiness that Mi bskyod rdo rje wishes to assimilate the Prāsaṅgika Madhyamaka emptiness referred to in dGe lugs writings, since emptiness in dGe lugs texts is said to be the absence of inherent existence *(y)* as pertaining to a particular substratum for analysis (the pot – *x*). For dGe lugs scholars there is no other or higher emptiness than this. Tibetan teachers like Mi pham and probably Mi bskyod rdo rje himself stress that this emptiness, which is simply an absence of inherent existence, is a relative emptiness and therefore, on Madhyamaka grounds, itself delusory. It could not thus be the final ultimate truth. Otherwise why did the Buddha say in the *Laṅkāvatārasūtra* that the *itaretaraśūnyatā* is to be abandoned? The real final ultimate truth is said in many Mahāyāna texts to be beyond the relative, beyond all duality, all verbal differentiation, and this clearly cannot be the relative *nyi tshe ba'i stong pa nyid* which is mere absence of inherent existence. Hence the significance of Mi pham's introduction of the *nyi tshe ba'i stong pa nyid* at this point, for it is the point at which Śāntideva and his commentators accept that emptiness too, as relative to a negandum, is delusory. In introducing the idea that this is the *nyi tshe ba'i stong pa nyid* – which is indeed relative to something – Mi pham is able to draw on a long tradition in Indian Buddhism which states that the *itaretaraśūnyatā* is not the highest Mahāyāna liberating emptiness, but is to be abandoned, and a long tradition in Tibetan thought which would oppose this emptiness – also associated with the emptiness discovered through intellectual analytic investigation, a process of negation – to an ultimate reality intuited nondualistically in the pristine gnosis of direct insight, an ultimate which is not and never has been relative to anything and is therefore obviously not delusory, which is not set-forth as the terminating point of a process of delusory means of valid cognition like inference, which is not the *object* of any cognition as it is not within the range of subject/object duality, the ultimate which is the emptiness which shines forth when entity and non-entity (negation) are calmed (see Mipham on *BCA* 9:35). In mentioning the expression *nyi tshe ba'i stong pa* in commenting on *BCA* 9:140 Mi pham has alerted his readers to what sort of emptiness is being negated in this verse. In commenting on the next verse of Śāntideva's text Mi pham will clearly introduce that pristine gnosis – whether Śāntideva's text suggests or requires it or not.

BODHICARYĀVATĀRA 9:141 (TIB. 140)

tasmāt svapne sute naṣṭe sa nāstīti vikalpanā /
tadbhāvakalpanotpādaṃ vibadhnāti mṛṣā ca sā //

des na rmi lam bu shi la /
de med snyam pa'i rnam rtog ni /
de yod rnam par rtog pa yi /
gegs yin de yang brdzun pa yin //

Thus, a son having died in a dream, the conception /
Which thinks he does not exist /
Puts a stop to the occurring of a conception that he does exist. /
[Nevertheless] that ('also' – Tib.) is delusory. //

For 'conception' the Sanskrit uses the term *vikalpanā* in the first half-verse, and *kalpanā* in the second. The Tibetan, no doubt for metric reasons, uses *rnam (par) rtog (pa)* (*vikalpanā*) in both. Either way, the terms refer broadly to acts of discriminative conceptual construction and constructive hypostasisation which echo the 'conceptually constructed entity' (*kalpitaṃ bhāvaṃ*) of *BCA* 9:140.[78]

The interpretation of this verse is fairly non-controversial. The three verses *BCA* 9:139–41 form a set which serve as a methodological interlude in the Mādhyamika refutation of causation, and Prajñākaramati speaks of this third verse as clarifying our topic by way of a summary (*upasaṃhāravyājena/mjug bsdu ba'i zur gyis*). The example of a son who is born and dies in a dream is said by Nāgārjuna in a verse from his *Catuḥstava* to originate with the Buddha himself.[79] Vibhūticandra gives a very clear statement of the argument of this last verse, and we can note in passing that it is sufficiently close to a summary of Prajñākaramati as to suggest once more that Vibhūticandra was following the latter:

> A son who is present in a dream, having been born, dies. When this occurs, with the conception which dreams that he does not exist there is eliminated the conception that the son does exist. Even though there is eliminated the conception of [his] existence, that is [itself] delusory since of that son in a dream there was neither birth nor cessation. Moreover, the same [example of] death in a dream can be applied to a real (*bden* – true) son. Thus do *dharmas* arise and perish. Even though this is not a means of valid cognition, still there is no fault in absence of inherent existence.[80]

We should note that there appears to be a considerable degree of agreement among commentators that what is said to be delusory in the second half-verse of *BCA* 9:141 is the *conception* that the son does not exist, or that conception as applied to all *dharmas*. Thus Kalyāṇadeva tells us that if there exists a conceptual-construction of a [real] entity, then there would be the conception that 'It does not exist'. But that also is delusory.[81] This is however rather problematic. If 'delusory' here means – with Tsong kha pa and rGyal tshab rje – lacking in inherent existence then dreaming of the death of a son is no more and no less delusory than anything else.[82] Of course Vibhūticandra says this.[83] But the point here is that so long as we restrict ourselves to lacking inherent existence the death of a son in a dream is *as real* as the death of a son in so-called 'real life'. On this level there is no reason why we should opt to see 'real life' death as dream-like (and therefore presumably less-distressing) rather than dream death as real life. Thus we can assume that when Śāntideva *et al.* speak of a dream death as delusory they mean more than just lacking in inherent existence. They mean dream-like, in the sense of less than fully real. But if that is so then there is a problem in speaking of the *conception* of dream death as delusory in that sense. I can understand that the birth and death of a dream son may be delusory, but the conception here, i.e. the ocurrence of certain mental events in a dream, would appear to be on a different level. The *conception* of the death of a dream son is a presupposition of the mistaken understanding that occurs in the dream (if it *is* a mistaken understanding) that the death was real. Because I dream of *x* we can, I suppose, speak of *x* occurring in a dream, though this may be a rather misleading way of putting it since *x* is presumably not actually occurring at all.[84] But it certainly does not follow that I am dreaming that I am dreaming of *x*. Rather the reverse. If I *am* dreaming of *x*, then I am really dreaming of *x* (the alternative is an infinite regress). However we look at it, the conception, i.e. the dreaming, would appear to be real at least in a way which would not apply to that which is being dreamt of, and it can be argued that any ontology which obscures this point is obscuring something rather fundamental.[85]

Tibetan comentators use this third verse in particular in order to answer the *pūrvapakṣa* concerning why, even though all the means of valid cognition are not means of valid cognition, it is still nevertheless worth meditating on emptiness (cf. *stong pa nyid / sgom pa*). It is a variation on Nāgārjuna's point in his *Vigrahavyāvartanī* that just because things are empty they can still have refutative power, that is, even delusory entities can have effects – as in the case of dreams.[86] As Thogs med puts it, 'meditative cultivation of emptiness is acceptable because it can act as an antidote to truth-grasping', as is the case in a dream where dreaming of his non-existence at death dispells the conception of a son's existence. Even though that apprehension of his non-existence is delusory, still it is able to lead to the abandonment of the apprehension of his existing.[87]

Of course, it is bSod nams rtse mo who is particularly concerned with the issue of justifying meditation on emptiness against the opponent, for he it was who separated-out the objection by the *pūrvapakṣa* that meditation on emptiness would be pointless as a different *prasaṅga*. And just as he sees *BCA* 9:140 as in its entirety a reply to the first *prasaṅga* – in which Śāntideva accepts the opponent's conclusion – he also sees *BCA* 9:141 as a reply to the second *prasaṅga* in which it is shown that even though the means of valid cognition are not means of valid cognition, and all things appear to be merely conventional and delusory, still it does not follow (*khyab pa ma grub* – there is not established a pervasion) that the meditative cultivation of emptiness has no point. Indeed, he adds with reference to the dream conception which negates the existence of the son, since it is able to act as an antidote to the superimposition which apprehends (or grasps after) something as existent there exists a part which is not mistaken (*yod par 'dzin pa'i sgro 'dogs kyi gnyen po byed pas 'khrul pa med pa'i cha yod de;* p. 511:3). This is an astonishing comment, particularly given bSod nams rtse mo's apparent dismissal of all the means of valid cognition as not means of valid cognition in his acceptance of the *pūrvapakṣa* when commenting on *BCA* 9:140. We have seen already that for Candrakīrti 'delusory' (*brdzun*) and 'mistaken' (*'khrul pa*) are equivalents (see above, note 23), and if all the means of valid cognition are delusory then they must also be mistaken. Nevertheless bSod nams rtse mo is in a sense right. He has realised that while what is set-forth by the means of valid cognition may be mistaken, the Mādhyamika has a problem if he or she maintains that the arguments (in the case of the inferential means of valid cognition) are also mistaken, i.e. invalid. The means of valid cognition may be delusory, i.e. not inherently exist, and they may show-forth conclusions which are delusory, that is, exist non-inherently. But this is not the same as saying the conclusions are *invalid*, or indeed false.[88] bSod nams rtse mo has discerned a problem which was to concern Tibetan scholars up to Tsong kha pa and beyond – the problem of the status of Mādhyamika arguments and the conclusions they want to draw given Mādhyamika (and particularly Prāsaṅgika) premisses. bSod nams rtse mo must have realised himself that in making this point about the arguments having a part which is non-mistaken he appears to be at variance with Prāsaṅgikas like Candrakīrti. bSod nams rtse mo is known to have followed his teacher Phywa pa Chos kyi seng ge in writing his commentary to the *Bodhicaryāvatāra*, and the latter was apparently strongly opposed to the Prāsaṅgika Madhyamaka approach of Candrakīrti.[89] It is on this point that we may well be able to detect one of those issues on which Phywa pa Chos kyi seng ge opposed the Prāsaṅgikas. bSod nams rtse mo comments that:

> The arising of the generic referent (*don spyi*) called 'empty' which puts a stop to the negandum, and that positively determining empty which craves that as an external reality, are also delusory. [Nevertheless] there is destroyed the opportunity for arising for superimpositions of grasping after reality (*dngos por 'dzin pa*). There is no contradiction in the existence of a part which is a means of valid cognition in the case of mere critical examination, the part which dispels superimposition of grasping after existence. This conforms to the Svātantrikas.[90]

Thus bSod nams rtse mo specifically derives his favoured approach to this issue from the Svātantrikas. By way of contrast he mentions but devotes rather less space to the Prāsaṅgika treatment of the same issue. Given his own suggestion that part of the means of valid cognition is not mistaken (they do indeed lead to valid conclusions), which he traces to the Svātantrikas, bSod nams rtse mo at this point seems to favour the Svātantrika strategy, although unlike Phywa pa Chos kyi seng ge one cannot say that bSod nams shows signs of being 'strongly' opposed (Jackson) to the Prāsaṅgikas. Thus, bSod nams rtse mo simply comments that the Prāsaṅgikas say that 'the expression "is delusory" [in *BCA* 9:141 cd] means that it is the "yoga mere-conventional" (*rnal 'byor kun rdzob tsam*). Even that brings about the stopping of another erroneous constructive reification.'[91] In other words, emptiness is not a means of valid cognition. It's actual ontological status is as it is seen by that vision of the world possessed by 'those śrāvakas, pratyekabuddhas, and bodhisattvas who have abandoned the nescience possessed of defilement', the latter being the bodhisattvas above the seventh *bhūmi*.[92] It is 'merely conventional', not even conventional truth, for it has no truth status. Nevertheless, bSod nams rtse mo's Prāsaṅgika wants to argue, even that seems to be able to put a stop to another erroneous construction. If the arguments that show that things lack inherent existence work, then they work. Whether they work is in the final analysis of concern to those for whom they are convincing. The fact that their implication means that things finally have no more status than 'mere conventionalities', existing from the conventional point of view alone, does not mean that the arguments cannot be successful. That is the way it is.

What this vision of the Prāsaṅgika approach does is simply repeat the point that arguments which exist solely from our unenlightened conventional point of view can still have pragmatic effects. It does not say *how* that can be. It does not answer the 'Svātantrika' objection that in such a case arguments must be valid, and therefore the means of valid cognition must be means of valid cognition in some sense. The arguments have their effects because their conclusions are considered to be true. But for arguments to establish their conclusions non-fallaciously is what we *mean* by being valid. If an argument is valid then the inferential means of valid cognition must in *some* respect be a genuine means of valid cognition. The alternative is for it to be impossible to derive a conclusion of absence of inherent existence, and impossible to generate any counter-argument (such as saying that his/her argument rests on the *truth* of emptiness) to the opponent who states this impossibility. The one who says that there are no valid arguments at all can only state it, but cannot give any rational grounds why that should be the case. If grounds are given, and valid conclusions are drawn, then (as Tsong kha pa realised so well) there must be valid means of cognition *in some sense*. In this respect bSod nams rtse mo is here right to favour what he sees as the Svātantrika approach in opposition to the mere assertion of the Prāsaṅgika (if bSod nams rtse mo and Phywa pa Chos kyi seng ge have correctly discerned the difference here between Svātantrika and Prāsaṅgika, a point which Tsong kha pa himself would question).

For Mi pham any suggestion of going beyond entity and negation, *x* and not-*x*, is a chance to introduce that third value which in its very impossibility as that which is neither of two contradictories forces the mind to a new level beyond which there can be none higher, the level of the Great Madhyamaka, the level of that gnosis which is the calming of all verbal differentiations (*spros pa thams cad zhi ba'i ye shes*). Mi pham has his opponent construct an objection in order clearly to facilitate an understanding of this point. Thus, the opponent objects, what is to be done with having cultivated in meditation such thoughts as 'All entities do not exist' (cf. Tsong kha pa), given that existent entities and their negations (non-entities) are both the same in that they are delusory, and both lack reality (*yang dag pa min*)?[93] The reply, Mi pham says, is that people bring about the fetters of *saṃsāra* by a craving for things which they have been obsessed with (*goms pa*) since beginningless time. As an antidote to that, there is a mere concern or cultivation (*goms pa tsam,* punning on *sgom pa*, meditative-cultivation) aimed at absence of inherent existence.[94] Both entity and negation are delusory, so it is like the case of the son who is born and dies in a dream. Therefore, Mi pham observes, just as a fire which had inflamed a bundle of two pieces of wood consumes them both, so too the fire of *prajñā* which had analytically investigated the absence of truth in all entities consumes without exception the dense forest of all objective realities which are set forth as entity or negation. Then, when one abides in the gnosis which is the calming of all verbal differentiations, there is the Great Madhyamaka free of all assertions.[95] And Mi pham quotes to this effect from a *sūtra* of the Prajñāpāramitā type, thus assimilating the *gzhan stong* Great Madhyamaka into the message of the Prajñāpāramitā. The quote concludes: 'There is seen as objective realities neither agent nor all *dharmas*. This is the conduct of the supreme Perfection of Wisdom' (*byed pa po yang mi dmigs chos kun mi dmigs te // 'di ni shes rab pha rol phyin mchog spyod pa yin* – p. 88). The comparison for Mi pham is with that Perfection of Wisdom which is clearly *not* supreme, which centres solely on emptiness as the ultimate truth, seen as the negation of inherent existence and therefore still a negation (*dngos med*) contrasted to an entity (*dngos po*), a relative emptiness (*nyi tshe ba'i stong pa nyid*). Mi pham considers Nāgārjuna was of the same opinion, for he quotes from *Madhyamakakārikā* 15:10:

To say 'it exists' is to grasp at permanence /
To say 'it does not exist' is the view of annihilation /

Therefore the wise should not rely /
On either existence or non-existence. //[96]

For Mi pham the point is to finish with existence and non-existence, abiding instead in non-conceptual gnosis which by definition can only occur when *all* concepts – which must involve either existence or non-existence – have come to an end. Śāntideva's verses have shown the relativity and dream-like nature of all negation, including the negation which is emptiness, while at the same time not denying the relative value of this supreme negation. Madhyamaka seeks transcendence of dualities which must be relative by nature. It therefore points beyond the negation which is emptiness to something higher, by definition non-dual and non-conceptual, and thus not open to the criticisms levelled at all existences and all negations. That beyond, Mi pham wants to say, as the completion and transcendence of Mādhyamika analyisis, is where the wise person should abide, in non-dual primeval gnosis (*ye shes*).[97]

Conclusions

If we stand back and look at Śāntideva's *Bodhicaryāvatāra* 9:139–41 the verses are not difficult to understand. An opponent makes a general point about the Madhyamaka approach. Given that Nāgārjuna and even Mahāyāna *sūtras* seem to maintain that the means of valid cognition are not means of valid cognition, and the results of so-called means of valid cognition are in fact delusory, it is dificult to see how the Mādhyamika can argue for emptiness. To argue for emptiness requires inference and to cognise emptiness requires direct yogic awareness. These are both normally included under the means of valid cognition which quite naturally form the first topic in any attempt by an Indian philosopher to set forth his system. The opponent wants to argue quite reasonably that Madhyamaka as a system (*darśana*) – like any radical scepticism – cannot get started. The Madhyamaka teaching of emptiness is thus not acceptable. Śāntideva's response is broadly to agree with the premisses while denying the conclusion that emptiness is unacceptable. He makes no attempt to defend the means of valid cognition (as one suspects Tsong kha pa and perhaps bSod nams rtse mo really thought he should), but points out that negation depends on a conceptually-constructed negandum and therefore as dependently-originated both are delusory. This is a general point about negation, of which it is implied that the negation which is emptiness is an example. But the fact that both are delusory *affirms* emptiness rather than denies it. Since negation and negandum are delusory and are of course conceptually-constructed entities, they occur within the realm of the conventional. Both are empty, including therefore emptiness itself. Nevertheless, as Nāgārjuna pointed out in his *Vigrahavyāvartanī*, the fact that something occurs only conventionally does not mean it lacks causative or in this case refutative power. As an example where negation occurs although we all agree that both negandum and negation are not real, there is the case of the death of a son in a dream.

This is all perfectly good Madhyamaka, which is not to say that it does not have philosophical problems associated with it, problems which became clearer – along with the range of possible answers – as time passed. For example, even in the case of a dream, while the son, his birth, and death are all just dreams, the fact that 'In a dream a son was born, and when he died he was present no longer' would appear to be completely real. That his death in the dream negated his existence in the dream is not a dream. Applied to emptiness, the negandum and negation (emptiness) may be delusory, but the *fact* that emptiness negates the negandum would appear to be true, and a true conclusion requires either valid argument or true premisses, and preferably both. These are issues of the acceptability of the means of valid cognition, a topic which appears of course to have been sidestepped by Śāntideva.

We have seen that Śāntideva's early Indian and Tibetan commentators followed the Master fairly closely, and with the possible exception of bSod nams rtse mo's introduction of a 'Svātantrika' strategy respecting the partial acceptance of the means of valid cognition, there seems to have been little objection to adopting Śāntideva's aceptance of the *pūrvapakṣa*'s premisses concerning the inadmissability of the means of valid cognition. For Tsong kha pa, however, things were very different. We know that Tsong kha pa considered himself to have had a revelation from Mañjuśrī in person concerning the final truth of the Prāsaṅgika Madhyamaka perspective, and the key to that perspective was said to lie in the identity of emptiness and dependent-origination. Thus the very beginning and (in a sense) the end of Madhyamaka for Tsong kha pa lies in neither over- nor under-negating through realising that emptiness is the negation of inherent existence but not of entities themselves. Entities certainly *exist* as non-inherently existing and dependently originated. Alternative understandings of Madhyamaka all must eventually fall into one or other of the faults of under- or over-negation (and sometimes, in different respects, both). This approach of Tsong kha pa and the dGe lugs tradition after him entails in particular a stress on what remains, what exists, in the teaching of emptiness. And what remains is the conventional world, seen not through unenlightened eyes as inherently existing, but rather seen as it really is, as a merely *conventional* world.

When Tsong kha pa's approach is applied to *Bodhicaryāvatāra* 9:139–41 we find that there is no longer any reason why, for Tsong kha pa, Śāntideva should accept the comments of the *pūrvapakṣa* concerning the means of valid cognition. Those means *can* only occur as part of the conventional (as dependently originated they must be empty of inherent existence, but they cannot be emptiness itself, which for Tsong kha pa is the only ultimate truth), but as part of the conventional there is no reason why they cannot be perfectly effective, valid, and lead to conclusions which are true. In other words, since the means of valid cognition can only occur conventionally, for Tsong kha pa and his tradition it is simply not true that the means of valid cognition are not means of valid cognition. In order to remain faithful to his Indian sources, therefore, Tsong kha pa clarified the assertion that the means of valid cognition are not means of valid cognition, by explaining that they are not inherently existing, or *ultimately* means of valid cognition.[98] Which of course is true, but since they could not be inherently existing means of valid cognition anyway Tsong kha pa has effectively neutralised the premise employed by Śāntideva's opponent. Moreover Tsong kha pa further undermines the *pūrvapakṣa*'s position by stressing a point central to Tsong kha pa's ontology – the equivalence of 'delusory' (*mṛṣā* – 'fiction(al)') and 'lacking inherent existence'. To call something delusory does not *as such* mean that it is less real than anything else, since both conventional and ultimate are delusory in the sense that they lack inherent existence. The result of all of this is that unlike Śāntideva, Tsong kha pa does not at all agree with the *pūrvapakṣa*'s premisses, let alone his (or her) conclusions.

It is not surprising, granted this, that Tsong kha pa's understanding of Śāntideva's reply in *BCA* 9:140 would not coincide perfectly with Śantideva's own intentions. Śāntideva *accepts* the opponent's premisses, and wants to confirm that like all negations, emptiness is delusory as well. His introduction of the dependence of negation on negandum is in order to move straight away to the delusory nature of both. There is no statement here that 'delusory' equals 'lacking in inherent existence', and there is no objection to the opponent's statement that the means of valid cognition are not means of valid cognition at all. Śāntideva agrees with the opponent's premisses and seeks to underline this agreement with a move away from the negandum towards negation and the ultimately delusory nature of both. Tsong kha pa, as we have seen, does not at all agree with the *pūrvapakṣa*. Thus for Tsong kha pa *BCA* 9:140 must perform a different function. Fortunately it can fit perfectly within his project of neither over- nor under-negating. *Bodhicaryāvatāra* 9:140 ab provides for Tsong kha pa an Indian authority in order to support the need to identify well the negandum – inherent existence, not existence as such – in meditation on emptiness. No doubt this was helped by the Tibetan version of *BCA* 9:139, which in reading *stong pa nyid / sgom pa* related the whole discussion to a situation where the meaning and viability of *meditation* on emptiness was very much in the background. Unlike Śāntideva, the importance of this half-verse for Tsong kha pa is in order to suggest a move *towards* the negandum, an appreciation of its nature and characteristics. Thus this half-verse from Śāntideva becomes in dGe lugs writings a *locus-classicus*, but a *locus classicus* for what? It is not a *locus classicus* for Śāntideva's own unique understanding. Śāntideva cites it in passing, intending that all will agree that it is necessary to have a conceptually-constructed negandum in order to have negation. Clearly, as Prajñākaramati points out, Śāntideva considers that he is putting forward a common view expressed by the man or woman in the street, and Śāntideva passes straight from this to the negation of the negandum. *BCA* 9:140 ab is also not *itself* the *locus classicus* for Tsong kha pa's interpretation of negation and negandum in meditation on emptiness. He and later writers do not seem to offer an *interpretation* of it as such at all. This is a short half-verse, which is rather *used* simply inasmuch as it is cited by Tsong kha pa and his later followers, or incorporated into the construction of their overall system. Thus the value of this half-verse from Śāntideva lies in the fact that 'Śāntideva' said it. What it states is useful to Tsong kha pa, and the great Prāsaṅgika authority who said it can be employed as an authority. *Bodhicaryāvatāra* 9:140 ab is a *locus classicus* but it is the *locus classicus* for nothing more and nothing less than itself.

BCA 9:140 ab can be used by Tsong kha pa in order to help his project of constructing a coherent Madhyamaka system which will avoid over-negation, avoid negating entities when it is only inherent existence which is to be negated. The other half-verse, *BCA* 9:140 cd, portrays negation itself as delusory. This enables Tsong kha pa to stress that emptiness too is not an inherently existent reality, an Absolute, as some other Tibetan teachers – inspired by certain interpretations of the *tathāgatagarbha* and various Tantric doctrines – seemed to want to maintain. The second half-verse, therefore, is tailor-made for stressing the avoidance of under-negation, an avoidance of the fault of not negating emptiness in the same way as other things have been negated. All things, without exception, lack inherent existence.

Since Tsong kha pa does not agree with the attack by the *pūrvapakṣa* in the preceding verse, it is as well that *BCA* 9:140 can be used in a way which is so central to his overall ontology. It required some skill in hermeneutics – the negandum here has to be understood strictly and solely as inherent existence, the negation emptiness – but Tsong kha pa was probably the greatest hermeneuticist in Tibetan history, and what we find repeatedly in examining the contributions of Tsong kha pa and his successors to the interpretation of Tibetan texts is their extraordinary originality and skill in attempting to construct a *rationally coherent system* of Buddhist thought and practice which takes in the whole range of Buddhist literature. Often in looking at the *Bodhicaryāvatāra* we find that Tsong kha pa and rGyal tshab rje are attempting to do something rather different from what is found in other Tibetan and indeed Indian commentaries. Always, it seems that what Tsong kha pa is trying to do involves modifications of understanding in terms of greater overall systematic coherence, and often greater rational philosophical coherence as well. For cultures and ages which see innovation as a fault this may be problematic. But when innovation is seen for what it is – simply innovation, sometimes good, sometimes bad – Tsong kha pa's innovations in the interpretation of Tibetan thought (and those of his brilliant successors) must surely be appreciated for their astonishing genius.

Five

The Absence of Self and the Removal of Pain

How Śāntideva Destroyed the Bodhisattva Path

No one, I think, would deny that to remove one's own pain does not in itself count as a moral act, while to soothe the pains of others would in general count as engaging in actions which are morally virtuous. Our Buddhists however – Śāntideva and his commentators – want to argue that morality requires that I make no distinction at all between removing my own pain and soothing the pains of others or, put another way, moral consistency requires that in acting to remove my own pain I must also act to remove the pains of others, and no *morally significant* distinction can be drawn between the two imperatives. We find Śāntideva arguing for this as part of his reasoning for the moral (and spiritual) transformation which is called *bodhicittotpāda*, the arising of the mind set on enlightenment, the mind which seeks perfect Buddhahood precisely because only perfect Buddhahood is finally the fulfilment of the moral imperative, the imperative to strive unceasingly to remove the sufferings of all sentient beings *without discrimination*.

I shall call the position that morality requires that if I am to remove my own pain I·must (moral imperative) act to remove the pains of others without discrimination the 'universal thesis'. Śāntideva and his commentators want to argue for the universal thesis based on (i) rational consistency arising at least in part from (ii) how things actually are, how the world is. In other words, Śāntideva takes as an assumption that the disinterested nature of morality is fulfilled by rational consistency, and a moral imperative can be drawn from what is, in the broadest sense, an ontological position. Śāntideva would hold, *pace* Hume, that it is very definitely possible to draw an *ought* from an *is*, that the way things are has moral implications and those implications can be – will be – derived through disinterested reason. Our failure to act in conformity with the moral imperative is measured by the extent to which we fail to understand the way things really are, and thus the extent to which we are blocked (through 'beginningless ignorance' and habitual tendencies from time immemorial) from disinterested reason. The centrality of the role of rationality in the moral imperative from this Buddhist perspective is made very clear, for example, by the 'Brug pa bKa' brgyud scholar Padma dkar po, commenting on *Bodhicaryāvatāra* 8:102–3: 'Therefore it is not rational (*mi rigs*) that one should remove the pain of oneself and not remove the pain of others. It is rational that because it is pain it is to be removed. . . It is rational that if it [i.e. my pain] is to be prevented, all [pain] also is to be prevented *(des na rang gi sdug bsngal bsal / gzhan gyi sdug bsngal mi sel ba mi rigs / sdug bsngal yin phyir de bsal bar bya rigs so . . . gal te bzlog na'ang thams cad bzlog par rigs).*

Moral actions, at least the aspired perfect moral actions, occur under the glance (perhaps the stare) of the eye of reason. The 'eye of reason' here is what has sometimes been called in Western philosophy the 'God-eye', the eye which is the paradigm of perfect objectivity, but better spoken of in this context as the Buddha-eye, the eye which – because it is perfectly objective – is also perfectly moral.[1]

1 Bodhicaryāvatāra 8:101–3

I want to undertake a close critical examination of the coherence of one of the arguments given by Śāntideva and his commentators – one of the appeals to rationality – for a logical inconsistency in removing the pain, the actual physical pain, of myself alone and ignoring pains of others. First, let us see what Śāntideva himself says:

> saṃtānaḥ samudāyaś ca paṅktisenādivan mṛṣā /
> yasya duḥkhaṃ sa nāsty asmāt kasya tatsvaṃ bhaviṣyati //
>
> rgyud dang tshogs ces bya ba ni /
> phreng ba dmag la sogs bzhin brdzun /
> sdug bsngal can gang de med pa /
> des 'di su zhig dbang bar 'gyur //
>
> A continuant and a collective – such as a [caste] row (*paṅkti*) or an army – are fictions (*mṛṣā*) /
> The one of whom there is pain (*duḥkha*) does not exist. Therefore of whom will there be the ownership of that? //101//
>
> asvāmikāni duḥkhāni sarvāny evāviśeṣataḥ /
> duḥkhatvād eva vāryāṇi niyamas tatra kiṃ kṛtaḥ //

sdug bsngal bdag po med par ni /
thams cad bye brag med pa nyid /
sdug bsngal yin phyir de bsal bya /
nges pas 'dir ni ci zhig bya //

Pains without an owner are all indeed without distinction /
Because of its quality as pain indeed it is to be prevented. What limitation can be made there? //102//

duḥkhaṃ kasmān nivāryaṃ cet sarveṣām avivādataḥ /
vāryaṃ cet sarvam apy evaṃ na ced ātmāpi sattvavat //

ci phyir kun gyi sdug bsngal ni /
bzlog par bya zhes brtsad du med /
gal te bzlog na'ang thams cad bzlog /
de min bdag kyang sems can bzhin //

If one asks why pain is to be prevented (Tib.: 'the pain of all is to be prevented'), it is [accepted] (Skt.: 'by all') without dispute /
If it is to be prevented, all also is thus. If not, oneself also is like [other] beings //103//

On the surface Śāntideva's argument is quite straightforward: As we all know – we are all good Buddhists here – there is no such thing as a Self, an independent, enduring and real unchanging referent of the indexical first-person pronoun. We are each of us an ever-changing composite of various radically impermanent psycho-physical components extended in space and time. But a composite thing itself is a fiction, in itself it is nothing at all.[2] Thus, Śāntideva wants to argue, we cannot rationally talk of the *owner* of a pain.[3] It follows that Śāntideva wants to hold an extreme version of the no-ownership theory for sensations. Pains are for him quite literally without owners at all. Since under such circumstances we cannot refer to the owners of pains, we can refer only to pains. But pains *qua* pains cannot be distinguished in terms of which are and which are not to be removed. If a pain is to be removed at all, then all pains are to be removed. And pain *is* to be removed, for pain is unpleasant and no one wants what is unpleasant. That is agreed by all, and all as a matter of fact do set out (or wish) to remove (what they consider through beginningless ignorance to be 'their own') pains. Thus if it can be removed, and one is able to remove it, pain is to be removed. The very nature of pain entails that on the no-ownership view if one is to be rationally consistent then in preventing or eradicating any pain at all ('one's own pain') it is not possible to draw a limit at the eradication of just some pains, but one is obliged to eradicate, or strive to eradicate, all pains.

Śāntideva's argument is an argument intended to move directly from wisdom – insight into how things actually are – to morality through rational consistency, an argument directly from the Buddhist ontological insight to altruism. It is simple yet clever. One can readily see its initial appeal which can be quite disturbing in its imperative for a 'revolution of the basis' (*āśrayaparivṛtti*) from egoism to altruism if one is to have any claim not just to morality but indeed to rationality itself. As a triumph of rhetoric over reason the argument may be persuasive. It is as noble as it is incoherent, and I shall argue that seen through the purely rational stare of the Buddha's eye which Śāntideva and his commentators invite us to aspire to and to do the argument is nevertheless fatal to the bodhisattva path and to the bodhisattva's project of concern for others.[4]

2 Ontology

Śāntideva's argument rests on a series of presuppositions and premisses which, while so common in Buddhist thought they might be held to be foundational, are nevertheless it seems to me at least in part highly questionable. Central, of course, is the non-existence of the Self and the non-existence of composite entities, wholes. I want to explore further what conception of 'existence' is at play here, why Śāntideva should hold the counter-intuitive position that wholes simply do not exist, and what unexpected and indeed undesired implications might follow. We can begin by highlighting the following absolutely central point:

(i) Śāntideva's argument will only work if mṛṣā, *(fiction) is taken as meaning complete non-existence.*

The point needs to be stressed, since we are familiar from other sources with the view that *mṛṣā/(b)rdzun pa* in a Madhyamaka context need not mean complete non-existence. Thus Candrakīrti in his famous verses at *Madhyamakāvatāra* 6:23–5 speaks of conventionalities (i.e. everything other than ultimate truths, emptinesses) as being seen by those who perceive 'fictions' (*brdzun pa*). All conventionalities are therefore fictions. Perceivers of fictions are of two types, those whose sense-organs are functioning properly and those whose organs are deranged. The fictions seen by the first category are correct in the eyes of the world, they are correct conventionalities (in comparison with the fictions of the second type).[5]

Thus tables, chairs and mountains seen by cognitions which in everyday life are held to be valid (there is no disfunction in the means of cognition), are correct conventionalities, but still 'fictions'. Indeed we can immediately see from what Śāntideva says above that a great many things (probably all) which we normally consider to be genuine realities, the 'furniture of our world', are going to be fictions for Śāntideva since they are wholes, composites made up out of parts. This includes, of course, the cosmos – the 'totality of things' – itself. Yet it is common, particularly in Tibetan dGe lugs sources, to state that while correct conventionalities are indeed fictions this does not mean that they are utterly non-existent. And this must be the case from what Candrakīrti says, since some very real problems would follow for Madhyamaka if it maintained that even correct conventionalities are completely non-existent, so non-existent (if one can coherently use such an expression) that even distinctions conventionally valid cannot be made between them. Nāgārjuna himself was at pains to argue in *Madhyamakakārikā* 24 and the *Vigrahavyāvartanī* that this conclusion, with its nihilistic implications, need not follow for the Mādhyamika, and the way he did this was through distinguishing between existing conventionally inasmuch as things while not inherently existent nevertheless have their functions and validly enter into everyday transactions, and on the one hand existing ultimately, found under what Tibetans refer to as 'ultimate analysis', and on the other simply not existing at all on any level, not found by even a conventionally valid cogniser. From this perspective (certainly as it is understood in dGe lugs texts) Madhyamaka does not claim that conventionalities found by conventionally acceptable means of valid cognition simply do not exist at all. Rather, in this context to be a fiction means 'to appear one way and exist another' (Napper 1989, p. 109), 'conventional phenomena are not truths, but are falsities (*rdzun pa, mṛṣā*) because they do not exist as they appear' (Newland 1992, p. 3). Thus a table as seen by the conventionally acceptable means of valid cognition of an unenlightened being will be a fiction because it will not exist the way it appears (it will appear as if existing from its own side, as independently self-subsistent, 'inherently' existent, while actually it exists as a conceptual imputation superimposed upon its 'bases of imputation'), but that fiction will nevertheless exist. It can enter perfectly adequately into pragmatic transactional usage and therefore will not be the same as a completely non-existent thing.[6]

It is common at least in dGe lugs Madhyamaka to apply the same approach to issues of the Self.[7] It is agreed on all counts that there is no such thing as a Self, some *really* existent ultimate and individual referent for the indexical 'I', an inherently existent thing which can be found ineliminably to be there as an identifiable entity even when subjected to most probing of philosophical analysis.[8] But I do clearly nevertheless exist. I am a conventionality, and as a conventional entity I am called in dGe lugs texts not the 'Self' (*bdag*) but the 'person' (*gang zag*).[9] Thus Daniel Perdue (1992, p. 364), again relying on dGe lugs sources, states:

> All systems of Buddhist tenets assert selflessness. Even though self in general is a synonym of person, the meaning of 'self' in the term 'selflessness' is different; thus, this is not a doctrine that persons do not exist. Rather, persons do exist and are impermanent phenomena. The meaning of 'selflessness' is variously identified in the different [Buddhist] schools of philosophy, but all agree that, at least, the person is devoid of being a permanent, partless, independent self. It is such a 'self' that does not exist. Persons exist, but a permanent, partless, independent self does not.

The person does indeed exist as a conventionality, it is the person who lives, breathes, needs to have his or her pains removed, and becomes enlightened. It is, if you like, what is referred to when I speak of 'myself', but not my Self. Thus I am indeed a fiction, but once more I am a fiction not inasmuch as I simply do not exist but rather inasmuch as I experience myself to exist one way and actually exist another way. A well-known dGe lugs doxographic manual defines the person (at least as far as the world which we occupy is concerned), the *conventionality* which is referred to by the indexical use of 'I' as finally and according to the most perfect understanding (that of Prāsaṅgika Madhyamaka) 'the mere-I which is conceptually imputed in dependence upon the five [psycho-physical] aggregates which form its own basis for imputation' (dKon mchog 'jigs med dbang po p. 69: *rang gi gdags gzhi phung po lnga . . . la brten nas btags pa'i nga tsam de gang zag gi mtshan gzhir 'dod*). I, myself, may be a 'mere-I', a conceptual imputation upon the spatio-temporal continuant of 'my' parts, but as such I exist. Thus one can make perfectly good distinctions between people. Regardless of the fact that Archibald and Freda, who are unenlightened, think they are truly existing Selves while actually they are just conceptual imputations upon two spatio-temporal psycho-physical continuants, still, there are *two* imputations at play here. *Why* there should be two, rather than one or thirty-three, is not here at issue, although *inter alia* there are obvious biological and evolutionary reasons why the living being who is Archibald is spoken of as one both by himself (as 'I', 'me') and by others (as 'you', 'Archibald'), and Freda also is spoken of as one. Within this framework of everyday life, everyday conventional transactions, there are genuine, real distinctions between Archibald and Freda. Archibald is portly and lives in London; Freda is extremely thin and lives in Edinburgh. These are genuine distinctions. To apply the attributes of Freda to Archibald is simply wrong.

My point here can be generalised as follows. The existence of the person thus understood as a conventionality, even if there are no True Selves, enables all the normal everyday transactional distinctions to be made. This is why insight into the absence of any Self does not entail seeing that no one exists at all and therefore does not undermine the Buddhist path. Correspondingly, it seems clear that if there is not only no Self but not even a person in the sense understood above then everyday distinctions of the relevant type cannot be made. It makes no sense to teach, for example, without even seeing the existence of a person or persons to be taught; it makes no sense to help without any awareness *on any level* of a person to be helped. If a Buddha does not perceive any difference at all between Archibald and Freda then even a Buddha is wrong, for inasmuch as there are both Archibald and Freda there are indeed differences between them. It would seem that those differences are to be respected as important to being Archibald and Freda and may – indeed must – be relevant to helping them.[10] And if a Buddha does not perceive Archibald and Freda at all, simply does not see them or hold them as existing at all, then once more a Buddha must be simply wrong. Nevertheless it is of course quite coherent to argue that teaching and helping do not require any conception of a True Self which is taught or helped, and indeed conceptions of True Selves are arguably antithetical to skilful helping.

There is a view that the Buddhist teaching of no True Self, if seen and understood directly in the fullest possible way, would logically entail freedom from all egoistic selfishness. Śāntideva himself seems to hold this view. Yet actually the fact, if it is a fact, of no True Self does not in itself have such an entailment. In spite of the common English equivalence of 'selfless' and 'unselfish', the absence of True Self is not the equivalent of, nor does it entail, unselfishness. It might be thought to be *immoral*, but there is no contradiction whatsoever in accepting as true a teaching of no Self (*anātman*) – even seeing it directly in the fullest possible way – and being selfish.[11] If I am selfish I give a precedence to the interests of this person, me, over the rights and interests of that person, Archibald. In itself this has absolutely nothing at all to do with holding to the existence of a Self. In order to give precedence to (a) this person over the interests and rights of (b) that person, all I have to do is be capable of making a distinction between (a) and (b). This distinction can be made in various ways, but in our common experience it rests on whatever normal everyday distinctions are indeed made between (a) and (b), between me and Archibald. Therefore if there is any difference at all between me and Archibald, if we are different persons, I can still be selfish. I can still put myself first. On the other hand to fail to recognise any difference at all would simply be false, and would also destroy all transactional conventions (at least as regards me and Archibald).

Thus, if we now return to *(i)* above, we can see I think that if there is even a conventional person then one could still talk – of course in everyday transactional terms – of the owner of the pain, and one could thus give priority selfishly to one owner of pain over another. If I can distinguish at all between myself and you – and clearly there is and has to be a distinction (accepted by [dGe lugs] Madhyamaka) even without True Selves – then I can give priority to myself even if that is held to be selfish. The 'ought' of unselfishness simply does not follow from the 'is' of *anātman*. And if as a matter of fact unselfishness does follow from [understanding] absence of self that is a contingent matter rather than one of logical entailment. What we want to know is *why* I should not be selfish, and that is not answered by the perspective of no Self – or rather it would only be answered by the perspective of no Self if that perspective entailed that it would be wrong to make even everyday conventional distinctions between me and others, in other words, if the perspective of no Self meant that I simply did not exist. Anything less than this and there would be no entailment at all.

This can be seen quite clearly if we write 'P is in pain' as P(φ), and 'S is in pain' as S(φ). Śāntideva's 'The one of whom there is pain does not exist. . . . Because of it's quality as pain indeed it is to be prevented. What limitation can be made there?' will work only if we can remove 'P' and 'S' from the statements entirely.[12] To represent 'P' and 'S' as classes containing subclasses 'inherently existent P' and 'conventionally existent [i.e. noninherently existent] P' etc., and argue that we need only remove inherently existent P, remaining with 'Conventionally existent P is in pain' [cP(φ)] will not do. cP(φ) and cS(φ) are still different. Here we can still make valid conventional distinctions between P and S.

Thus Śāntideva's 'fiction' (*mṛṣā*) – notwithstanding its meaning elsewhere in Madhyamaka – here *must* involve complete non-existence, as P and S above do not exist and need to be struck from the statements P(φ) and S(φ).[13] This is for reasons not of textual hermeneutics but rather philosophical coherence. Nevertheless in actual fact the simple non-existence of Archibald and Freda, you and me, is of course completely false. One does not have to be an out-and-out Cartesian to find it quite self-contradictory. Note that the issue here is not one of the status of you and me (the Self), but simply one of reference, the ability to refer for any purpose at all to you and me.[14] Unless we are to accuse him of disingenuousness however we have to assume that Śāntideva has what seem to him to be plausible reasons for what turns out to be an absurd conclusion. His reason is contained in the first *pada* of *BCA* 8:101. Composite things are wholes made up out of parts. As psycho-physical individuals we are actually each of us composite things. But in reality there is no such thing as a whole. Note here, for it is important, that in introducing the present discussion through the psycho-physical individual understood on the model of continuant and collective Śāntideva's hypothetical opponent takes for granted the denial of the True Self. This is a Buddhist opponent, an opponent who wishes nevertheless to argue for the person, understood as a conventional existent identical with or constructed out of or on top of the psycho-physical composite. In denying the opponent's argument in actual fact Śāntideva has to deny the person in addition to the Self.

3 Continuants and collectives

A continuant (*saṃtāna*) is a sequential ordering of events, ordered in the series before::after. It is possible to imagine examples where the ordering is temporal, and also a spatial ordering. Thus for a Buddhist like Śāntideva the cause-effect series of mental events, where each event is both effect of a previous and cause for a further event within the series, and each causal event perishes before the occurrence of its resultant event, would be an example of a continuant showing a temporal ordering of before::after. Another example might be an *articulated* sentence or word-token. One uttered phoneme precedes the next, is the cause of the next and has itself ceased when its subsequent phoneme comes into existence. According to some of his Indian and Tibetan commentators, in speaking of a continuant Śāntideva is precisely thinking of the mental continuant – where the before::after series is explicitly a temporal series – while reference to a collective (*samudāya*) is intended to indicate the physical body, where in contrast the ordering would seem to be a non-sequential structuring based, I would imagine, on something like purpose and optimal performance (although Bu ston, in *this* context rather simplistically, refers to the *samudāya* (*tshogs*) as simply the 'uniting of many into one' (*mang po gcig tu 'dus pa ni / tshogs yin la;* p. 469)).[15] Thus Sa bzang mati paṇchen can speak of 'a single continuant of the mind which consists of former and later temporal phases of itself' (*rang gi tshe snga phyi'i sems kyi rgyud gcig pas*: p. 277), a point echoed much more recently for example by gZhan phan chos kyi snang ba who precisely then couples this mental continuant in temporal series with 'a collective of the body, consisting of feet, hands and so on' (*rkang lag sogs kyang lus kyi tshogs pa gcig:* p. 393).[16] The dGe lugs lama Thub bstan chos kyi grags pa makes the situation even clearer when he speaks of the continuant or stream wherein there arises a sequentially ordered series, one following the other, of a plurality of former and later momentary cognition-events (*shes pa skad cig snga phyi du ma gcig rjes su gcig brgyud nas rim gyis 'byung ba la rgyun nam rgyud ces:* p. 532). By way of contrast, in the case of a collective there is no suggestion at all of sequential ordering in a before::after sequence, whether that sequence is understood in temporal or spatial sense. The foot does not by nature come *before* the hand, either in time or space.

This systematic linking of Śāntideva's reference to a 'continuant' with the mental series, and 'collective' with the body is not universal among commentators however. The Indian commentator Kalyāṇadeva specifically refers here to the 'continuant of body *and* mind' (*lus dang sems kyi rgyud:* f. 61a), while Bu ston has his opponent introduce the continuant by explaining that even though there is no Self, no 'deep further fact' (Parfit) or perhaps even 'psychological substance' (Descartes, and Lowe) as a separately existing entity with determinate identity expressed in terms of ownership behind the personal series of mental and physical events, 'nevertheless there still exists a "continuant" which is a stream that is the union of the before and after sequence of body and mind' (*bdag med kyang lus dang sems kyi snga phyi 'brel ba'i rgyun rgyud ces bya ba zhig yod la:* p. 469).

Since the explicit linkage of Śāntideva's 'continuant' with the mind involves a linkage with what is a *temporal* before::after series, it is interesting that as an example Śāntideva chooses a caste-row (*paṅkti*) – which is a *spatial* before::after sequence. The translation of *paṅkti* by 'caste-row' here however is tentative, although I rather like it. The word can be used for any token-row, any row where its members are tokens of the same type and therefore fall under the same class. I am presuming that a group of things would not be classed together and therefore conceptually bound into one continuant if they had nothing in common at all. My suspicion – though I can scarcely prove it – is that Śāntideva intended to refer here to the homely example of a row of members of the same caste, as he refers also to the army (*senā*) as an example of a collective. Remembering that most monks would be familiar from childhood with the Brāhmanic social organisation of the village from which they came, perhaps the first suggestion of *paṅkti* would be the lineal organisation of caste and kinship members at a village feast.[17] Possibly some evidence for this interpretation can be found in the Tibetan translation. The Tibetan translates *paṅkti* by *phreng ba*, an expression which also translates the Sanskrit *mālā*, a garland or – commonly in the Buddhist context – a rosary, but also indeed a row or series (as in the case of a series of words). This gives rise to a problem however with the Tibetan translation of Prajñākaramati's *Pañjikā*. There, the additional examples implied by the expression 'such as' (*ādi/la sogs*) employed in Śāntideva's verse are glossed by 'such as a garland/rosary or forest and so on' (*mālāvanādayo/phreng ba dang nags la sogs pa*).[18] The reduplication of *phreng ba* here with its use in the verse is of course quite absurd, and Bu ston, who appears to have used the Sanskrit text in writing his commentary, while he does not discuss the reduplication, wisely omits to make reference to this second use of *phreng ba*.[19] It is just possible that one reason for the translators using *phreng ba* in translating *Bodhicaryāvatāra* 8:101 was that they felt *paṅkti* to be a cultural term which would not be understood by Tibetans, referring, that is, not just to a 'row' but to a caste-row at a village feast. Thus the translators chose to translate with a reference to a garland or rosary which they felt would be more accessible to their Tibetan audience.[20] After all, if *paṅkti* in the root-text here suggested immediately to the translators simply a 'row' or 'sequence', there are other Tibetan expressions which could have been used as a translation, such as *rim pa*, thus avoiding the problems in the use of *phreng ba* in Prajñākaramati's commentary, where it translates *mālā* very precisely. I suspect that the culturally-determined country village use of *paṅkti* was predominant in the minds of the translators, and also in Śāntideva's search for a homely example to place alongside his reference to an 'army'. If so, then Prajñākaramati's commentarial illustration of a *paṅkti* with a series of ants in file (also taken up by some of the later Indian and Tibetan commentators) can be seen as originally a joke which might have appealed to the anti-Brāhmanical Buddhist monks, likening castes in file at a feast to ants playing follow-my-leader.

4 Wholes simply do not exist

According to Śāntideva and his commentators there is simply no such thing as a continuant or a collective, let alone a psycho-physical aggregate of continuant and collective extended in time and space. Yet this is very strange, since most things – most 'medium size' things – met with in everyday life are composites. It is even more strange when we remember that, say, water molecules are composites of hydrogen and oxygen atoms and are therefore for Śāntideva simply non-existent. Thus we are going to find that the very physical basis of life, the universe and everything simply does not exist. This is not just the philosophically plausible (though it seems to me false) contention that aggregation does not make anything new over and above the composite elements. Rather, aggregation simply does not make anything at all, since otherwise there could be conventionally existent persons and – let me repeat – Śāntideva's argument would not follow. Why, according to Śāntideva and his commentators, is the whole – the continuant and collective – a fiction, simply non-existent? The discussion by Prajñākaramati is for later scholars both foundational and comprehensive. According to Prajñākaramati:

(i) There does not exist any unitary ultimate reality called a *continuant*.
(ii) This is of the nature of a stream which is the ordered succession of moments occurring under the aspect of cause and effect.
(iii) It is not apprehended separately from that.
(iv) Thus, having recourse to one word for those moments a convention is employed by the mind for the purpose of everyday transactions with the word 'continuant'.
(v) It is a conceptual reality.
(vi) One should have done with craving for it. . . .
(vii) Thus also, there does not exist one reality which is a *collective* apart from the collected members themselves.
(viii) This is because it is not apprehended separately from those.
(ix) Since it cannot bear critical examination by way of conceiving it as identical or different from the subject, it will not be spoken of here.
(x) Therefore this also is a conventional existent, as formerly.[21]

Given that we have seen that for Śāntideva there can be no question of the psycho-physical composite existing but as a mere conventionality, one might be forgiven at this point for some confusion in reading Prajñākaramati's comments. Thus at (i) we are told that what is being negated is not the continuant as a conventionally existent construct, but rather an ultimate reality (*paramārthasat*), as something which can be found under an 'ultimate analysis' (ix). Prajñākaramati actually states that the continuant is a 'conceptual reality' (*prajñaptisat;* (v)), and the collective is a 'conventional existent' (*saṃvṛtisat;* (x)). The classical Madhyamaka *svabhāva :: niḥsvabhāva* binary structure is quite clear here, but it is also quite inappropriate.[22]

Prajñākaramati's terminology is that of Vaibhāṣika Abhidharma.[23] I have discussed the central Vaibhāṣika binary distinctions (which are equivalent in that they mark the same opposition) between *paramārthasat :: saṃvṛtisat, dravyasat :: prajñaptisat, sasvabhāva :: niḥsvabhāva* elsewhere.[24] Here we should note that these binary distinctions – which in origin arise from the basic Buddhist claim that the apparently fundamental, primary reality of the Self can actually be reduced to a spatio-temporal series of psycho-physical elements – are closely related to issues of certainty and irreducibility, that is, the ability or otherwise to resist a process of literal, or analytic conceptual, reduction. To say that *x* exists in the fullest possible sense (i.e. it has *paramārthasat*) is to say that no matter how hard we try we cannot reduce *x* to some other elements which one way or another can be said to be its components and therefore, it is claimed, can be said to have *a more fundamental* (foundational, i.e. *dravyasat*) reality. We know that something has only conventional (*saṃvṛti*) or conceptual (*prajñapti*) reality when it can be divided into its component parts and then the original object is no longer experienced. In the light of this reduction the experience of the original object is lost. What this means, of course, although it is not put in quite this way, is that if such a reduction can take place then clearly there does not remain the original object still there alongside its parts. Thus, it is argued, apart from its parts the original object is nothing and therefore the original object is just a way of conceptualising, or seeing, its parts and cannot be granted the same sort of reality as the parts themselves. To quote from the summary of the Vaibhāṣika view contained in the doxographical digest (*Grub mtha'*) of dKon mchog 'jigs med dbang po:

> The definition of conventional *satya* [*kun rdzob bden pa/saṃvṛtisatya*] is as follows: It is an object where, if it can be destroyed or analysed into its separate parts by the mind, so the cognition of the nature of that thing must be abandoned. For example, a clay pot and a rosary. If the clay pot is destroyed by a hammer then the cognition which apprehends it as a clay pot is abandoned. If the rosary is analysed into each of its beads then the cognition which apprehends it as a rosary is abandoned. The definition of ultimate *satya* [*don dam bden pa/paramārthasatya*] is as follows: It is an object where, [even] if it could be destroyed or analysed into its separate parts by the mind, then the cognition of the nature of that thing would not be abandoned. For example, atoms which have no directional parts, partless moments of consciousness and those such as space (*ākāśa*) which are nonconditioned (*asaṃskṛta*). . . That being the case it is maintained that conventional *satyas*, even though not ultimately established are nevertheless established as true (*bden* – *satya* – actual), since this school maintains that every entity is truly established.[25]

Note the example of the rosary here, since of course it occurs again in discussing *Bodhicaryāvatāra* 8:101, and also dKon mchog 'jigs med dbang po's last comment. It is not maintained in Vaibhāṣika Abhidharma that to say that something has conventional or conceptual existence is a euphemism for saying that it does not exist at all. Things like rosaries, forests, armies, and any other continuants or collectives – even the person itself – while they are conventionalities inasmuch as they are made up of ontologically more fundamental elements, are definitely held to exist. They are not fictions (*mṛṣā*) in Śāntideva's sense of the term. And in this respect, as we have seen, Vaibhāṣika Abhidharma is surely correct.

There is another respect in which the Vaibhāṣika here is, if not necessarily correct, at least not necessarily wrong either. Rosaries genuinely are made up out of beads, forests out of trees, and pots out of atoms. It is truly the case that if you take apart the 108 or so beads of the rosary there does not remain an additional thing called the 'rosary itself'. While true, this is however quite trivially so. It is trivial to state that there is not an additional thing (an additional part, or 'super-part'?) called the 'rosary itself' over and above the parts. Thus what Prajñākaramati states at (i), that 'there does not exist any unitary ultimate reality called a continuant', at (iii) 'it is not apprehended separately from that', and similar comments at (vii) and (viii), are all trivially true. Of course the whole 'in itself' is nothing at all. A whole is a *whole*; by definition there is no whole *in itself*. The parts are precisely its parts. It is part of the meaning of 'parts' that they are all the elements, factors or whatever which make-up *x* as its constituents (which is not to say that there are not other types of things – relations between parts, for example – which are necessary in addition to the parts themselves in order to make a whole). If there were an additional thing called the '*x* itself' then without that additional thing there would be no *x*, no rosary. Thus that additional thing would be a constituent of *x* and therefore not the whole but a further part. Thus it is trivially true – a result of the meaning of 'part' and 'whole' – that there is no thing called a 'whole' in addition to the parts. There is no paradox here. Nevertheless a follower of Vaibhāṣīka Abhidharma – let us call him 'Vasubandhu' – is perfectly entitled to involve in distinguishing between wholes and parts a distinction of two types of 'reality'. It is a matter of definition – perhaps not to be recommended as a potential source of confusion, however – if Vasubandhu wishes to call wholes *'saṃvṛtisat'*, *'prajñaptisat'* etc., and phenomena which are thought to be analytically irreducible *'dravyasat'*, *'paramārthasat'* and so on.[26]

The distinction is however more than just one of different types of reality. It contains a strong dimension of value. The word *'paramārtha'* in particular conveys in Sanskrit the sense of the supreme thing, purpose, goal and meaning. If a contrast is drawn between *paramārtha* and *saṃvṛti* there is an implicit but very definite value judgement being made. If something has *saṃvṛtisat* it may be useful but it is not to be *supremely valued*. Just as his discussion of *Bodhicaryāvatāra* 8:101 relies completely on the structures of Vaibhāṣika Abhidharma ontology, Prajñākaramati's derivation of the 'ought' of value from the 'is' of his ontological categories can be seen at (v) and (vi). Since the continuant is a conceptual reality, one should have done with craving for it. The principle underpinning this comment is the Buddhist horror of impermanence and our attempts to ignore or deny impermanence as the source of all suffering. It is plausible to argue that all (or perhaps most) composites, inasmuch as they have been put together by various forces of composition, will eventually fall apart. Thus composites by their very nature are obviously subject to impermanence. Inasmuch as craving for what is impermanent leads to suffering in the light of its very transitoriness, it is as well to avoid craving for any composite. Therefore the rationale for distinguishing between wholes and parts, composites and simples, on the basis of types of existence, and the introduction of an axiological dimension through valuing one type of existence more than another – together with playing on the superficial paradox that the whole is *nothing in itself* and therefore is thought to be somehow not fully real – has its basis in the wider Buddhist spiritual context of decreasing attachment and therefore, it is argued and hoped, decreasing suffering. Within this context it is certainly not *wrong* of the Buddhist to speak of composites as 'merely conventionalities', lacking the prestigious type of existence. This is a matter of how we choose to define and use our terms. It would be wrong, however, if the Buddhist was misled by this to go to the far extreme and deny that conventionalities have *any existence* at all. This, unfortunately, is what Śāntideva does. But if he does not do this then his argument is going to loose whatever initial plausibility it might possess.

5 Conceptual existents, artefacts and natural kinds

Let us look now at an ambiguity here in referring to something as a 'conceptual existent' (*prajñaptisat*). On the one hand to describe something as a conceptual existent in this context could mean merely (i) that *x* is not a simple. It has the particular sort of existence which occurs 'in dependence upon' more fundamental elements, parts. In other words, in some sense *x* can be reduced to its components. If *x* has parts at all then, as we have seen with the Vaibhāṣika, it is to be granted only the lesser sort of existence. On this basis a mountain, for example, would be a conceptual existent, as indeed would be molecules.

On the other hand if *x* is described as a conceptual existent it could mean (ii) that *x* which is a composite made of parts is seen and spoken of as one thing simply as a manner of speaking, perhaps for practical purposes, but this unity is entirely a matter of the synthesising activity of minds. Thus if all minds suddenly went out of existence there might (must?) hypothetically (but not as a matter of fact actually for the Mādhyamika) remain the component parts but there would no longer remain *x*. This is indeed what I take it is meant in Madhyamaka by referring to something, indeed all things – such as the person – as existing as a mental imputation in dependence upon the imputing power of the mind and the bases of imputation.[27] In a case like this *x* is not just spoken of as one, it is actually given its unity by the conceptualising, the imputing activity of minds. It makes no sense to talk of *x* as actually *being* one thing apart from the intentions of minds – to all intents and purposes human minds – which find it convenient for *x* to *play the role* of one thing.

It seems clear to me that while the first sense of 'conceptual existent' may be defensible and useful as a form of valuation, an indication of the tendency of composites to fall apart, and also in drawing attention to the very composite nature itself of something, this sense of 'conceptual existent' is perfectly compatible with the actual and continued existence, quite independently of minds, of mountains and molecules, as well as every other natural kind (gold, water, and, I think, trees and persons). The second sense of 'conceptual existent' is not, and I do not believe such an explanation is warranted simply because something is a composite made up out of parts. The parts which make up a mountain genuinely are parts making up a mountain. The parts exist independently of minds, their relationships exist independently of minds, and the mountain exists independently of minds. All this is perfectly compatible with there being no mountain apart from and alongside its parts, and of course with the impermanence of the mountain when its parts come apart.

Indeed it seems to me quite implausible to maintain (perhaps like Berkeley) that mountains *came into existence* when minds appeared, more implausible still to think that water as a combination of hydrogen and oxygen did. Under such circumstances it would also be difficult to avoid some sort of solipsism or quasi-solipsism, since I should have to hold that other people taken as psycho-physical wholes also came into existence when my mind – as an individual and indivisible mental event (supposing that should make sense!) of reification or construction (reifying them) – came into existence.[28] I take it that biologically as far as we understand it certain things must pertain in order for there to be any minds at all, and I am sure that those very conditions for minds include many composite things. [29] Thus it seems to me it simply is not the case, nor are we required to say, that just because a thing is a composite it comes into existence in accordance with interpretation (ii) above. Indeed to maintain that composite entities are given their *very existence* by the process of conceptual imputation runs up against problems associated with the origins of the process itself. What process of conceptual imputation, if no one had ever seen mountains, could first (chronologically or conceptually) give rise to a mountain? Of course, it is possible to conceive of something no one has ever seen (a unicorn, for example) on the basis of composition from things which have been seen. But as an explanation of the origin of *everything*, or the origin of all composites which is just about everything, the unicorn model will be of no help.[30] Indeed we want to argue that at least in the case of natural kinds/objects (among which I would be inclined to include persons – see Wiggins 1980; Guttenplan, ed. 1994, p. 556) the composite where applicable is conceptually prior to the parts. It is possible to have branches, leaves and trunks, and to speak of branches, leaves and trunks, because we have trees. If there were no trees first then it would be the branches, leaves and trunks that would go out of existence.[31] If there were no trees then it would not be possible to conceptualise a tree, on the basis of its component parts or otherwise. And it also seems clear to me that if there were no persons given first then we could not even begin to conceptualise a person in dependence upon feet, hands, and the stream of mental events.

Yet it is arguable that this second sense of 'conceptual existent' *will* work for artefacts, things which have actually been put together directly (or indirectly – consider something planned and constructed by robots) by beings animated with some sort of intelligence. Artefacts are commonly characterised by a particular function, and all the examples of continuants and collectives given by Śāntideva and his commentators – a caste-row, or row of ants, an army, a rosary and, I would argue, even a forest – are examples of artefacts.[32] But, and this is crucial, the person (or self, or indeed human being – these are not of course intended here as equivalents) as it is normally understood is patently *not* an artefact. It is something like a member of a natural kind. Artefacts appear to be parasitic upon the existence of natural kinds. In the case of the caste-row, it is made up out of persons, precisely beings which are not artefacts. The same applies to the ants in the row of ants, the trees in the case of a forest, and the soldiers, elephants and so on in the army. Moreover it seems clear that the relationship between the persons who make up the caste-row is quite different – perhaps we could call it 'external' – to the relationships which exist between the various elements which are involved in our concepts of a person ('holistic'?). Although the examples given are perhaps analogies intended to illustrate one particular feature only (the bringing together into a unity of what is in actual fact diverse), it is strikingly obvious that the caste-row itself is existentially and it seems to me ontologically too quite unlike the individual persons who make up the caste-row. The caste-row is a cultural construct for a purpose which comes together and (after the village feast) parts. It is a social reality and has no natural structure or intrinsic homeostatic regulation.[33] Its members do not form one holistic entity in anything like the same way as the members of a functioning human body, and it is quite clear that this difference is absolute and not simply a matter of degree. As Jonathan Glover says, 'the [human] body is not like a swarm of bees [a row of ants!] whose members can go off in different directions. It is *natural* to treat the body as a unit because it moves about as one' (1991, p. 74; italics PW). This unity of the body, indeed the whole person, at a time and to a greater or lesser degree over time, is not the result of some conceptual construction for pragmatic purpose. That is how it is given naturally.[34] It is given as a whole *prior* to deconstruction into parts. It is not just that the situation is numerically more complicated, there are *more* members of the human body than members of our village caste-row. The caste-row, unlike the caste-members, is not *alive*, and to ignore this fact is to ignore something vitally important.[35] Human beings, for example, along with many other natural kinds which are alive reproduce their own kind which as the result of genetic programming resemble them – caste-rows and other artefacts do not.[36] These points simply cannot be portrayed as incidental or irrelevant to the (ontological and other) status of persons compared with caste-rows (and it is not necessary to be able to define clearly what 'life' is in order to understand directly its truth). One is reminded here of essentially the same distinction made by Aristotle at *Physics* 2:192b, a distinction which even allowing for a rather archaic conceptual framework is surely basically correct:

> Some existing things are natural, while others are due to other causes. Those that are natural are animals and their parts, plants, and the simple bodies, such as earth, fire, air and water; for we say that these things and things of that sort are natural. All these things evidently differ from those that are not naturally constituted, since each of them has within itself a principle of motion and stability in place, in growth and decay, or in alteration. In contrast to these, a bed, a cloak, or any other artifact – insofar as it is described as such, i.e., as a bed, a cloak, or whatever, and to the extent that it is a product of a craft – has no innate impulse to change . . .[37]

Clearly for Aristotle a member of a natural kind differs from an artefact precisely in that a natural kind has the principle of life (depending on what is to count as 'life' in the case of each natural kind) within it. Yet if that is even remotely like the truth then in the case of, say, human beings there must crucially be a sort of unity to the human being in order that the human being can be alive in the way that humans are actually alive, a sort of unity which is lacking in an artefact like a caste-row. And there is another relevant and important way in which natural kinds differ from artefacts. As Samuel Guttenplan has pointed out, 'What is crucial to the notion [of natural kind] is that the shared properties [of natural kinds] have an independence from any particular human way of conceiving of the members of the kind' (Guttenplan, ed. 1994, p. 450). That is, even if we do wish to represent all wholes as through their very composite nature only conceptual existents (*prajñaptisat*), in recognising the human being as a natural kind one is precisely recognising it as a conceptual existent in only the *first* of the two senses delineated above (i.e. it is nevertheless ontologically mind-independent) and this non-dependence for its actual existence on human ways of conceiving is precisely crucial in distinguishing natural kinds from social artefacts like caste-rows.[38]

There is an additional problem which might result from taking the person on the model of the caste-row in particular. It is plausible to argue that the identity of the caste-row is gained through the identity of the set of its members. Thus we can speak of it being the *same* caste-row if it contains the same members.[39] If that is right, then since a set is defined by its members it follows that if one member dies or is replaced we have a different set, a different caste-row. But it seems clear that the identity of persons, psycho-physical individuals, cannot be simply a matter of the set of their members, the set of causally-related mental events plus physical parts. For if that were the case then no person could change in the slightest degree (the loss of one hair of the head) without becoming another person. While initially that might seem acceptable to our Buddhist, not only does it seem implausible that I become another person if I loose a toenail, but it would then be correct for me to avoid punishment by claiming *quite literally and properly* that I was no longer the person who committed the crime (although *very* much like him), memory would become fantasy, the Buddhist path would become impossible since *I* could not become enlightened, my wife would be replaced by someone else very like her but minus a hair – and so on and so on. No one seriously thinks or acts as if that were the case, and there is actually no *need* to do so. This is not just due to a lack of metaphysical insight or a failure to truly internalise the Buddhist teachings. The natural response is to say that although I have lost a toenail I am still (in all relevant respects) the same person who committed the crime, it is still my wife even though she has lost a part, and so on. But if that is the case, as it surely must be, then the person cannot change with a change in parts and therefore the person cannot by definition be identical with the set of the parts. That cannot be how it is and we are not committed to it if we cease to identify persons with the set of their members (presumably at time T). Incidentally, such an identification of persons with sets would also entail that the caste-row would no longer be identical with the set of its natural members, since each member is a person. Thus if one of the members looses a hair or a toenail and therefore becomes another person the entire caste-row changes. But if the caste-row changes when a member looses a hair then it cannot be identical with the set of its obvious natural members, and since the set changes when one of its members changes one hair becomes a member of the set which makes up the caste-row. Note that while this might seem absurd, the way to avoid the absurdity is simply to reject the principle which gave rise to the absurdity, the principle of taking the person as a collection and/or continuant on the model of a caste-row.

6 Time, change and the identity of a continuant

It might be thought that while there are problems with the unity and identity of any whole made up out of parts, there are particular problems with things extended in *time* where the parts are not spatially separated although coexistent but rather the parts are temporal events which arise and cease while we continue to talk about the *persistence of the thing* itself. Put another way, if a continuant is changing all the time, how can we truthfully refer to it as the same?[40]

For example, there is a view sometimes found that there is a particular problem in the existence of a temporal continuant, since at any one time the past stages of the continuant will have ceased and the future stages not yet come into existence.[41] Thus the temporal continuant consists of something most stages of which do not exist, and *qua* existent it reduces to only the present momentary stage. The present momentary stage cannot itself be a temporal continuant (for fear of infinite regress), *ergo* there is no such thing as a temporal continuant. This argument as it stands is confused. *If* there is a temporal continuant then it consists precisely in something extended over time. Thus it is part of the very meaning of 'a temporal continuant' that some stages which constitute it are past and some stages are future. Since of course past stages have ceased and future stages have not yet come into existence (that is what we mean by 'past' and 'future') there is clearly no problem as such in that being the case. A problem would only arise if the past stages had *never existed*, and the future stages *never came into existence*, that is, if the past and future stages were mere non-existents, completely unexampled. It would be under those circumstances that you would not have a temporal continuant, for most of the stages which constitute it simply would not exist. Thus it is necessarily false that a temporal continuant needs to have all its stages existing at the same time. All that is necessary to a temporal continuant is that either it has stages which existed previously, or – if we are now at the first stage – that it has stages which come after, and that it has stages which will exist in the future, or – if we are now at the last stage – that it has stages which came before. [42]

In order to be able to refer truthfully to a continuant as the same over time it is necessary, of course, that it remain the same in at least *some* respect, and it certainly has remained the same in *some* respect if it can be identified correctly as that same thing (by whatever way we normally correctly identify things of that sort as the same).[43] For example, if I correctly identify the person arriving at the party as Archibald, the friend I invited yesterday and therefore as a continuant, then something – no doubt including something significant for identification – has remained the same (perhaps he still has the same beard). However it might be objected (particularly by our Buddhist friends), that all is *in every respect* impermanent, changing incessantly from moment to moment. Although we may not notice it, the beard has changed too. Note that the beard here has to have changed completely, in every respect. If there is some respect in which it remains the same then of course we do not have a case of change in every respect. Even aspects of the beard which might not seem to have changed (its colour, its exact position on the changing face?) must have changed also. Surely under those circumstances precisely because a thing does not remain the same in any respect from moment to moment, it can only strictly speaking be utterly false to refer a temporal continuant as the *same* (person, or whatever).

The problem with this response (supposing it is even coherent at all or at least plausible) was realised as early as Plato, in his reply in the *Theaetetus* (179D–183B) to the extreme version of the Heracleitean flux espoused by Cratylus. According to this picture of Cratylus, as recounted by Aristotle in his *Metaphysics*, 'seeing that the whole of nature is in motion, and that nothing is true of what is changing, they [Cratylus *et al.*] supposed that it is not possible to speak truly of what is changing in absolutely all respects' (trans. Barnes 1979, p. 68; for Plato see also Burnyeat 1990). But, as Plato points out, this position is quite literally contradictory. If x is changing all the time in every respect then it is indeed not possible to identify x at all, let alone as the same over time. Thus not only is it not possible to *say* that x is changing all the time in every respect, but the situation referred to is not true either since there *is* no *x* in order for it to change. [44] If there is no way at all that something can be identified then that thing simply does not exist. If *that* is what I am as a person, something that changes all the time and in every respect, then Śāntideva is right and I quite simply do not exist. However, we have seen already and we shall see further that taking persons (me, you) as literally non-existent is utterly incoherent and is going to have dramatic repercussions for the path of the bodhisattva. Thus in order for something to exist it must have some stability, it must remain the same in *some* respect. If on the other hand there is no *x* at all, then it is not true that *x* is changing all the time and in every respect.

It might be objected that this would be to miss the point of a position like that of our Buddhist. It is granted that things *appear* to be stable. They can thus be identified. It is then possible to discover (by rigorous reasoning involving the nature and operation of causation) that nevertheless those things identified and supposed to be stable are actually changing constantly and in every respect. This response however is not going to work. It tries to have its alms-offering and eat it – it wants stability while at the same time denying it. Thus if we can identify *x*, then *x* must be in some respect stable. If we then through reasoning find that *x* is not in any respect stable then our original identification must have been wrong. There is no *x*. Therefore contrary to appearances we have *not* found out that *x* is changing in every respect. *Nothing* has turned out to be changing in every respect. But if that is the case then it must become impossible to discover that *x* is changing constantly and in every respect. The opponent's position is still strictly contradictory. There is also another way of arguing the same point. If *x* appears to be stable, yet is found to be changing constantly and in every respect, are the changes themselves *real* or *mere appearance*? If the changes are real, then it must be possible to identify *x*, that which is changing. As Aristotle was so aware, there is no such thing as change without a subject of change, and what is to count as a change in a particular subject depends upon what type of subject it is. Thus if the changes are real, *x* cannot be changing constantly and in every respect. If there is change at all, if 'impermanence' is to have any meaning, then it cannot be instantaneously total. But if the changes are mere appearance (whatever that might mean) then one cannot argue from the appearance of stability through rigorous reasoning to a conclusion that things are *actually* changing constantly and in every respect.[45]

Thus any continuant, anything which in everyday life is capable of being identified as the same over time, must genuinely remain stable in *some* respect(s).[46] It is therefore possible to argue that one can genuinely and properly refer to a thing as the same even though it is changing all the time inasmuch as that thing can be identified as the same based on criteria of identification which remain (perhaps relatively but sufficiently) constant. Take the case of a river, which ever since Heracleitus' obscure sayings 'It is not possible to step into the same river twice' and 'On those who step into the same rivers, different and different waters flow' (Barnes 1979, p. 66) seems to have been thought particularly apt as an example of constant change.[47] The river, of course, taken as a geographical entity is actually an example of Śāntideva's collective, with parts spread out spatially, rather than a temporal continuant. But if we take the river with reference to an observer watching the waters flow past, then as an experienced river it is closer to a temporal continuant. (The experience of) some waters is past, some present, some yet to come. There is no experience of a river, it is argued, but only of a series of 'present waters' which are ever changing. But why should it follow that there is therefore no river at all, or there is a problem in referring to the river, or saying truthfully that 'I saw the river', or (said one day) 'That is the River Thames', and (said the next day at the same place or further along the bank) 'That is the River Thames'? Clearly the answer is that the River Thames cannot be identified with the present water (stage). Tomorrow the 'present water stage' will be different, and if the River Thames were *identified* with the present water/river stage then it would indeed be wrong to say tomorrow that it is the same River Thames, since clearly it will not be the same water/river stage. Thus, as Quine has pointed out, Heracleitus is right in that one cannot step into the same river stage twice, but he is wrong in saying that this cannot be done to the same river.[48] The River Thames as I have portrayed it here is a temporal (and spatial) continuant, not a momentary river stage. That is what it is to be the River Thames, that is the *sort* of thing a river is, and terms for that sort of thing refer and are used in a different way from terms for the momentary river stages (*that* sort of thing). If we can apply this to the case of the person, I am a temporal continuant, that is the sort of thing it is to be me (among other things!) and in identifying me, and referring to me as a unity, one, the same and so on this is obviously not the same as referring to the present momentary stage of me (whatever that might be). The sort of thing it is to be a temporal continuant is not the sort of thing it is to be a momentary thing, but it does not follow that because of this there are no such things as temporal continuants. Indeed we can only speak of the present river stage, we can only identify it, because of the river. River stages are parasitic on rivers. It is because rivers exist that river stages exist (this is a substantial not a trivial point). It is because persons exist that the various transitory psycho-physical events exist.

Clearly, rivers are *not* constantly changing in literally all respects. The river as a geographical phenomenon remains relatively stable. The banks might crumble and the river change its course over time, but relative to the changing waters they are stable (and if something is relatively stable then relative to what it is relatively stable it is absolutely stable). Moreover the changes occur in a regular and lawlike way.[49] Relative to my *experience* of the river also a great deal is stable. I can remain in one place, or move my head, or walk up and down the banks, or look at a map, and the river is given to me in various ways which form an identifiable unity. If my experience of the river had no stable elements in it at all (the banks, me perceiving it etc.), then it is difficult to see how that would count as an experience of the river or indeed of anything at all.

One of the implications of all of this is that the river is not identical with the present river stage, nor could it be identical with the set of present river stages – all the water, what would be seen by a series of observers lined along the entire length of both banks, for example. If I point at a river (this can be done linguistically as well as manually), or identify a river *as the River Thames*, I am by no means necessarily pointing at a river stage, or identifying a river stage, or the set of river stages (either present stages or all the stages throughout history). As David Wiggins has pointed out (1980, pp. 30ff; p. 35), when we say that the river is the water the 'is' here is not the 'is' of identity but rather the 'is' of constitution. Thus the river is *constituted* of water, but is not *identical* with the water (the set of the river stages).[50] For example, when all the water which constitutes the present river has reached the ocean it would not be correct to say that the river is in the ocean. Thus they could not be identical, but a river is still water since the word 'is' is used in many more senses than that of identity. Moreover, if the river were the set of present river stages then if the set changed it would no longer be the same river (a set consists precisely of the members of that set). Thus we could no longer refer to the River Thames at all tomorrow, or after a great storm which increased the waters, or after a drought, even when the waters returned. And the river also could not be identical with the set of river stages throughout its length, breadth, and history. These are indeed constantly changing (most of them are in the ocean, or have evaporated, and so on), yet the river *qua* that river has not constantly changed (it is not partly in the ocean, partly in the clouds etc.). It is still the River Thames, and contrary to what some might think this is not in any respect paradoxical. To be the River Thames, that sort of thing, is not the same thing as being a river stage or a set of river stages. Thus the whole is not identifiable with a part, or the set of the parts. Yet clearly, the river is not an additional thing alongside the set of the parts. We have seen already above that it is trivially true to state that the whole is not an additional thing alongside the parts. But as we have seen also this is not to say that there is no more to a whole than the simple sum or collection of the parts. For there to be a whole other elements from different categories need to be involved, such as various functional relations and positions between the parts (cf. Hamlyn 1984, pp. 56–7).

Some would seem to find the suggestion that one thing is neither the same nor different from another paradoxical, indeed outright contradictory. Remember Prajñākaramati on *Bodhicaryāvatāra* 8:101:

> (iii) It is not apprehended separately from that. . . .
> (viii) This is because it is not apprehended separately from those.
> (ix) Since it cannot bear critical examination by way of conceiving it as identical or different from the subject, it will not be spoken of here.

Yet that the whole cannot be apprehended separately and yet is neither the same nor different from the parts is precisely what we find and should expect in the case of wholes and parts, and it is neither paradoxical nor contradictory and certainly does not have the radical implications of the non-existence of the whole. Wholes are identified differently from the way we identify parts, the criteria for identity are different. Things can be said of wholes which cannot be said of parts.[51] A paradox might occur only if something is found to be neither the same nor different to another thing when those things are both of the same sort. Take the following case, derived from a famous discussion by Gilbert Ryle:

a) She went home in a taxi.
b) She went home in a huff.

Supposing a learner of the English language, having understood perfectly well the sentence represented by a), asked if a huff is the same or different from a taxi? The answer surely is neither (or 'No!' to both questions). If he or she objects that this is paradoxical we have to explain that a huff is not the same sort of vehicle as a taxi, nor is it a different sort of vehicle (or indeed any different sort of *thing*). This is an example of what Ryle calls a 'category mistake'. Taxis and huffs fall into different categories. The usage of 'huff' in English is different from that for 'taxi', and 'in a huff' is a colloquial expression which just appears to parallel 'in a taxi' but which is actually used in a very different way. Thus it is simply not enough to argue that a subject is paradoxical (or does not really exist) simply because it is neither the same nor different from something else. It needs to be shown first at least that they are of the same category, or the same sort.[52]

7 The continuant/collective model and the unity of the person

I have argued, therefore, that there is no problem in taking a continuant and a collective as wholes and giving them identities which are not just arbitrary constructions but genuinely reflect the way things are. Such wholes do indeed exist. Nevertheless, it is clear that there are serious problems with the Buddhist's view (apparently shared by Śāntideva and his opponent) that the living human being (let us ignore animals and other sentient beings for this discussion) can be treated as a continuant on the model of a caste-row, or a collective on the model of a forest or rosary. For it is clear that in everyday experience and also in biological and evolutionary terms the person I am is a holistic whole which has a much, much tighter and more complex unity than is allowed for in the Buddhist model.[53] It is difficult to see how the continuant-collective model is going to be able to explain that unity in a manner which will not beg the question. Take the case of a continuant of mental moments linked on the Buddhist model by causal links 'of the right sort' (to use a favourite but probably question-begging expression of Derek Parfit).[54] Let us represent the mental continuant with its causal links as it is suggested by Śāntideva's examples by:

(i) MT(i)→(MT(ii)→(MT(iii)→n

where 'MT(i)' refers to the mental moment at time (i) and so on, the arrow indicates the causal relationship, and 'n' n-further moments. Actually this model of the way our minds work as a mental continuant appears to be false, or at least it is not obviously correct. It seems obvious that in our actual experience our minds do not run in a simple linear series of mental events, one at a time. Many mental events seem to be occurring at the same time.[55] Thus we need to make the model more complicated. Let us try:

(ii) MT(i)→MT(ii)→MT(iii)→(n
NT(i)→NT(ii)→NT(iii)→n

where NT(i) is another mental event occurring at the same time as MT(i). In addition in reality it appears that one mental event, perhaps more, may be the result of many causes, and have one or many effects. And so on and so on. In addition we also have a bodily continuant occurring:[56]

(iii) MT(i)→(MT(ii)→MT(iii)→n
NT(i)→NT(ii)→NT(iii)→n
BT(i)→BT(ii)→BT(iii)→n

where BT(i) refers to a bodily event occurring at T(i) and so on. Note that even if we do not accept that the mental series has two or more mental events occurring at the same time, we still have:

(iv) MT(i)→MT(ii)→MT(iii)→n
BT(i)→BT(ii)→BT(iii)→n

Now, if (iii) or (iv) provide anything like an admittedly enormously simplified model of what is going on, then we have the following problem:

Problem: What, in a non question-begging manner, exactly provides the unity – any unity – possessed by the person both at T(i) and over the entire series T(i) to n?

To show the nature of the problem let us take the simpler situation given in (iv) above, and hypothetically see it as the situation of Archibald. We can indicate this by adding 'A's at the appropriate points:

(v) AMT(i)→AMT(ii)→AMT(iii)→n
ABT(i)→ABT(ii)→ABT(iii)→n

Now let us also add the situation with Freda:

(vi) FMT(i)→FMT(ii)→FMT(iii)→n
FBT(i)→FBT(ii)→FBT(iii)→n

The two meet at a party:

(vii) AMT(i)→AMT(ii)→AMT(iii)→n
ABT(i)→ABT(ii)→ABT(iii)→n

meet (or should it be 'meets')

FMT(i)→FMT(ii)→FMT(iii)→n
FBT(i)→FBT(ii)→FBT(iii)→n

Our problem is what exactly gives the identity here to the two series represented in (v) and in (vi)? Putting it bluntly, why is it that Archibald's and Freda's series do not get mixed-up? Why do we not have:

(viii) AMT(i)→FMT(ii)→AMT(iii)→n

or even:

(ix) FMT(i)→ABT(ii)→FMT(iii)→n

Initially we might appeal to the causal links. Thus we cannot have the situations represented in (viii) and (ix) since the causal links are not of the right sort. AMT(i) can only produce another event or events in the AM series. Note that in appealing to the putative unity provided by causal links we are already pointing to the inadequacy of the artefact-model given by Śāntideva with his caste or ant-row, army, rosary or forest. There is no causal link, or at least no obvious and relevant causal link of the right sort, between the elements of a caste-row, rosary, forest or army. These are, if you like, heaps, rather than causally linked constituents (see Stone 1988, pp. 521–2). But clearly while it would be trivial to speak of a causal series as indeed one causal series, this particular recourse to causal links in order to speak not of one *causal* series but one *personal* series here is question-begging, since it requires that we make use of the concept of the *AM series* and links 'of the right sort' which is precisely what we are seeking to explain. Moreover the suggestion that the causal series is only mistakenly taken as a personal series – a recourse to the *avidyā* theory – is not going to work precisely because it too begs the question – it requires the person for ignorance to take place. It is necessary to have a person first in order that a particular causal series can be *taken as* also a personal series. It is only *persons* who can take it this way. Indeed it can be argued that there can be even a causal relationship between mental events only *because* they are the experiences of the same person. What we need is not an explanation of the personal series as a causal series, but precisely an explanation of what it means to say that this particular causal series is a *personal* series. And the causal links being of the 'right sort' and so on *requires* the concept of the same series, and they are only of the 'right sort' which are in that particular personal Archibald-series. Our problem is how to explain the unity apparently represented by (v) and (vi) without appealing to the concepts of the same series and that particular personal series in order to give that unity. Why should a causal series be united into a personal series?[57] Furthermore, appealing to the causal series does not in itself anyway explain why we should give any sort of *unity* even to AMT(i) with AMT(ii), let alone AMT(i) with AMT(iii), and that of course the unity of a *person*. Why should we give a unity to two events just because one causes another, especially where causation is understood on the very loose model of 'this being, that occurs; with the non-occurrence of this there is the non-occurrence of that'? Supposing a brick thrown at me causes a bump on the head. I do not see the collision of the brick with my head and the bump as forming one unified whole (let alone a whole which is a person). Or take the case where I feel well and my wife is happy because of that. My mental event is a cause of a mental event in the case of my wife. It is directly a case of one mental event causing another, since it is my actual feeling well which causes my wife's happiness. It is not just that my wife *thinks* that I feel well (a mental event for her) which brings about her happiness. Nor is it that I *report* that I feel well which brings about her happiness (even if these form the mechanism by which she comes to know that I feel well). She would not be happy here if I did not *actually* feel well. The report is the means by which she comes to know that I feel well, but it is my actually feeling well which (in this example) is the cause of her happiness. The fact that my actual feeling brings about her actual feeling can certainly be explained using the 'this being, that occurs; with the non-occurrence of this there is the non-occurrence of that' formula. So this all takes place according to the model MT(i)→MT(ii). And yet we do not see these as mental events in the same series of one person. Or take the case where, as is held in the Vaibhāṣika Abhidharma, for example, among the causes of a perception is the object of the perception. Yet again, we do not incorporate the object of the perception (say, Freda) into the personal continuum of the perceiver (Archibald). Yet the only *grounds* for not doing this must surely be that, while there is a causal connection, the causal connection is not 'of the right sort'. Thus the burden of linking the psycho-physical factors into persons falls not to causation as such, but particular *sorts* of causation. It is difficult to see what this would amount to in detail without somewhere along the line relating in a question-begging way causal relations 'of the right sort' not only to a series already seen as one, but *an actual personal series*, a series seen as a person.[58]

Note here that we have MT(i) and MT(ii). I cannot refer to *A*MT, since the whole point at issue is the unity of the person, Archibald.[59] We are inclined to accept the unity of AMT(i) and AMT(ii) here only because we see them already as part of the *same personal series*, that is, we give a unity by appealing to the fact that they are a unity (and indeed of a particular sort) already. When Hume, inspired by his empiricism, looked and found no self but only a series of linked impressions, there was already a self there doing the looking – Hume, the referent of Hume's use of the indexical 'I' – and providing the unity for those impressions. Those impressions were given already as part of the same personal series. As an empiricist Hume did not stop to ask whether looking was the best way of finding a self if there is one. Nevertheless failing to find P, particularly when the search is limited to a search of a particular sort, and finding that there is *no* P, are not the same thing. Likewise when the Buddhist monk, say, in meditation observes the flow of mental events, there is certainly a self, a unified person, doing the observing and the unity of the psycho-physical events is given already, a presupposition of the process of observation. In actual fact both Hume and the Buddhist presuppose a unity as a condition of their analysis which they appear to be unable to reconstruct again from the reduced elements of their analysis. Of course, in saying that Hume and the Buddhist presuppose the self no commitment is made here to the *status* of the self, what a self is, or what it is to be a self, and certainly there is no necessary commitment to a Self, a Cartesian or quasi-Cartesian entity. But it is simply mistaken to dissolve away the self into a series of events linked by non-specific causal connections. If we observed and listed exhaustively all our psycho-physical events and their causal connections this would not give us the self, the person, since it would not follow that the person could be adequately reduced to psycho-physical events and their causal connections, or fully explained in their terms. This would be the case even if the person supervened upon psycho-physical events and their causes and there were no person in any sense apart from psycho-physical events and their causes.[60]

Let us return to MT(i)→MT(ii). We say that they are Archibald's or they are mental, but both require the concept of the personal series in order to make any sense. However since at our rather small party we have just two series, MT(i)→MT(ii) etc. and cannot refer to *A*MT(i) and *F*MT(i) it appears to be impossible to see why MT(i) will give rise at the next moment to the MT(ii) of (question-begging) 'it's' series rather than the MT(ii) of the 'other' series. One response might be to say that *whatever* is the result at the next moment of an MT(i) will by virtue of that very fact be the MT(ii) of 'it's' series. This would be to put the entire burden of unity simply on the causal connection as such. One immediate problem here however would be that we could never know in advance whether the one series is not going to cross over, as it were, or invade the other series. Put bluntly Archibald cannot know in advance whether or not at the next moment his mental series might not incorporate an event of 'Freda's' mind, presumably with her habits and memories! Of course, this is absurd but how can we specify the source of the absurdity on the Buddhist's premisses? Another problem which is related to the possibility of causal activity outside the series and also multiple effects (which will be introduced below) is that there is no reason for knowing in advance that the MT(i) of the one series might not give rise both to the MT(ii) of the same series and also the MT(ii) of the other series as well. If we put the burden of unity entirely on the causal connection then here we would have a unity between both the MT(i) and MT(ii) of the first series and also the MT(i) of the first series and the MT(ii) of the second series. Both series would then have to be Archibald. It would then seem that we have two Archibalds, or has one Archibald become Freda? Is Freda now identical with Archibald? I don't know.

Moreover even if we take just Archibald himself, how can we explain the unity given in (v) above when we actually have at least two series, those of mind and body? This is a particularly acute version of our problem. We cannot appeal to the unity of the same series through the causal links here, since the series and causal links pertain to the mental series and physical series taken separately, and not together. Thus why do we not construct one person out of Archibald's mental series and Freda's physical series? We cannot, of course, say that one is Archibald's series and the other one Freda's! As they stand – and without begging the question – there is no closer linkage between Archibald's mental series and his physical series than Archibald's mental series and Freda's physical series. As it stands, what this means is that the relationship between my body and my mind at any one time or through time is purely contingent matter, indeed accidental and finally arbitrary. Or at least, it is a matter of conventional pragmatic construction but, note, not a construction by me, since to appeal to me here would once again be to beg the question. This seems to be quite absurd (and also incidentally to be at variance with neurological science). So instead we must employ a suggested possibility of causal links across the mental and physical series, perhaps:

(x) AMT(i)→ABT(ii)→AMT(iii)→n

and

FBT(i)→FBT(ii)→FMT(iii)→n

and so on. This would after all appear to correspond more closely with the discoveries of neuroscience, since we do indeed find that stimulating parts of the brain can produce mental events. However, two initial problems spring to mind here. If we tried to give some sort of unity to Archibald's psycho-physical series by allowing causal links across the 'body-mind' divide we would still have no way of restricting 'permissible' links to something like (x) rather than, say, (ix) without stipulating that the permissible links must occur *within the same personal psycho-physical series*, which would precisely be to beg the question again. Secondly, unless we want to maintain that there is a gap in the mental series between AMT(i) and AMT(iii), we will have to accept that AMT(i) has two causal results, the one being ABT(ii) and the other (not represented here in (x)) being AMT(ii). We might refer to the one (AMT- effects) as horizontal or 'within the series' and the other (ABT-effects) as vertical or 'outside the series' (for a parallel example in Vaibhāṣika Abhidharma see Williams 1981, p. 246). Under these circumstance what we would require is an explanation of how and why one mental event can have these quite different types of effect, what we mean by talking of 'within' and 'outside' the series here given that it is the very notion of the same personal series which we are seeking to explain, and also why, again without begging the question, we should restrict AMT(i) to causing the physical event ABT(ii) and not the physical event FBT(ii).

Another point. We have been discussing the problem of explaining in a way which does not beg the question the unity of the complex psycho-physical continuant(s) over time given the Buddhist understanding. But of course Śāntideva also refers to the collective, the spatial whole which is the bodily complex. In the case of the body, *at any one time* extended in space, it would not be possible on Buddhist grounds to explain the unity of the body in terms of a causal series since generally, and certainly in Madhyamaka, it is not held that cause and effect can exist at the same time and anyway it is not clear what it could mean in a way which would not beg the question to refer to say, the spleen as the cause of the eye. Thus even the (already weak) causal link as a possible basis for unification could be of no help here. Of course, it might be possible to appeal to something like the unity of purpose of the elements of the body at time T in order to supply a basis for unity, but in the case of the living human being that unity of purpose is possible just *because* the body is a living holistic structure, and could not be constitutive of it.[61] It is because at time T a body is presented as a unified whole that we can abstract from it the constitutive elements which gain their role and meaning in terms of that unified structure. Neither conceptually nor chronologically do we construct the living body at T out of its constitutive elements. The whole is here prior to the part.

8 Korsakov's syndrome – a relevant digression

I have argued that a model of the person, the conventional person, in anything like the form of Śāntideva's continuant plus collective supplied by the Buddhist causal series – even with the added cement of beginningless ignorance – would be quite incapable of explaining the holistic integrated whole of the normal living human being, and even that of great bodhisattvas, and would appear to lead to implications of confusion of persons which, incidentally, would play havoc with the theory of karma and its results. But the 'normal living human being' is an achievement conditioned by genetic, biological and social as well as personal psycho-physiological factors.[62] There are clinical cases where that achievement fails. One particularly interesting case in this context is Korsakov's syndrome, particularly associated, ironically, with chronic alcoholics who also have an inadequate diet notably with thiamine deficiency:

> In its modern use the term 'Korsakoff syndrome' refers to a group of symptoms – known alternatively as the amnesic syndrome – which includes inattentiveness, memory defect for recent events, retrograde amnesia and other disorders of recall and recognition, and disorientation in time, place, and situation. Confabulation, grandiose ideas, and an inappropriate cheerfulness are prominent symptoms in some cases (Gregory, ed. 1987, p. 413).

One with Korsakov's syndrome has been described by the clinical neurologist Oliver Sacks as being 'reduced to a "Humean being"', wherein, as Hume states of all of us, as far as our impressions tell us 'we are nothing but a bundle or collection of different sensations, which succeed each other with an inconceivable rapidity, and are in perpetual flux and movement' (quoted in Sacks 1986, p.28). For

Hume, cool reflection would indicate that this is all we actually appear to be. But, Sacks comments, '[t]his is clearly not the case with a normal human being, because he *owns* his own perceptions. They are not a mere flux but *his* own, united by an abiding individuality or self' (1986, p. 119; italics original). Korsakov's syndrome shows that the Humean being, lacking the unity we normally take for granted, is in a hopelessly disadvantaged position, and seriously impaired. He or she is, to use Sack's rather appropriate expression 'a lost soul'.

A frequent particularly debilitating and distressing part of Korsakov's syndrome can be the constant loss of memory from moment to moment (or sometimes a complete forgetfulness of events after a particular date in the past). Thus each moment a sufferer of the syndrome (in one of Sack's cases, a Mr Thompson) is, as it were, a new person and frantically tries to invent a past, 'such a patient *must literally make himself (and his world) up every moment.* [H]ere is a man who, in some sense is desperate, in a frenzy. The world keeps disappearing, losing meaning, vanishing – and he must seek meaning, *make* meaning, in a desperate way, continually inventing . . . ' (Sacks 1986, pp. 105–6; italics original). Such a person, Sacks observes, looses all sense of the distinction between real and unreal, true and untrue, important and trivial, relevant or irrelevant. In one case the patient reported not feeling anything at all about [the enjoyment of] life and 'I haven't felt alive for a long time' (p. 35).[63] In the case of Mr Thompson there was 'some ultimate and total loss of inner reality, of feeling and meaning, of soul . . . one never feels, or rarely feels, that there is *a person* remaining' (pp. 108/110). Now compare the situation with Archibald above:

(v) AMT(i)→AMT(ii)→AMT(iii)→n
ABT(i)→ABT(ii)→ABT(iii)→n

Clearly it is important to this Buddhist model that at T(ii) AMT(ii) and ABT(ii) are *completely* different from, although the causal results of, AMT(i) and ABT(i). Thus it appears that actually the very next moment the self, or person, who is Archibald is completely different from the previous self or person who was Archibald. Of course, AMT(ii) is indeed the causal result of AMT(i), although as we have seen being simply the causal result is far to loose a connection for our purposes, and being a causal result 'in the right way' is going to be impossible to specify without bringing in more than just a causal connection as central to the concept of the same person and specifying in a question-begging way (such as causation within the same personal series) what is to count as causation 'in the right way'. Thus on the model of (v) above the person at T(ii) must effectively be a different person from that at T(i). The situation is very much like that of Korsakov's syndrome, although much more acute since at least in the case of Mr Thompson he presumably had some rudimentary sense of identity provided by the same body. None of the cases of Korsakov's syndrome recounted by Sacks is anywhere near the extreme case of *completely new* generation each moment suggested by the Buddhist model (but cf. the poor, unconscious Alice referred to by van Inwagen in footnote 64 below!).

Note that on (v) above we cannot appeal to memory to provide the necessary unity. Since in fact the persons at T(i) and T(ii) are completely different, there can be no memory although, as with Mr Thompson, there could be pseudo-memories, fantasies masquerading as memories. For a *memory* of having done *x* it is necessary that one is the same person who actually did *x*. But at every moment I perish. [64] And without memory it is difficult to see what sense we can make of conceptually uniting the entire series, or the entire series so far, and calling that the 'self' or the 'conventional person'. We cannot even mistakenly give a unity to the

(v) AMT(i)→AMT(ii)→AMT(iii)→n
ABT(i)→ABT(ii)→ABT(iii)→n

series. There would be no more grounds for doing this than for uniting or mixing the AMT-series with the FMT-series. Or complete fantasy. Mr Thompson was not able to look back over his life, his series of psycho-physical events, and unite them as the history of one person. It seems that for Śāntideva too because there is only the causal series and each moment is completely new no such synthesis can take place.[65] One person cannot be discovered, and there is no one person. Poor Mr Thompson was not just a Humean-being, but – were it not for the fact that Śāntideva holds that persons do not exist at all – he would be a Śāntideva-being as well. We are tempted to suggest that if he simply relaxed and perhaps ceased his frenzy of creating fictional persons for himself, Mr Thompson would be – if not enlightened – much, much nearer to the truth as Śāntideva understands it than the rest of us. He would also be significantly incapable of normal life or meaningful interaction with anyone else.[66] And we should also note among the many disastrous results for Śāntideva in the present context of the destruction of memory might well be the following: – It seems that the drug hyoscine, which is an anaesthetic, operates precisely through the effect it has on the brain's memory functions. What it produces is a form of amnesia where each passing moment is forgotten. In so doing hyoscine destroys the brain's ability to recognise, and thus to recognise pain. Unrecognised pain is arguably no pain at all. Therefore for a being with no memory there could also be no pain. Even if unrecognised pain *is* still felt, and that feeling is unpleasant, it is at least arguable that instant forgetfulness is as good as not feeling the pain at all. Hyoscine was, after all, used as an *anaesthetic* (see Dennett 1978, pp. 214–5, and Gregory, ed. 1987, p. 24). If complete impermanence is true, and we take it with Śāntideva that there is actually no self, there can also be no pain either. As we shall see, if Śāntideva's premiss of no self is true, then he cannot draw the conclusion that we should remove pain universally, for there is no pain.

9 The need for a subject

Śāntideva's position is an extreme version of the no-subject view. But any serious attempt at a no-subject view, even in a version considerably less extreme than that of Śāntideva, would appear to be quite implausible. As we have seen, in the dGe lugs version of Madhyamaka it is important to recognise the actual (conventional) existence of the person, the individual subject of experiences. In stressing this, dGe lugs scholars are absolutely right – but they are at variance with Śāntideva. I am going to argue at greater length subsequently that pain has a *necessary* connection with a subject who is in pain, and that anything resembling a literal understanding of a no-subject position is quite incapable of making any sense of the concept of pain. Inasmuch as Śāntideva himself is therefore incapable of making any sense of the concept of pain, Śāntideva cannot make any sense of the removal of pain which is a *sine qua non* of the bodhisattva path. The case of the dying Mrs Gradgrind in Dickens' *Hard Times* is well-known among philosophers. Mrs Gradgrind declares that she thinks there is a pain in her room somewhere, but she is not sure whether she is the one who has got it or not (Bk. 2, Ch. 9). This is of course absurd, as Dickens intended it to be. It is part of the very concept of a pain that it is the pain of a subject. While it is certainly possible to be unsure whether one is in pain or not, it makes no sense to speak of pains as if they are free-floating. It does not just *happen* to be the case, a contingent matter, that pain P is *my* pain, and that very pain P (the pain-token, the pain itself) could have been someone else's pain. I do not catch my pains, as I might catch a passing feather. If there is a pain, part of the having of the pain is its being had by a subject. This point seems indubitable. It is contained in Kant's comment (*Critique of Pure Reason* B131–2) that a contentless 'I think' must be capable of accompanying all my experiences and, as Kant stressed, and it should be stressed again here, from this fact alone, while the essential subjectivity of mental events follows tautologously, nothing follows about the status, the nature or constitution, of the subject, whether for example it is merely a self or really a Self.

For the moment I wish to remain at this level of experiences in general. It seems to me that it makes no sense to talk of any experience which is not the experience of a subject, and if pain necessarily requires a subject it would appear implausible *à priori* that other experiences would not also require a subject. Thus my argument here concerning experiences in general will receive also indirect support from my subsequent argument concerning pain. It makes no sense to refer to happiness, to refer to feeling cold, to refer to desire, to refer to compassion, without these being the happiness, feeling cold, desire, compassion of some subject. The fact that all experiences require a subject, they are experiences of some sentient being, is of course behind Descartes' conclusion that if he can doubt then he must exist. Doubt requires the subject of doubt. Just as there are no free-floating pains which happen to be caught as they pass, there are also no free-floating doubts.[67] Descartes' mistakes – if mistakes they are – came not from this, which might be thought to be trivial, but from his conclusions concerning what followed about the 'substance' which he instantly inferred he must be, a subject, indeed a Self, whose essence consists solely in thought and which is completely separate and indeed of a completely different order from the body.[68]

Galen Strawson has referred to the contention that '"[a]n experience is impossible without an experiencer" or subject of experience (Frege quoted in Strawson 1994, p. 129)' as 'Frege's thesis', and describes it as a truism: 'This is a necessary truth. Its appearance of necessity is not the product of some kind of grammatical illusion, and it holds equally for man and mouse'. Strawson is right, though in explicating the thesis he appears to be reduced to simply restating it:

> There cannot be experience without a subject of experience, because experience is necessarily *for* someone or something – an experiencer or subject of experience. Experience necessarily involves experiential

> what-it-is-like-ness, and what-it-is-like-ness is necessarily what-it-is-like-ness *for* someone or something. Whatever the nature of this experiencing something, its real existence cannot be denied (italics original).

I shall subsequently try to show more fully why at least in the case of pain there is a *necessary* connection between pain and a subject who is in pain. Compare here also the obvious absurdity of referring to a subjectless *belief*. If there is no subject for the belief that the moon is made of cheese then no one believes it, i.e. there is no actual belief that the moon is made of cheese. Of course, it therefore follows for Śāntideva that if there is no subject for beliefs there is no actual belief in, say, karmic cause and effect, and indeed karmic cause and effect is as unbeliev*able* as the claim that the moon is made of cheese. Strawson for his part is concerned to point out that Frege's thesis is perfectly compatible with different views on what the subject actually *is*, what I have called the 'status' of the subject. It is, for example, quite compatible with the subject as a physical or psychophysical thing. Frege's thesis follows from the nature of experience itself, and it is not committed to any particular view concerning materialism or otherwise, or any view of the subject as a substance. Nevertheless, it is incompatible with Frege's thesis, and therefore if Frege's thesis is a necessary truth it is necessarily false, to state that a full account of an experience itself as it occurs purely at the level of experience can take place without mentioning the subject and without distinguishing the subject of experience from the experience's experiential content. All experiences require a subject of experience, and all experiences have the potential for distinguishing between the experiential content and the subject.[69] *Pace* Śāntideva, it is necessarily false to think that a full account of a pain can be given without mentioning the subject of that pain. And that is just as well, since, as Strawson points out, 'if, per impossibile, there could be pain experience without an experiencer, there would be no point in stopping it, because no one would be suffering' (p. 133). On Śāntideva's extreme no-subject view there is no one undergoing pain, and thus there is no point is stopping pain. But more on that later.

The argument that there cannot be a subjectless mental event, mental events are not that sort of *thing*, might be thought to run counter to an often-stated criticism of Descartes which appears to originate in the philosopher Lichtenberg. This criticism is that Descartes cannot argue from the occurrence of mental events to a *subject* which has them. From doubting we can infer the existence of the occurrence of doubting, but we cannot infer as such that *I* doubt. Likewise, although pain may indeed have a subject, we are not entitled to infer a subject of pain from the occurrence of pain itself. The additional inference is not contained in e.g. the occurrence of doubt, or the pain, itself and is as such unwarranted. If pain occurs, pain occurs. What more do we want with an 'I' that feels pain? This argument as it stands, however, while directed against Descartes' *inference* of a subject, does not entail that it makes any sense to speak of experiences as actually free-floating. Moreover even within these terms of reference Lichtenberg's argument is not going to work. If Lichtenberg is right then it should be possible to state first-person statements involving mental predicates in neutral (non-first-person) terms without loss of significant meaning. It is trivial to say that a mental event must happen in *some* mind, and significant meaning will be lost if Lichtenberg's reduction renders us incapable of distinguishing between events which happen in my mind and those which happen in the mind of someone else. Yet, as Glover (1991, p. 51) points out, if a group of people each thinks of a word and those words together would make a sentence, it does not follow that anyone has thought of the whole sentence. There is a difference between:

a) 'I think "The rose is red"', and
b) i) 'It is thought "The"';
   ii) 'It is thought "rose"';
   iii) 'It is thought "is"'; and
   iv) 'It is thought "red"'.

In reducing a) to terms which make no reference either directly or implicitly to a subject it becomes impossible to distinguish between a) and b) where each word thought in b) is thought by a different person (even if they are in the right order). Thus with Lichtenberg's reduction no sentence is thought at all. Actually thinking the sentence can only be expressed with reference to the one subject who thinks all the words in the right order.[70] From doubting, Descartes can indeed infer that *he* is doubting, since it is from *here* (i.e. Descartes) that the doubt is taking place. It is simply not the case here that just someone is doubting.[71]

All experiences are subjective, essentially of a subject and, in spite of Śāntideva's wish otherwise, subjects are different. In a world where subjects could not be distinguished (a 'Śāntideva-world', the level of *prajñā*, the *buddhabhūmi*?) there could also be no experiences. We could no longer have grounds for speaking coherently of consciousness at all, not because we are there at the level of nondual *jñāna* which is beyond all linguistic superimposition but simply because we can make no sense of consciousness without experience, and no sense of experience without subjectivity, and no sense of subjectivity without subjects. The subjective quality of an experience is what makes it an experience, and is thus essential to consciousness. An experience which lacked subjectivity would not be conscious. As the neurologist Antonio Damasio points out, if the brain simply generated images without the dimension of subjectivity we could not know them as *our* images and there would thus be serious doubt as to whether we could ever be conscious of them as images at all. Indeed, Damasio is prepared to go further. He observes that years of opposition to the idea of the self as a little person inside the brain having our perceptions and feelings has made some theorists very wary of the whole concept of the self. But this is not necessary. The self can be as much a transitory construct as we like. In fact the self 'is, rather, a perpetually re-created neurobiological state'. But '[w]hat should cause some fear, actually, is the idea of a selfless cognition' (Damasio 1995, pp. 99–100; cf. pp. 227–9, 236 ff.). For it is precisely the self which endows experiences with their essential subjectivity (p. 227).

10 Unity and the self

If experiences, including pain, require subjects we can call that subject the self (not necessarily, note again, the Self!), or perhaps the person. But the self is not simply the subjectivity of experiences. As Kant argued, the fact that all my experiences are necessarily given as *mine* means that the subject, the self, provides a unity to what is diverse. Prajñākaramati will accept that we can use the expression 'self' for everyday pragmatic purposes, with actual reference to the five psycho-physical aggregates, the components of embodied individuals.[72] But we have seen already that in fact this will be fatal to Śāntideva's argument, since that argument is intended to lead to altruistic action which makes no distinction between different persons, and is thus taking place not at the ultimate (*paramārtha*) level but at the level of convention (*saṃvṛti*). In other words, if *any* distinction can be made between persons *conventionally* then Śāntideva's argument for altruism is not going to follow. Thus for Prajñākaramati to admit a distinction between persons conventionally based on what must be different 'bundles' (Hume) of the psycho-physical aggregates is to dissolve away Śāntideva's entire argument. We have seen already that in spite of Śāntideva and Prajñākaramati it does not seem that there is anything wrong as such in speaking of a whole constituted through parts as one thing (one tree, one mountain). Nevertheless there is at least more to a person than simply a bundle composed of psycho-physical parts.[73]

Clearly, it is possible to unite any properties, thoughts, or experiences into a set, yet the self cannot simply be just any old set of properties, thoughts, or experiences.[74] In real life (ignoring Surrealist paintings) I could not be composed of a set of properties which included those of the table I am sitting at (or your thoughts). Yet why not – if I can be composed of *inter alia* arms and legs – given the Buddhist premisses? The front parts of the table may be closer to me than my feet, and if my hand is on the table I am in actual physical contact with it. It may be objected that my hand can feel (it participates in one life, as Locke might say), whereas the wood of the table cannot. Perhaps this objection begs the question, presupposing the unity of the person as a living being. But anyway suppose some nerves have been severed in my hand and I have lost all feeling in that part of my body. Still, I would see the hand as part of me. Why not the table? And so on. Remember, any answer to the question why we see particular sets of properties, thoughts, or experiences as persons and not other sets must not beg the question by presupposing conceptually the existence *already* of a particular person, self, or even 'personal' set of properties, thoughts, or experiences. Thus we cannot appeal to 'karmic determination', beginningless ignorance, or socio-cultural factors, for example. And there is another problem. Even if we can bring together a group of items into a bundle, and speak of one bundle, what has that to do with me? *A* bundle does not equal *my* bundle. From the perspective of the bundle theory, for me to think that P is the case is simply for a thought that P is the case to occur as part of the bundle. But it seems clear that in actual fact 'P is thought about' is not at all equivalent to 'I think about P'. This will only the case if 'P is thought about' occurs in *my* bundle (see Stroud 1977, p. 132). The uniting into a bundle is not in itself going to explain at all the origin of persons and personal sets. More is required – and (without begging the question) more has not been forthcoming.

The Buddhist cannot argue that the self, the conventional person, is the set of psycho-physical properties, thoughts, or experiences occurring at time T, since if there is a change in the members of a set the set ceases to be the same set. Given the Buddhist view of impermanence we would be back with the self instantaneously ceasing to exist (at T(i)), and the impossibility of change in a person occurring at all. We have seen already the chaos – such as the impossibility of memory and even consciousness itself – that would produce. The same would be the case if the self were the set of psycho-physical properties, thoughts, or experiences which had occurred up to and including T (say, T as 'now'), since T is always ceasing and being replaced by the next T. But clearly there would be problems too if the self was the set of psycho-physical properties, thoughts, or experiences occurring over a whole lifetime, the complete set, since that would mean that so long as death had not occurred one would not be a *complete* self (or person, if it makes any sense to talk of incomplete selves or persons in this context), and all the properties, thoughts, or experiences of an entire life become essential to its being that person. While it might be possible to define 'self' in such a way that those not dead are incomplete selves, this would scarcely correspond to our normal everyday use of 'self' or person' (it is after all the conventional self the Buddhist is trying to explain here) and would seem to have little to recommend it. And what about incompatible properties such as being six feet tall and not being six feet tall but being three feet tall? Archibald, the conventional person we all know and some have great affection for, cannot be both. Yet both properties truly pertain to Archibald over his lifetime, so if the conventional person is the bundle of all properties, thoughts, or experiences over a lifetime the conventional person contains many incompatible properties. Of course, there is a temptation to say that Archibald is six feet tall now, and was three feet tall many years ago. But this answer cannot be used without referring to Archibald at different stages during his life. This requires that we employ *first* the concept of 'Archibald', and there is no person Archibald until the end of his life.

There is another problem with a set version of a bundle theory as an explanation of selves. What if two complete sets were the same? It is not possible to rule this out in advance. It is perfectly possible to conceive of two people who had all the same properties, thoughts, or experiences. Under such circumstances on the Buddhist premisses the two persons should be the same person. But they are not. If the two persons *were* the same person there would not be two persons but only one person. Of course, we would not then have two complete sets! One possible answer might be that if we have two complete sets then they must be distinguished from each other by at least one characteristic, i.e. that they are *two* sets (and not one). But this requires that we specify what it is to speak of two sets, rather than one. Take the following: The most plausible suggestion is that they are two sets rather than one because they occur at different places – one is *here*, the other is *there*, and/or one is at *this* time, the other at *that* time. This is not going to work. It entails that in order to specify the sets as different (in order, remember, to speak of them as different selves) we have had *first* (i) to refer to the complete sets; and (ii) to distinguish them using the indexicals 'here' and 'there', and 'this time' (i.e. 'now') and 'that time' ('then'). But this begs the question, since in order to refer to a set using the first-person indexical 'I', for example, I have had *first* to be able to distinguish the set, and distinguish it *inter alia* by the use of other indexicals 'here' and/or 'now', which in this context are no different from the indexical 'I' and indeed can only be specified sufficiently precisely by substituting exactly for 'I'. To distinguish the two otherwise identical sets we have to *presuppose* that one set is *my* set (or the set of whoever) and the other the set of Archibald.[75]

Even if it were possible to overcome these problems, there is a final problem with the bundle theory here which is both pertinent to our present considerations and it seems to me conclusive. The bundle theory – as far as we can tell Śāntideva's and Prajñākaramati's theory – is *not going to be able to account satisfactorily for attributions to oneself of absence of pain*. As James van Cleve points out, there appears to be no way Hume – or the Buddhist – can translate a sentence like 'I am not now feeling pain' into the impersonal language of the bundle theory. Clearly, it is perfectly meaningful for me to say that I am not now feeling pain, and it may well be important for the bodhisattva to say so him- or herself, or to allow that others, the objects of their beneficial actions, can say so. Until the bodhisattva has reached the level of knowing directly the feelings of others (if this makes sense – how can I know directly another's pain?), the bodhisattva will want to rely on first-person reports that, yes, thanks to the bodhisattva's benevolent action the pain is no longer felt. Yet without allowing for the perfectly *meaningful* and indeed referential use of '*I* am not now feeling pain' this cannot be done. 'Pain is not now felt' is not an equivalent, since unless the bodhisattva has simultaneously removed all pain it is indeed still felt *by others*. Even 'Pain is not now felt here' will not be an equivalent unless 'here' is explained as strictly identical to 'by *me*'. And that would be to beg the question. Otherwise where is 'here'? I cannot say that the fact that pain is not felt by me entails as equivalent that there is no sentient being at all, perhaps very small, feeling pain 'here'. Van Cleve suggests that 'This sensation is now occurring and is not co-instantiated with pain' may be a good try, but it is clearly not an equivalent for 'I am not now feeling pain' since it states positively that some sensation is now occurring, and while that may indeed be true and even a true implication of the original statement it is not an *equivalent* of it. [76] The implications of all this for Śāntideva need to be clearly underlined. If in order to speak of pain and its removal in impersonal terms we abandon what we would normally consider to be the legitimate referential use of the indexical 'I' – as Śāntideva wants and requires as part of his thesis concerning the need to remove pain universally, without bias – then whatever the other problems of Śāntideva's theory we will also be *unable to say* what we normally do say when we utter 'I am not now feeling pain'. It seems to me that loss would be serious for both us and Śāntideva.

We have seen throughout much of this essay that the great problem for the no-ownership bundle theory of whatever form is explaining what exactly unites the bundle into one thing.[77] Of course, *pace* Śāntideva there is no problem in referring to a collection as one thing, but in stating that we do not state *why* a bundle should be bound together as a unity, let alone why that particular unity. But the key to this in the case of the person, surely, was given by Kant at the beginning of this section above. So long as we speak only of the elements which make up the bundle, and the bundle as the aggregate of those elements, we shall not have a principle of unity. What actually unites the bundle of properties, thoughts, or experiences into one is that they all pertain one way or another to the same subject. For the moment let us put the limbs of the body to one side. We have seen already that the limbs participate all in the same *life*. If we concentrate on thoughts and experiences then their essential subjectivity means that as part of their very nature they are all given as *mine* (or yours, i.e. 'mine' for you etc.). As Chisholm (1969, p. 19) puts it, the items within the bundle are in fact states of the person – 'person-stages', if you like – while what unites all the person stages into one is that they are all experienced by a (i.e. the same) person. I do not experience another person's experiences. My experiences are experienced by me. If this is correct then, Chisholm points out, 'the existence of particular bundles of perceptions presupposes ... the existence of selves of persons that are not mere bundles of perceptions.'[78] Note that to state that the person is not a mere bundle of perceptions in the Buddhist context need not logically *in itself* require adherence to a Self, a permanent, partless independent Self which is different from the aggregates (this would be what Kant sees as Descartes' mistake). As we have seen, to recognise that the person is a different *sort* of thing from 'person-stages' (if it makes any sense at all to talk of 'stages of a person') need no more imply the existence of another thing separate from and alongside, as it were, the person-stages than does recognising the river as different from the river-stages, or a whole as different from the parts, involve the existence of a separate whole alongside the parts, or a separate river as well as the waters. The person could be constituted by the psycho-physical constituents without being identical to them.

Nevertheless, when all is said and done even though it may be possible to speak of a continuant as a unity, it seems to me that it is nevertheless not possible to see the person *simply* on the model of a river – as a continuant which is a whole, a unity constituted of a series of 'person-stages' into which it can be reduced, and a collective made of spatially separated limbs which happen to be in temporary connection.[79] First, it is only possible for me to remember doing *x* if *I* actually did *x*, and 'a previous stage of a whole called "me" of which I now am the present stage did *x*' is not the same as saying 'I did *x*'. Indeed, the present stage is not responsible for what the previous stage did, and it is hard to see why the present stage of a whole should be punished, for example, for what *the whole's* previous stages did. The present stage, while one of those which constitutes the whole, precisely is not the one which committed the crime. Nor did the whole commit the crime. It was the previous person-stage which committed the crime. However it is looked at, the person understood simply as a whole lacks the sort of unity a person actually must have and is experienced to have.[80]

Moreover on the model of the person as constituted by a series of different person-stages it would not be me acting now to avoid some future pain, but the present person-stage called 'I' acting to avoid that pain. However what will actually occur in the future will not be me undergoing some excruciating pain, but a future person-stage which will use the term 'I' or 'me' undergoing that pain. This is because although it may be correct to see the person as a whole constituted by person-stages, at any one time we do not have the whole person but only the person-stage. But that is absurd. If there is only the present person-stage which instantly or even fairly soon ceases, and no present me which endures for the significant amount of time, then acting to avoid future pains does indeed (at least so long as we rely on hedonistic criteria) become irrational. The present person-stage will not experience the future pains. There *must* be more to it being rational for me to act now to avoid excruciating pain in the future than a present person-stage acting so that a completely different future person-stage will not suffer pain. This is the case even if the present person-stage is related to the future person-stage by something closer than a rather weak form of causal connection ('this being, that occurs; with the non-occurrence of this there is the non-occurrence of that'). Why anyway should the present person-stage care one little bit about a completely different future person-stage even if there is some sort of causal connection between them? While if I am already a generous and kind person I may want to act to help future person-stages avoid pain – as I might want to help others now although (*pace* Śāntideva) it is not actually the case that they are me – it will no longer make any sense to speak of *me* avoiding future pain. This is the case for the Buddhist even conventionally, since it is the 'conventional self' as a whole constituted of person-stages that we are discussing here. But clearly it *does* so make sense to speak of me avoiding excruciating future pain. In actual fact my concern is that it will be *me* experiencing the pain – just as it is my concern that my wife will be with me tomorrow, not some causally linked future person-stage of her.[81] In terms of future care, it seems quite clear to me that mere causal connection is not in itself what counts. I can be sure that it will not be some future person-stage which will no doubt refer to itself as 'I' (as indeed 'your' future person stages will also refer to themselves with as much justice as 'I') which will be in pain if 'I' am due to have a wisdom-tooth extracted without anaesthetic tomorrow. It will be *me*, and we can all recognise that these two cases are completely different (and their difference is not just due to beginningless ignorance). We all know that, and far from it being irrational to fear the operation tomorrow the fear would be extremely rational (almost primevally so, even for a good Buddhist), and rightly so, and we would be correct – indeed wise – to take steps to avoid it even if for some strange medical reasons the operation turned out to be still advisable.[82]

Take also the case of conceptual thought, together with reasoning, decision-making, and engaging in choices. In order for me to engage *at all* in conceptual thought (and thus, from a Buddhist point of view, *if* conceptual thought is a sign of unenlightenment, in order for me to be unenlightened at all) I must be capable of abstracting from one particular case and applying it to another, and using a term or concept more than once. This is also the case in order to use any language at all. How does Śāntideva think that the very language he is using could be acquired without both his own and others' existence and indeed the actual continued endurance of the subject he is and they are? In order to acquire the use of language and engage in conceptual thought I must remain as the same person for a significant period of time, and that remaining as the same person cannot reduce simply to the use of the same name (question-begging) for a series of separate albeit causally related person-stages. In order to engage in the reasoning which requires conceptual thought and which for Śāntideva is capable of bringing about a correct understanding of the way things really are, the *sine qua non* of any form of enlightenment, it is necessary that there is an actual significant identity between the person at one stage of the reasoning process and that at the next. An extremely short momentary person-stage where nothing of the first stage remained in the second would not be capable of conceptual thought, would not be capable of entering into the common lived world where conceptual thought takes place, would not be capable of imposing conceptual existence (*prajñaptisat*) on things like persons or indeed caste-rows, forests, and armies, would not be capable of reasoning, and would not be capable of seeing things the way they really are.[83] As Grant Gillett puts it (1987, p.83):

> A single individual must be the same thinker who uses a term now with a given intent and also at other times and places, if that term is to come under the rules or normative constraints which ensure consistent use. . . I may have no experience or 'impression' or 'intuition' of an 'inner me', but I can be sure, nevertheless, that there *is* an essential unity in all my thought. My thought, to be coherent, must be the thought of a persistent rational being subject to independent normative constraints on his thought contents (italics original).

Take also the use of the word 'I'. This is learnt through personal experience but also through public application. It refers to a person who is capable of having both mental and physical predicates applied to it and which appears to be quite irreducible (see P.F. Strawson 1959, Ch. 3). I use the word 'I' to refer to myself, but I have *learnt* the use of it through its use by others and trial and error in something like whatever way a child normally learns the use of terms. No doubt I may have been corrected either directly or implicitly in its use before I fully acquired the use and meaning of the term. Clearly in order for this usage to be acquired – and it certainly is acquired, surely we all know what it is for it to be acquired correctly, and its correct acquisition and application is absolutely necessary for normal human transactions – it is necessary that 'I' refers to the same identifiable and reidentifiable particular, identifiable and reidentifiable both by myself and others. Moreover I do not have to apply some sort of inference or criterion each time 'I' is used by me in order to know whether it is actually being used correctly or not, or whether it is the same or different I as was referred to last time 'I' was used by me. If that were the case *who* could apply such a criterion? All my experiences are mine, are given as mine, just as all my memories are mine without requiring inference or criterion (Kant). It is part of the very givenness of my experience that it is mine, and meaningless to speak of it as mine if the 'me' instantly ceases. Under such circumstances it would thus become meaningless to speak of 'my experience' at all, and therefore as there are no free-floating subjectless experiences (and your experiences, for example, are just the experiences you call 'mine') it would also be meaningless to speak of any experiences at all.

Similarly even learning the use of a sensation-word like 'pain' depends upon the existence of persons, repeatedly identifiable using *inter alia* the first- and third-person indexicals. The word 'pain' does not well-up from within each one of us as a private term for a particular sort of momentary individual private sensation. If that were the case then we could never know that we were using the term in the same way and for the same thing as others, and use of the term 'pain' would become impossible. Rather, we must learn the use of a term like 'pain' through its repeated public use, in the case of its use by others, and then applying it to ourselves through trial and error until eventually our own usage corresponds with the public and publicly acceptable usage as *the same*. If something like this (if much more complicated and sophisticated) is the case, then without the use of 'pain' for the *same* thing as applied by and to other persons I could not learn the use of the term, and without learning the use of the term I could not have the concept of pain (as such) at all. Śāntideva's free-floating pains – pains deprived of their subjects and thus their subjectivity – must also be pains cut adrift from not just their private but also their public contexts. Under such circumstances it is difficult to know how to make sense of speaking of them as 'pains' at all (cf. Glover 1991, p. 48). There would not even be strange sensations which had not been identified as pains, since there would be no one to experience such sensations. And with no one to experience the sensations, and no identification of them as pains and therefore (generally) unpleasant, it is difficult to see what sense we can make of Śāntideva's suggestion that these 'pains' should be eliminated.

11 On pain

Śāntideva has argued that without Selves there are no selves, with no selves there are no persons, and with no persons we cannot distinguish between 'my pain' (my *duḥkha*, of which pain is a sub-class) and 'your pain'. Nevertheless, we do as a matter of fact all set out to remove (our own) pains. That is a basic fact of human nature. Thus we are morally obliged if we are to be logically consistent to remove the pains of others as well. I shall argue at greater length that without persons we have no subjects for mental predicates like 'is in pain', and therefore without persons not only can we not distinguish between 'my pain' and 'your pain', but we cannot make sense of pain at all. The basic fact that we do (normally) as a matter of fact set out to remove our own pains is because Śāntideva's analysis of the person and pain is wrong, and if Śāntideva were right not only could we not remove pain but we would have no need to do so. Quite contrary to what Śāntideva says at *Bodhicaryāvatāra* 8:102, that 'Pains without an owner are all indeed without distinction. Because of its quality as pain indeed it is to be prevented', pains without an owner simply do not exist and therefore we cannot apply the argument that pain is to be prevented simply because of its subjectless quality as pain. I do not prevent ('my own') pain because it has some abstract 'quality of pain', but rather because it hurts, i.e. it is a first-person unpleasant experience. If neither I nor anyone else could make sense of pain hurting – and the hurting quality of pain is a sensation, *intrinsically* subjective – then not only would pain not exist but even if it did exist there would be nothing unpleasant about it and therefore no need to remove it. It is simply contradictory to argue with Śāntideva that there are no subjects and then refer to pain as being to be removed because of its quality as pain. We can only make sense of its negative quality as pain with reference to the unpleasant experiences of subjects. However if we cannot make sense of pain at all then the bodhisattva path becomes meaningless. Thus for Śāntideva to take his own argument and its implications seriously would be to destroy the bodhisattva path.

I want to argue that there is a *necessary* relationship between pains and the subject of pains. Although this seems quite obvious, it is probably incompatible with a bundle theory, and we can do more than simply repeat its obviousness. I shall argue for this necessary relationship using three arguments which while linked will nevertheless stand independently of one another and in the form in which I develop them may indeed not even be entirely compatible:

(i) Far from there being no such things as persons, but only subjectless pains, I shall suggest that the truth is the exact reverse. There are no such things as pains, but only subjects (persons, cats, limbs etc.) in pain. Once we understand our language properly we will no longer be misled by the noun 'pain' into thinking that it refers to some thing which can float free of its subjective context. You can meet a person hurting, but you cannot meet a pain.

(ii) Pains (or the having of pains) are events, and events as changes cannot occur without a subject. Changes are happenings that occur to subjects.

(iii) The identification, individuation and reidentification of pains require mention implicitly or explicitly of the subject, the person who is in pain. There is no such thing as a pain in a subject-free bundle. Without the subject, pains cannot be identified and individuated, and pains without identity are pains which do not exist.[84]

As a prolegomenon to our discussion, however, I want to make one point quite clear. If we ignore for a moment any question of what sort of individual a pain is, and think of a pain as simply hurting, then it should be quite clear that pains exist. They exist in epistemologically the strongest possible sense. While it is not true that pains are indubitable in the sense that one cannot doubt whether one is in pain or not (I can certainly be unsure whether what I have is a pain or, perhaps, an intense itch), it is absolutely true that one cannot have an hallucinatory pain (one cannot hurt hallucinatorily). If one experiences pain there cannot be any doubt as to whether the pain is real or not. This is because the failure of sensations to correspond with extramental reality, as happens in the case of hallucinations,[85] cannot occur with pains since the experiencing of pain *is* the pain. It would be quite wrong to think of pains as parallel to monkeys in 'I see the monkey'; thus: 'I feel the pain'. In this confused understanding the pain becomes the *object* of a sensation (just as phenomenalists like Hume used to talk quite confusedly of perceiving *perceptions* or impressions instead of perceiving things – tables etc.), and thus just as one can see the monkey (in an hallucination) without there being a monkey present, it might be thought that it could be possible to feel the pain without there being a pain there. But the parallel grammar here is misleading. I do not feel the pain in the sense that the pain becomes the object of a feeling, as I might feel the tree. Feeling the pain is just having the pain, hurting. Indeed I would suggest that it is the very failure to be sensitive to the potentially misleading parallel in grammar between 'I see the monkey' and 'I feel the pain' which has contributed in a large part to the thought that there might be free-floating pains as there are free-ranging monkeys. More about that below. But it seems clear that if one has the sensation of pain then that is all there is to it. There is no further question of the correspondence or not of the pain with a further putative real pain. Of course, it is certainly possible to have pains associated with hallucinations, as in the case of the amputee's pain felt in a phantom limb. But while the location of the pain is misidentified – it cannot really be in the shin of an amputated leg – the pain is quite real and could be treated with appropriate painkillers. Galen Strawson is surely uncontroversially right when he states that:

> No account of reality can be correct if, for example, it denies that experience of pain is really (or ultimately) real, or holds that there may be some sense in which we are *entirely* wrong about the real nature of pains we undergo even as we undergo them. For their real nature unquestionably includes their experiential character, whatever else it may include. And as regards their experiential character, how they seem is how they are. . . . the seeming is itself and ineliminably a real thing, and whatever the nature of the universe, it is what we denote when we use the word 'pain'. . . . There is simply no room for total error, for the seeming is unquestionably real, and the seeming just is the reality in question (1994, p. 51; italics original).

This is allied to the old sense-datum point, that while I may be hallucinating a table there can be no doubt at all that I am being presented-to with certain data. Because a pain is itself the sensation, to be presented-to with pain-data is to have a pain. Thus, if Śāntideva's argument entails that pains are not real – indeed really real in the fullest sense that pains can be real – he *must* be wrong. It is as simple as that.[86]

(i) There are no such things as pains, only subjects hurting

Take the following:[87]

(i) I see the monkey;
(ii) I feel the pain.

I have argued above that while the English grammar of these two sentences is parallel, that parallel is potentially misleading.[88] The noun 'monkey' is a class-term which refers to a class of things, as it happens natural kinds which are capable of independent action, reproduction and so on. A monkey is a physical object with a physical location, and the following is true of our monkey: If the monkey is in a cage, and the cage is the zoo, then the monkey is in the zoo.

Now take the case of a pain. If the pain is in the knee, and the knee is in the trousers, is the pain in the trousers? I take it not. Something has gone wrong with the parallel. Something would be awry even if – in order to bring the parallel to 'I feel the pain' closer – (i) above were 'I feel the tree', for if the tree were in the forest and the forest were in England, the tree would also be in England. Again, if the monkey is in the cage I can (*inter alia*) open the cage and see the monkey. Can I open my knee and see the pain? Once more, I take it not. But if we object that pains are not physical things and therefore should not be expected to have a physical location like a monkey, then how can we say that the pain is *in the knee* at all? [89] What about the following problem: Can a pain be experienced by more than one person, as a monkey can be seen by more than one person? It seems clear that while I can have my pain, and you can have your pain, we cannot both have each other's pain. The pain is not a public object like our monkey (which, note, is not to say that I am committed to the pain as a *private* object either). Clearly, pains cannot be things in the same way that monkeys and trees are things, and 'in' cannot be used in the same way when we talk about a monkey being in the cage, and a pain being in the knee. What sort of thing is a pain?

Well, I suggest that the only reason we might think that a pain is some sort of a 'thing' at all is because of the parallelism between sentences like (i) and (ii) above. But (as Candrakīrti was so well aware), we are not committed to basing our ontology on grammar. We do not have to maintain that pains are *things* at all, in *any* sense. There is nothing in our experience which suggests that we should. Contrary to what Buddhists might urge, if we sit down and calmly observe what is going on we simply do *not* find (free-floating or independently identifiable) pains. We find that I, the meditator, have knees that are hurting. Thus, as Chisholm (1957, p. 123) points out, we can remove at a stroke questions concerning the peculiar status of pains as things. It seems likely that all statements which use 'thing-language' of pains can be replaced with a form of adverbial – or perhaps verbal – language. Thereby we can read a sentence like 'I have a pain' as something like 'I sense painfully'. I have a sharp pain can be read as 'I sense painfully, sharply', or in other words, 'I hurt [or 'am pained'] sharply'. Thus the original 'I have a pain' can become, in a manner which is perfectly satisfactory for our purposes in eliminating reference to occult objects like pains, 'I hurt'. Similarly, 'I have a pain in my knee' can perfectly adequately be read as 'I hurt in my knee', or possibly (in order to keep to a strictly adverbial analysis) even 'I hurt knee-ly', or something like that.[90]

With these translations we are no longer left with strange *things* like pains at all. All the above problems dissolve. 'I hurt in my knee' does not entail that it should be possible to operate on the knee and find a thing called a 'pain'. The fact that I hurt in my knee and my knee is in my trousers no longer entails that some additional thing connected with the hurting must be in my trousers themselves. Thus it no longer makes sense even to ask the question whether pains can be free-floating or not. In 'I hurt in my knee' there is nothing left which even *might* be free-floating.[91] It becomes incumbent on the one who would resist this rephrasing to show how something essential is lost in no longer referring to pains as things. Śāntideva's position absolutely requires that it makes sense to talk of pains floating free from the subjects whom we normally speak of as possessing the pains, and indeed that such talk is truer to reality. It has to be meaningful to talk of pains while not requiring reference at all to the patently differing subjects of pains, differing persons undergoing pain. If the adverbial analysis or something like it is correct, then not only are there actually no pains to float free, but all pain expressions involve 'hurting-modifications' of some subject. That subject could be e.g. a limb, but it seems to me that to give a full specification of the subject will eventually involve a reference to the *person* undergoing the hurting-modification. If this is right – or even if, as it surely must be, *any* subject at all is required for hurting-modifications – then inasmuch as persons/subjects differ Śāntideva's desired conclusion will not follow. Otherwise, if there are *no* subjects at all, then inasmuch as we have seen that pains can be translated into hurting-modifications of subjects it follows that there can be no pains. We know already that the non-existence of pains in the sense of the complete non-existence of hurting would be the *reductio ad absurdum* of Śāntideva's thesis and entail its obvious falsehood.

Thus our conclusion here must be quite the opposite of Śāntideva's thesis. If hurting occurs, and it certainly does, then inasmuch as hurting is a modification of a subject, or expressed in a verb which requires for its full analysis the specification of a subject, there necessarily has to be a subject. But we are not committed to there being any such thing as a pain, only hurting.

The reason why there appears to be a necessary relationship between pains and the subject in pain therefore is that reference to pains can be translated into either adverbial expressions modifying a verb which requires a subject of the action ('I hurt sharply'), or they can at least be translated into verbal expressions, again which require a subject (i.e. 'I hurt'). Expressions like 'hurt', 'hurts', 'is hurting' etc. are Fregean functions which are incomplete and clearly require completion in order to make full meaningful sentences. As we shall see later, one corollary of this is that without reference to a subject who is hurting it thus becomes impossible to remove hurting or, in Śāntideva's language, to remove pains.

(ii) Pains as events

Consider the case of an actual pain, the actual having of a pain, the pain-token. Whether or not we accept that this is in fact *identical* with a brain-process – 'the firing of C-fibres' as it is misleadingly called for short in much philosophical literature, which would clearly be the case of an event occurring – we can convincingly argue, I think, that if the actual pain itself is to be any individual at all it must be an event. That is, even if we reject the adverbial analysis given above and still want to speak of pains as identifiable particulars, the only sort of things they could be would have to be events. Events occur unlike, say, physical objects (or 'things' in a narrower sense). A pain is a sensation, and the (occurrence of a) sensation is an event; '[a]n event is anything that happens, an occurrence; something that occurs at a certain place during a certain interval of time' (Lombard, in Kim and Sosa 1995, p. 140). Event-tokens are individual particulars – they can thus be portrayed as some sort of 'things' in the widest possible sense as identifiable individuals (see the next section). It should also be clear from Lombard's definition above that events are in fact changes. The sort of 'thing' an event is, is a (non-relational) change.[92] As Lowe 1991 points out, events are not substances in the Aristotelian sense precisely because events do not persist through qualitative change. Rather, events *are* the changes themselves which substances undergo (p. 88). It is also the prevailing view among contemporary philosophers that cause and effect are events (see David Sanford in Kim and Sosa 1995, p. 79). [93] Under such circumstances if an actual pain is itself isolatable and identifiable as a cause or an effect, as it certainly must be for Śāntideva, then the pain must indeed be an event.

We have seen already above that changes require subjects of change. It is meaningless to talk of a change without a subject. But an event is not a physical individual and an event in itself does not have a spatial location. Events gain a derived spatial location from inhering in the subjects of which they are changes, assuming of course that the subjects have a spatial location. Thus in order for an event to occur at all in a physical place, the event must have a subject which is spatially located. In order for a pain to be physically located anywhere, the pain must have a physical subject. And it makes no sense whatsoever to talk of pains having no spatial, i.e. physical, location in any sense. We cannot say 'I have a pain' when we cannot even in principle refer to an 'I' or to a location in the body where the pain is occurring.

Moreover we have seen that in order for a change to take place, a subject has to endure for more than one moment. In a momentary entity there could be no changes, for the momentary entity would have ceased to exist, not *changed*. Note the implications of this for Śāntideva. If we can speak of individual pains they can only be events. Since pains are therefore changes, we can make no sense of pains without subjects.[94] Free-floating pains once more become incoherent. There is a *necessary* relationship between pains and subjects of pain. Moreover the subject must endure for more than one moment and be such that a pain as a change can occur. On Śāntideva's argument this would make the subject a temporal continuant and therefore non-existent. Thus for Śāntideva pains as well cannot exist. We are back at our *reductio ad absurdum* of Śāntideva's position.

And there is more. If having a pain is a change then pains too cannot be instantaneous, literally momentary in that sense. There cannot be a change which is instantaneous. As Lombard puts it (in Kim and Sosa 1995, p. 141), 'the time at which an event occurs can be associated with the (shortest) time at which the object, which is the subject of that event, changes from the having of one to the having of another, contrary property. Since no object can have both a property and one of its contraries at the same time, there can be no instantaneous events, and every event occurs at some interval of time.' Thus the pain itself must last for a period of time. But if the same pain lasts for a period of time, the subject also must last for a period of time. We cannot make sense of one and the same pain lasting for more than one moment but the pain having a series of instantaneous subjects! However, since for Śāntideva the subject cannot last for any period of time since that would make it a temporal continuant and there is no such thing as a temporal continuant, there cannot be an enduring subject and therefore of course there cannot be an enduring pain. Thus, since there cannot be an instantaneous pain either, once more we find that for Śāntideva pains cannot exist.[95]

(iii) Without subjects there can be no identification and individuation of pains

For something to be individuated requires at least that it be identified and normally capable of being reidentified. If there is no way at all for a thing to be identified even in principle then that thing has no existence (cf. Quine's 'no entity without identity'). To be a pain is to be identified as a pain and to be individuated as *this* pain. But reference either directly or indirectly to the subject is essential for the identification and individuation of pains. Without subjects pains cannot be identified and individuated even in principle, and thus without subjects there can be no pains. In throwing out the subject, Śāntideva throws out the pains because he no longer has any basis for making sense of the concept of 'pain'. It is not possible to argue, as does Śāntideva and his commentators, that even though it is true that subjects do not exist, still we do all as a matter of fact remove ('our own') pains and therefore we are morally obliged to remove the pains of others. If there is no subject then we do not have any pains.[96] The very fact that we clearly do remove *our own* pains shows incontrovertibly that there must exist subjects, since there must be a subject in order to have a pain at all. Something must have gone very seriously wrong with Śāntideva's argument. Since, as we have seen, Śāntideva's argument will only work if we cannot identify subjects, persons, at all, and the very existence of pain implies the identification of persons, Śāntideva's argument will only work if pain does not exist. But if pain does not exist Śāntideva's argument is unnecessary. Clearly, however, pain certainly does exist. And in granting that we all do as a matter of fact strive to eliminate our own pains, Śāntideva is showing that his own argument is incoherent. Thus when in *Bodhicaryāvatāra* 8:103 Śāntideva concedes as an essential point in his thesis that we all do as a matter of fact strive to remove our own pains, although he proceeds as if the truth of his argument has been established and he can now incorporate this common behaviour into the very moral imperative which he wishes to establish, in actual fact Śāntideva shows nothing more than the impossible contradiction which his argument is in, which needs identifiable persons at the same time as arguing for their absence.

Supposing someone said to me completely out of the blue that there are three pains. This is meaningful (I know the meanings of the English words; the syntax is grammatically complete) but woefully inadequate. It would have little or no informative content. My natural response would be to ask questions like 'What sort of pains?', 'Where?' and 'Whose?'. I could not even know in this case what it meant to speak of three pains, rather than one or one thousand. Even the concept of pain here requires to be completed, its content to be filled, and it seems clear any content which is to be given to the claim that there are actually three pains will require reference directly or indirectly to persons. Thus Archibald might begin by pointing to a door and saying that there are three pains *in there*. But supposing I were to enter and find the room empty (apart from myself, of course). Then I could make no sense of three pains in there. Supposing I were to find two tractors and a honeycomb. Again, I could make no sense of the comment. I need to find at least one sentient being, in addition to myself. This need is not contingent. It does not just happen to be the case. It is *necessary* in order to make sense of what I am looking for. If there is just one person then I might be able to ask questions which will help me understand why the reference was to *three* pains, rather than more, or less. If the three pains are occurring now, then this will invariably involve identification of three separate pains with reference to three identifiably different bodily locations. If there are three people in the room I might conclude – again, fallaciously without further evidence – that there is just one pain per person. Either way, it seems patently obvious that it is only possible to identify the pains – and to individuate them – with reference to pain-possessors, subjects.[97] Indeed, those philosophers who adopt a functionalist approach to mental states would be inclined to *identify* being in pain with the state proceeding from certain sensory inputs and having pain-behaviour as results. Hence we find Hilary Putnam's observation that pain is a functional state of the whole organism.[98] But bizarrely for Śāntideva there is no 'whole organism', only a disembodied pain! Without the person in pain not only could we not even know what sense to make of a pain-report, but there could be no individuation of such a free-floating pain. The word 'pain' would become literally meaningless. And, alas, what Śāntideva says in *Bodhicaryāvatāra* 8:102–3 must be literally meaningless for *himself*, given what he considers he has shown, if he is to be rationally consistent.

Now a rather different but allied point. Since temporal continuants are not permitted, on Śāntideva's criteria each pain must either be a single unchanging thing through time, or a momentary individual, a specific momentary pain-token. We can take it that for Śāntideva the Buddhist a pain as a single unchanging thing through time would be unacceptable, particularly when we have seen already that the subject of pain is for him unreal precisely because it is actually a temporal continuant and not a unity. A pain unchanging through time while the subject of pain is momentary is absurd. Pains must be impermanent, and for any Buddhist this inclines towards portraying the pain as changing from moment to moment. But if the pain were to be taken as a specific and unique momentary pain-token then how could a pain ever be identified as a 'pain'? In order to apply the concept of 'pain' to something, that thing has to be seen to be an example of a pain-type. It has to be capable of being *identified*. Thus there has to be more than one pain, and in order for this to be the case all examples have to be examples of 'pains' (i.e. things to which the concept 'pain' can *correctly* be applied). Even if the pain is momentary it cannot be unique. Moreover there must be more pains than just my own pains, for if there were only my own pains I could never learn the concept and I could never know that the concept 'pain' had been correctly applied. Diṅnāga and Dharmakīrti are quite right in thinking that a completely unique specific individual with no actual characteristic at all in common with anything else (a *svalakṣaṇa*) would have to be beyond all concepts, for in its very uniqueness (its 'intrinsic tokenhood'!) a *svalakṣaṇa* could not be specified as being of a type. If that were the case, the *svalakṣaṇa* would also have to be beyond language, for it would be completely beyond identification at all.[99] A Quine would take this as a *reductio ad absurdum* of the *svalakṣaṇa* itself, for such an identity-less entity simply could not be an entity. Similarly in the case of pain, if one is unable to apply the concept 'pain' to a pain, then the pain cannot be identified as a pain at all.[100] In order to apply the concept 'pain' to a pain there has to be more than one pain (and indeed more than one person who experiences pains). And if it cannot be identified as a pain, it also cannot be *re*-identified as a pain.[101] But without an ability to identify (and generally reidentify) *x*, it is difficult to see how it makes any sense to say that we have a case of *x*. That is, if something is *in all respects* unique, there can be only one example of it and therefore in fact there can be no example at all. But Śāntideva wishes to argue in *Bodhicaryāvatāra* 8:103 that since we do as a matter of fact seek to eliminate ('our own') pains, we are also morally obliged to seek to eliminate the pains of others. Unfortunately, however, it transpires that not only are we unable to identify ('our own') pains, but even if we could the momentary uniqueness of pain *x* could give us no grounds for identifying others of the same type; pain *y*, pain *z* and so on. Each is completely unique, *sui generis*. I have no grounds for saying that what 'other people' experience is an example of what 'I' experienced when 'I' experienced a pain. Śāntideva is wrong therefore to state (8:102) that each has the quality of pain. That requires the concept of 'pain', and the concept of 'pain' requires that we can identify at least two cases of pain as being of the same type. It is difficult to see on Śāntideva's premisses how this could be done, particularly when, as we have seen, we cannot distinguish either different subjects for the pain-tokens, or the same subject over time. I am simply not allowed by Śāntideva to speak of 'my pains' and 'others'' pains'. And here indeed behaviourist objections come into play. With disembodied free-floating pains we are asked to believe that it makes sense to speak of pain, and indeed more than one pain, completely divorced not only from subjects as such but, of course, from familiar pain-behaviour. Protecting the site of a pain, writhing, screaming, avoiding the source of the pain – all the behaviour which along with the actual sensation of pain (the *quale*) make up what we think of as pain-experience, are part of what it is to be a pain – all these are irrelevant to Śāntideva's thesis. Yet these are central to what it is to be a pain, and when the actual sensation itself is lacking without a subject it is difficult to see that anything is left to count as the free-floating pain. We have failed to identify and to individuate pains.[102] Śāntideva has therefore ruled out any possibility of talking about a multiplicity of pains or persons in pain. He is therefore unable to count pains at all. We cannot even say that each pain has a *similar* quality of e.g. hurting, being unpleasant etc., for all this requires an ability to identify, reidentify, and count pains, hurts, unpleasant sensations and so on. Thus Śāntideva is unable any longer to apply the concept of 'pain'. Moreover it must be obvious even to Śāntideva that it makes no sense to talk of me *feeling* another person's pain. Thus it would not be enough to say that in actual fact one does not need the concept of 'pain' in order to identify pains. They can be identified simply by feeling them. If Śāntideva wants to urge the removal of pains without reference to *who* is experiencing them, he cannot employ experience as the means of identification. I can only experience my own pains. That is a truism.[103] Thus it is indeed necessary even for a great bodhisattva to employ the concept of 'pain' in order to identify pains. Without being able to do so, even the great bodhisattva can make no sense of *Bodhicaryāvatāra* 8:102–3. Without even being able to identify pains, no sense can be given to the removal of pains. This is not only because there is nothing to remove, but also because if pains cannot be identified and individuated, it would be impossible to identify and individuate a removal of a pain. Without reference to persons what is to count as the removal of a pain? And without being able to identify and individuate the removal of pains even the great bodhisattva would be unable to fulfil his or her pledge to remove all *duḥkha* and thus all pains.[104]

12 Conclusion: How Śāntideva destroyed the bodhisattva path

Śāntideva has eliminated the subject in order to appeal for the removal of pains without discrimination of myself and others. His argument will fail immediately if this discrimination can still be made in terms of anything which will enable me to isolate myself from others, and this can be done with *any* identifying description (what about, for example, 'the person who experiences pain-token *x*, where pain-token *x* is presently being experienced by the person currently writing this essay'?). Let me repeat the point again, for it is central and its importance can easily be forgotten or missed. It is simply not true that Śāntideva's elimination of the subject, the person, or whatever, is occurring only on the level of the ultimate truth, the final way of things. Śāntideva intends his elimination of the person to issue in altruistic actions. But it is within the everyday transactional conventional realm that actions – and therefore the salvific actions of the bodhisattvas and Buddhas – take place. An elimination of the person as ultimate, leaving the acceptability of a conventional person, is completely irrelevant to his purposes and indeed quite possibly antithetical to the conclusion Śāntideva wishes to establish. I can *quite consistently* accept that I do not have an isolated monadic True Self and yet, *qua* Williams, this person here, repeatedly and selfishly put the interests of myself (if not my Self) before the interests of all others.

Thus it is simply not the case that Śāntideva is denying the *ultimate* existence of the person and urging the removal of pain without discrimination. He has also to be denying the conventional transactional existence of the person. Thus *there can be no distinguishable and therefore differentiating subjects for pains either ultimately or conventionally*. Therefore Śāntideva is arguing that it is consistent to remove pain without discrimination because we cannot logically – if we want to be rational animals – discriminate between persons. There simply are no persons.

However, I have argued that it is absurd to refer to pains without the subjects who are in pain.[105] Thus on Śāntideva's premisses we are left with the impossibility of making sense of pain. If the first part of Śāntideva's argument is correct then the conclusion of altruism which he wishes to draw becomes impossible, and the removal of pain as an integral part of the bodhisattva path itself looses any meaning. Indeed reflection suggests that if the implications of Śāntideva's argument at *Bodhicaryāvatāra* 8:101–3 are consistently thought through – particularly in terms of their complete elimination of the person as subject – their effect on the bodhisattva path might be even more catastrophic than the mere meaninglessness of pain. Here are just a few random reflections and jottings on the further *consequences* of Śāntideva's argument, if we are to be good bodhisattvas and rationally consistent, as Śāntideva and the Buddhists wish and exhort us to be:

(i) If pain is to be eliminated regardless of the subject who is in pain, as being simply a free-floating disembodied pain, then pain is to be eliminated *because it is pain*, regardless of *context*. I do not want to enter into an elaborate discussion of the nature of masochism and masochists who seem to like pain, except to say that if there are such beings who actually like the sensations that we all call 'pain' (not just that they feel pleasure when we would feel pain) presumably the bodhisattva would strive also to eliminate their pain even if the very elimination of it caused them suffering. Of course, the bodhisattva would also strive to remove *that* suffering as well, but short of changing them – their very nature – the bodhisattva can only remove the second sort of suffering by giving them the first sort. And of course the bodhisattva cannot change their nature as masochists, since the bodhisattva cannot take into consideration the context, the fact that they *are* masochists. Our bodhisattva sees no masochist, for he or she sees no person. Thus if there are any masochists the bodhisattva cannot relieve *all* their sufferings, and thus cannot fulfil the bodhisattva vow to remove the sufferings of all sentient beings.

(ii) Our problem here is that on Śāntideva's premisses, pain has to be seen as *intrinsically* bad. There is nothing about pain which makes it something to be eliminated apart from the fact that it is pain, for the only thing about a free-floating pain is its nature as pain. However, the intrinsically bad nature of pain seems to be wrong. Take the case of morphine poisoning. It is a simple fact that in the case of someone with morphine poisoning the antidote is to *give* them pain, thus 'soaking-up', as it were, the excess morphine. In the case of pain *x*, it is only the context – which includes necessary reference to the person in pain – which will tell whether *x* is or is not the antidote to morphine poisoning. Thus if pain is to be eliminated regardless of persons in pain, the bodhisattva would be unable to administer pain in the appropriate context, or would seek to remove the therapeutic pain, and thus would be unable to help the person with morphine poisoning.[106] Note also other cases where cognisance of the person in pain might be thought to be intimately bound up with removing their pain. Supposing a person were in pain due to an electrical shock. As I understand it, commonly in serious electrical shocks the person, say, in contact with the live wire cannot let go of it. Thus the removal of the pain might be thought to be involved with safely removing the person's hand from the wire. Without cognisance of the fact that *this* person is in pain – and of course that involves necessarily a cognisance of the fact that it is not *me* who is in pain – the correct strategy I should pursue as the bodhisattva for removing the pain could not be followed. Note also, of course, that intentional action is embedded in persons as well. When we speak of the actions of a Buddha or a bodhisattva we mean the actions of a person (as subject) as the locus of the actions. Without persons to act as their loci, there can be no actions of Buddhas and bodhisattvas. It makes no sense for Śāntideva to speak of acting for the benefit of others, removing pains because of their quality as pain, if he denies the person as locus for the action. The point is important. As we have seen, Śāntideva's exhortation to act is on the same level as his denial of personal differences which would make us act to remove our own pains and not those of others. Thus Śāntideva is exhorting selfless action at the same time, at the same level, *and on the very same grounds* (that we have no distinctive self) as he is in fact (although not in intention) denying its basis. Note also incidentally – to return to a previous point – that intention issuing in volition and then action requires a series of temporal points and must involve the same person throughout (otherwise *inter alia* one person would have the intention, another act, and so on). Intentional action is therefore impossible on the basis of a theory of complete momentariness, with the person as a temporal continuant nothing more than a fiction. We find that on Śāntideva's premisses there could be no such thing as an immoral action, or a virtuous action, or the actions of Buddhas and bodhisattvas.

(iii) Take the following imaginary case (derived from a discussion in a different but associated context by Bernard Williams): I am a great bodhisattva (I said it was imaginary), and the job of a great bodhisattva *inter alia* is the removal of pain. I have been captured by a fiendish scientist who plans to exchange my brain with that of Hitler. I take it that Hitler enjoys *inflicting* pain. I am told that at the end of the brain-exchange there will be left one person whose job is the removal of pain, and one person who enjoys inflicting pain. I am asked which one do I wish and hope to be when I wake up? It seems that it is required of a great bodhisattva (it follows not just from his or her nature but also from his or her vow) that the great bodhisattva should wish to be the person who removes pain, not the person who inflicts it. Unfortunately, however, since reference to persons is not permitted (is not *rational*) by Śāntideva's argument, the great bodhisattva cannot express a preference. The great bodhisattva can at the very most express pleasure that *someone* will be removing pain (and dismay that *someone* will be inflicting it), but cannot wish *him- or herself* to be the one who removes pain. And this seems very strange. A bodhisattva vows not just that that all sentient beings should be free of suffering, but that he or she will bring it about. This no longer makes sense in the present context. On Śāntideva's premisses I cannot fulfil my vow as a bodhisattva in the situation of a brain-exchange. And it no longer makes sense not just with reference to the hypothetical fantasy case of a brain-exchange. How, on Śāntideva's premisses, can it make sense for me to vow that in a future life *I* shall remove pain? Such a vow is necessary for the bodhisattva in order to embark on the long path to full Buddhahood for the benefit of all sentient beings. I need to vow that after death I shall continue on the path of removing pains. But even if it were to be true that after the death of the being I am now someone with a causal connection to me might remove pains, without reference to persons (in fact, not just persons but in some sense the *same* person) it can make no sense for *me* to vow to remove pains in a future life.[107] On Śāntideva's premisses, when I take the bodhisattva vow I am doing something irrational, since it requires reference not just to the person I am, which is itself irrational, but also the person I will be in a future life – as if I and that person are the same – which is doubly irrational. Thus if Śāntideva's argument at *Bodhicaryāvatāra* 8:101 is rational, then it is no longer rational even to take the bodhisattva vow! Note also another similar case. Supposing a Hitler decides to torture one out a group of ten people. The great bodhisattva, who is present, is unable to express a preference that it should be him or her who is to be tortured. All the bodhisattva can do is lament that anyone is to be tortured at all. On Śāntideva's premisses self-sacrifice become impossible, since self-sacrifice precisely requires that I distinguish myself from others and that I sacrifice myself on their behalf. Śāntideva cannot have it both ways. If it is rational, correct according to reason, to make no distinction between oneself and others in the removal of pain, because there is no such thing as a self, then it is also rational on the same grounds to make no distinction between oneself and others in the case of self-sacrifice. Without a self, there can be no self-sacrifice.

(iv) Supposing I cause a particular pain. If pains are intrinsically wrong, then I commit an intrinsically wrong act. Thus I commit an intrinsically wrong act if I cause a pain to Hitler, or a fully armed concentration camp guard, or to an innocent child. Supposing we can make sense, on the theory of intrinsically wrong free-floating pains, of quantities of pain. One pain is more intense or longer lasting than another. Then for me to cause a pain of x quantity to a concentration camp guard in the act of murdering an innocent child, and for me to cause a pain of the same x quantity to the child herself, are equally wrong since we are unable to take into consideration the persons involved, and thus the context within which the infliction of pain is occurring. Consider also the following. The concentration camp guard is very tough. The child is not. The pain inflicted by the guard on the child is much less than would be necessary for me to inflict on the guard in order to bring the torturing to an end. But it should follow from Śāntideva's argument that I am unable to inflict a greater pain to remove a lesser, or two pains to remove one. Let us now reverse the case. On Śāntideva's argument, the *removal* of pain in these two contexts is equally imperative and of equal value. Thus supposing someone is preventing the guard from inflicting pain on the child, and in doing this happens to inflict exactly the same amount of pain on the guard himself. The bodhisattva, as a further person present, would have as much imperative and moral duty to prevent the pain meted out to the guard by the child's protector as to prevent the pain inflicted on the child by the guard himself: 'Because of its quality as pain indeed it is to be prevented. What limitation can be made there?' But surely something has gone very wrong here. We want to say that who is undergoing pain, and the context within which the pain is occurring, has *direct* relevance to the removal of that pain, if the pain is to be removed, and the morality of doing so. It seems to be *immoral* to prevent the pain inflicted on the concentration camp guard if that is the only way (and let us suppose for our example that it can reasonably be expected to be a successful way) of preventing the pain of an innocent child. Not only is Śāntideva's argument philosophically and psychologically incoherent, not only would it destroy the bodhisattva path and, as we shall see below, the bodhisattva' salvific action, but it is also immoral and unjust. It would be unjust because the guard in inflicting pain, and the one who inflicted pain on the guard, would in this respect be equally wrong, and equally guilty. Compare also the case of the same amount of pain inflicted by a vicious criminal, and a doctor in the course of emergency treatment.

(v) Take the following case. Supposing there are three people, A, B, and C. At time T(i), A is in pain. At T(ii) the pain of A has ceased, but B is in pain. Let us say that the pain is the same type of pain, and of the same quantity and quality, as that experienced by A.[108] Likewise, at T(iii) the pain of B has ceased, A is still free of pain, but C has 'the pain'. Now, on Śāntideva's premisses without reference to the three different people A, B, and C it would be impossible to distinguish between these three pains and one long pain lasting from T(i) to T(iii). Clearly, reference to the times alone will not do it. This difficulty of distinguishing between three pains and one long pain is itself a problem, since supposing actually I am B, and I experience the pain at T(ii). It is a simple fact that there is a real difference between the two pains at T(i) and at T(iii), and that at T(ii), and I know it in the most direct manner possible. As we have seen, it is a simple fact that to experience a pain oneself is different from someone else experiencing a pain. If someone other than me is experiencing a pain, I can wonder whether it is A, or C, and make a mistake. But if *I* am experiencing a pain, I cannot wonder whether it is me, and make a mistake (remember Dickens' Mrs Gradgrind). But take the case of a fourth person, who happens to be an omniscient Buddha who wishes to act to remove the pains of others. According to Śāntideva's position, even the omniscient Buddha cannot distinguish between the three separate pains and one long pain, although there definitely is a difference. I should know, since I am B and I experienced the pain at T(ii), a pain which now has thankfully gone. Thus the Buddha does not know something which happens to be true, and therefore is less than omniscient. Moreover, although the pain at T(i) ceases at T(ii), and the pain at T(ii) ceases at T(iii), without reference to different persons the Buddha or bodhisattva cannot know that this is the case. Among the implications of this is that the Buddhas and bodhisattvas cannot know if he or she has succeeded in removing a pain or not. In the case of pain at T(ii), without reference to the person even the Buddha cannot know when it started or when it ended. *Prima facie* there are problems in seeing therefore how the Buddha at T(ii) could remove the pain at T(ii). The notion of *an individual pain* at T(ii) is completely lacking. Since he or she cannot distinguish between the three pains, and one long pain, pain has actually ceased only at T(iii), the end of the series. Even the omniscient Buddha will not know that *a* pain has ceased at T(ii). And in actual fact since there will still be some pain in the infinite cosmos, and thus for all the Buddha knows one very long pain, for a Buddha or bodhisattva there can be no way of telling the success of their salvific actions to remove even the slightest pain until *all* pain is removed. But then we have another problem. Actually I can make no sense of 'all pain' except as a series of individual pains. It cannot be that at some time in the indefinite future, as a result of the actions of the Buddhas and bodhisattvas, some individual thing called 'all pain' – with no connection to the actual pains experienced throughout history by sentient beings – will disappear! Thus the salvific activity of the Buddhas and bodhisattvas will have a criterion for success and know of its own success when all pain, understood as the temporal series composed of the pains of all sentient beings, has come to an end. But not only does the Buddha not see the individual members of this series (they cannot be identified and individuated apart from persons), but according to Śāntideva's own argument, a temporal series is a continuant and thus does not exist. Thus the Buddhas will know that they have succeeded in their vows and aspirations when they discern that through their salvific actions something which never existed *even conventionally* has finally ceased! Therefore we find that even the Buddhas and bodhisattvas cannot make sense of the removal of individual pains, or have criteria for success in their removal, and also cannot make sense of the removal of the complete series of all pains, or have criteria for success in its removal. We are left with the possibility of speaking of and knowing success only with reference to the removal of the very last pain in the series. Under such circumstances it seems that success, the fulfilling of the bodhisattva vow itself to remove all the pains of all sentient beings, becomes difficult to imagine. At least, there appears to be a criterion for success and knowledge of its accomplishment in removing only one final pain. We can make no sense of speaking of the Buddhas and bodhisattvas removing a pain during the series, since there is no sense to the concept of a pain's ending *during* the series. The situation is even worse if actually the series of pains is infinite through time, since then the Buddhas and bodhisattvas could neither identify and individuate pains (for all they know it might be one infinitely long pain, stretching infinitely into both past and future), nor ever know at all whether they had succeeded in removing even one pain.

(vi) In the case of free-floating pains it seems obvious that in cases where both cannot be removed at the same time, the greater pain should be removed before the lesser pain. We cannot make any distinctions based on who is experiencing the pain. In particular, we can assume that *qua* pain, the pain of animals is like that of humans. At least, if we are to refer to free-floating pains it must be taken that way. Therefore absolutely no priority can be given to the removal of human pains over animal pains, or moral condemnation to inflicting human pains over inflicting pains on animals. Thus not only does it follow that there is absolutely no moral difference between inflicting the same amount of pain on an animal in the case of vivisection and doing the same to a human being (say, a baby) *regardless of the circumstances*, but if, for example, the bodhisattva is faced with a straight choice between removing a great deal of pain experienced by a rat and identifiably less pain, although still a lot, experienced by his or her own baby then it would actually become immoral to give preference to the baby over the rat, again regardless of circumstances (the rat might carry plague). Similarly, even among humans, it would be immoral of us to make distinctions. Thus supposing a concentration camp guard is in greater pain than his innocent victim. And supposing, perhaps, that the innocent victim is your own daughter (three years old). The very least we should do, as good bodhisattvas, is remove the pain of the concentration camp guard first. If your daughter subsequently died due to the delay, although not with any further pain, nevertheless if you are Śāntideva you would have done the right thing. You removed pain simply because it was pain, without making distinctions and creating preferences between fictitious persons. Presumably if they were in equal amounts of pain then, like Buridan's ass, we would die before we could work out which to give the priority to.

Also take another case. Supposing a mad scientist had discovered a particularly effective drug for the instant curing of headaches, made from something contained only in the brains of human babies from a particular racial group. This is far and away the fastest acting headache cure available, and the mad scientist is so impressed with it that he dispenses it free of charge. Supposing also that the mad scientist, full of compassion, had developed a painless way of killing the babies. Thus the actual preparation of this drug would cause no physical pain to anyone at all, and all the babies chosen were orphans supported by the state with no living relatives and kept since birth individually isolated, seen by no one apart from the mad scientist and his equally mad assistant. Due to an operation which went wrong twice both mad scientist and his assistant are incapable of actual affection for these babies, so they will not suffer even mentally in killing the children. Supposing then that a sentient being found himself with a clear, identifiable, although quite mild headache. Supposing also now that you are a great bodhisattva. It is the duty of the great bodhisattva to remove pain regardless of the person who is experiencing the pain. It becomes your moral duty therefore, in accordance with your bodhisattva vows, to act to remove that sentient being's mild headache. It is, after all, pain. Moreover, it follows that the longer the pain lasts the worse the situation becomes simply through the pain's duration. A pain of two minutes is by definition worse than a pain of one minute. It is therefore perfectly proper for you to use the new wonder drug which acts instantly (and even to encourage and help in its production). Indeed, it would be immoral of you as a great bodhisattva not to use the drug as soon as you could get hold of it. Note that there is only one pain in this whole situation, the mild pain of a sentient being. Thus you must act to remove that pain. Not to do so would be wrong, while to do so not only would be right but would be completely right. With reference only to disembodied free-floating pains there can be discerned nothing wrong here whatsoever. Indeed, the mad scientist might *be* the bodhisattva in this situation, for he simply removes pain and there is no 'compensatory' pain inflicted. The bodhisattva acts to remove pain because of its quality as pain, that is all there is to it. Thus if removing *any* quantity of pain requires the painless killing of *any number* of innocent beings, the bodhisattva should do so. Persons do not enter into the equation. That is all there is to it.[109]

(vii) Supposing a person were in a great deal of pain, and the only drug which would remove that pain will not be available for six months. Since the longer the pain lasts, the worse the situation is by definition, as without reference to persons or contexts a greater quantity of pain must be worse than a lesser quantity, it follows that the bodhisattva should remove the pain immediately if at all possible, and the sooner it can be removed the better. Thus it would be better if the pain ceased now, rather than in six months time. The only drug which can do this is unavailable, but of course there is always euthanasia (with or without the consent of the patient, who is irrelevant in all of this and who should not be taken into consideration by the

> bodhisattva). Thus if the pain is free-floating, intrinsically wrong, necessarily of the nature to be removed, then it would be morally better for the bodhisattva to kill the patient now (painlessly, or with less pain than is currently experienced), thus removing all pain, rather than wait six months as part of a process which will increase the aggregate amount of pain.[110]

Has Śāntideva really destroyed the bodhisattva path? Well, if he himself takes his reasoning at *Bodhicaryāvatāra* 8:101–3 seriously, accepts it and follows it through consistently, then I think we have seen so many reasons enough to show that Śāntideva has indeed completely destroyed the path to full Buddhahood for the benefit of all sentient beings. Without persons even conventionally there are no pains. Without pains there is no removal of *duḥkha*. Without removal of *duḥkha* there is no Buddhahood. On the other hand with pains there are persons. With persons at least conventionally there are differences between persons. With differences between persons it is not possible to argue for the moral imperative to remove pain based on the argument of *Bodhicaryāvatāra* 8:101–3. Without the moral imperative to remove pain there is no moral imperative to remove *duḥkha*, which includes pain. If Śāntideva holds that the path to Buddhahood requires rational consistency, and his argument *is* rationally consistent, then the implications destroy *inter alia* the Mahāyāna. If Śāntideva himself does not follow through those implications, then he himself abandons appeal to rational consistency – and this too is to abandon an important element of the bodhisattva path. In fact we have just seen that this undermining of the bodhisattva path would be the case even if Śāntideva did not take his arguments seriously, or follow them through rationally, inasmuch as Śāntideva's argument suggests that at the very least we should not take cognisance of different persons (or as far as possible minimise cognisance of different persons) in making moral choices.

It seems clear from all of this discussion that quite a lot has gone wrong as a result of Śāntideva's position. Not only is it incoherent to treat pains as if they are free-floating, but – as anyone who has ever received training in counselling knows – to help others effectively requires *not* that we discount their individuality as the persons they are but actually to focus on that individuality most closely. The good counsellor – dare I say, the good bodhisattva – is someone who can actually discount to an unusually effective extent their own intervening concerns in order to focus on the other *in their very uniqueness*. This requires a very vivid awareness of the other as an individual. It is not helped by denying uniqueness to either of us. The pain which we seek to remove is intrinsically embedded in the actual individual in front of us, who is different from other individuals and, of course, different from us. However the bodhisattva is going to develop the most effective way to work for the benefit of others, in order to be an effective helper he or she is going to have to recognise and start from the individual person, the fact that each person is an individual with unique circumstances, problems and potential. Anyone who actually works in the caring professions knows that.

In general Buddhist philosophy has tended to urge a concern with the individual and concrete rather than abstractions – with the *svalakṣaṇa*, for example, rather than the universal – but here we find Śāntideva directing us to pain rather than the suffering individual. But pains are essentially embodied and context-dependent, and in fact this reduction to free-floating pains is precisely itself a move from the specific towards the abstract. And as we have seen, removing abstract pain reduces to removing pain in abstract, for with abstract pain we cannot identify any actual persons in pain nor can we identify and individuate pains or the removal of pains. Thus if we are not careful what we will end up with is a vague disembodied altruism – through vague pain to 'the suffering of all' and a 'concern for all sentient beings' – which is divorced from the helping of anyone in particular. It is interesting that, whether intended or not, this is in fact conceptually and, I fear, psychologically the implication of Śāntideva's argument. This tendency in Buddhist thought to de-individualise – to a reduction that creates a whole plethora of new abstractions (from *dharmas* to *svalakṣaṇas* and beyond) – even with the best of motives, can perhaps be a legitimate matter of some concern. It seems to me that altruism (as in the relationships between religions) actually begins with a concern for others as being indeed who and what they are, different from us yet still loveable in all their strangeness, not a reduction of them to versions of ourselves, or something no different from ourselves, or all of us to some abstract unity, or something already familiar. Altruism begins in a wise recognition of differences, and it should not surprise us to find that Śāntideva's strategy here, superficially attractive though it may appear to be, is unable to generate a rational basis for altruism. To subordinate our own interests to the interests of others may indeed be helped in some cases by the teaching of no Self, but when that teaching is interpreted as denying the significant differences between people that those I wish to help value, it precisely looses not only our own egoistic concerns but also our concern with the *other* which is a condition of altruism. It has to be possible to recognise the other as a unique individual and at the same time to subordinate any inordinate concern for ourselves.

That altruism *requires* an honest recognition of differences, and concern requires a one-pointed concentration on the other who is different, seems clear to me. *Why* we should be altruistic at all has still not been answered, but the way Śāntideva appeals to the teaching of no Self at *Bodhicaryāvatāra* 8:101–3, is not as such going to work. Still, in finding at the end of our meditation inspired by Śāntideva some approaches which do not work perhaps some light may also be thrown on ways that might. We can but look on the bright side.

Notes

Preface

1. See here the notes and introductions to the Crosby and Skilton translation, and Saito 1993.
2. In particular, I find that closer study in the fifth essay has made me much less sympathetic to some form of Buddhist/Humean/Parfitian reductionism concerning the self than I was previously (in paper 2, for example).

One: On *Prakṛtinirvāṇa/Prakṛtinirvṛta* in the *Bodhicaryāvatāra*

1. Lhasa edition of the *Legs bshad gser phreng*, folio 35b: spyir myang 'das bzhir gsung rab las 'byung ste / rang bzhin dang mi gnas pa dang / lhag bcas dang lhag med kyi myang 'das so // de la dang po ni / chos rnams kyi rang bzhin spros pa mtha' dag dang bral pa'o // gnyis pa ni / sangs rgyas dang byang sems kyi myang 'das so // tham gnyis la gnyis las / theg dman gyi dbang du byas pa ni / This passage has been noted by David Seyfort Ruegg (1969), p. 450. On the translation of *spros pa* (*prapañca*) as 'verbal differentiation' see Williams (1980b), esp. pp. 30–4
2. See the Vaidya edition of the *Bodhicaryāvatārapañjikā* (1960):

   tan na kiṃcid ataḥ sattvāḥ prakrtyā parinirvṛtāḥ //104//

   ataḥ asmāt karaṇāt sattvāḥ prāṇinaḥ prakṛtyā svabhāvena parinirvṛtāḥ parimuktasvabhāvāḥ / niḥsvabhāvatālakṣaṇasya prakṛtinirvāṇasya sarvasattvasaṃtāneṣu sadā vidyamānatvāt /

   –Tib.: de ni cung zad min de'i phyir /
   sems can rang bzhin mya ngan 'das //103//

   de'i phyir zhes te / rgyu des na sems dang srog rnams rang gi ngo bo nyid kyis mya ngan las 'das pa yin la / yongs su grol ba'i rang bzhin yin zhing / rang bzhin med pa'i mtshan nyid rang bzhin gyis mya ngan la 'das pa / sems can thams cad kyi rgyud la rtag tu yod pa'i phyir ro /
3. Vaidya edition, Ch.24 verse 4cd: evam śūnyeṣu dharmeṣu nirvāṇaṃ saṃprakāśitam // See also verse 6ab: sarvadharmāḥ svabhāvena nirvāṇasamasadṛśāḥ /

4. For a discussion of these issues in the context of *Madhyamakāvatār-abhāṣya* 6:181–2 see Williams (1982), pp. 67–80.
5. For a short recent discussion of Tibetan views on the *tathāgatagarbha*, particularly from a dGe lugs point of view (the position of rGyal tshab rje), see Doboom Tulku (1985), pp. 24–8. Doboom Tulku also has studied works by Mi pham, Kong sprul and Shākya mchog ldan. He suggests that Rgyal tshab rje does not want to maintain that the emptiness of the mental continuum *alone* is the *tathāgatagarbha*. Rather this term can also apply to various potencies within the mind.
6. See Williams (1989a), pp. 1–9.
7. For dates I am relying on David Seyfort Ruegg (1981b).
8. I also consulted the *Spyod 'jug 'grel pa Rin po che'i phreng ba* by the dGe lugs lama rGyal mkhan po Grags pa rgyal mtshan (1762–1837), New Delhi, 1979. It was disappointing. On the relevant verses he simply quotes at length the commentary by rGyal tshab rje. 1996 note: On the controversy between Mi pham and certain dGe lugs lamas see now Williams 1996. A study of Mi pham's interpretation of Madhyamaka by John Whitney Pettit is nearing completion and promises to be most interesting when published.

8b. 1996 note: This half-verse has not been well-translated: cf. 'If what has ceased from an ultimate point of view should be subject to saṃsāra from a conventional point of view . . .'. The Tibetan is telegrammatic: 'If ultimate – nirvāṇa; saṃsāra – conventional . . .'. I am grateful to Richard Gombrich for suggesting to me that I look again at the translation of this verse Incidentally, the discrepancy between the Sanskrit verse numbering and that of the Tibetan results from a mistake in manuscript copying. See the translation by Crosby and Skilton (who do not reproduce the mistake in their verse numbering, which consequently corresponds to the Tibetan), pp. 113–4.

8c. Another 1996 note: My use of '::' throughout my work indicates a binary opposition, as is common in e.g. structuralist writings.

9. mya ngan las 'das pa ni rang bzhin gyis stong pa yin pa'i phyir skye ba dang 'gag pa la sogs pa dang bral ba yin la / don dam par ni don dam pa'i bden pa yin te / rang bzhin gyis mya ngan las 'das par gdod ma nas zhi ba'i phyir ro / folio 200a.
10. It is probably also *nirvāṇa* because it is a 'blowing-out' of the concepts of inherent existence through emptiness, like fire without fuel, an image frequently used in our commentaries, particularly on *BCA* 9:35. Compare all of this with the discussion by Candrakīrti in his *Madhyamakāvatārabhāṣya* on 6:112. Candrakīrti quotes from the *Ratnameghasūtra* to the effect that all *dharmas* are calm from the beginning, free of birth, *prakṛtyā parinirvṛtāḥ*. Therefore they are always without birth (*de phyir 'di ltar ston pas chos rnams kun / gdod nas zhi zhing skye bral rang bzhin gyis / yongs su mya ngan 'das pa gsungs gyur pa / de phyir rtag tu skye ba yod ma yin //*). In his commentary he explains that 'all *dharmas* are calm' is because they are the sphere of calm gnosis (*jñāna/ye shes*). This is because they are not born. They are not born because they are fundamentally ceased or ceased from the point of view of inherent existence, that is, empty of

inherent existence (*rang bzhin mya ngan 'das*). The gloss on this is that if something had an inherent existence (*rang bzhin* or *ngo bo*) that hypothetically could be born. But it does not, so there is no birth. In other words he thinks of *rang bzhin* – *prakṛti* – as an equivalent of *svabhāva*, and *prakṛtinirvāṇa/prakṛtinirvṛta* as equalling ceased, i.e. not born from the point of view of *svabhāva*, or inasmuch as they have *svabhāva*. Candrakīrti goes on to explain that there is never any birth. Thus there is *prakṛtyā parinirvṛta*. The expression 'from the beginning' means that it is not just the case that *dharmas* are not born from the point of view of the yogin's gnosis, but also from the transactional (conventional) point of view *dharmas* are not born with their own inherent natures (*rang gi bdag nyid kyis*). 'From the beginning' is a synonym for 'from the first'. Things are always like this; it is not that they are one way for enlightened beings and another for unenlightened beings. 'Always' here carries both a time reference and also a soteriological implication. Thus for Candrakīrti, because things are always completely ceased from the point of view of inherent existence, there is never any birth of such inherently-existent things. Because there is no birth their absence of birth forms the object of the yogin's gnosis. Because this entails that their object is a non-object, the gnosis is calm (ff.286b–7a). Thus for Candrakīrti here, things are free of birth and death because they are *nirvṛta/nirvāṇa*, rather than the other way round. There is little difference, however. For *dharmas* to be *nirvṛta*, ceased, is for them to be subject to neither birth nor death. This fact psychologically carries with it resonances of *nirvāṇa*. They are thus '*nirvāṇa*' because *nirvṛta*.

11. (Vaidya ed.) iha hi sarveṣāṃ prapañcānāṃ nimittānāṃ ya upaśamo'pravṛttis tan nirvāṇam / sa eva copaśamaḥ prakṛtyāivopaśāntatvāc chivaḥ / Cf. *Anon.* f.180b: spong lugs kyi don dam par ni mya ngan las 'das pa yin zhi dang zlog nas
12. The same sense of *prakṛti* is implied, it seems to me, by Candrakīrti at *Madhyamkāvatārabhāṣya* 6:112.
13. For the textual material from the *Ratnagotravibhāgavyākhyā* here see Ruegg's *La Théorie*, pp. 257 and 421: tatra prakṛtiviśuddhir yā vimuktir na ca visaṃyogaḥ prabhāsvarāyāś cittaprakṛter āgantukamalāvisaṃyogāt.
14. I do not know which work by rNgog these are from. Did he write a commentary on the *Bodhicaryāvatāra*? (1994 note: It seems he did, although at the moment it is lost. I am grateful to David Jackson for verifying this for me from a text in his possession.) Ruegg refers in *La Théorie* to a commentary to the *Ratnagotravibhāga*, but I do not have access to it.
15. Reading a number of Tibetan commentaries from different times one after the other, incidentally, it is even more obvious than usual how distinctive are dGe lugs commentaries in continually drawing attention to the fact that Madhyamaka negation occurs only from an ultimate point of view. What is negated is *inherent* existence, *ultimate* existence, being *truly* established. No opportunity is lost to clarify through drawing attention to this point.
16. It is interesting in the light of our previous discussion concerning *nirvāṇa* as freedom from birth and death that Tsong kha pa employs here not the

Tibetan *'gag pa* – cessation (Skt. *nirodha*) – as used in the Tibetan translation of Prajñākaramati, but rather *rga ba*, the normal Tibetan expression for old age, thus implying also death, the end of life. Tsong kha pa is thinking of *prakṛtinirvāṇa* as a *nirvāṇa*, a freedom from old age, sickness and death. Possibly this is explained by the context of the opponent's criticism.

17. It is a little unclear where Mi bskyod rdo rje stood on the *rang stong/gzhan stong* controversy. In his commentary to the *Madhyamakāvatāra* he strongly criticises well-known exponents of the *gzhan stong* position such as Shākya mchog ldan. Nevertheless he also wrote another work expounding and defending the *gzhan stong* interpretation of the *tathāgatagarbha* and the Madhyamaka (the *dBu ma chen po* – see later), and attacking Candrakīrti. See my 1983a paper, pp. 125–45, esp. note 39.
18. For a thorough discussion of the *gzhan stong* interpretation of the *Ratnagotravibhāga* with particular reference to the bKa' brgyud materials, see S.K. Hookham (1990).
19. Which is not to say that there is necessarily here any distinction to be made. The Sanskrit verse could read *prakṛtyā parinirvṛta* rather than *–nirvṛta* for purely metrical reasons, or the Tibetan could be subject to metrical constraints. In general, of course, Tibetan is perfectly capable of making linguistically the distinction if required.
20. bden par grub pa cung zad kyang med pa de'i phyir / sems can thams cad bden pa'i spros pa thams cad dang bral ba'i rang bzhin gyis mya ngan las 'das pa'o / (f. 24a).
21. cung zad kyang rang bzhin gyis grub pa yod min de'i phyir sems rang bzhin gyis stong pa de nyid rang bzhin mya ngan las 'das pa'o / (p. 258). I find this comment a little difficult. The obvious way of reading it would be to take *de nyid* as meaning 'that very', thus 'That very empty of inherent existence mind is the *prakṛtinirvāṇa*.' This, however, does not harmonise with the dGe lugs view that in this context the *prakṛtinirvāṇa* is not the mind but the emptiness of inherent existence of the mind. Actually it would be much better to omit '*de*' and read '*stong pa nyid*'. As it stands, '*de nyid*' must refer in some way to the *nature* of the mind as empty of inherent existence.
22. don dam par *cung zad* kyang yod pa *ma yin* pa *de'i phyir sems can* rnams *rang bzhin* te / rang gi ngo bo nyid kyis *mya ngan las 'das* pa grol ba'i rang bzhin yin yang sgro btags pa'i nyon mongs pa'i bag chags kyis nyams par byas bas ma grol bar brjod kyi / don dam par ma yin no // (p. 556). The material in italics represents portions of the verse commented on (with *ma yin* for *min*).
23. Cf. also Padma dkar po: de'i phyir sems can rnams gdod ma nas rang bzhin gyis mya ngan las 'das pa'o / (p. 160). Sentient beings are *nirvāṇa* by nature from the very beginning. The same point is stressed by *Thogs.* (p. 348) who, strangely, in his commentary makes no mention of *rang bzhin myang 'das* by name (in spite of Stephen Batchelor's adding the dGe lugs interpretation in brackets to his translation from *Thogs.* in his 1979 translation, p. 153. It is one thing to read Śāntideva through dGe lugs eyes, but it is clearly another issue to read Thogs med, who was a Tibetan commentator and not a dGe lugs pa, some centuries earlier than rGyal tshab rje, through the eyes of rGyal tshab).

24. sems kun rdzob glo bur ba de ni dpyad na cung zad kyang grub pa min de'i phyir dang / don dam chos nyid ni nam yang 'gyur ba med pas sems can rnams ni sems kyi rang bzhin 'od gsal mya ngan las 'das pa'i snying po can du grub ste / yum las / sems ni sems ma mchis pa ste sems kyi rang bzhin ni 'od gsal ba'o zhes pa ltar ro / (p. 381). For a discussion of this material from the *Aṣṭasāhasrikā* see Ruegg's *La Théorie*, pp. 413ff.
25. It is clear in Sa bzang mati paṇchen's text that we have a final stage in the *Ratnagotravibhāga* and *tathāgatagarbha* interpretation of the *prakṛti-nirvāṇa*. This shows the powerful influence of the *tathāgatagarbha* concept in Tibet in influencing the interpretation of texts which originally show no clear evidence of *tathāgatagarbha* thought. It also provides a basis for the placing of texts (in this case a Prāsaṅgika Madhyamaka text) in terms of Tantric practice where expressions like the 'clear-light nature of the mind' become particularly important. I am not denying that it is *possible* to interpret Sa bzang's text here in a way perfectly compatible with Tsong kha pa. He could be referring simply to emptiness, absence of inherent existence in the mental continuum. But I think such an interpretation is highly unlikely, especially when it is taken in the light of his comments on other verses which we shall look at subsequently. There also remains the difference of language used. In spite of what is often thought, difference of language carries with it other differences. It is not simply an arbitrary matter. In fact what we seem to find is that while the *Bodhicaryāvatāra* tradition of Prajñākar-amati influences the dGe lugs interpretation of the *tathāgatagarbha*, in Sa bzang mati paṇchen it is the reverse. It is the *Ratnagotravibhāga* which influences here his interpretation of the *Bodhicaryāvatāra*. The dGe lugs is firmly based in Prāsaṅgika Madhyamaka. Other traditions sometimes found the *Ratnagotravibhāga* a useful text for bridging the theoretical framework of Sūtra and Tantric approach.
26. See, for example, Bu ston: rnam dpyod kyi rten med pa'i phyir yod med sogs su dpyod pa'i blo mi skye zhing / (p. 560).
27. rten chos can bden pa med pa'i phyir na dgag bya dang bkag pa gnyis rang bzhin nyid kyis mi skye ste de yang rang bzhin gyis mya ngan 'das par brjod la / don de rtogs nas goms par byas pa la glo bur dri bral gyi myang 'das thob par yang brjod do / (p. 261 – *bkag pa* here must refer to the negating mind).
28. The absence of *parikalpita* in the *paratantra*. For a discussion of Cittamātra in general, and these points in particular, see Williams (1989b), ch.4, esp. pp. 86, 89–90.
29. sarvasamāropaniṣedhaṃ vidhāya vastutvaparijñānāt kṛtakṛtyatvāt pravṛt-tinirvṛttyabhāvāt na kvacit sajyate, nāpi virajyate / tac ca nirvāṇam ucyate, sarvavyavahāranivṛtteḥ sarvatra nirvyāpāratayā praśāntatvāt tad eva nirvāṇam abhidhīyate // The Tibetan is slightly but not significantly different: sgro 'dogs pa thams cad dgag pa byas nas dngos po'o / de kho na nyid yongs su shes pas bya ba byas pa'i phyir / 'jug pa'i ldog pa med pa'i phyir gang la yang re ba med pa ste / gang la yang 'dod pa ma yin la / de yang mya ngan las 'das par brjod de / tha snyad thams cad log pa'i phyir ro / thams cad du bya ba med pa'i phyir rang bzhin gyis zhi bas de nyid la mya ngan las 'das par (the blockprint appears to follow this with

ba, or should it read *rab*?) brjod (f.257a-b). The expression *rang bzhin gyis zhi ba*, calm by nature, in the Tibetan (the Sanskirt lacks 'by nature') may have suggested to rGyal tshab rje the *prakṛtinirvāṇa*, but in context it is clear that Prajñākaramati is here referring to *nirvāṇa* itself.

30. Prajñākaramati himself did not feel the problems which gave rise to a later Tibetan appeal to the *prakṛtinirvāṇa*. In the case of rGyal tshab rje these were connected with problems in Tibet going back to Ho-shang Mahāyāna and the eighth-century debates (see Williams (1989b), pp. 193ff), affected by the influence of the *Ratnagotravibhāga* on Tibetan thought in general and in this case Madhyamaka interpretation, exacerbated by a reaction against *gzhan stong* absolutism and a need to establish what to rGyal tshab rje was thought to be a pure Prāsaṅgika Madhyamaka. Here we see what was possibly a Tibetan *contribution* to the interpretation of Madhyamaka. It is not enough to use Tibetan commentaries as if they necessarily give us clear and unambiguous access to the original meaning of Indian Buddhist texts.
31. To be fair, Kalyāṇadeva is unclear. He states that 'the investigating mind also has not arisen with inherent existence. That which has not arisen is declared to be *nirvāṇa*' (*rnam par dpyod pa yang rang bzhin gyis ma skyes ba yin la / ma skyes ba de ni mya ngan las 'das par bshad do /* (f.82a)). There is no doubt this *could* be interpreted as referring to the *prakṛtinirvāṇa*, but the actual expression is not used.
32. In Sa bzang's Tibetan quote: phyi ma phyi ma'i rten yin la / ngo bo nyid ni med pa yin / skye med 'gags med gzod nas zhi / rang bzhin mya ngan 'das pa 'grub / (p. 382). Cf. *Sphuṭārthā* on *Abhisamayālaṃkāra* 4:2: go rim bzhin du ngo bo nyid med pa dang / ma skyes pa dang / ma 'gags pa dang / gzod ma nas zhi ba dang / rang bzhin gyis mya ngan las 'das pa'i mtshan nyid. In Yaśomitra (1977), pp. 77–8.
33. rten dmigs yul bden par med pa'i phyir na yul can gyi blo yang mi skye ste / yul dang yul can la sogs pa skye ba med pa'i chos nyid de yang rang bzhin gyis mya ngan las 'das par brjod de gdod ma nas spros pa nye bar zhi ba'i phyir ro / (p. 384).
34. spros pa thams cad zhi bas na/ rnam dpyod de'ang chu la rlabs bzhin du chos nyid kyi ngang du rang bzhin gyis mya ngan las 'das par brjod do / (p. 76).
35. For Mi pham the expression *de yang* – 'that also' – is clearly taken to refer to the investigating mind, which is thus said to be *rang bzhin gyis mya ngan las 'das*. For rGyal tshab rje, on the other hand, it is equally clearly non-arising with inherent existence (*rang bzhin kyis mi skye*). What *de yang* is taken to refer to tells us what the commentator considers to be meant by *nirvāṇa* in this verse. Padma dkar po (p. 161) refers simply to non-arising. Sa bzang takes it to be the *dharmatā*, thus distinguishing his position *prima facie* from that of Mi pham. For dPa' bo it is the innate, non-contingent (*gnyug ma*) nature of *dharmas* (p. 874), presumably the same as the *dharmatā*; for Bu ston the complete calming of all minds of craving desire and absence of craving desire (p. 560); while for Thogs med it is that calming in the absence of arising of both object and awareness (p. 350). Clearly commentators differ considerably on what is being said to be *nirvāṇa* in *Bodhicaryāvatāra* 9:111.

36. de ltar sgro skur gyi zhen pa log pa na chos rnams kyi rang bzhin bsal bzhag byar med pa stog zhing 'od gsal ba tsam 'di ni chos rnams kyi gnyug ma ste de yang gzod ma nas mya ngan 'das pa nyid tu brjod to / (p. 874).
37. For a more precise discussion of differences in Madhyamaka see Williams (1980b).
38. de ltar yul blo'i mdun na med na / de'i 'dzin pa'i blo mi skye bas / sgrib pa las grol bar 'gyur ro // (p. 523).
39. de la 'ga' zhig sems 'gags pas ye shes kyang med par 'dod mi thad de / rnam shes glo bur ba'i sems spangs pa'i cha nas bzhag pa'i mya ngan las 'das pa dang / don dam ye shes kyi sku mngon du gyur pa'i cha nas bzhag pa'i / rdzogs pa'i sangs rgyas ni don gcig pa'i phyir ro // (p. 343).
40. Mi pham p. 28: (de las gzhan bden par grub pa'i rnam pa gzhan med pas na) bden 'dzin gyi dmigs pa'i gtad so mtha' dag med par spros pa ma lus pa rab tu zhi ba yin te / = rGyal tshab p. 228: (de'i tshe bden par grub pa'i rnam pa gzhan med pas) / bden 'dzin gyi dmigs pa'i gtad so mtha' dag med par rtogs par spros pa mtha' dag rab tu zhi ba yin te / In saying that the dGe lugs perspective and that of, say, Mi pham and Sa bzang are very different here I am not saying that a subsequent scholar could not succeed to his satisfaction in harmonising them. That is another matter.
41. stong nyid mngon sum du rtogs pa'i gang zag gi ngo na stong nyid la gnyis snang gi spros pa yang zhi la stong nyid don spyi'i tshul gyis rtogs pa la ni gnyis snang ma khegs kyang nges don bden pa'i spros pa khegs pa yin no / (p. 228). rGyal tshab subsequently goes on to attack the earlier Tibetan scholar sTod lung rGya dmar for holding the view that emptiness is truly established. Clearly, rGyal tshab says, he does not understand even the slightest tenet of the Mahāyāna.
42. so so rang rig pa'i ye shes tsam gyis rab tu phye ba smra bsam brjod du med pa nam mkha'i dkyil lta bu mnyam pa nyid do / gnas lugs mthar thug pa de lta bu yin pa (p. 28).
43. dngos dang dngos med du zhen pa sna tshogs pa'i tshul bzlog pa'i phyir stong nyid bcu drug tu bshad pa lta bu ste / spros pa mtha' dag khegs pa'i zung 'jug chos kyi dbyings de ni theg pa chen po'i rtogs rigs khyad par ca yin la / der dbu ma chen po zhes tha snyad byed pa yin te / (p. 29).
44. Since it is outside the range of verbal differentiations, this reflexive awareness is not affected by the refutations of reflexive awareness found in Madhyamaka texts such as the *Bodhicaryāvatāra* and the *Madhyamakāvatāra*. For more on reflexive awareness in Tibetan thought see Williams (1983b), pp. 321–32 (1996 note: For even more, see also Williams 1996, which includes a reprint of the 1983 paper).
45. For a brief further account of the *gzhan stong/rang stong* dispute in Tibet see my *Mahāyāna Buddhism*, pp. 105–9.
46. Quotations from the *Madhyamakakārikā* are from the edition by J.W. de Jong (1977).
47. des na de lta bu'i stong pa nyid kyis ni spros pa mtha' dag chos kyi dbyings su nub nas sgrib pa gnyis po yongs su spangs shing mi gnas pa'i myan 'das thob par byed de / (p. 29). The sinking into the *dharmadhātu* here parallels the investigating mind with the nature of the *dharmatā* in Mi pham's commentary on 9:111. Thus the extremes of verbal differentiation too are of the same nature as the ultimate – pure

reflexively aware clear-light gnosis. The two obscurations referred to are the obscurations of moral taints and the obscurations concerning the knowable. Overcoming both of these is in the Mahāyāna the attainment of Buddhahood.

48. The 'three circles' here are possibly agent, action and object of action, but more likely the three actions of body, speech and mind.
49. shes rab dri ma med pa'i blo de nyid kyang gzod ma nas ma skyes ma 'gags pa'i ngo bo nyid tu rtag tu zhi ba yin pa de kho na'i dbyings su de ltar zhi ba yin no / (p. 676).
50. It may also place him at variance in a different way with rGyal tshab's comments on *Bodhicaryāvatāra* 9:2, where rGyal tshab *does* want to maintain that the ultimate truth comes within the range of the mind. Discerning the ultimate does not entail the cessation of the non-dual mind. This is not at all the same, however, as saying that there remains a real inherently existing mind. For a discussion of these points see Williams (1982).
51. In the main body of my text I have not deemed it necessary to discuss the commentaries on *Bodhicaryāvatāra* 9:150 (=Tib.149), although these are also apparently relevant to our purposes:

 evaṃ na ca nirodho'sti na ca bhāvo'sti sarvadā /
 ajātam aniruddhaṃ ca tasmāt sarvam idaṃ jagat //

 de ltar 'gag pa yod min zhing /
 dngos po'ang yod min de yi phyir /
 'gro ba di dag thams cad ni /
 rtag tu ma skyes ma 'gag nyid //

 Thus there does not exist cessation, and never (Tib. omits 'ever' but adds 'also ') does there exist entity /
 Therefore all this world (Tib. 'all these beings') is (Tib. 'always are') not arisen and not ceased //

 Among our Indian authors Prajñākaramati, and among Tibetans, rGyal tshab rje and Thogs med, all refer to the *prakṛtinirvāṇa/prakṛtinirvṛta* in commenting on this verse. In general none of the commentators really adds anything to what we have seen already in examining the other verses. dPa' bo, however, does make one additional enigmatic comment: 'All *dharmas* always transcend the mind, there does not exist speech, thought or utterance, by nature (*ngo bo nyid kyis*) [they are] simply purified from the beginning' (*chos thams cad ni rtag tu blo las 'das pa smra bsam brjod du med pa ngo bo nyid kyis gzod ma nas rnam par dag pa kho na'o* (pp. 907–8)). Mi pham, of course, also employs the expression 'there does not exist speech, thought or utterance'. What *precisely* does dPa' bo mean by saying that 'all *dharmas* always transcend the mind'? For Mi pham this would be because all *dharmas* are *themselves*, in their nature, the ultimate Reality, the ultimate gnosis, as waves on water. For rGyal tshab it is because all *dharmas* are primevally lacking inherent existence. He would have to take 'mind' as equalling dualistic mind. It would however be a rather ambiguous and obscure way of putting it. In context dPa' bo is stating that all things, even *saṃsāra* and *nirvāṇa*, are just diversifying constructions which accompany reification. His appeal is to going beyond all, even the most rarified, diversifying constructions. But once more he has not expressed himself very lucidly.

Two: On Altruism and Rebirth

1. On the story well-known to Tibetans of Śāntideva floating up into the sky and disappearing while teaching the *Bodhicaryāvatāra*, see for example Tāranātha (1970), p. 218.
2. Bodhicaryāvatāra 8:97:

   tadduḥkhena na me bādhety ato yadi na rakṣyate /
   nāgāmikāyaduḥkhān me bādhā tat kena rakṣyate //

   gal te de la sdug bsngal bas / bdag la mi gnod phyir mi bsrung /
   ma 'ongs pa yi sdug bsngal yang / gnod mi byed na de cis bsrung //

3. bSod nams rtse mo p. 488a: gsum pa khyab pa'i rgyu mtshan nyid bsgrub pa / gal te gang zhig bdag la gnod pa de bsrung bya yin pa'i rgyu mtshan yan (= yin) gyi gzhan mi 'dod pa tsam gyis bsrung bya yin pa'i rgyu mtshan ma yin te / des na gzhan gyi sdug bsngal gyis bdag la mi gnod pa bsrung bya ma yin no snyam na / bSod nams rtse mo seems to have followed in his commentary Phywa pa Chos kyi seng ge (1109–69), who was apparently critical of the Prāsaṅgika approach and therefore presumably a Svātantrika. It is noticeable in his discussion on these two verses how much bSod nams rtse mo employs the structures, terminology (*khyab/rgyu mtshan* etc.) and flavour of the *pramāṇa* tradition in a way perhaps familiar from much later dGe lugs writing but absent from all the other commentaries examined on these verses (with perhaps the exception of Bu ston), including that by rGyal tshab rje.
4. *Ibid.*: bdag la gnod pa tsam bsrung bya yin pa'i rgyu mtshan yin pa bkag pas 'dod bya ma yin pa bsrung bya yin pa'i rgyu mtshan shugs las grub pa'o / de'ang dngos su bdag la mi gnod pas bsrung bya ma yin pa'i rgyu mtshan du 'dod pa 'gags so /
5. See Prajñākaramati's *Bodhicaryāvatārapañjikā*: yato nāgāminaḥ kāyasya paralokabhāvino narakādijātasya duḥkhātmakasya [duḥkhānme] tasyopāttasya kāyasya kācidbādhā saṃbhavati, tasya anyatvāt / = Tibetan Cone bsTan 'gyur, microfiche edition produced by The Institute for Advanced Studies of World Religions, New York, mDo vol. 26, folio 165b: gang gi phyir / ma 'ongs pa ste 'jig rten pha rol gyi lus dmyal bar skyes pa'i sdug bsngal gyi bdag nyid 'dir skyes pa'i lus po 'di la cung zad kyang gnod par mi srid de / de gzhan yin pa'i phyir ro /
6. Of course, in Tibetan Tantric theory there is a physical continuation into future lives through the very subtle wind. This is an interesting theory, but the very subtle wind is so different from the normal gross bodily continuum as to be irrelevant here. The very subtle wind explains the medium of consciousness transference, it does not provide in the case of normal (say, human or animal) rebirth any coherent sense of continuity between the body that has died and the one reborn, and it certainly would not deny a radical gap between the one who dies and the one

reborn, a gap which does not normally exist within *one* lifetime of bodily continuity.

7. bSod nams rtse mo, p. 488a: mi gnod pa la bsrung bya ma yin pas khyab na tshe phyi ma dang rang nyid rgas pa la sogs pa'i dus kyi sdug bsngal de chos can / bdag gis ma bsrungs par thal / da ltar gyi lus mi gnod pa'i phyir gzhan gyi sdug bsngal bzhin no /
8. Bu ston p. 469: ma 'ongs pa skye pa phyi mar dmyal bar skyes pa'i lus kyi duḥkha chos can / da ltar gyi lus des ci ste srung mi srung bar thal / da ltar gyi lus la gnod pa mi byed pa'i phyir ro /
9. Sa bzang mati paṇchen p. 276: de lta na ma 'ongs pa yi dus su bdag nyid ngan song du skye ba'i sdug bsngal yang da lta'i lus 'di la dngos su gnod pa mi byed pa'i phyir na de cis srung ste bsrung ba'i don du mi dge ba spong ba la 'bad pa mi byed par thal bar 'gyur ro / Another commentator who adds *da lta(r)* to his gloss is the great sixteenth century historian dPa' bo gTsug lag phreng ba. Like Bu ston and Sa bzang, he seems to take *da lta* to refer to present lives, although he is not as explicit (p. 589): gal ste gzhan gyi sdug bsngal sel mi dgos te bdag la da lta mi gnod pa'i phyir snyam na / 'on na bdag gi ma 'ongs pa ngan song gi sdug bsngal srung pa'i phyir sdig pa spong ba yang mi rigs par thal ste des bdag la da ltar mi gnod pa'i phyir ro /
10. Cone mDo 27, f. 249b: gal te gzhan mi bsrung na dmyal bar ma 'ongs pa'i lus kyi sdug bsngal gyis da lta mi gnod pas de ji ltar bsrung / mi dge ba las log pas so /
11. rGyal tshab rje p. 182: rgas pa'i tshe sdug bsngal byung dogs nas gzhon pa'i tshe nor gsog pa dang / de bzhin du sang dang phyi dro sdung bsngal byung dogs nas di ring dang snga dro'i dus nas sdug bsngal sel ba'i thabs la 'bad par mi rigs par thal / phyi ma'i dus kyi sdug bsngal ma'ongs pa'i sdug bsngal yang snga ma'i dus kyi gang zag de la gnod par mi byed na de byung dogs nas cis bsrung bsrung mi rigs par thal lo /
12. It is worth noting the use of *gang zag* and the adoption of a wider application in rGyal tshab rje, for it is often thought that one of the features of the dGe lugs tradition has been a return to a rather faithful and perhaps even slavish adherence to the Indian sources. Clearly rGyal tshab rje knows his Indian sources, but his commentary is very much his own with some rather important aspects lacking in the Indian materials.
13. See Geshe Rabten (1978), p. 131: gdags gzhi phung po lnga po gang rung la brten nas btags pa'i nga.
14. For a detailed study of the status of *saṃvṛti* in the work of Tsong kha pa see now Helmut Tauscher (1990/91), pp. 169–202.
15. See Wilson (1980), especially pp. 13–14.
16. Sa bzang, p. 276: mi 'dra ste gzhan gyi sdug bsngal gzhan gyis mi myong zhing bdag gi sdug bsngal de ni bdag gcig pus rtag tu myong ba'i phyir ro snyam na /
17. rGyal tshab, p. 182: tshe dir bdag gis phyi ma'i sdug bsngal gyi rgyu ldog par ma byas na phyi mar bdag gis sdug bsngal myong dgos pas
18. Bodhicaryāvatāra 8:98:

    aham eva tadāpīti mithyeyaṃ parikalpanā /
    anya eva mṛto yasmādanya eva prajāyate //

bdag gis de ni myong snyam pa'i / rnam par rtog de log pa ste /
di ltar shi ba 'ang gzhan nyid la / skye ba yang ni gzhan nyid yin //

[1994 note] Looking back on it some years after writing this paper, I seem to have followed the Tibetan in translating the first part of this verse and all but ignored the Sanskrit. I do not know why that should be (apart from my preference for Tibetan). Anyway 'The notion "it is the same me even then" is a false construction, since it is one person who dies, quite another who is born.' (Crosby and Skilton trans.). It does not appear to make significant philosophical difference to the following discussion.

19. Of course, those who hold to metaphysical Self claims usually maintain that suffering precisely *does not* happen to the enduring and truly real Self. So for many, if not most, Self-claim-holders the existence of a Self is not relevant to the claim that 'I will experience suffering in the future'. This is not to say, however, that it may not be relevant to making sense of the claim that I have survived *death*, such that derivatively I can speak of experiencing suffering in a future life. But the relationship between the 'I' that we speak of when we say 'I have survived death', and the 'I' when we say 'I shall receive suffering in a future life' must clearly be a complex one (and not one of simple identity) for those Self-claim-holders who hold that the Self does not experience suffering.
20. This is not to say, of course, that the Buddhist (a Mādhyamika, for example, with his or her understanding of latent, innate Self-grasping) could not argue that our behaviour shows an un- or subconscious assent to concepts of an enduring Self. It might be argued that certain behavioural patterns (the cult of the new, for example) can only be rendered systematically coherent by assent to a Self, and once this is pointed out to a person he or she, in order to act rationally, would either have to abandon certain behaviour patterns (abandon grasping after new material goods) or abandon the claim not to hold to a permanent enduring Self. It is arguable that not all philosophical beliefs need to be held consciously in order to be held. I have touched on this issue again in a different context – once more in a footnote – in Williams (1992a), p. 203.
21. Blackmore (1991), p. 119. On p. 123 Blackmore comments that the sense when we wake up in the morning that we are the same person who went to sleep is largely based on bodily continuity, familiarity of place and setting, and memories.
22. This is not a matter of simply changing names from Williams to Archibald, of course. And the expressions 'me-constructions' and 'other-constructions' are just devices here. Obviously from the other's point of view I am the focus of 'other-constructions' as the other, Williams.
23. This is not to say that I could not have sympathetic pain sensations, or even, supposing I was a great yogin and the other had great faith, I could 'take-on' the other's pain such that the other ceases to have pain and I have pain instead. But I am not literally receiving *their* pain. Their pain has ceased. Mine has started. And there could be problems. If I am a great yogin with a good set of teeth (perhaps I practise the *Lotus Sūtra*,

where it is specifically stated that good teeth come to the sūtra's practitioners) and I start to hurt and the other's pain ceases, the other's teeth will continue to decay. Perhaps mine will be extracted. But, we say, it is the *other* who has bad teeth, the result of the other not cleaning them. Precisely!

24. rGyal tshab rje, p. 183: 'di ltar shi ba'i gang zag de'ang gzhan nyid la skye ba phyi ma'i gang zag de'ang ni gzhan nyid yin pas de gnyis gcig tu mi rung ba'i phyir ro / 'di ni so so tha dad yin pas gcig gi sdug bsngal cig shos kyis sel mi rigs pa la
25. For Derek Parfit see in particular 1984 and 1971, pp. 3–27. The connection of Parfit's work with Buddhism is noted in Parfit (1984), pp. 273, 280, 502–3. It appears that the first Buddhologist to explicitly notice this connection was Steven Collins (1982), p. 177. Collins, influenced I think by Parfit's work, speaks subsequently of past selves as in fact subjectively the same as contemporary others (p. 190). Śāntideva would appear to agree, although his concern is rather with future selves since those are the selves which we now attempt to protect against future sufferings. Collins seems unaware of the support from Śāntideva. His very valuable book goes into a number of these and other issues in great detail from the point of view of the Theravāda tradition, and seems to have been read by Parfit himself. This is one area where Buddhist thought is of direct and explicit relevance to the very latest controversies in Western philosophy. Recently the relationship of Parfit's views to Buddhism have been the subject of a philosophically sophisticated study by Nigel Tetley (1990). Tetley argues that Parfit's views are in certain crucial respects not as close to those of Buddhism as Parfit seems to think. For a clear but respectfully critical summary of Parfit's views see the very readable book by Jonathan Glover (1991 reprint), pp. 101–6.
26. I think I can make sense of continuity through the death process as it is usually understood and into, say, an intermediate state, at least if the intermediate state body is held (and it often is not) to be akin to the present body – like, say, the astral body spoken of by certain writers – and there are no radical discontinuities in the mental continuum. And I do not think I have a problem with cases of rebirth – maybe in certain god or hell-realms – where there is psychological continuity of a coherent type with the being who died, even if the new bodies do differ. And I can accept that the (re)born being arises in causal dependence upon the being who died. But the break between 'me in an intermediate state body' and 'me as a beetle' is just too great for *any* meaningful sense that it is me who is reborn. In the case of (re)birth someone is born in causal dependence upon me in a different way, certainly, from the way my children who are contemporary others are born in dependence upon me. But that someone is not me. Arguably that person is no more me than my children are me. We can speak this way sometimes ('his children are him reborn') as a manner of speaking, but that is all.
27. I ignore the issue of purported 'memories' of previous lives. This is a large and complicated topic. To call them memories is of course to beg the question. Clearly *I* could not remember being another person in a

previous life. I am not sure it makes much sense to talk of a beetle remembering it was a king, or a king a beetle. Does it make much more sense to talk of a foetus remembering it was a king, or even a king remembering being another king in a previous life? The point here is, I think, a conceptual one. I am not here denying that (re)birth may be conditioned by a previous life, that the (re)born being may have inherited certain habits and talents, and may even have mental events relating to the lives of other persons who died before this person's birth which are in certain respects *like* memories, although few if any of these could occur in cases of radically different species (king/beetle), and it is debatable whether they could occur in the case of radically different types of beings from the same species (king/foetus). This last point is rather important, for it suggests a radical psycho-physical discontinuity even in the case of rebirth within the same species (king/king). If there is a radical discontinuity, I suggest, we can talk of birth, but not *re*birth.

28. It might be objected here that I am looking to base rebirth on a rather Western and egoistic idea that the reborn being has to be *me*. But in Buddhism it is said that the reborn being is neither the same nor different from the one who died. This would be to miss the point. I have argued that the sense in which the reborn being is said to be not different from the one who died is in the sense of causal connection, which is not what we normally mean by 'not different'. When a cause produces an effect normally this is a case of difference, although a difference where there is a causal connection. In fact for the Buddhist the reborn being is indeed not the same as the one who died, i.e. is different in all relevant and meaningful senses of 'different'. The reborn being will not be me. In fact the reborn being will be as different from me as contemporary others, although different in a different sense (the reborn being will exist in causal dependence upon me in a way that contemporary others do not). *And this is what Śāntideva and rGyal tshab rje say too.*
29. rGyal tshab rje, p. 183: skad cig snga phyi so so tha dad pa'i mgo mtshungs kyi rigs pas 'gog pa yin gyi / don dam la ltos nas 'gog pa gzhung gi don min no / rGyal tshab uses the word '*bdag*' a number of times in his discussion, but each time it is being used simply for the personal pronoun (*bdag gis*).
30. Of course, I could not live through the death process and yet feel in any real meaningful sense that it is *not* me. But I could fail to have psychological continuity at all, in other words my sense of 'me' could fail to survive the death process. The (re)born being would then be a different person. This appears to be what rGyal tshab rje is saying.
31. For example, even if I did have a Self and it were the same Self in future lives, the Self is not the conventional person, and it is the person who experiences the sufferings of future lives. The person who does the deed is different from the person who receives the results even on a Self theory, unless the Self is held to be an active doer and experiencer. But this would have other doctrinal problems for Self-theorists, and the more nearly this putative Self approaches the status of 'doer/experiencer' the more it becomes another name for the person, and the less likely this Self could be the same in future lives.

32. The Tibetan *rnam par rtog* is usually a translation of *vikalpa*. For a discussion of these terms in Buddhism see my 1980 paper. In favour of interpreting Śāntideva's argument in *Bodhicaryāvatāra* 8:98 as concerning the *ātman* I might cite what I say there: 'In all Mahāyāna texts *parikalpa* tends to be specifically associated with the *ātman* as a unity created out of the *skandhas*' (p. 29).
33. Sanskrit text: aham eka eva sarvadā, tenātra bhinnatvaṃ nāsti śarīrayoḥ / = Tibetan: bdag ni dus thams cad du gcig yin te / lus dag la tha dad pa yod ma yin la / That *aham* here is taken as equalling the Self (*ātman*) is clear from subsequent comments (*ātmano* . . .), and in Tibetan the same word *bdag* is used throughout. But as we have seen the Sanskrit of Śāntideva's verse uses *aham* and thus (like rGyal tshab rje) it does not explicitly mention the Self.
34. Bu ston, p. 469: bdag ni / dus thams cad du gcig pas de'i lus de yang bdag yin pa'i phyir bdag gis duḥkha de ni myong ngo / Thus Bu ston's opponent wants to deny that the Self itself experiences suffering (see note 17 above). We can say that I will experience suffering in the future life because although it is the body which experiences suffering, and the body will be different, there is an underlying continuing and unchanging Self such that we can call the future body derivatively 'I'.
35. Sa bzang, p. 277: dpyad na bdag rtag pa gcig pu ma grub pa'i phyir ro / de'i rgyu mtshan'di ltar 'di nas shi ba'i phung po'ang ma 'ongs pa la ltos te gzhan nyid yin la phyi mar skye ba'i phung po yang ni da ltar ba la ltos te gzhan nyid yin pa'i phyir ro /
36. Prajñākaramati does not make the situation any better by going into some detail on how the referent of the Self-notion is simply the five aggregates, like an illusion (*māyopamapañcopādānaskandhamātrālambanatvād asya = sgyu ma lta bu nye bar len pa'i phung po lnga tsam dmigs pa'i phyir ro*), and giving the traditional Buddhist explanation of how the (re)born being is born in dependence upon contaminated actions. This asserts how rebirth comes about on the Buddhist explanation without reference to a Self. It states that there is no Self, but does not argue that the opponent is wrong to think that in a future life it will be me who will receive the results of present actions. The matter is one of conventional persons, not Selves. It *could* be that in a future life it will be me receiving the results in the same way that it will be me tomorrow who will receive the results of what I do today, if in a future life I am the same person. It has nothing (here, directly) to do with the Self.
37. dPa' bo, pp. 589–90: bdag ni 'das ma 'ongs da ltar thams cad na gcig tu bden no snyam pa 'di ni phyin ci log gi rnam rtag (rtog) chen po yin ste / 'di ltar bdag ni skye'o zhes 'dzin pa skye ba'i dus kyi bdag 'dzin de skad cig de nyid tu 'gag la de nas ring zhig na bdag ni ngar la bab pa'o zhes dang de yang 'gags nas bdag ni rgas pa'o zhe dang de 'gags nas bdag ni 'chi'o snyam pa dag rim par skye mod kyi bdag 'dzin de dag snga ma snga ma 'gags nas phyi ma phyi ma skye bar mthong (590) bas bdag 'dzin gcig ma yin par mngon sum gyis myong ba'i phyir dang / bdag tu bzung bya'i lus sems kyang skyes ma thag pa na sems mi gsal lus nyam chung / ngar la bab pa na sems gsal zhing lus mkhregs / rgan po'i tshe

gnyi ga mthu chung / 'chi ba'i tshe gnyi ga'i stobs nyams pas phyi ma'i tshe snga ma'i gnas skabs 'gag par mngon sum gyis myong bas lus sems mi rtag par rang gis mngon sum gyis nges pa'i phyir ro /

38. Note also that, as he points out, Parfit's position would also support abortion, 'abortion is not wrong in the first few weeks, and it only gradually becomes wrong' (Parfit (1984), p. 347). This would not be acceptable to (traditional?) Buddhism, but this is just one of a number of morally unwelcome conclusions (euthanasia?) for Buddhists which could follow from thinking through fully the view that in one life there can be a series of selves (complete impermanence), and the being in a future life is a different person from the one who died. If a continuum entails different persons, if personhood is the result of an imputation, a construction upon a series of aggregates, then personhood can be acquired gradually and lost even within one lifetime, and certain moral repercussions which are repugnant to most Buddhists *may* follow. Not necessarily, of course, for additional premisses could be brought into play. For example, wherever there is consciousness aggregate (rather than full personhood) killing should not take place. But it is worth thinking about.
39. Glover, 1991, pp. 103–4.
40. Parfit 1984, p. 347,
41. J. Glover, *op. cit.*, p. 105.
42. Compare here Geshe Kelsang Gyatso: 'Although the person of our future life who will experience the results of actions we have committed in this life will not be the person of this life, nevertheless it will be "us" who experiences those effects. If we deny this, we deny a fundamental principle of Dharma, that the results of an action cannot ripen on another person' (Gyatso 1993, p. 16). Yet this remains at the level of assertion and no value is given for the scare-quotes on 'us'. It is clear from what Geshe Kelsang says that it will *not* be us, and the results of an action do in fact ripen on another person [1994 note].

Three: An Argument for Cittamātra

1. Quotations from the Sanskrit text of the *Bodhicaryāvatāra*, as well as the Sanskrit text of Prajñākaramati's commentary, are taken from Śāntideva (1960). The Tibetan text of the *Bodhicaryāvatāra* is from the version published with the commentary by rGyal sras dNgul chu Thogs med in Śāntideva (1982). For the Tibetan of Prajñākaramati see the Cone edition,mDo vol. 26.
2. See Tsong kha pa (1973), pp. 33 ff. This corresponds to pp. 211 ff in Thurman (1984).
3. See Rong ston (1979), pp. 69–70: gzung 'dzin gnyis su snang ba ni chos can / 'khrul pa yin te / don la med pa'i gzung 'dzin gnyis su snang ba'i phyir / dper na zla ba gnyis snang bzhin no // gnyis snang de nyid kun nas nyon mongs pa'i rgyu yang yin te / gnyis su snang ba la brten nas gnyis su zhen pa skye la de la brten nas chags sogs skye ba'i phyir ro // dper na sgyu ma'i glang po cher snang ba dang / rmi lam du rta glang snang ba

sogs la brten nas zhen pa skyes te kun nas nyon mongs pa 'byung ba bzhin no // 'khrul pa'i gtan tshigs gnyis pa ston pa ni / yod pa'i bdag med mi snang ba'i phyir yang 'khrul par grub (p. 70) bo // dper na yod pa'i tho yor mi 'dzin par med pa'i mir 'dzin pa bzhin no // don la med pa dang snang tsam du yod pa ya bral ba las 'khrul pa mi skye bas 'khrul pa skye ba la gnyis ka tshogs dgos par bstan pa ni / med pa 'ba' zhig la'ang med par (amended from *yod par*) 'dzin pa'i 'khrul pa mi 'byung ste / med pa la med pa nyid du 'dzin pa ni ma nor ba yin pa'i phyir ro // yod pa 'ba' zhig la yod par 'dzin pa'i 'khrul pa mi 'byung ste / yod pa la yod par 'dzin pa 'khrul pa ma yin pa'i phyir ro // des na don la med pa dang snang tsam du yod pa'i gnyis tshogs las don la med pa la yod par 'dzin pa skye dgos so // don la med pa dang snang tsam dag las gang yang rung ba zhig med na med pa la yod par 'dzin pa'i 'khrul pa mi 'byung ngo // de bzhin du gzung 'dzin gnyis med kyang gnyis su snang ba'i 'khrul pa med na rgyu med pas kun nas nyon mongs 'byung ba yang mi 'thad do // 'khrul pa med na 'khrul pa'i gnyen po ma 'khrul pa yang med pas de las byung ba'i rnam par byang ba yang mi 'thad do //

4. For a version of this argument see Śaṃkara 's *Brahmasūtrabhāṣya* to 3:2:22 translated, for example, in Radhakrishnan and Moore (1967), p. 537.
5. For a detailed discussion of the Vaibhāṣika ontological categories and their interrelationships, based largely on the explanations of Saṃghabhadra, see Williams (1981), pp. 227–57, especially pp. 237 ff.
6. (tatra) prajñapter vastu nāstīti niradhiṣṭhāṇa prajñaptirapi nāsti / From the N. Dutt edition of the *Bodhisattvabhūmi*, Patna: K.P. Jayaswal, 1966 p. 31, quoted in Thurman (1984) p. 212. The Tibetan as quoted by Tsong kha pa in his *Drang nges legs bshad snying po* is even more specific: 'If there is held not to exist the substratum (*gzhi*) for conceptual designation then because there would not exist a substratum conceptual designation also would not exist' (*(de la) 'dogs pa'i gzhi med du zin na ni gzhi med par 'gyur bas 'dogs pa yang med par 'gyur ro* . . .(p. 34)).
7. *Bodhisattvabhūmi*, p. 31, quoted in Thurman (1984), p. 213:evam vādinaḥ/ prajñaptimātram eva sarvam etacca tattvaṃ / yaścaiva paśyati sa saṃyakpaśyatīti / teṣāṃ prajñaptyadhiṣṭhānasya vastumātrasya abhāvāt saiva prajñaptiḥ sarvena sarvaṃ na bhavati /
8. de dag gi gzung cha med kyang don dang sems can dang bdag dang rnam par rig par snang ba'i rnam par shes pa'i ngo bo de ni chos can / rdzas su grub pa yin te / yang dag pa min pa'i kun tu rtog pa yin pa de'i phyir / gzung dang 'dzin pa gnyis ji ltar gnyis su snang ba de bzhin du yod pa min la / snang gzhi kun tu rtog pa ye med min te / 'khrul par byung ba'i phyir ro // 'khrul pa'i rnam par shes pa de zad nas grol ba thob par 'dod do // From the *dBus dang mtha' rnam par 'byed pa'i rnam bshad Mi pham dgongs rgyan* on *Madhyāntavibhāga* 1:4, T.G. Dhongthog Rinpoche printing (1979), p. 6. Note that the comment at the end of this passage does not entail the destruction of all consciousness in enlightenement nor, even if it did, would this mean that Cittamātra finally does not claim that the substratum has any greater ontological status than anything else (as we find in Yogācāra-Svātantrika Madhyamaka). Just because certain conditioned *dharmas* in Vaibhāṣika Abhidharma are completely destroyed in an enlightened being, it does

not follow that for Vaibhāṣika Abhidharma all these *dharmas* become *prajñaptisat* and there is no fundamental ontological disagreement with Madhyamaka. The substratum in Cittamātra is the substratum to both falsehood and enlightenment. As *dravyasat* it has a fundamentally different ontological status from *prajñaptisat*. See the discussion in Williams (1989b), pp. 89–90.

9. The tendency to see the history of Mahāyāna thought as a series of complementary footnotes to Nāgārjuna should, I think, be firmly resisted. It is sometimes also suggested that the polarisation of ontological opposition between Madhyamaka and Yogācāra Cittamātra was developed by Tibetans. This too I find quite unconvincing. Prajñākaramati argues that when the expression 'like space' is used in *Bodhicaryāvatāra* 9:28cd, because this would in fact be absence of inherent existence 'there would be reduction to our tenets' (*ākāśavad iti niḥsvabhāvatvād asmatsiddhāntānupraveśaḥ*), that is, the Madhyamaka. Thus Prajñākaramati is quite clear, as we should expect from the other side in the *Bodhisattvabhūmi*, that a teaching of complete *niḥsvabhāvatā* (= *prajñaptimātratā)* is a feature of Madhyamaka which contrasts it with the Cittamātra view of the texts we have been examining. I see no reason to doubt that this contrast was present already in the *Bodhisattvabhūmi*.
10. Tsong kha pa (1957), folios 9a-b: 'khor ba sogs rdzun pa rnams dngos po ste bden grub re'i rten can nam gzhi can yin te / 'khrul pa thams cad la gzhi bden pa re yod pas so //'khor ba de ni gzhi bden pa la brten pa la gzhan du mi rten na nam mkha' dang 'dra bar dngos po med par 'gyur ro // The commentary by rGyal tshab rje (1973), p. 224 here is almost identical.
11. See Tsong kha pa's *sDe bdun la 'jug pa'i sgo Don gnyer yid kyi mun sel*, fiche 16, folio 1b.
12. The full context reads: tadā saṃsāro'nyathā bhavet, cittādanyaḥ syāt, vastuno'nyatve avastu syāt, cittasyaiva ca vastutvāt / katham iva? ākāśavat gaganam iva / Śāntideva (1960), p. 195.
13. ya eṣa cittāśrayaḥ saṃsāro'bhidhīyate, sa kiṃ vastu avastu vā? vastvapi cittaṃ tadanyadvā? tatra yadi vastu cittam eva, tadā na cittād anyaḥ saṃsāras tadāśrayaḥ, cittam eva saḥ / cittaṃ ca prakṛtiprabhāsvaratayā vyavadānasvabhāvatvān na praheyam / atha cittād anyaḥ, tadā cittavyatiriktasya anyasyābhyupagamāt siddhāntakṣatiḥ/ atha avastu, tadā saṃsāro nāma na kiṃcid asti, kharaviṣāṇavat / ata evāha ākāśavat iti / yathā ākāśaṃ prajñaptisanmātram asat, na kvacid arthakriyāyāṃ samartham, tathā saṃsāro bhavataḥ syāt / See also the Tibetan version, folios 208b–209a. Note that Prajñākaramati uses the opponent's premisses against the opponent himself. It is a view of the opponent that if all is *prajñaptisanmātra* it would be non-existent and therefore completely lacking in causal efficacy. Subsequently the opponent replies by pointing out that if saṃsāra is grounded in a real entity – mind – as support then it could have causal efficacy (*syād etat yadi nāma avastu, tathāpi vastusadbhūtacittasamāśritatvāt tasya arthakriyāsāmarthyaṃ bhaviṣyatīty*). Clearly the opponent's model is the dependence of *prajñaptisat* on *dravyasat*. If all had only *prajñaptisat* then nothing would exist at all. But if *prañaptisat* can be grounded in *dravyasat* then

entities which enjoy only secondary existence can indeed have causal efficacy. The dGe lugs commentary by the contemporary lama Geshe Kelsang Gyatso (1980), pp. 274–5 makes this *dravyasat/prajñaptisat* contrast and relationship quite explicit (although it is not found explicitly stated in his main sources, which must be Tsong kha pa and rGyal tshab rje), and provides further evidence for the suggestion that it is this which underlies Tsong kha pa's reading of the verse. The model is pure Abhidharma. In the Vaibhāṣika case if there were no *dharmas* there would be nothing. But because there are *dharmas*, tables and chairs – which are nothing *in themselves* – nevertheless are something. It is debatable whether in subsequent verses Śāntideva or his commentators ever really come to grips with the force of the opponent's argument.

14. See the *Bodhicaryāvatārasaṃskāra*, Cone mDo 27, folio 71b: 'dir sems tsam pa na re / gal te dngos po la brten na ni de nyid (? – this is a very obscure print) kyis 'khor bar 'gyur la / de la ma brten na ni 'khor ba nyid nam mkha' dang 'dra bar 'gyur ro zhes... The reconstructed name of the author as Kalyāṇadeva is not certain. Among other Indian commentators Vibhūticandra in his *Bodhicaryāvatāratātparyapañjikā Viśeṣadyotanī* seems definitely to be following Prajñākaramati (Cone mDo 27, folio 265a). Vairocanarakṣita, on the other hand, appears to split the half-verse so that the first part is the hypothesis of the Cittamātrin, and the second the Mādhyamika reply. See his *Bodhicaryāvatārapañjikā* (Cone mDo 27, folios 142a-b). We shall see subsequently that in Tibet Sa bzang mati paṇchen takes a similar approach.
15. For the whole of Thogs med's discussion (Śāntideva (1982), p. 323): rtsod pa dgod pa ni / gal te gnyis snang 'khor ba ni 'khrul gzhi gnyis med kyi shes pa dngos pa'i rten can yin gyi / gnyis snang de ni rten dngos po yod pa las gzhan du na nam mkha' dang 'dra bar gzung 'dzin gyi dngos por snang ba yang med par 'gyur ro zhes pa'o // In Williams (1992) I followed the twelfth century dating given in the introduction to Stephen Batchelor's translation of the *Bodhicaryāvatāra*, which used this commentary (Batchelor (1979). I am now inclined towards the fourteenth century (1295–1362) dating given somewhere, I think, by Leonard van der Kuijp. For bSod nams rtse mo (1968) see p. 498a. This Sa skya hierarch uses language here which is very familiar from the *Dharmadharmatāvibhāga* and its *Bhāṣya*, including even the example for falsehood of confusing a heap of stones for a man, but seems to trace the Cittamātra argument here to Sthiramati (slob dpon bLo brtan).
16. See Bu ston (1971), p. 519.
17. Sa bzang mati paṇchen, p. 340: gal te rnam shes don dam du bden pa med na de la brten pa'i 'khor 'das kyi rnam gzhag mi 'thad par 'gyur bas // gzung 'dzin du snang ba'i 'khor ba 'di ni ngo bo bden par grub pa med kyang gnyis med kyi shes pa bden pa dngos por grub pa la brten nas bya ba byed pa can yin la // de spangs pa las mya ngan las 'das par yang rnam par 'jog go zhe na // 'o na 'khor ba de ni bden pa'i dngos po las gzhan du gyur ba yin na ...
18. See Williams (1992). Mi pham uses rGyal tshab rje, but sometimes subsequently to turn the argument round in a way which would not at all be favoured by his dGe lugs predecessor.

19. From Mi pham (1975), p. 24: gal te 'khor ba 'di ni gzhan dbang gi sems dngos por grub pa'i rten can yin gyi / gzhan du na nam mkha' bzhin du ci yang med par 'gyur gyi 'khor ba'i snang ba 'di 'byung mi rigs te / rten gzhi med pas na 'jim ba med pa'i bum pa dang / snal ma med pa'i snam bu bzhin no snyam na /
20. Bu ston, who is usually quite quick to notice differences between Indian commentators, and Indian commentators and Tibetan commentators, makes no mention of it.
21. Padma dkar po (1982), pp. 141–2: kho na re / ji ltar sgyu ma bden pa min yang ma brtags pa'i ngo na de blta bya / de bzhin du lta byed yid du 'thad pas / (142) gal te ma brtags ma dpyad pa de srid 'khor ba sems kyi dngos po la sprin lta bu brten pa can 'khor ba'i bya ba byed / de ni gzhan du brtags shing dpyad na de sangs nas sems rang nam mkha' dang 'dra bar dag par 'gyur bas 'khor ba'i bya ba mi byed / des mya ngan las 'da'o zer ro //

Four: Identifying the Object of Negation

1. With thanks to my friends Tom Tillemans and Georges Dreyfus, who first asked me what I thought of *Bodhicaryāvatāra* 9:140.
2. See Shākya mchog ldan's *dBu ma'i byung tshul*, p. 215. Otherwise, it is claimed, one could not know that the emptiness cognised is in fact the emptiness spoken of by Nāgārjuna. This interesting reference is noted by José Cabezón (1992), p. 442.
3. Cabezón, p. 442. See also Mi pham in his commentary to the *Bodhicaryāvatāra*, discussed in Williams (1992), pp. 545 ff (reprinted above).
4. The translation of *abhāva* by 'negation' seems more appropriate in this context than the more literal 'non-entity' which I have used elsewhere, in commenting on *BCA* 9:35 in my paper 'On *prakṛtinirvāṇa/prakṛtinirvṛta*' for example, but the translation 'absence' would be almost as appropriate and might have some other advantages such as distinguishing from the translation 'negation' in contexts where the Tibetan verb *'gegs pa* and its derivatives (*dgag bya* – the object of negation – etc.) are used. Clearly the term 'negation' as I am using it embraces more than just linguistic negation. *A* negation is a situation of absence.
5. See Tsong kha pa (1990), p. 579: dper na / gang zag 'di mi 'dug snyam du nges pa la med rgyu'i gang zag de shes dgos pa ltar / bdag med pa dang rang bzhin med pa zhes pa'i don nges pa la'ang med rgyu'i bdag dang rang bzhin de legs par ngos zin dgos te / dgag par bya ba'i spyi legs par ma shar na de bkag pa'ang phyin ci ma log mi nges pa'i phyir te / This corresponds to the translation by Elizabeth Napper (1989), p. 176. For some other references, there is a similar discussion in mKhas grub rje's *sTong thun chen mo* (Cabezón, p. 92) and also his *Lam ngan mun sel* (mentioned *ibid.*, p. 441), where Śāntideva's half-verse is quoted, and also briefly in 'Jam dbyangs bzhad pa's *Grub mtha' chen mo,* text and translation in Hopkins (1983), p. 633.

6. See, for example, Candrakīrti's *Prasannapadā* on *Madhyamakakārikā* 20:18: tatra śūnyam ucyate yatsvabhāvena nāsti /.
7. phyin ci log bden 'dzin gyi sgro dgag bya sgro btags pa'i *dgag bya'i* dngos po *bden grub* la *de'i rnam pa blo la shar pa'i sgo nas* ma reg *cing ma nges* par *bden grub* // de *med pa* yi dngos med *bden par med pa blos rtogs pa'i sgo nas* 'dzin *par nus pa* ma yin *no* // (zhes gsungs pa'i phyir ro). Tsong kha pa (1972), p. 198. See also the translation by Napper, p. 312.
8. Indeed one might offer as an alternative philosophical reading (cf. translation) of *BCA* 9: 140 ab: 'If we cannot apply the concept, there is no understanding of the negation of that.' This may not be too far from what Śāntideva has in mind
9. For more on the notion of 'concept' once more applied to some Tibetan debates, see Williams (1992a), p. 193. Of course, one could argue that inherent existence is rather unusual in that in order to have even the *concept* of inherent existence in order to negate it I need to know a great deal about it, in fact I need to know about it all the things which the dGe lugs tradition holds I need to know. But in order to argue this one would have to do more than simply quote Śāntideva.
10. A point clearly realised by Geshe Kelsang Gyatso who, in his English commentary (1980), p. 313 (based mainly on rGyal tshab rje) introduces the relevant critical verse here by referring to 'other Schools' rather than 'Sāṃkhya', as previously.
11. It is worth noting when looking at this verse, incidentally, that in spite of the unanimous commentarial tradition, there is nothing in Śāntideva's text which states that *BCA* 9:139 is the view of an opponent. Given Mādhyamika style one could easily come up with an interpretation which reads this verse as an assertion of Śāntideva himself. Or with some imagination one could read *both* this verse and *BCA* 9:140 as the view of an opponent.
12. don dam par sgom pa ni / 'grel pas dngos po la bshad pas dngos po ste / chos rnams thams cad rang bzhin med pa'i stong pa nyid tshad mas nges pa yang mi 'thad par 'gyur te / bod dpe ltar na / stong nyid rdzun pas sgom par mi 'thad do // Bu ston (1971), p. 574.
13. See Leonard van der Kuijp (1983), p. 11.
14. Padma dkar po (1982) often shows signs of producing a very much simplified version of Bu ston's commentary – as in his comments on these verses. Note, incidentally, that in his commentary to the ninth chapter of the *Bodhicaryāvatāra* the present Dalai Lama (1988, p. 102) – or more likely his translator, B. Alan Wallace – uses the Sanskrit version of *BCA* 9:138(Skt. 139). The commentary itself ('Then there is no point in meditating on emptiness') suggests however that His Holiness himself was using the Tibetan version of the verse!
15. Prajñākaramati's *Pañjikā*: (*BCA* verse 139 ab) yadi pramāṇam api paramārthataḥ pramāṇaṃ na bhavatīti bhavatāṃ pakṣaḥ, nanu tatpramitaṃ mṛṣā, pramāṇasyāprāmāṇye tatpramitaṃ tena pramāṇena paricchinnaṃ mṛṣā alīkaṃ prāpnoti / kim ataḥ syāt? (*BCA* verse 139 cd) yadi pramāṇasyāprāmāṇye tatpramitaṃ mṛṣā, tadā yeyaṃ bhāvāṇāṃ dharmāṇāṃ tattvataḥ paramārthataḥ śūnyatā sarvadharmaniḥsvabhā-

vatā tasmāt pramāṇān niścitā, sāpi nopapadyate, na saṃgacchate / sarvapramāṇopadarśitasya mṛṣārthatvāt sāpi sarvadharmaniḥsvabhāvatā tadvicārakapramaṇopadarśitaiva iti samāno nyāyaḥ // The Tibetan is slightly different, although not significantly so: gal te tshad ma yang don dam par tshad mar mi 'gyur ro zhes pa khyed kyis phyogs yin na / de gzhal brdzun par mi 'gyur ram / tshad ma tshad ma ma yin pa nyid yin na des gzhal ba ste / tshad ma des yongs su bcad pa brdzun zhing bden pa ma yin pa thob bo // gzhan cir 'gyur zhe na / de'i phyir de nyid du dngos rnams stong pa nyid ni 'thad pa ma yin /(f. 272 b) gal te tshad ma ma yin de nyid yin na/ des bcal ba yang brdzun pa yin no // de'i tshe gang 'dir de nyid du ste / don dam pa yin la / dngos po rnams ni chos yin te / stong pa nyid ni chos thams cad rang bzhin med pa yin la / tshad ma de'i nges pa de yang 'thad pa ma yin zhing / rigs pa ma yin te / tshad ma thams cad kyis nye bar bstan pa yang brdzun pa yin pas so // chos thams cad gang na med pa de yang de dpyod pa'i tshad ma nye bar bkod pas rigs pa mtshungs pa yin no zhe na / (Cone mDo 26, folios 272 a-b).

16. See Vibhūticandra's *Bodhicaryāvatāratātparyapañjikā Viśeṣadyotanī*, Cone mDo 27, folio 281 a: don dam par rang bzhin med pa stong pa nyid tshad ma nges pa gang yin pa de'ang med par 'gyur ro //
17. For important discussions of these issues, with particular reference to Tibetan debates, see the work of David Seyfort Ruegg, particularly 1981a, pp. 205–41, and 1991, pp. 281–310. See also my 1985 paper, pp. 205–25, and the paper by Chizuko Yoshimizu (1993).
18. Tibetan commentaries I have examined which also add *paramārthataḥ* (*don dam par*) are those by: Tsong kha pa (folios 28a-b); rGyal tshab rje (p. 269); Sa bzang mati paṇchen (p. 396); gZhan phan chos kyi snang ba (p. 455); and Mi pham (p. 85. Mi pham's commentary is followed word for word by that of his pupil, Kun bzang dpal ldan (p. 631. For a translation of the ninth chapter of this text see Khenchen Kunzang Palden and Minyak Kunzang Sönam 1993). dPa' bo gTsug lag phreng ba (p. 903) uses *yang dag par* instead of *don dam par*. In the commentaries by Bu ston and Padma dkar po, however, there is no reference to the means of valid cognition not being means of valid cognition ultimately, but rather the reference is instead to *transactional* (i.e. conventional) means of valid cognition not being means of valid cognition: tha snyad pa'i tshad ma thams cad tshad ma min na (Bu ston, p. 574. cf. Padma dkar po, p. 168). This could mean that Bu ston and Padma dkar po would accept the strong interpretation that even conventionally there are no means of valid cognition. But not necessarily. What they could mean is that the means of valid cognition *which are conventional* (i.e. accepted and acceptable in the world) are not in actual fact means of valid cognition (i.e. ultimately).
19. Commentators gloss *tattvataḥ/de nyid du* in a variety of ways: Vairocanarakṣita (Cone mDo 27, folio 175b) and Kalyāṇadeva (Cone mDo 27, folio 85b) make no mention of it. Thogs med, Padma dkar po, bSod nams rtse mo and rGyal tshab rje mention it but give it no specific gloss; Prajñākaramati, Vibhūticandra, Bu ston and Mi pham gloss it with *paramārthataḥ/don dam par*, Tsong kha pa has *ji lta ba bzhin du*, referring to the meditative cultivation of emptiness *as it really is*; Sa

bzang mati paṇchen has *de kho na nyid du*, according to reality, truthfully; while gZhan phan chos kyi snang ba gives *de kho na nyid de don dam du na*. dPa' bo gTsug lag phreng ba's comment is interesting: *dbu ma pa nyid kyi rnam par dpyod pa de nyid ltar du dpyad na* – 'if one should examine it in accordance with that very analytic investigation of the Mādhyamika himself', thus ignoring any reference to 'the ultimate point of view'. 1996 note: For an alternative translation of *mṛṣā* as 'fiction(al)' see the next paper.

20. See Vairocanarakṣita's *Bodhicaryāvatārapañjikā*, folio 175 b: khyod kyis stong pa nyid la yang yid brtan ci yod ces.
21. One should not forget, incidentally, that actually Bsod nams rtse mo was writing *earlier* than Vibhūticandra.
22. buddher agocaras tattvaṃ buddhiḥ saṃvṛtir ucyate // Tibetan: don dam blo yi spyod yul min / blo ni kun rdzob yin par brjod // bSod nams rtse mo (p. 511:2) does not state that his opponent's reference is to *BCA* 9:2, but it is quite explicit: *khyod dbu ma pas blo ni kun rdzob yin par 'dod ces*. He is the only commentator I have examined who makes this link here with a verse earlier in Śāntideva's text. On some of the controversies among Tibetan writers concerning the interpretation of this verse see my papers 'Non-conceptuality' (1992a), pp. 196–8; and 'Silence and truth' (1982), pp. 67–8
23. Continuation of the quote from bSod nams rtse mo above: blo 'khrul par khas len na / 'o na spros pa gcod pa'i rjes dpag tshad ma'ang 'khrul par thal lo // That all the conventional is mistaken is stated by Candrakīrti in his *Madhyamakāvatāra* 6:23 ff., where conventional truth is said to be the object of delusory (*brdzun*, i.e. *mṛṣā*) perception (1978, p. 75). It is clear that for bSod nams rtse mo the expresion *brdzun* (delusory) in *BCA* 9:139 equals *'khrul pa* (mistaken).
24. Does this mean that bSod nams rtse mo would accept interpretation (ii) of Prajñākaramati's commentary? Not necessarily, since while the means of valid cognition which sets forth emptiness is mistaken as is all the conventional, there is an additional problem in this case that the means of valid cognition which sets forth emptiness purports to go beyond the conventional.Therefore this means is not *in all respects* the same as the means of valid cognition which sets forth conventionalities. Nevertheless there remains a feeling that bSod nams rtse mo's opponent may wish to accept a stronger interpretation than interpretation (i), a stronger interpretation which hints that *all* means of valid cognition whatever the level are not means of valid cognition at all. This is supported by the absence of any gloss here of *BCA* 9:139 ab with reference to an ultimate point of view. If the opponent does hold a stronger interpretation then it is significant for, as we shall see, bSod nams rtse mo himself in his commentary on the next verse *accepts* the opponent's argument of the first *prasaṅga* entirely.Yet bSod nams rtse mo subsequently adopts an approach which he claims is Svātantrika, which has the means of valid cognition only *partly* not means of valid cognition. See later.
25. The derivation of two arguments from the whole verse may well have been made easier not only by the reference in the Tibetan translation to the 'meditative cultivation of emptiness', a completely new factor

entering the equation, but also the Tibetan interrogative final particle (*'am*) in *'gyur ram* at the end of the first half-verse, which can also be used to express disjunction.

26. yang na gtso bo la sogs pa mi bden na bkag pa dgag bya la (p. 511:3) ltos pas dgag bya mi bden pas de bkag pa'i stong pa nyid kyang mi bden par thal la / de 'dod na de nyid du zhes pa ste 'o na stong pa nyid bsgoms pa don med par thal zhes rgol ba'o // Note that there is no gloss of *de nyid du,* and nowhere is there any mention that these arguments apply only on the ultimate level. *Don med* could be translated by 'lacks a referent' rather than 'pointless', and it is probable that both senses are intended. Nevertheless, to say that meditation on emptiness lacks a referent would in one sense be to repeat a point made already (emptiness is untrue). In another sense those Mādhyamikas who accept that emptiness is beyond duality and beyond the mind might well grant that meditation on emptiness lacks a referent, so this would not in itself stand as a criticism. Finally, bSod nams rtse mo is here glossing the expression *nopapadyate/ mi 'thad 'gyur* – 'will not be acceptable', for which 'pointless' is better than 'lacks a referent'. Therefore the primary meaning here seems to be that if emptiness is untrue then meditation on it is pointless.
27. See Quine (1963), pp. 1 ff. It is, he comments, a tough beard which has frequently dulled Occam's razor.
28. *MMK* 24:18: yaḥ pratītyasamutpādaḥ śūnyatāṃ tāṃ pracakṣmahe /
29. For construction in general, and these '*kalpa*' terms in particular, see Williams (1980b), esp. pp. 26 ff. On *kalpanā* in the *BCA.Pañjikā* see the reference given there to the commentary on *BCA* 9:109: kalpanā āropikā buddhiḥ / kalpitaṃ tayā samāropitam /
30. kalpanākalpitaṃ samāropitaṃ bhāvam aspṛṣṭvā kalpanābuddhyā agṛhītvā tadabhāvo na gṛhyate nālambyate / (Tibetan f. 272 b) brtags te rtog pas sgro btags pa'o // dngos po ni chos yin la / ma reg pa ste / rtog pa'i blos ma bzung bar de'i dngos po (add 'med' with the Sanskrit version) 'dzin pa ma yin te / dmigs pa ma yin no //
31. tathāhi ghaṭam āropitarūpeṇa parikalpya tatsaṃbandhitayā ghaṭābhāvaṃ pratipadyate lokaḥ / (Tibetan) 'di ltar yang bum pa btags pa'i ngo bos yongs su brtags nas de dang 'brel ba bum pa med pa 'jig rten pas rtogs te / Once more this is beginning to look a little like Plato's beard. According to Quine one of the main entanglements of this beard is to think that since negation is of something, and therefore the negandum must in some sense *be* in order to be negated, what it must be is 'an idea in men's minds' (p. 2). Nevertheless, while this may be a danger for the construction of a theory on the *meaning* or logic of negation based on Prajñākaramati's comments, his point here is simply to appeal to our everyday minimal understanding of the *psychology* of negation. Prajñākaramati is explicit about how he wishes only to appeal to everyday understanding. Everyday understanding involves some sort of mental act which (super)imposes a conceptual appreciation of the negandum.
32. Vibhūticandra folio 281 a: sa phyogs la brtags pa'i bum pa med par rtogs so // 'jig rten la grags pa'i dpyad pas / der bum pa'i gzugs gang yang med do //

33. ghaṭasya vicārena lokaprasiddhenaiva yadā na kiṃcit svarūpam avatiṣṭhate, tadā tadabhāvaḥ tadviparyayarūpaḥ sutarāṃ na kaścit / tadevopadarśayann āha tasmād ity ādi (v. 140 cd) / (Tibetan) bum pa la rnam par dpyad pas 'jig rten la grags pa nyid / gang gi tshe cung zad kyis ngo bor mi gnas pa de'i tshe med pa nyid yin te / de las phyin ci logs gi ngo bo shin tu 'ga' yod pa ma yin no // de nyid brtags pa bstan pa'i phyir / de'i phyir zhes bya ba la sogs pa gsungs te /
34. yasmāt kalpitabhāvavivekena abhāvo gṛhyate, tasmād bhāvo mṛṣā asatsvabhāvo yaḥ, tasyābhāvaḥ sphuṭaṃ mṛṣā (Tibetan) gang gi phyir brtags pa'i dngos po'i dbye bas dngos po med pa 'dzin pa ('ma' omitted with the Sanskrit) yin pa de'i phyir brdzun pa'i gang la dngos po gang na med pa'i dngos po gang yin pa'o // de yi dngos med gsal bar brdzun // The Tibetan is slightly different, and makes no reference *here* to the important introduction of the absence of inherent existence.
35. Continuation of above: tasya niḥsvabhāvasya bhāvasya abhāvo virahaḥ sphuṭaṃ niścitam mṛṣā asatyaḥ / tasyāpi parikalpitarūpatvāt / evaṃ ca bhāvābhāvayoḥ parikalpitarūpatve sarvadharmaniḥsvabhāvataiva avatiṣṭhate // The Tibetan appears rather less clear: de'i ste dngos po med pa'i rang bzhin gyis dngos po med cing bral ba gsal ba ste / des par brdzun zhing bden pa ma yin pa yin te / de yang yongs su brtags pa'i dngos po yin pa'i phyir ro // 'di ltar yang dngos po dang dngos po med pa dag yongs su brtags pa'i ngo bo la chos thams cad rang bzhin med pa nyid kyis gnas pa yin no // See also similar comments in Vibhūticandra, particularly: de ltar dngos dang dngos min brtags pa yin pas / rang bzhin med pa kho na gnas par 'gyur ro //
36. yadā na bhāvo nābhāvo mateḥ saṃtiṣṭhate puraḥ / tadānyagatyabhāvena nirālambā praśamyati // (Tibetan) gang tse dngos dang dngos med dag / blo yi mdun na mi gnas pa / de tse rnam pa gzhan med pas / dmigs pa med par rab tu zhi / Broadly speaking, this is equivalent to *nirvāṇa*. For a discussion of this verse see my paper 'On *prakṛtinirvāṇa/ prakṛtinirvṛta*', original publication pp. 541 ff (reprinted above).
37. See Jacques May (1959), p. 16.
38. Note, incidentally, the easy way Prajñākaramati moves from (ii) above to (iv), from the complete non-existence of the negandum to the absence of inherent existence of the negation, or the absence of inherent existence of the negandum to the negation's complete unreality. Prajñākaramati does not make the clear, systematic distinction between absence of inherent existence and complete non-existence so beloved of the dGe lugs tradition.
39. (mDo 27, folio 85 b) brtags pa'i dngos po rnams brdzun pa (omitting 'ma') yin pas de'i dngos po med pa nyid ni shin tu gsal bar brdzun pa yin te / med pa ni yod pa la ltos pa yin pas dngos po ma grub pas na de'i med pa yang mi 'grub bo // It is beginning to look even more like Plato's beard. This would appear to make it impossible to negate the existence of anything without thereby affirming its existence! But all Śāntideva's principle concerning negation shows is that negation depends on *the existence of the concept* of what is being negated, not the existence of the negandum itself.
40. It is conceptual, but that is not to say that what we are talking about here is *simply* the expression of negation in language, even if it does often manifest itself that way.

41. I am ignoring the issue of what it means to say that the table is there in a world bereft of consciousness. The Berkeleyan alley is fortunately irrelevant to the present discussion.
42. Negation is not the same as destruction, of course. Not only minds engage in destruction (as we all know).
43. In spite of the rather strident views of certain contemporary hermeneuticists, I think it is meaningful and often helpful to talk of what a thinker of the past did or did not have in mind. It seems to me to be perfectly meaningful, for example, to say that Nāgārjuna did not have in mind an overall argument for theistic devotionalism. If we can talk meaningfully about what he did *not* have in mind then it seems to me we can talk meaningfully about what he *did* have in mind. Of course we verify our theses about what a thinker had in mind primarily by argument from their literary remains. And of course there may be much more implied by those remains than was in the mind of the author. And an author often does not know what he or she had in mind until the text is finished and read. And of course the category of 'what was in mind' is unclear, particularly at the edges. I see no insuperable problems about any of this, and no problem which would put a bar on hypotheses based mainly on the texts about what a thinker had in mind. And I do think it can be helpful to speak in terms of what the author had in mind, providing we are not naive enough to think that what we are searching for is a set of clear private mental events corresponding to unuttered sentences.
44. The stages of this move are made clearer by Kalyāṇadeva: 'If there were not determined and examined entities through an act of constructive reification, one would not be able to apprehend the negation of a conceptually-constructed entity (on the model of "That does no exist"). In spite of that one knows the nature of it as emptiness, and from that apprehension entities will be known as delusory.' (gang gi phyir rtog (? – unclear blockprint) pa'i dngos po rnams kyis bcal shing yongs su ma dpyad par de med pa nyid ces brtags pa'i dngos po med pa nyid 'dzin par mi nus kyi / de'i rang bzhin stong pa nyid du shes shing 'dzin pa de las dngos po rnams brdzun par shes par 'gyur ro) The move from negation in general to absence of inherent existence is not specifically clarified, however. Kalyāṇadeva continues with the material quoted above on the negation also being delusory in dependence on the delusory negandum. Thus, unlike Prajñākaramati, Kalyāṇadeva does appear to relate his answer specifically to the process of developing an understanding of emptiness, and he is more concerned with the specific reference of *bhāva* and *abhāva* to issues concerning inherent existence and emptiness. But he does not suggest this is the only use of these terms in this verse.
45. He accepts that emptiness is delusory, although as we shall see he does not accept that in terms of the path to liberation this makes emptiness no different from any other delusory entity. He accepts that the means of valid cognition are ultimately not means of valid cognition. But he does not seem to accept that the inferences obtained by the means of valid cognition which set forth emptiness are descriptively false. He does not

discuss the point, but implicitly he must accept that although emptiness is delusory it has been validly set-forth. This supports the view that Prajñākaramati must accept the interpretation that would see the means of valid cognition as genuine means of valid cognition from a conventional point of view (interpretation (i)).

46. An interesting point, since it suggests the possibility of developing an interpretation of emptiness based on the idea that the term 'emptiness' can be used in two ways: (i) for a particular type of *abhāva*, a negation correlated to a negandum; and (ii) that situation of universal emptiness which is seen when it is appreciated that negandum and negation are both mutually dependent and therefore empty. Some such way of thinking (combined with ontologising tendencies which come from other contexts) may be behind those Tibetan traditions of the 'Great Madhyamaka' (*dBu ma chen po*) which are inclined to speak of the emptiness which is absence of inherent existence as a lower 'relative' emptiness (a *nyi tshe ba'i rnam grangs pa'i stong pa nyid*) and not the actual final emptiness which as the ultimate truth is absolute. See here Mi bskyod rdo rje in Williams (1983a), pp. 134–4, and in particular Mi pham in my 'On *prakṛtinirvāṇa/prakṛtinirvṛta*', pp. 545 ff of the original printing (reprinted above.) See also later. This might be compared with the comments by Vairocanarakṣita on *BCA* 9:140 ab, who seems very unwilling to admit the opponent's argument which entails that emptiness is itself delusory. He notes that 'we do not say emptiness is the negation (*bkag pa*) through entity and absence (negation, *dngos po med*)': (dngos po dang dngos po med pa dag gis bkag pa ni stong pa nyid yin no zhes mi brjod de). Thus there is a slight implication here that if emptiness is for Vairocanarakṣita ultimately beyond *bhāva* and *abhāva* (in one sense a normal Madhyamka position, but it is interesting that Vairocanarakṣita stresses it here) there remains open the claim that *this* emptiness, the ultimate emptiness, is not touched by the opponent's assertion that emptiness is delusory. Emptiness is ultimately not a negation, so it is ultimately not correllated to a negandum, it is ultimately not set forth through a process of negation, and it is thus ultimately not dependently originated and delusory. The process of negation really does involve, as Vairocanarakṣita says, a *superimposition* (*sgro btags*).
47. These points appear to be strongly implied in Śāntideva's verse and Prajñākaramati's discussion of it, but they are made particularly explicit in dGe lugs texts (see later), partly as a response to those who would like to argue, as did the *dBu ma chen po* mentioned in the last note, for a real inherently-existing absolute reality called emptiness. Someone like Mi pham for example might object that, nevertheless, if emptiness is a negation, what is the emptiness which is revealed when *all* negandum and negation are said to be empty?
48. Among Tibetans, the one who probably follows Prajñākaramati most closely in Bu ston, who like Prajñākaramati indicates that this *BCA* 9:140 ab is a general account of negation based on everyday common sense. Bu ston himself makes no reference to the specific examples of inherent existence and emptiness, except simply to follow

Prajñākaramati at the end of his comments with a mention of absence of inherent existence abiding because existent and non-existent entities are conceptually-constructed (*dngos po yod med brtags pa yin pas rang bzhin med pa nyid du gnas so*). The negandum and negation spoken of in this half-verse are illustrated with a pot and absence of pot at a particular locus (*sa phyogs brtags pas de'i bum med rtog par 'jig rten pa'i grags pas so* (p. 574) – cf Prajñākaramati, quoted above, note 31. Bu ston appears also to have used here Vibhūticandra as well. See above, note 32).

49. bSod nams rtse mo p. 511:3: blo thams cad sun phyung bas tshad ma ma yin pa'am dgag bya ma grub pas de bkag pa'i stong nyid yongs gcod kyi stong pa nyid de gzhal bya mi bden pas tshad ma ma yin par 'dod do. There is a temptation to see as significant bSod nams rtse mo's reference to a means of valid cognition which is 'positively determining' (*yongs gcod*). We know that there were Tibetan thinkers who wished to employ Dharmakīrti's distinction between *vyavaccheda* (*rnam par gcod pa*) and *pariccheda* (*yongs su gcod pa*) in order to argue that while the Madhyamaka might employ arguments *rnam par gcod pa* (purely in order to negate, i.e. – if we can follow Tsong kha pa – in order to simply negate inherent existence, for example), the (Prāsaṅgika) Madhyamaka does not employ arguments *yongs su gcod pa* (positively determining, i.e. to demonstrate that absence of inherent existence is the case). This issue is bound up with questions of whether the Madhyamaka has a position which it argues for, or whether it simply engages in negating the positions of opponents, and what is the nature of the apparent negations which occur in Madhyamaka. Tsong kha pa argues that the distinction is incoherent, and it is at the core of his attack on the theoretical methodology of many of his predecessors. See the sources cited in note 17 above, and Tsong kha pa's *Drang nges legs bshad snying po* (1991), pp. 220 ff especially pp. 223–4; translation by Thurman (1984), pp. 376 ff, especially p. 379. Thus one could argue that bSod nams rtse mo, in accepting the first *prasaṅga* of the *pūrvapakṣa*, on the basis of the quotation above might be included among those who deny that Madhyamaka has an argument of thesis which is positively determining, but would accept arguments as simply negating. However, while bSod nams rtse mo may indeed think this, I do not believe we can argue it on the strength of his comments of *BCA* 9:140 alone. Prajñākaramati also uses the expression 'positively determined' (*paricchinna/yongs su bcad pa*) in putting forward the views of the *pūrvapakṣa*, (see above, note 15), and it is probably from this source that bSod nams rtse mo decided to employ the term in this context. But there is no sign there of any correllation here in Prajñākaramati or bSod nams rtse mo with *vyavacchinna/rnam par bcad pa*. Ruegg has pointed out that Candrakīrti uses *pariccheda* in his commentary to the *Yuktiṣaṣṭikā* (Ruegg, 'On *pramāṇa* theory', p. 307, note 92), but there again there is no correllation with *vyavaccheda*. Thus it is difficult to read at this point any technical usage in the sense treated by Tsong kha pa, for example, into the employment of these terms in this *BCA* context. Nevertheless it may be this employment of the term by Prajñākaramati in commenting

on *BCA* 9:139 and his acceptance of the *pūrvapakṣa* in 9:140 which was a major factor contributing towards the technical usage of these terms in Tibet. For clearly if the Madhyamaka does not accept arguments which are positively determining, the issue of why it is Madhyamaka uses arguments and what their role might be remains open. What are the Prāsaṅgika arguments then, if they are found to be valuable in cutting the forces of unenlightenment and yet they are not accepted as positively determining? As we shall see from *Bodhicaryāvatāra* 9:141, they occur 'like illusions', but that does not explain what they are doing or what they are if they are not positively determining. Dharmakīrti already had a distinction between *pariccheda* and *vyavaccheda*; it may well have been precisely this context in the *Bodhicaryāvatāra* which suggested its employment in such a controversial way in Tibet. Moreover, as we shall see, there are some grounds in bSod nams rtse mo's comments on *BCA* 9:141 for thinking that he may have been moving towards a distinction between *yongs gcod* and *rnam gcod* based on Svātantrika grounds, probably under the influence of his teacher Phywa pa Chos kyi seng ge. See below, note 90.

50. dgag bya bkag pa 'dzin pa de brdzun no // ci'i phyir zhe na brdzun pa'i dngos po gang yin te / dgag bya brdzun pa'i phyir ro // de ci'i phyir zhe na / brtag pa'i dngos po dgag bya blos ma reg pa ste / dgag bya blos yul du ma byas par de'i dngos med 'dzin pa ma yin te / bkag pa la dmigs pa'i blo mi 'byung ste / Almost the same is said, although at shorter length, in Thogs med's commentary, including even the reference to the son of a barren woman. I suspect that here at least Thogs med may well have used the commentary by bSod nams rtse mo: blos btags pa'i dngos pa la ma reg ste de yul du ma byas par de'i dngos po med pa blos 'dzin pa ma yin te / mo gsham gyi bu ma bzung bas de shi ba mi 'dzin pa bzhin no // (p. 359). See also Padma dkar po's commentary, which stresses the role of the intellect in the process of negation, but also makes the strange unexplained comment that 'since there is not apprehended the negation of that if one has not perceptually appropriated the entity which is an object of conceptual construction for the mind, this is not like meditative cultivation' (*blo ngor brtag bya'i dngos po mi dmigs par de'i dngos po med pa 'dzin pa ma yin pas 'di sgom pa la mi mtshungs* – p. 168). Is Padma dkar po making a reference here to meditative practices like Mahāmudrā and rDzogs chen where an emptiness may be known directly without relying on negandum and negation, i.e. where one can realise an emptiness (*dBu ma chen po*?) which is beyond negation and negandum?
51. dgag bya ngos ma bzung na bye brag med pa spyir bkag pa'i phyir ro // des dgag bya brdzun na bkag pa yang brdzun te /
52. I am taking 'barren' here not in a contingent but a logical sense. A barren woman is one who *by definition* cannot have children, in other words if in some possible world a barren woman has a child she would not, by definition, be a barren woman. A barren woman who is cured is no longer a barren woman. Thus there cannot be the son of a barren woman by definition (although there could, of course, be the son of a woman who was previously held to be barren).

53. de la brten pa'i (28b) dngos po [med] ste bden med de yang gsal bar rdzun pa ste rang bzhin med par grub par thal lo. I have amended the text to *dngos po med* because that must be correct, and is certainly the intention, even though my other copy of Tsong kha pa's text, the microfiche edition available from The Institute for Advanced Studies of World Religions, also lacks the *med*.
54. Nor could it even be an inherently-existent pot, since emptiness is not the negation of an inherently existent pot. The emptiness of a pot is the negation of an inherently existent pot. Emptiness is *niḥsvabhāvatā*, the negation of inherent existence. As Tsong kha pa says (see note 5 above), the negandum which has to be known well is the Self, or inherent existence. Thus in negating the inherent existence of the pot, the negandum (*dgag bya*) is inherent existence and the substratum for negation (*dgag gzhi*) is the pot.
55. Always assuming that this part of the commentary is by rGyal tshab rje and is not by Tsong kha pa himself. It is repeated word for word, with a few very minor variants, in the *Shes rab le 'u 'i zin bris*, contained in the collected works of Tsong kha pa, microfiche edition vol. pha, folios 37 b-38 a, which is described as notes on Tsong kha pa's lectures on the ninth chapter of the *Bodhicaryāvatāra* written by rGyal tshab rje.
56. (p. 269) kho bo cag la stong nyid 'jal ba'i tshad ma rdzun pa dang des bzhag pa'i stong pa nyid kyang rdzun pa yin par ches 'thad de / rtog pas bden pa'i dngos po bkag pa'i dgag pa nges pa de dgag bya'i rnam par shar ba la rag las pa'i phyir / rGyal tshab rje seems to want to say here that the negation is an ascertainment, i.e. a mental event, which is itself empty because it arises in dependence. As we shall see, emptiness itself is also empty, existing in dependence on the empty entity and also the negandum. But rGyal tshab does not appear to actually say so *here*.
57. See the references in note 5 above, and also the annotated *Lam rim chen mo*, pp. 198 ff. On the *don spyi* ('meaning generality' (Klein), a term introduced into Madhyamaka from the tradition of Dharmakīrti), defined by the much later dGe lugs scholar Phur bu lcog as 'the superimposed factor which, although not a pot, appears as like a pot to the thought consciousness apprehending a pot' see Klein (1986), especially pp. 123–6. In introducing the idea of the arising of a *don spyi* of inherent existence as the meaning of *BCA* 9:140 ab, therefore, dGe lugs writers are specifically indicating the need to generate an image of inherent existence which while not itself inherent existence (inherent existence does not exist at all) appears like inherent existence to the consciousness conceiving it. Thus for this reason alone *BCA* 9:140 ab on dGe lugs premisses requires an act of imagination, an active and positive move of the imagination towards considering the negandum.
58. Translated by Hopkins in the Fifth Dalai Lama (1976), first revised edition p. 10. Material in brackets added by translator. Jeffrey Hopkins has written a great deal on the dGe lugs view of the stages of meditation on emptiness. For an extensive discussion of these issues see his *Meditation on Emptiness*.
59. brtags pa'i dngos po bden grub la rtog pas ma reg par te bden grub kyi rnam pa ma shar bar bden stong de'i dngos por bden med de rtog pas

'dzin pa ma yin pa'i phyir / Note that rGyal tshab rje's text here refers to the non-arising of an *aspect* (*rnam pa ma shar bar*) where earlier the reference was simply to arising (*rnam par shar ba*). There may be a textual corruption. On the equivalent of *bden grub* – true establishment – and *rang bzhin grub* – inherent existence, see Hopkins, *Meditation on Emptiness*, p. 36.

60. Incidentally, in order to have a complete correspondence in the interpretation of Śāntideva's text by Tsong kha pa and rGyal tshab rje, one would have to say that the negandum, inherent existence, is delusory, that is, lacks inherent existence. Tsong kha pa had stressed that to be delusory is to lack inherent existence, and we know that he did not want to identify this with complete non-existence. Thus as an interpretation of Śāntideva Tsong kha pa and rGyal tshab rje should read the verse as saying that the negandum – inherent existence – lacks inherent existence, and negation – emptiness – also lacks inherent existence. This does not mean that inherent existence does not exist in any sense. And inasmuch as it is necessary to contact the negandum in order to negate, so it is necessary to contact a non-inherently existing inherent existence (which is taken as inherently existing)! This is not at all what Tsong kha pa *et al.* want to say about inherent existence, and suggests some further problems for such an interpretation of Śāntideva's text.
61. snga ma'i dpe ni rtog pa la mo sham bu'i rnam pa ma shar bar mo sham bu shi ba'i rnam pa mi 'char ba bzhin no. But there is a possible problem in using the son of a barren woman example. While inherent existence is for rGyal tshab rje completely non-existent, emptiness *does* exist conventionally. So the emphasis must be mainly on the example illustrating dependence. But for that a different example would have been less problematic. Note also, incidentally, that it is difficult to see what the aspect (*rnam pa*) or generic impression of a son of a barren woman could be, given Phur bu lcog's definition in note 57 above.
62. dgag bya bkag pa'i bden stong bden par grub na rigs (reading with the *Zin bris*) shes rjes dpag la bden stong snang ba bden par grub dgos la /
63. yadi aśūnyaṃ bhavet kiṃcit syāc chūnyam api kiṃ cana / na kiṃcid asty aśūnyaṃ ca kutaḥ śūnyaṃ bhaviṣyati // (Tibetan) gal te stong min cung zad yod / stong pa cung zad yod par 'gyur / mi stong cung zad yod min na / stong pa yod par ga la 'gyur // Tibetan text included with the commentary by the First Dalai Lama (1987), p. 105. rGyal tshab rje quotes only the first line, in the insignificant variant: *gal te mi stong cung zad yod*. I make no comment here on whether or not this verse can support the interpretation which rGyal tshab rje wishes to draw from it. Another time, perhaps.
64. As we have seen, since emptiness is the same as absence of inherent existence, then if emptiness were not true of each entity they would *be* inherently existent. Perhaps this is *one* reason why those who followed the *dBu ma chen po* in Tibet had to argue that their Absolute Reality which is beyond all conceptual fabrications is a higher but different emptiness to that one which is the absence of inherent existence of each thing (the Prāsaṅgika emptiness), since it is beyond all conceptualisa-

tions while the emptiness which we have been looking here at is very much a negation and thus part of the realm of conceptualisation, and therefore relative to each thing. See later, and note 46 above.

65. Sa bzang mati paṇchen p. 396: de kho na nyid du na gnyen po stong pa nyid sgom pa'ang bden pa med pa de'i phyir mi 'thad par 'gyur ro zhe na /
66. dpyad na brdzun pa yin yang re zhig gnyen por 'gyur ba ni mi 'gal te dgag bya bum pa la sogs pa brtags pa'i dngos po la (p. 397) ma reg cing ma dpyad par // de bkag pa yi dngos med 'dzin pa ni srid pa ma yin la //
67. dgag bya bden pa'i dngos po ma grub pa de'i phyir brdzun pa'i dngos po gang yin pa de bkag pa yi dngos med stong pa nyid kyang gsal bar brdzun pa nyid yin mod // 'o na kyang de sgom pa ni 'thad de bden par 'dzin pa'i gnyen po byed pa'i phyir ro //
68. In showing elsewhere a *gzhan stong/dBu ma chen po* tendency towards absolutism, Sa bzang mati paṇchen would also have been accused by Tsong kha pa with under-negating as well. This accusation of both cardinal errors was often hurled by dGe lugs writers at the Jo nang pas in Tibet, and Sa bzang mati paṇchen may well have been a pupil of the great Jo nang teacher Dol po pa Shes rab rgyal mtshan. For Sa bzang's 'absolutism' see my 'On *prakṛtinirvāṇa/prakṛtinirvṛta*', original printing pp, 532–5, and 542–4 (reprinted above). On the accusation of both faults levelled at the Jo nang pas, see Thu'u bkvan bla ma's *Grub mtha'*, translated by D. S. Ruegg (1963), p. 85.
69. p. 903: nam kha'i tha snyad la ma bsten na nam kha' dngos med du yang 'jog mi nus pa'i phyir /
70. de'i phyir brdzun pa'i dngos po snang tsam pa de la sems can rnams bden par zhen pas 'khor bar ltung la de nyid mi bden pa sgyu ma tsam du shes na de yi gnyen por 'gyur mod kyang dngos por snang ba brdzun pa de'i dngos med du btags pa stong pa nyid de yang gsal bar brdzun pa yin la
71. sgyu ma'i seng ge sgyu ma'i glang po che gsod pa ltar bden par rtog pa'i dngos 'dzin gyi gnyen por stong nyid du shes pa'i dngos 'dzin de 'jug pa yin no //
72. See Mi bskyod rdo rje's *Dwags brgyud grub pa'i shing rta*, p. 134: shar tsong kha pa chen po rjes 'brangs dang bcas pa ni stong nyid yod pas de'i rten dngos po'i rang bzhin yang khas len par byed pa dang / jo nang pa dang shā kya mchog ldan sogs bod phal cher stong nyid bden par grub pa las don dam par gzhan kun rdzob kyi chos thams cad med par smra bas / Cited and discussed in Williams (1983a), p. 128–9.
73. In his youthful work defending the *gzhan stong* teachings, the *dBu ma gzhan stong smra ba'i srol legs par phye ba'i sgron me*, Mi bskyod rdo rje was definite about the limitations of Candrakīrti's approach, and how the *gzhan stong* perspective goes beyond what can be found in Candrakīrti. For a short discussion of the *gzhan stong* perspective in the context of the *tathāgatagarbha* see Williams (1989b), pp. 105–9.
74. See my 'On *prakṛtinirvāṇa/prakṛtinirvṛta*', original printing pp. 545 ff. The association of *gzhan stong* and Great Madhyamaka is also found clearly stated in Mi bskyod rdo rje's work mentioned in the previous note.
75. dir bdag cag gis tshad mas grub don stong nyid ces dmigs gtad kyi yul bden grub gcig la grub mtha' 'cha' ba ni med de / gang gi phyir na / brtag

par bya ba'i dngos po bum sogs lta bu de la ma reg pa'am ma brten par ni bum med lta bu dngos po de yi dngos med yan gar du nam yang 'dzin pa ma yin te / p. 86.

76. de phyir bum med dang bum pa'i stong pa lta bu'i rnam grangs pa'am nyi tshe ba'i stong pa de'ang gzhan dngos po de bkag pa'am bsal be'i cha yin pas / 'di ltar rang bzhin gyis rdzun pa'i dngos po gang yin pa de'i dngos med kyang gsal bar de nges par rdzun yin par 'dod do //
77. See Williams (1983a) pp. 134–7.
78. For a more precise discussion of *vikalpa(nā)* – discriminative conception – see my 'Some aspects of language and construction' pp. 27 ff, cited in note 29 above.
79. *Acintyastava* verse 25: utpannaś ca sthito naṣṭaḥ svapne yadvat sutas tathā / na cotpannaḥ sthito naṣṭa ukto loko'rthatas tvayā // (Chr. Lindtner ed. (1982), p. 148.) Prajñakaramati quotes the second part of the verse together with some other verses, but strangely makes no mention of the essential point concerning the dream-son: utpannaś ca sthito naṣṭa ukto loko'rthatas tvayā / kalpanāmātram ity asmāt sarvadharmāḥ prakāśitāḥ // kalpanāpy asatī proktā yayā śūnyaṃ vikalpyate / Lindtner traces the scriptural reference to *Samādhirāja* 9:17, which is also cited elsewhere, including Candrakīrti's *Prasannapadā*. Prajñākaramati also includes a lengthy quote which appears to be from a *sūtra* as yet unidentified, in which a number of the themes of these three verses from Śāntideva are introduced, including the idea that ultimately the means of valid cognition are not means of valid cognition. The only other commentator to mention a *sūtra* quote in support of their position is Mi pham, who for his part also cites a lengthy section from a different *sūtra* of the Prajñāpāramitā type.
80. Vibhūticandra folio 281 a: rmi lam du gnas pa'i bu skyes nas 'chi na de med rmi ba'i rtogs pas bu de yod par rtog pa 'gog par byed do // yod pa'i rtog pa 'gog par byed kyang de brdzun yin bu de'i rmi lam du ma skyes pa dang ma 'gags pa'i phyir ro // yang na bu bden la rmi lam du shi ba la 'di sbyar bar bya'o // de ltar chos rnams skye ba dang 'gag pa'o // 'di tshad ma ma yin kyang rang bzhin med pa la skyon med do //
81. de bzhin du gal te dngos por brtags pa yod na de med do zhes bya ba rnam par rtog par 'gyur te / de nyid kyang brdzun pa yin no // (folio 85b). See also Vairocanarakṣita folio 175b: 'o na rnam par rtog pa nyid de kho nar yod par 'gyur ro snyam na / de yang brdzun zhes gsungs so //
82. Tsong kha pa comments on this verse that object and subject in the cognition of emptiness, and truth-grasping, are the same inasmuch as they both lack inherent existence. Nevertheless as regards its being seen as an antidote leading to abandoning it is like in the case of the son in a dream (des na stong nyid rtogs pa'i yul yul can dang bden 'dzin dag rang bzhin med par mtshungs kyang spang gnyen du mthong ba ni / rmi lam gyi bu... folio 28b). Thus for Tsong kha pa the point is that while negandum and negation both lack inherent existence, still the negation can have casual efficacy, and the case of the son in a dream is given simply as an example to show how this can be. Neither he nor rGyal tshab rje repeat the comment made by Prajñākaramati and others that the same applies to a son who dies in real life as one who dies in a dream

– in other words, apparently, all *is* a dream. Compare Tsong kha pa's reading with the similarities and difference of that by Sa bzang mati paṇchen: 'Even though the true entity which is conceptually-constructed by cognition (read '*rtog pa*' – constructive reification?), and emptiness which is the mere negation of that, are the same as actually nonexistent (*don la med par*), there is no contradiction in [emptiness] occurring as an antidote leading to abandoning (rtogs pas btags pa'i bden dngos dang de bkag tsam gyi stong nyid kyang don la med par mtshungs kyang spang gnyen du 'gyur ba ni 'gal ba med do // – p. 397).

83. Following, probably, Prajñākaramati: yang na bden par mngon par 'dod pa'i bu nyid rmi lam du shi ba la 'di thams cad sbyar bar bya'o. See also Bu ston p. 574, who makes the general conclusion of this point very clear. '*Thus*, even when awake, all conventions of existence and non-existence are conceptually-constructed,': yang na bden par 'dod pa'i bu rmi lam du shi ba la sbyar ro // de bzhin du sad pa'i gnas skabs na'ang yod med kyi tha snyad thams cad btags pa yin no // They are apparently conceptual constructions because they are no different from dreams. See also gZhan phan Chos kyi snang ba p. 455: rmi lam gyi bu ni ma skyes pa dang ma 'gag pa'i phyir ro // de ltar na chos thams cad kyi skye ba dang 'gag pa rtogs pas rtog (instead of 'rtag') par blta bar bya'o //
84. Was in Hobbes who said somewhere that if a man says that God told him something in a dream, all that follows is that he dreamt that God told him something? And yet this indicates a particular attitude to dreams and their contents which is at variance with many other times and places.
85. Of course the Mādhyamika has a response to this. Madhyamaka is quite capable on a conventional level of making a distinction between dreams and 'reality' without seeing such distinctions as having any fundamental ontological significance. Moreover if the opponent takes such reasoning above as an argument for the inherent existence of something mentalistic, there are plenty of Mādhyamika arguments against the inherent existence of mental events of which conceptions are a sub-class. The Mādhyamika will argue that lacking inherent existence means not to be found under the type of analysis which would find *x* were it inherently existent, and it is up to the opponent to put forward a candidate for inherent existence which can be analysed. When he or she does so, it turns out – as in the case of mental events – not to be found (but cf. pain, referred to in the next paper, note 86). And we have already seen an argument that if the negandum is delusory the negation (i.e. in this case the mental event) must be delusory – what applies to the one applies to the other. But what of the mind (the opponent might object) which is doing the analysis, *whatever is being analysed*, a mind which is always presupposed in the act of analysis itself? There is moreover a problem (understood, I think by Tsong kha pa who stresses that when the Mādhyamika says that all things are a dream what is meant is that things are *like* a dream inasmuch as they appear one way but exist in another) in arguing that because something lacks inherent existence it is for that reason less than real, a dream. The general principle underlying the opponent's objection here is that the mental

event which is, for example, deluded must have a different ontological status from that about which it is deluded. This is a general principle which is, I think, behind Cittamātra ontology. I have touched on it in my paper 'An argument for cittamātra – reflections on *Bodhicaryāvatāra* 9:28 (Tib. 27) cd', reprinted above, and also in the next paper.

86. See, for example, *Vigrahavyāvartanī* verse 23 (example of illusory entities). Much of what is discussed in *BCA* 9:139–41 can be seen to have its predecessor in Nāgārjuna's reply in the *Vigrahavyāvartanī*, including also the discussion of the means of valid knowledge, and the response made clear by Prajñākaramati on *BCA* 9:140 that the opponent's objections in fact rest on the *truth* of emptiness rather than refuting it.

87. (p. 359) bden 'dzin gyi gnyen po byed pa'i phyir te des na dper na rmi lam du bu shi ba rmi ba la bu de med snyam pa'i rnam rtog ni bu de yod par rnam par rtog pa'i gegs yin la / med 'dzin de yang brdzun pa yin yang yod 'dzin de spong nus pa bzhin no // I have translated *'dzin pa* sometimes as 'apprehension' and sometimes 'grasping' depending on context. Note that Thogs med holds that it is the 'apprehension of non-existence' (*med 'dzin*) which is said to be delusory in the last line of the verse. This is ambiguous. It could mean – as in the case of our previous discussion of the conception of the son's death – that the *apprehension*, i.e. certain mental events, are delusory, not fully real. In which case this would be open to the same objections suggested about 'conception' earlier. Or it could mean the apprehension of *non-existence*, i.e. apprehending that the son is non-existent now, having been existent previously, is delusory (that is, a *dream*). On this interpretation Thogs med is right, and it is a superior interpretation to the alternative.

88. For Tsong kha pa, of course, when the means of valid cognition are said to be delusory this means that they lack inherent existence. On that basis Tsong kha pa is able to accept the means of valid cognition, and not just in the sense that they can only set-forth conventionalities (see, for example, mKhas grub rje and others in Cabezón, pp. 117–20 and notes 404 and 412). Thus the means of valid cognition can positively determine absence of inherent existence, emptiness. The result of all this is that Tsong kha pa neutralises the claim found in other Mahāyāna sources that the means of valid cognition are not means of valid cognition, since all this means is that they are not *inherently existing* means of valid cognition, which is not relevant to their being means of valid cognition at all (except inasmuch as lacking inherent existence means for Tsong kha pa that they occur as part of a casual flux which therefore enables them to actually *be* means of valid cognition). This understanding found in Tsong kha pa was not how bSod nams rtse mo saw it. Basically, Tsong kha pa answers the objection of Phywa pa Chos kyi seng ge (see next) against the Prāsaṅgika by claiming that it is no objection at all since this is not the Prāsaṅgika view. His opponents would see this granting of a status to the means of valid cognition as a Svātantrika element in Tsong kha pa's view, that is, in trying to construct a coherent system of Prāsaṅgika epistemology Tsong kha pa has capitulated to Svātantrika. But I have suggested earlier that

Prajñākaramati would probably have accepted the move, at least for conventional matters. Where Tsong kha pa is probably different is in granting that the means of valid cognition can even set-forth ultimates (emptinesses). In other words for all their faults they are capable of doing all that anyone could expect from them.

89. See Jackson (1985), pp. 22–3 and note 13.

90. de bzhin du stong zhes dgag bya khegs pa'i don spyi shar ba dang de phyi rol tu zhen pa'i stong pa yong gcod de brdzun yang dngos por (4) 'dzin pa'i sgro 'dogs skye ba'i go skabs bcom ste yod par 'dzin pa'i sgro 'dogs sel ba'i cha rnam dpyod tsam la tshad ma'i cha yod pa mi 'gal lo zhes bya ba ni dbu ma rang rgyud pas sbyor la / There is a very strong temptation to read *rnam dpyod tsam* as *rnam gcod tsam*, which is pronounced in exactly the same way. In that case bSod nams rtse mo would be following what he sees as a Svātantrika strategy in order to introduce a distinction between the means of valid cognition used in order to positively determine (*yongs gcod*) emptiness, and an acceptable use of the means of valid cognition in order to merely negate (*rnam gcod tsam*), thus dispelling the superimposition of grasping after reality. We have seen already that this distinction applied to *Prāsaṅgika* Madhyamaka is made by certain early Tibetan Mādhyamikas, and is criticised by Tsong kha pa. The issue of the status of Mādhyamika arguments if all the means of valid cognition are not means of valid cognition remains nevertheless. It is possible that as a result of bSod nams rtse mo's – or Phywa pa Chos kyi seng ge's – employment of a Svātantrika strategy originally seen as a criticism of Prāsaṅgika (based on Dharmakīrti's use of the terms *pariccheda* and *vyavaccheda* – Phywa pa Chos kyi seng ge was an important logician) this distinction was subsequently introduced into Tibetan Prāsaṅgika as Prāsaṅgika Madhyamaka became more well-known and eventually predominant in Tibetan thought (see note 49 above. On the distinction between Svātantrika and Prāsaṅgika Madhyamaka, which appears to have originated in Tibet, see my 1989a paper, pp. 1 ff. Note, incidentally, that it was common particularly pre-Tsong kha pa to refer to the tradition of Dharmakīrti as the *tshad ma'i lugs* – the system of those who follow (the means of) valid cognition (see for example Sa skya Paṇḍita in his *bKa' gdams do kor ba'i zhus lan*, quoted in Jackson, p. 32). Thus inasmuch as it was recognised that Madhyamaka is not the system of Dharmakīrti, so Madhyamaka is not 'the system of those who follow the means of valid cognition'. Inasmuch as it was recognised that Madhyamaka is required to follow means of valid cognition *in some sense*, it would have been natural to turn to Dharmakīrti for a structure which would make this possible). Thus bSod nams rtse mo would be claiming that means of valid cognition in Prāsaṅgika Madhyamaka *are* possible in that they involve mere negations which dispel the superimposition of truth-grasping or grasping after reality. Even if we do not read *rnam dpyod tsam* as *rnam gcod tsam*, still more or less the same point can be made in that bSod nams rtse mo is making a distinction between the means of valid cognition inasmuch as they are not means of valid cognition – presumably those which set-forth a positively determining empty, which

craves the generic referent as an external reality which puts a stop to the negandum – and the part which is acceptable as a means of valid cognition and is the part which dispels superimposition and is the case of mere critical examination (*rnam dpyod*). Structurally there is still some opposition being drawn between the means of valid cognition in a sense which is acceptable, and in a sense which is not. And there is an opposition between the *mere* means of valid cognition which dispels superimposition, and that which seeks to do more. This structural opposition is enough to suggest the *rnam gcod/yongs gcod* distinction. Note also in the quotation, incidentally, the idea of the arising of the generic referent which is so important for Tsong kha pa, although here related to emptiness and not at all related to the need to produce the generic referent of the negandum in order to know it fully so that negation can take place.

91. de la brdzun pa yin zhes bya ste rnal 'byor gyi kun rdzob tsam yin la des kyang log rtog gzhan gyi gegs byed do zhes bya ba'o //
92. See Williams (1980a), p. 328. For the specific idea of the perception of the conventional by the *yogin* bSod nams rtse mo is probably thinking of *BCA* 9:3–5, especially verse 5 (things are seen 'like illusions' (*māyāvad*)). For the notion of 'mere conventional' he is clearly thinking of the principal Prāsaṅgika source for this interpretation, Candrakīrti's *Madhyamakāvatāra* and *Bhāṣya* on 6:28.
93. Mi pham, p. 86: 'o na dngos po kun med ces bsgoms pas ci bya ste / dngos yod dang dngos med gnyis ka rdzun par mgo mnyam zhing gnyis ka yang dag pa min pa'i phyir zhe na
94. re zhig thog med nas goms pa'i dngos zhen gyis srid par 'ching bar byed pa de'i gnyen por dngos po rang bzhin med par goms pa tsam ste / dngos dngos med gnyis char rdzun pa
95. des na shing gnyis zung du sbar ba'i (amended from *bdar ba'i*, which makes little sense) mes shing gnyis ka bsregs pa bzhin du dngos kun bden med du rnam par dpyad pa'i shes rab kyi mes dngos dngos med du bzhag pa'i dmigs pa'i gtad so thams cad kyi nags 'thib po ma lus pa bsregs nas spros pa thams cad zhi ba'i ye shes la gnas pa'i tshe na khas len thams cad dang bral ba'i dBu ma chen po yin no // (p. 87).
96. astīti śāśvatagrāho nāstīty ucchedadarśanam / tasmād astitvanāstitve nāśrīyeta vicakṣaṇaḥ // (Tibetan) yod ces bya ba rtag par 'dzin / med ces bya ba chad par lta / de phyir yod dang med pa la / mkhas pas gnas par mi bya'o // The Tibetan *gnas par mi bya'o* carries with it the sense of 'should not abide', which is useful to Mi pham as he wants to speak of the wise abiding *instead* in gnosis (*ye shes la gnas pa'i tshe na*). The Sanskrit *nāśrīyeta* carries more an implication of 'should not rely on' (a cognate is the word *āśraya*, support).
97. No doubt it is the same as Shākya mchog ldan was talking about with his 'experiential Madhyamaka, based on nonconceptual meditation' referred to above, and also his reference to that type of Madhyamaka which is based on the doctrine of emptiness found in the Kālacakra and rDo rje gur (Cabezón p. 415).
98. Which is not at all the same, of course, as saying that they are not means of valid cognition concerning the ultimate, as some previous Tibetan

scholars seem to have thought. As we saw earlier, this interpretation by Tsong kha pa appears to be contained implicitly in Prajñākaramati's comments on *BCA* 9:139, but Tsong kha pa is possibly more radical in explicitly holding that the means of valid cognition can set-forth ultimates (emptinesses) as well as conventionalities. See Cabezón, especially pp. 117 ff, and 371 ff, together with associated notes.

Five: The Absence of Self and the Removal of Pain

1. One is tempted to speculate that a being who is perfectly objective would have to see things from every position, and not itself occupy any place. The Buddha-eye is the eye which is everywhere and nowhere. Would this not be omniscience? And a being who is perfectly objective would presumably also be perfectly just and – at least for our Buddhist – be perfectly good as well.
2. I have chosen in this context to translate *mṛṣā* – more usually 'delusory' or 'false/falsity' – by 'fiction(s)' specifically because it recalls the case well-known in philosophical writing, and as we shall see very appropriate to the present context, of Hume's treatment of personal identity – since persons clearly change and are therefore not identical – as a fiction superimposed upon a succession of like impressions: 'Our chief business, then, must be to prove, that all objects, to which we ascribe identity, without observing their invariableness and uninterruptedness, are such as consist of a succession of related objects' (Hume 1969, p. 303), 'The identity, which we ascribe to the mind of man, is only a fictitious one' (p. 306), 'Since our attributions of identity result only from the easy transition of the mind from one perception to another, and since resemblance and causation are the only relations that in this case can facilitate such a transition, it follows that resemblance and causation alone must be enough to produce in us the "fiction" or "mistake" of a continuously existing self or mind' (Stroud 1977, p. 122).
3. I have translated *duḥkha* by 'pain', and throughout this essay I mean by 'pain' what we normally refer to as *physical* pain, the sort of sensation which occurs when we are flayed alive or step with bare feet on a drawing-pin. Putting scepticism about other minds to one side, I take it we all know what that sensation is. I am perfectly aware, however, that 'pain' is inadequate in general as a translation of the Buddhist technical term *duḥkha*. There are various types of *duḥkha*, of which pain (*duḥkhaduḥkha*) is only one. Pure sensations of pain form a class of mental events which are a subclass of events occurring under *duḥkha*. Thus my translation of *duḥkha* in the verses as 'pain', and my stressing that I intend here the physical sensation of pain, mean that my translation is not intended *in general,* or in isolation, as a precise translation of these verses. The translation is contextualised within the following discussion. I shall argue that the reasoning of Śāntideva and his commentators – for all its praiseworthy and noble motives – is incoherent in that granted Śāntideva's premisses he can no longer make

sense of the physical sensation of pain at all, and therefore the removal of pain. Thus since pain-events form a subclass of events occurring under *duḥkha* properly understood, if Śāntideva's account is incoherent for the subclass then it becomes incoherent for the class taken as a whole. In other words, if by his reasoning Śāntideva cannot make sense of physical pain and its removal, he will be unable to make sense of *duḥkha* and its removal even though *duḥkha* is for the Buddhist more than just physical sensations of pain.

4. In their appeal to rationality Śāntideva and his commentators invite us to engage with them in the reasoning. If their argument *is* rationally compelling then we have to become universal altruists if we are to claim rational consistency. If we do not even aspire to become universal altruists and yet still wish to claim rational consistency then we have to show flaws in the argument. Even if we like the idea of becoming universal altruists but need to base it on good reasons, then we must engage with the reasoning and with the [grounds for] truth of Śāntideva's argument and conclusion. To respect Śāntideva's argument but not to engage with it intellectually, to 'meditate' on it but not seriously to question its truth, i.e. simply to worship it, is not only to fail to take Śāntideva and his arguments seriously – surely the lowest form of respect, an insult – but also to fail to open oneself to the *possible* transformative effects of his argument, the meditation.
5. *M.A.* 6:23–5: dngos kun yang dag brdzun pa mthong ba yis / dngos rnyed ngo bo gnyis ni 'dzin par 'gyur / yang dag mthong yul de de nyid de / mthong ba brdzun pa kun rdzob bden par gsungs // mthong ba brdzun pa'ang rnam par gnyis 'dod de / dbang po gsal dang dbang po skyon ldan no / skyon ldan dbang can rnams kyi shes pa ni / dbang po legs gyur shes ltos log par 'dod // gnod pa med pa'i dbang po drug rnams kyis / gzung ba gang zhig 'jig rten gyis rtogs te / 'jig rten gnyis las bden yin lhag ma ni / 'jig rten nyid las log par rnam par gzhag //
6. This is the standard dGe lugs Madhyamaka approach to conventionalities. I am not sure even given Madhyamaka thought that it is very coherent. For example, to be capable of entering into everyday pragmatic usage *is* to exist in every sense of existing whereby existing can be distinguished from i.e. being an hallucination. It is common in Madhyamaka to speak of conventionalities as being such since they 'are not found under [ultimate] analysis', taken as a form of analysis which probes with the plenum of philosophical rigour whether or not the object of the analysis really exists or not. But while to be capable of entering into transactional usage might not be existence according to some rather restricted senses of 'existence', it is still to exist. Thus if something 'merely' enters into transactional usage, i.e. it can be used and that use *works,* it seems to me this *is* to be found under analysis (it could not be used and work if it did not even *exist*).
7. In talking about 'dGe lugs Madhyamaka' in this way, of course, I generalise. It should not be taken that I think there is one universal complete system of Madhyamaka held in common by all dGe lugs thinkers from Tsong kha pa to the present day. But one can nevertheless speak perfectly precisely of 'dGe lugs Madhyamaka' just as one can

speak of 'Roman Catholic thought' without holding that all Roman Catholics have a system which is in all respects identical.

8. For a detailed study of the different levels of the Self which are uncovered and then refuted in mature dGe lugs thought see Wilson 1980. The Self as a 'permanent, partless and independent phenomenon' is merely the coarsest level of negandum.
9. 'Person' is often used in philosophical circles in a way which would distinguish a person from merely being an animal or, for the Buddhist perhaps, a sentient being. Thus while there are some philosophers who would accept that there are animals (such as some chimpanzees, possibly) who could turn out to be persons on some acceptable definition of 'person', still generally to be a person is a very particular and fairly advanced state of being which could certainly not be identified simply with being self-conscious inasmuch as one has a rudimentary and often innate and preverbal sense of one's own identity. A person is, perhaps, with Locke 'a thinking intelligent Being that has reason and reflection and can consider itself as itself, the same thinking thing in different times and places' (Locke 1977, p. 162; see also Ayers 1991, pp. 254 ff., esp. pp. 290–2; cf. Campbell 1994, p. 178, where persons require first-person thinking, 'autobiographical thought'; and cf. also Shoemaker in Kim and Sosa, ed. 1995, pp. 380–1). To all intents and purposes persons here are a particular class of human beings and higher beings – such as for theists God. (Not all humans even under this definition would be persons. Consider the case of a severely brain-damaged human being. Note in passing that in everyday English and life, however, we feel a certain unease to say the least about denying that a brain-damaged or perhaps a comatose individual is a *person*. We consider that personhood has implications for moral duties and rights which should not be denied to any *human*). For the moment then we should note that the translation of *gang zag* by 'person' follows standard practice among Tibetologists and gains its significance structurally as meaning the identity that sentient beings have given that there are no Selves in the technical sense that they are denied by Buddhists. Note however that there is nevertheless good philosophical precedence for this broader use of 'person'. In his influential discussion of the person in *Individuals* Ch. 3, P.F. Strawson speaks of the concept of a person as 'the concept of a type of entity such that *both* predicates ascribing states of consciousness *and* predicates ascribing corporeal characteristics, a physical situation etc. are equally applicable to a single individual of that single type' (1959, p. 102; italics original). Strawson's point is that the person is a sort of irreducible thing (it has, for Strawson, a logical primitiveness that is presupposed by both mental and physical predicates and cannot simply be reduced to either; cf. Lowe 1989, p. 116) about which both mental and physical ascriptions can be made, and it is the *very same thing* which is the subject of these mental and physical ascriptions (see p. 89; italics Strawson. See also Wiggins 1987). It seems to me that this characterisation of the person will apply to any being which is sentient and has a physical body. That will suit our purposes very well. Moreover the person is the *subject* of such mental and physical ascriptions. In

particular, for Strawson states of consciousness must be ascribed to something, and that thing is the person – the very same person to which physical ascriptions are made. This incorporates excellently the subjectivity of mental events which I shall discuss subsequently. Thus it seems to me there is no problem in speaking of the dGe lugs conventional self as the 'person', a *subject* of mental and physical ascriptions. Hamlyn 1984, p. 199 in fact notes that this applicability of 'person' to animals has been seen by some as a criticism of Strawson's usage, for it does not correspond with our normal usage in English. Hamlyn seems to prefer the term 'self' to 'person' here, and providing we are careful to distinguish the self in this sense from the isolated, independent monadic Self of a Cartesian or quasi-Cartesian sort there should be no problem with the term 'self' (but cf. Harré 1987, pp. 99–100, who works with a rather more restricted notion of 'self' and seems to be prepared to grant that chimpanzees can be rudimentary persons but not rudimentary selves). I shall make the relevant distinction, which corresponds to that between the dGe lugs 'Self' and the 'conventional self' by using upper case for the former and lower case for the latter (of course, Sanskrit and Tibetan do not have upper and lower cases). Thus I shall speak of 'person' and 'self' in ways which are to all intents and purposes interchangeable. I shall use 'subject' mainly for the subject of mental ascriptions, although that too overlaps with 'person' and 'self'. All this is to be distinguished from the Cartesian (or perhaps Sāṃkhya) Self. Incidentally, it is sometimes felt to be paradoxical (in Buddhist meditations on the selflessness of persons, for example) that the same word 'I' sometimes appears to refer to the body and sometimes to the mind. Strawson would say that the word 'I' refers to the person ('this person here'), and it is precisely the peculiar and irreducible nature of a person that mental and physical ascriptions can be used of the very same thing. So, 'I am hungry', 'I am happy', 'I am six feet tall' all refer to this person here, and this very same person here can sometimes be the subject of mental ascriptions ('happy', and possibly 'hungry'), and sometimes physical ascriptions (possibly 'hungry', and 'six feet tall'). That is just how it is with persons – they are unusual in that respect! The Buddhist's need to pin down *one* referent, or *one type* of referent, and drawing earth-shattering significance from failing to do so, is just the result of failing to understand the nature of persons, what sort of thing is sufficient to answer the question posed at time T: 'What is the referent of "I"'. Incidentally again, the fact that mental and physical ascriptions are made of the same thing, and require the concept of the logically primitive concept of the person in order to do so, suggests the impossibility of explaining the unity of the person on the basis of any Humean or indeed Buddhist 'bundle theory' of psycho-physical attributes linked simply by causal or other relationships. See later. With Strawson's persons as unique subjects of mental and physical ascriptions compare E.J. Lowe's extremely helpful 1991 paper, which would see the person as a 'psychological substance': 'a person is a substantial individual belonging to a natural kind which is the subject of distinctively psychological laws, and governed by persistence conditions which are likewise distinctively psychological in character' (p. 105). But while this is compatible with Descartes' Self, Lowe does not in fact think they are the same, since Lowe's person is not essentially immaterial. Rather, 'persons are a wholly distinctive kind of being fully integrated into the natural world' (p. 107). It seems to me this is not so far from Strawson's position, and it is also compatible with animals and other sentient beings as (sub-classes of) persons, and it is thus suitable for our purposes. On persons as 'natural kinds' – a position I am sympathetic to and indeed influenced on this by Locke through Wiggins and Lowe – see subsequently. On Strawson's and Lowe's approach, it would not even be correct to think of persons as some sort of whole, constituted by their parts, or 'person-stages'. I shall discuss the person as a whole subsequently. At the moment, I would incline towards the Strawsonian position here too. For a discussion of the possibility of non-human persons see Wiggins 1980, pp. 173 ff., and 1987: 'an alien intelligence is not a person. A person is a creature with whom we can get onto terms . . .' (para. 16). Maybe, but not *necessarily*, in the broader sense in which I am using 'person' here.

10. Clearly, if there were no differences at all between them then by the identity of indiscernibles there would not be Archibald and Freda but just one, Fredabald.
11. Cf. here dPa' bo gTsug lag phreng ba p. 590: 'Since there does not exist any self (Self) anywhere even conventionally, that very grasping after self and possessions is irrational, and it is necessary to abandon it' (bdag ni kun rdzob nyid tu'ang gang na'ang yod pa min pas bdag dang bdag gir 'dzin pa de nyid mi rigs te spang dgos so) But it simply does not follow from the absence of any Self even conventionally that it is irrational to grasp after self and possessions, if by 'self' here we mean a concern with myself, this person. It might be *immoral*, but not irrational. Many, perhaps most, contemporary philosophers and scientists would vigorously deny accepting a Cartesian or quasi-Cartesian Self, and prefer to accept what a Mādhyamika would be quite happy to call a 'conventional self' as a socio-cultural or perhaps a biological construct. The fact that nevertheless they might often be quite selfish may be lamentable, but it is not a logical contradiction. To think that it is, or might be, rests on an equivocation which also occurs in Sanskrit between 'self' as in a metaphysical Self and 'self' as it occurs reflexively in words like 'oneself', 'myself' etc. This is simply a confusion. On the other hand if we take dPa' bo's comment to involve a denial even conventionally of any sense of oneself, a conventional person, then while this does indeed seem to be what Śāntideva has in mind, as we shall see it will lead to some extremely unwelcome implications.
12. This will leave us with two incomplete statements 'is in pain'. Of course they are indeed identical, as Śāntideva wants. They are also as they stand incoherent, or rather, lacking in full meaning since they are predicates which require to be completed by subjects. But the moment the subjects are brought in we are back with difference and a perfectly acceptable basis for selfishness. I shall return to this point later, drawing on adverbial theory to argue that pains are indeed not things

but, if you like, predicates requiring subjects and quite incoherent without them.

13. Does this indicate a difference between Śāntideva and Candrakīrti on the meaning and/or range of *mṛṣā*?
14. It is unusual in philosophy for a thinker to teach seriously and literally that he or she simply does not exist. Hume, in his famous treatment of personal identity, professed himself unable to find an *impression* of the selfsame self throughout his experiences yet independent of them, yet he would not have considered that he was literally contradicting himself when he said 'The identity which *I* ascribe to myself is only a fictitious one' (in Stroud 1977, p. 130; italics Stroud). Derek Parfit, in an approach which is often held to be somewhat similar to that of the Buddhist, has said controversially that '[w]e could therefore redescribe any person's life in impersonal terms. . . Persons need not be claimed to be the thinkers of any of these thoughts' (quoted by Grant Gillett in Peacocke and Gillett 1987, p. 76), yet as Shoemaker points out in his review of Parfit's *Reasons and Persons*, Parfit seems to be unclear whether he is saying quite literally that there are no subjects at all for mental events (Shoemaker 1985, p. 446). It is one thing to deny personal identity over time, or even to suggest that first-person statements can be translated adequately into those involving solely third-person expressions, and another literally to deny subjects for mental events, and it is not clear whether this is what Parfit wants to do. If so, then as I shall argue subsequently, there would be very serious problems for such an approach with reference to pain which, I shall urge, is intrinsically subject-involving. Thus if Parfit's position is literally that of no subject then in the case of pain he is quite wrong. But perhaps Parfit's view is closer to one described as 'arguably Parfitian' by Galen Strawson (and which seems to owe something to a remark by Kant in a footnote at *Critique of Pure Reason* A363–4): 'If we consider things at the purely experiential or purely mental level of description, it is not clear that we can identify anything that persists over long stretches of time as a single experiencer, whether in the case of cats or bats or human beings. It must, of course, be granted that "an experience is impossible without an experiencer." But maybe the best thing to say, when considering a succession of experiences that we naturally think of as the experiences of a single being at the purely experiential or purely mental level of description, is that each involves a different experiencer. This may be best, although we can certainly also say that they all involve a single experiencer insofar as we are considering them as the experiences of a single persisting physical thing, like a human being.' (1994, p. 133) Be that as it may I am by no means sure that the idea of a series of 'I's is coherent at all. If I were told that the very next second I would cease to exist, to be replaced by another I, but I shall notice no difference, I might protest (i) that not noticing any difference is scarcely very consoling, since *I* want to remain (the present I) and I will not, and the one who will not notice any difference will not be me; (ii) but who exactly is it who is not supposed to notice any difference?; and (iii) anyway it would certainly make one difference in that all memory claims would have to

become false (the suggestion that all my memory claims are false would require some sort of evidence, to say the least), and it would be pointless for me to plan for *my* future (see Chisholm 1976, pp. 104–5) – including becoming enlightened, helping all sentient beings etc.; and (iv) as Locke would point out, it would become unjust and mistaken to punish one I for the crimes committed by another I (this would be a very serious problem for the Buddhist approach to karma and its fruits). And so on and so on. Be that as it may, as Strawson makes very clear, the suggestion of a series of selves concerns what I have called the 'status' of the self and not the existence of a referable subject. It is indeed quite incompatible with a literal no-subject view of experiences.

15. Cf. Bu ston with Kalyāṇadeva f. 61a, who refers to the collective as the 'collection, such as the aggregate composed of the hands etc.' (*tshogs ni 'dus pa ste / lag pa la sogs pa'i phung po lta bu'o*). But compare also Mi pham's pupil Kun bzang dpal ldan (p. 470), who refers to the illustration of the collective with an army as conceptually superimposed upon a 'collection of many men who have taken up arms' (*tshogs pa yang mtshon cha thogs pa'i mi mang po 'dus pa la dmag ces btags*), an illustration which portrays the collective not just as an aggregate but as an *ordered functional, purposive* aggregate. Glossing the verse with reference to the continuant as the mind and the collective as the physical body is found already in Prajñākaramati's commentary: *paṅktivat saṃtānaḥ, senādivat samudāyaḥ* / The linking of the *ādi* with the *samudāya* appears to be merely for syntactical reasons, since the illustration of *ādi* with a garland (or rosary) and a forest would suggest here too a correlation with continuant and collective respectively.
16. This echoes almost word for word the earlier phrasing of Thogs med dpal bzang po: *rang gi tshe snga phyi rgyud gcig la rkang lag sogs tshogs pa gcig pa* (p. 288). Interestingly, rGyal tshab rje, while speaking of one collective as consisting of a *single person's* feet and hands [etc.; see Thub bstan chos kyi grags pa p. 532], continues by referring to old age and youth, as well as former and later temporal stages (of the mind?) as one continuant. In other words for rGyal tshab rje the continuant appears to be any temporal series of the person (*gang zag*) ordered in the sequence before::after: *gang zag gcig gi rkang lag tshogs pa gcig cing / rgan gzhon dang tshe snga phyi rgyud gcig yin pas:* p. 183. dPa' bo gTsug lag phreng ba also implies that he takes the continuant as the mental continuant. His opponent speaks of a [conventional] Self – in fact the person – which is the 'mere collective of the body and the continuum' (*lus kyi tshogs pa dang rgyun tsam bdag yin no snyam na:* p. 590). Kun bzang dpal ldan also implies as much, taking the continuant as a before::after temporal series, and contrasting it with the collective of feet and hands [etc.], stressing the unification involved in the notion of 'continuant' and 'collective' even though the events which make them up are multiple: *de ltar tshe snga phyi sogs gcig min kyang de dag rgyun gcig yin pa dang / rkang lag de dag tha dad yin kyang tshogs pa gcig yin pas:* p. 470.
17. See also here *Manusmṛti* 3:167 ff., where the concept of the 'rows' refers particularly to the lineage of Vedic transmission and recitation. As Vedic

lineage the *paṅkti* can also embrace of course a temporal as well as a spatial continuant.

18. Compare here Kalyāṇadeva's glossing of *ādi* by 'the flow of a river etc.' (*chu'i rgyun la sogs pa*). The use of a *mālā/phreng ba* is also found in Vibhūticandra's commentary (f. 250a) which follows that of Prajñākaramati so closely as to count *in the main* as a summary of Prajñākaramati.
19. In fact Bu ston chooses to split the application of the 'such as', giving (with Kalyāṇadeva) the example of the flow of a river for the *ādi* taken with the example of a continuant, and referring to a forest which is an aggregation of a plurality of trees for the *ādi* applied to the collective.
20. Among our commentators Kun bzang dpal ldan (p. 470) appears clearly to have taken the reference in the verse to a *phreng ba* as a reference to a rosary, since he speaks of 'conceptually superimposing one continuant which is a *phreng ba* upon a plurality of beads' (*phreng ba rdog du ma la phreng ba'i rgyud gcig ces btags pa bzhin*). The same interpretation can be found in his near contemporary Thub bstan chos kyi grags pa (p. 532). Perhaps it was current in the 19th and early 20th century *ris med* ('nonpartiality') circles in which they both moved.
21. *saṃtāno* nāma na kaścid ekaḥ paramārthasan saṃbhavati / kiṃ tarhikāryakāraṇabhāvapravṛttakṣaṇaparaṃparāpravāharūpa evāyam, tato vyatiriktasyānupalambhāt / tasmād eteṣām eva kṣaṇānām ekapadena pratipādanāya saṃketo kṛto buddhair vyavahārārthaṃ saṃtāna iti / iti prajñaptisann eva ayam / tena atrābhiniveśo na kāryaḥ / . . . / evaṃ *samudāyo*'pi na samudāyibhyo vastusan eko vidyate, tasya tebhyaḥ pṛthag anupalabdheḥ. tattvānyatvavikalpas tu asya avayavivicāreṇaiva gata iti neha pratāyate / tataś ca ayam api saṃvṛtisann eva pūrvavat / [= Tib Cone mDo 26 f. 166b] rgyud ces pa 'ga' zhig don dam par srid pa ma yin te / 'o na kyang rgyu dang 'bras bu'i dngos po 'jug pa skad cig brgyud pa'i rgyun gyi rang bzhin nyid 'di yin te / de la tha dad pa de ma dmigs pa'i phyir ro // de'i skad cig ma 'di rnams tshig gcig gis blo'i tha snyad bya ba'i don du rgyud ces brdar byas pa yin te / de ltar na 'di ni brtags par yod pa nyid yin la / des na 'dir mngon par zhen pa spong par bya ste / de bzhin du tshogs pa can la sogs pa'i dngos po gcig pur gyur pa yod pa ni ma yin te / de rnams las de tha dad par ma dmigs pa'i phyir la / de nyid rang gzhan du brtags pa'i cha shas kyi rnam par dpyad pas mi gnas pa'i phyir 'dir brjod par mi bya ste / de'i phyir 'di yang sngar bzhin du kun rdzob du yod pa nyid do //
22. For another nice example of the way in which Śāntideva's commentators here slide between the denial of a Self as a truly existing and independent referent for the indexical 'I' and the denial of a conventional self, or person, which will demarcate the difference between psycho-physical individuals see Sa bzang mati paṇchen p. 277: 'They are fictions. This is because that which does not exist established truly as one, is not a primary existent (*rdzas=dravya*). Thus the solitary self which is the experiencer of pain does not truly exist. Therefore by whom, as experiencer for this pain which is to be experienced, will there be the owner – there will not be anyone as owner' (*brdzun* pa yin gyi gcig tu bden par grub pa med de rdzas du ma yin pa'i phyir ro // de ltar *sdug*

bsngal myong ba *can* gyi bdag gcig pu *gang* yin pa *de* bden par *med pa des* na myong bya'i sdug bsngal *'di* myong ba po *su zhig* gis *dbang* du byed *par 'gyur* te su yang dbang bar mi 'gyur ro // Material in italics is from the verse). The answer to Sa bzang is, of course, that whether or not there is a 'solitary self', the experiencer of pain – the owner – is the person Archibald, or Freda, and when Archibald experiences pain this is not the same as when Freda experiences pain. I know for a fact that when *I* experience pain, it is not the same as when *you* experience pain. Having said that, it is indeed strange to speak of me as the *owner* of my pains. Many more examples of this slide from ultimate Self to conventional self and back again can be found among Śāntideva's commentators on these verses. A particularly interesting and I would imagine rather embarrassed example, given the dGe lugs care to distinguish between the conventional person which is not denied, and the Self which is, can be found in rGyal tshab rje's commentary (p. 183): 'Therefore the self, which is the person (*gang zag*) of whom there is pain, does not exist. By that independent person (*gang zag rang dbang ba*), who will there be the ownership of this pleasure and unhappiness?' (*sdug bsngal can* gyi gang zag gi bdag *gang* yin pa *de med pa*'i phyir / gang zag rang dbang ba *des* bde sdug *'di su zhig dbang bar 'gyur*). Either there is a person who experiences pain or there is not! All this is particularly unfortunate, since as we have seen, and shall see again, Śāntideva's denial as one of the conventional person is *crucial* to his argument. One suggestion is that Śāntideva's commentators simply did not understand what he was saying. They were not actually thinking; they were not actually engaging in the meditation. Another suggestion is that they understood what Śāntideva was saying only too well, but also its unwelcome implications.

23. But compare here the Hellenistic sceptic Sextus Empiricus: 'if a whole exists it is either distinct from its parts or its parts of it *are* the whole. The whole does not appear to be distinct from its parts, since when the parts are removed nothing remains which would allow us to reckon the whole as something distinct from them. But if the parts themselves are the whole, the whole will be merely a name and an empty designation, and will not have an individual existence . . . Therefore there is no whole' (*Outlines of Pyrrhonism* 3:98–9; trans. Hankinson 1995, p. 249).
24. Notably in Williams 1981, pp. 237 ff., although this distinction, the importance of which to Buddhist thought has, I believe, been much underrated, is central also to my historical discussions elsewhere, such as the 'Argument for Cittamātra' paper above, Williams 1996, p. 12–15, and Williams forthcoming.
25. Translation slightly modified from Williams 1981, pp. 237–8. The text used there was from the *Collected Works* 498–9: bcom pa'am blos cha shas so sor bsal ba na rang 'dzin gyi blo 'dor rung ba'i chos su dmigs pa de / kun rdzob bden pa'i mtshan nyid / mtshan gzhi ni / rdza bum tho bas bcom pa na rdza bum du 'dzin ba'i blo 'dor ba'i phyir dang / phreng ba'i rdog po so sor bsal ba na phreng bar 'dzin ba'i blo 'dor ba'i phyir / bcom pa'am blos cha shas so sor bsal ba na rang 'dzin gyi blo 'dor du mi rung

ba'i chos su dmigs pa de / don dam bden pa'i mtshan nyid / mtshan gzhi ni / rdul phran phyogs kyi cha med dang / shes pa skad cig cha med dang / 'dus ma byas kyi nam mkha' lta bu yin te / . . . des na kun rdzob bden pa rnams don dam du ma grub kyang bden grub tu 'dod de / lugs 'dis dngos po la bden grub kyis khyab pa khas len pa'i phyir / In the original paper I point out that this explanation can be traced back to *Abhidharmakośa* 6:4: yatra bhinnena tad buddhir anyāpohe dhiyā ca tat / ghaṭāmbuvat saṃvṛtisat, paramārthasad anyathā //

26. Things are rather different, however, for Madhyamaka. In Madhyamaka *all* phenomena without exception – all *dharmas*, all things – are said to have only *saṃvṛtisat/prajñaptisat*. While it is accepted that a provisional distinction can indeed be made between composites and the simples which make them up, still, inasmuch as composites for the Abhidharma lack their 'own unique and distinct identity' (i.e. they are *niḥsvabhāva*), it is thought that all things inasmuch as they are one way or another for Madhyamaka the results of causal conditioning must therefore also lack their own unique and distinct identity and be *niḥsvabhāva*. Nothing has the plenum of existence, all are simply conventionalities, conceptual existents. Clearly a switch has occurred here in the meaning of *svabhāva*. In the Vaibhāṣika Abhidharma to have a *svabhāva* was not to be causally independent but rather to be a fundamental, an irreducible analytical simple, which can serve as a constituent of those composites which inasmuch as they do not have that sort of existence in themselves are *niḥsvabhāva*. If something has a *svabhāva* it is free of a particular type of causation, causation through composition out of parts, not free of all causation altogether. Most Abhidharma fundamental existents (primary existents; *dravyasat*) are nevertheless the results of causal conditioning and are radically impermanent, succeeding one another as stages of a psycho-physical stream. Thus the well-known Madhyamaka equivalence of *niḥsvabhāvatā* with dependent origination would be unacceptable in Vaibhāṣika. And this is for good reasons. It is clearly incoherent to speak of all things as having merely *prajñaptisat*, all things as conceptual existents. The very meaning of '*prajñaptisat*' depends on its opposition to '*dravyasat*', and in order to have things which are constructs it is necessary to have those factors out of which they are constructed. Thus a follower of Vaibhāṣika can plausibly argue that if the Mādhyamika says that everything without exception is *prajñaptisat*, i.e. a construction, this must mean that nothing whatsoever exists since it is not possible for *all* things to be constructions. There would then be nothing left for them to be constructed out of. While for Vaibhāṣika composite entities – rosaries, and persons – can be said to *exist as composites*, this cannot be the case for Madhyamaka. Śāntideva is thus actually right to maintain *on Madhyamaka grounds* that composites are fictions in the sense that they simply do not exist. He is right, consistent, but it is nevertheless absurd.

27. See here Hopkins 1983, pp. 626 ff. for example. Cf Thub bstan chos kyi grags pa p. 532 for a clear statement of the person as a fiction on this basis: 'for there does not exist truly established as unitary the continuant and collective apart from their bases of imputation' (gdags gzhi de dag

las gzhan pa'i rgyud dang tshogs pa gcig tu bden par grub pa med pas so).

28. Of course, I suppose other people might exist also as single indivisible mental events of reification (but not as series, since series are themselves wholes and therefore come into existence in dependence upon minds). I find all this completely unbelievable, and I am not even sure it is conceptually coherent. I suppose that alternatively, perhaps, our Buddhist does not want to talk about 'my' mind at all, but just 'mind-in-general' as the reifying agent. Given the Buddhist antipathy to wholes/universals however I find this rather implausible.
29. Also see here the recent and very useful discussion in Searle 1995, Chs. 7–9 (on 'Does the Real World Exist?' and 'Truth and Correspondence'): 'Now, in order that we should understand these utterances [such as "My dog has fleas"] as having these truth conditions – the existence of these phenomena and the possession of these features – we have to take for granted that there is a way that the world is that is independent of our representations. But that requirement is precisely the requirement of external realism. And the consequences of this point for the present discussion is that efforts to communicate in a public language require that we presuppose a public world. And the sense of "public" in question requires that the public reality exists independently of our *representations* of that reality' (italics original).
30. Of course, I am perfectly aware of the Buddhist argument that there is no first beginning, and the only real origin is primordial ignorance (*avidyā*). But I am not asking for a chronological first beginning. I just want some sort of explanation of the conceptualising process which will help to make plausible what seems to me implausible but is often taken in Buddhist circles as axiomatic, the dependence of the very existence of mountains *simply because they are composites* on the occurrence of certain types of mental processes. I am not sure how *avidyā* is going to help here either, since *avidyā* is merely a repetition of the fact that misunderstanding, misperception, occurs. What I am interested in is the coherence of certain explanations of the process of misunderstanding.
31. A good way to illustrate this is with the old Heracleitian example of the river. It only makes sense to refer to river-stages, actual 'pieces' of water, because we have rivers. We cannot isolate our piece of water without eventually involving the river. But we can certainly refer to a river without referring to any particular piece of water.
32. See Peter Simons in Kim and Sosa, ed. 1995, p. 33: 'Artefacts are continuants, that is, objects persisting in time. . . The identity conditions of artefacts are however vaguer and more convention-bound than those of natural objects . . .' In choosing examples of artefacts in order to illustrate persons not only are Śāntideva and his commentators wrong, they might also be accused of begging the question or at least creating a rhetorical slant. Of course *if* a self/person were the same sort of phenomenon as a caste-row then it could plausibly be claimed that it is merely a conceptual construct existing in dependence upon conventional processes for simply culture-bound pragmatic purposes. But a person patently is *not* that sort of thing. Cf. also the case of the forest. It is

arguable that all the trees in a forest could be uprooted, one could wait a year, and replant the trees. When the trees have grown to a suitable height people would still refer to it as the same forest as the one which was cut down ('Sowdley Wood has recovered from that devastating felling ten years ago!'), in spite of the fact that not one tree is the same and there was actually an intervening year when there were no trees at all. And there would be nothing *wrong* in that. As Wittgenstein would say, language is completely in its place. This is to do with the criteria we employ for identity of forests. But there is nothing analogous in the case of persons. Since this is precisely an issue of identity – what it is to be the same person – our Buddhist is quite wrong to homologise the person to examples like the caste-row, the rosary, or a forest.

33. Cf. van Inwagen 1990, p. 87, 'Lives . . . are self-maintaining events. But not just any self-maintaining event is a life.' See also Locke's *Essay Concerning Human Understanding* 2:27:4 where Locke distinguishes between an oak tree and a 'mass of matter' precisely inasmuch as 'the one is only the cohesion of parts of matter any how united; the other such a disposition of them as constitutes the parts of an oak, and such an organisation of those parts as is fit to receive and distribute nourishment, so as to continue and frame the wood, bark, and leaves, etc., of an oak in which consists the vegetable life.' For Locke this means that it is not necessary to the identity of the oak that it remains numerically the same 'parcel of matter' (the same set of material parts, for example), as it would be if the oak were simply a mass of matter. The oak can change – it can grow – and still remain the same oak so long as it is the same kind of *living thing*. What it is to be the same living thing may vary. See also 2:27:8 on the animal as 'a living organised body'. The same can also be related to the person. For discussion see Lowe 1989, pp. 101 ff.
34. For the mind, see Campbell 1994, p. 167: '[T]here is a certain unity in all of one's judgements about what are in fact one's own mental states, judgements made otherwise than on the basis of observation. They must all be relativized to just the same thing. But this unity is secured by the fact that these judgements are, as we might say, implicitly in the first person. These judgements unite all the psychological states that one ascribes in this way as the states of a single person.' On the 'holism of the mental', the way in which mental events are all linked not (*pace* Hume and the Buddhists) simply causally but to the 'mental life of a single *person*' (italics original) see Lowe 1989, p. 117.
35. Remembering that for Śāntideva the spatial separation of the collective also means that a collective is unreal and the spatially disparate parts have no unity but fragment into separateness, I wonder how he would respond to the fact that it has been shown that what is learnt by one tentacle of an octopus can be performed by the others – but not when a particular part of the brain is removed. Clearly under normal undamaged circumstances the memory related to the one tentacle is instinctively *generalised* and applied to the whole organism as a single living creature with many tentacles. See the article 'Memory' in Gregory, ed. 1987, p. 456.

36. Robots could be programmed to do something analogous to animal reproducing, for example, but not genetically and it would only be analogous.
37. Translated Irwin and Fine in Aristotle 1995, p. 95. See also Locke 1977, 2:27:6: ' the identity of the same *man* consists . . . in nothing but a participation of the same continued life, by constantly fleeting particles of matter, in succession vitally united to the same organised body.'
38. See also Lowe 1989, p. 5: 'perhaps only *natural* kinds need to be accorded a wholly mind-independent status – though this of course raises the thorny problem of *how* we are to draw any objective distinction between natural and non-natural kinds. My own view is that the crucial distinguishing feature of natural kinds is that they are subject to *natural law*' (italics original).
39. I would like to think that this would be the same for *all* artefacts. But there are problems. If a ship at sea has one timber replaced we can scarcely say that the sailors return in a different ship. The heap of bits of a pot is not the same as the pot. In dGe lugs thought the fact that a heap of bits cannot literally be identical to the whole is the reason why the (conventional) person cannot simply be the aggregates, but rather is a conceptual entity imputed onto the aggregates (see Hopkins 1987, pp. 238–40). But this requires the dGe lugs notion of the conventional self as a conventional existent, which is, as we have seen, rather different from the position of Śāntideva. As Wiggins points out (1980, p. 44) in discussing a passage of Frege, with reference to the very pertinent case of a forest, *all* the trees could be replaced and while the aggregate (the set) of the trees would change as well as the class comprising the present trees, it could still quite justifiably be called the same forest (supposing, for example, one tree is replaced per year). Thus the forest is not the same as the aggregate of the trees or the class of the present trees. Yet, as Frege said, if we burn down all the trees in the forest we thereby burn down the forest (Wiggins, p. 32n.20) Therefore for this reason among others we can indeed maintain in a way which Prajñākaramati (see his point (ix) above) would consider absurd that the forest is neither the same nor different from the trees. If all this is correct and it would not apply in the same way to the caste-row then there are also interesting differences between the examples used to illustrate continuant and collective in *Bodhicaryāvatāra* 8:101.
40. A serious question for Hume too, who firmly held that there is a clear distinction between something remaining unchanged through time, and thus the same, and a succession of similar things. Perhaps because of their similarity we constantly confuse the second with the first and speak of something which changes as the same. Thus we end up with the 'fiction' of personal identity. See the useful discussion in Penelhum 1968, especially pp. 221ff. Penelhum points out (p. 224), as we have seen with the Buddhists, that if this were right then a changed person would be literally another person. This would have chaotic results – we would need to call ourselves by another name every time we noticed a change in ourselves!
41. For versions of this see, e.g. Kamalaśīla's *Tattvasaṃgrahapañjikā* on, for example, vv. 1989–1991.

42. Perhaps something additional needs to be said about the future stages of a temporal continuant. At any one time while the continuant is still taking place, since the future stages have not yet occurred, it is apparently open whether the future stages will in fact take place. If they do not, i.e. the continuant ceases at the present time, then of course we do not have the temporal continuant that would have occurred had the putative future stages taken place. We have a different temporal continuant, that is, one which ended now. Thus we cannot know for certain until it is completed what particular temporal continuant we have (although we can know, of course, what *sort* of continuant it is). Thus if we take the temporal continuant of a living human being, we cannot know until death whether that temporal continuant (as a whole) is of a three-year, eighteen-year, or ninety-year, duration although we can know that it is the temporal continuant of a human being. This is part of what we mean by the open nature of the future, and need not provide any particular problems for speaking of the temporal continuant as a whole and an existing thing.
43. Penelhum 1967, pp. 226–7 points out that while a group of objects is clearly made of a number of things, by giving it a class-name (based presumably on some shared feature) it becomes *in that respect* one. Thus 'This is a sentence' is four words, but one sentence. There is no contradiction in saying this, as there would be if one said quite literally and in the same respect there were four words but only one word. It can be six and one, depending on the *sort* of thing we are referring to (I shall return to the importance of distinguishing different sorts of things in discussing whether we have one or many below). Likewise a temporal continuant can be in different respects both many temporal stages and one, say, person. They are different sorts of things. Moreover it is not necessary that something remain unchanged in order to be called 'identical' or 'the same'. We need to distinguish between two different things being the same in some (a) specific sense, where they remain two things but are exactly alike in some respect (two similar things, like Hume's two stages of the human being), and two things which are the same in (b) the numerical sense, i.e. they are not really two things at all, but one (this use of 'specific' and 'numerical' is Hume's own). For something to remain unchanged is to be the same in sense (a), where if a change occurs there would be two things albeit alike in some respect: 'i.e. to be now exactly as one was at an earlier time. But I can remain the same in the numerical sense without doing so in the specific sense – I can be numerically the same but changed [that is, changed – I can have two different and perhaps contradictory features at different times – but still the same person]. In fact I cannot be said to have changed unless I am the same in the numerical sense [as we shall see below, it is necessary to the concept of change that something remains the same during the change. Something *undergoes* change. So if the thing does not remain the same in the numerical sense, it has not changed but it has ceased to exist and been replaced by another thing]. The only reason for saying that something is numerically different (something else, that is) when a change occurs, is if it is by definition an unchanging thing. . . . What kind

of changes can occur without our having to say that the thing has ceased to exist and given place to something else depends on what kind of thing we are talking about.' For a useful and very pertinent entry on numerical and specific identity see 'Identity' in Honderich, ed. 1995, p. 390.

44. See the definition of change given in Kim and Sosa, ed. 1995, pp. 83–4: 'An object undergoes change if, and only if, it possesses a property at one time and does not possess this property at an earlier or later time.' It follows from this definition first, that if there is to be change there must be a subject of change, second, that the subject of change has to last for more than one moment (it must therefore be a 'Śāntideva continuant') and third, that if a change in property means that the thing is no longer the same and therefore literally ceases to be that thing (Hume/Buddhist) then since on this basis the same thing *cannot* possess one property at one time and a different property at another time, there obviously cannot be change at all. Since for Śāntideva a temporal continuant cannot be treated as a unity (it does not even exist), and change requires temporal continuants treated as unities, it follows that for Śāntideva there can be no change. It is not clear how one can *become* enlightened then – but more about this sort of issue later.

45. It is tempting to argue (perhaps with a Dharmakīrti) that this is all quite acceptable, since actually when we say things are changing constantly and in every respect what this collapses into is a theory of momentariness where things are constantly being replaced by items which are very similar. But this too will not work. First, it makes no sense to speak of the momentary *svalakṣaṇas* as similar, or indeed anything at all, since if they are involved in a situation of complete and constant change they cannot be identified. This does not mean (*pace* Dharmakīrti) that the *svalakṣaṇas* are strictly beyond language. Rather they do not exist at all. It makes no sense to talk of *complete and total change* as involving a series of momentary entities like *svalakṣaṇas*. Second, as applied to the present case of an ever-changing person the nearest we could get to any relevant sense to the idea of constant replacement would be something like the theory of Alice, the 'staccato-being' mentioned in footnote 64 below. Here we find not only many consequences particularly unacceptable to Buddhists (the loss of karmic results, absence of moral responsibility, the impossibility of enlightenment and so on), but it would also render memory meaningless and crucially it would make no sense to refer to someone like Alice as in any way *conscious*.

46. This is not to say that there are not problems in explaining what it means conceptually, and how it happens psychologically or culturally (for example), that we give a unity over time to various internally changing things. For example, is it sometimes that the respect in which x remains stable is itself unchanging throughout the life of x, or are there changes in that respect (at a slower rate). If the latter, then we might have a series of overlapping respects in which change occurs and it is even plausible that nothing at all has remained completely unchanged throughout the life of x. Why we call it a unity, how the identification of x as the same takes place, and what this means, is still open to discussion. And nothing said here would want to detract from the

genuine problems about certain cases, personal identity (over a whole lifetime, for example) included.

47. For a Buddhist example in the present context of the river being used to illustrate constant change, and then applied to the case of the mind, see the quote from Sa skya paṇḍita in Thub bstan chos kyi grags pa's commentary to *BCA* 8:103: 'For example, even though certain fools might certainly consider that this waterfall carried away my clothes last year, and one forded this river the day before yesterday, the water which carried away the clothes last year is other, the river which was forded the day before yesterday is other. In like manner, the past mind is not me, and the future mind is not me. That being the case, they are other' (dper na blun po dag 'bab chu 'dis na ning nga'i gos khyer ro snyam pa dang nang par chu 'di brgal lo snyam du sems mod kyang / na ning gos khyer ba'i chu de'ang gzhan yin la nang par brgal ba'i chu de'ang gzhan yin no // de bzhin du 'das pa'i sems kyang bdag min la ma'ongs pa'i sems kyang bdag ma yin par gzhan yin no).
48. Quine 1963, p. 65. But cf. Chisholm 1976, pp. 143–5 for criticism of Quine's statement that the river could be identical to the *sum* of the river stages through time, and the adequacy of Quine's account as a response to Heracleitus' universal flux. And see Lowe 1989, pp. 79ff for criticism of Quine's need to introduce talk of river *stages* at all rather than simply water(s).
49. Cf. Wiggins 1995, p. 235: 'The river is in constant flux. The waters are constantly renewed. We may even suppose that consequentially upon this changing of constituents, the river changes in any and every property range, in depth, strength, speed, temperature, colour, noise-level, etc. These changes, however extreme, need not be lawless. Nor, incidentally, do they prevent us from singling out one and the same river [in order to speak of the river changing there must after all be a river]. To say that the river is changing constantly in every respect is not to say that it is changing in respect of being a river. Rather, that is precisely *not* a respect in which the constantly changing river changes, even under condition of total flux.'
50. A thought: If I someone asks me to show them the River Thames and I take them to a bluff above the river and say 'There it is', and the river has dried up in a drought, have I failed to show them the River Thames? My inclination is to say that I have showed them the river, but at this particular moment there is no water in it. If that is right, then *pace* Wiggins it would not even be true to say that the river is constituted of water. But my inclination may be wrong (cf. 'That is where the river usually is, but it has dried up at the moment'). Cf. Lowe 1989, p. 14. To return to Wiggins' point (which is still broadly correct), the implication of this, that two material objects – the river and the water – occupy the same space need not be a problem if they are different *sorts* of things. To generalise, there is no problem in whole and parts occupying the same space. That is what we would expect of a part/whole relationship. As we have seen, one would not expect to find a whole *alongside* but apart from the parts!
51. By what is sometimes called 'Leibniz's law', things differing in quality cannot be identical. In general this 'law' is accepted in contemporary

philosophy (although it has to be interpreted carefully in the case of change). Now, wholes frequently differ in qualities from their constituent parts. Take the case of a bundle of sticks. The bundle cannot be broken while each individual stick can. The property of 'unable to be broken' is possessed by the bundle, not by each of the parts taken separately. Thus inasmuch as something can be identified as the locus of its properties, the bundle is identified in a different way from each stick. Incidentally, the bundle is presumably also not simply the set of the sticks, since a mere heap of sticks, or the sticks widely dispersed, would not be the unbreakable bundle referred to here. Thus the bundle is not the same as one or all of the sticks. Yet it is not another thing alongside the sticks, and it can certainly not be identified apart from the sticks. Should we therefore maintain that there is no such thing as an unbreakable bundle? Or it is paradoxical? Or merely a concession to activity on the admittedly paradoxical transactional level? For examples of predicates which can be applied to persons which are not derivable from properties attributable to the putative constituent stages of persons (thus showing that persons cannot be *merely* fusions, sums, of constituent stages) take these from Wiggins' list: weak, clever, cowardly, opportunistic, a fair weather friend (1980, pp. 168–9; see also Shoemaker in Guttenplan, ed. 1994, p. 556).

52. Perhaps I should add a short note here on sortal terms. Basically, the criterion for identity of something depends upon what sort of concept the concept of that thing is. Thus whether X is to count as the same river or not over time or at a time depends upon the criterion for identity of rivers, and since rivers are a different sort of thing from water (the concept of a river is a different sort of concept from the concept of water) the criterion for identity of X will not be the same as the criterion for identity of the water, even if the water constitutes the river. Likewise, the criterion for identity of a person will not be the same as the criterion for identity of a 'person-stage', a mental event, a body part, their combination or whatever. Because wholes are a different sort of thing from their parts, the criterion for identity of wholes is different from the criterion for identity of the parts. Whether Archibald is the same person as the mysterious Mr X (or the same person himself over time) will depend on what is to count as being 'the same person', not as such on whether e.g. certain psycho-physical events or their bundle are the same or not (see Lowe 1989). Since wholes and parts are different sorts of things, it may be the case – indeed, it seems to me it is – that wholes may be neither the same nor different from their parts in a sense in which two parts of the same sort could not be neither the same nor different from each other (or one part over time could not be neither the same nor different). A sortal term (the expression comes from Locke; *Essay* 3:3:5) is a general term, usually a noun, the extension of which consists of things or substances which are all of one particular sort. Examples might be 'tree', 'horse' or (it can be argued) 'person'. Such terms tell us 'what the thing is', and as such supply a criterion for identity which will enable us to determine what is to count as an instance of that sort. To understand the meaning of the sortal term 'tree', for instance, is to

understand what is to count as an instance of a tree, and to know how to go about answering questions related to the identity of a tree. These sortal terms contrast with, for example, adjectives. In the case of 'tree' since we have a criterion of individuation and identity we know which things are being referred to by the term, we can count trees, and know how to go about answering a question whether one tree is identical with another (or identical over time). On the other hand, in the case of an adjective like 'green', for example (the examples are taken from Lowe 1995, pp. 93–7), we have no criterion of identity and we cannot from the term alone know which things are being referred to by the term, nothing about the meaning of 'green' alone tells us how to go about answering the question whether in its use twice it is two green things or the same green thing which is being characterised, nor can we even in principle count all green things. (How many green things are in a wood? Should a leaf count as one green thing, two green sides, two hundred green cells, two hundred and three – the thing plus the sides plus the cells – or what?). The term does not enable us to answer, nor is there *one* answer. Although there may be borderline cases of definition, there is nevertheless one answer as to how many trees there are in the wood. Eli Hirsch has clarified the thesis of 'sortal dependency' pertinently as follows: '[W]hereas a continuous succession of stages of trees typically must add up to stages of one and the same tree, a continuous succession of stages of brown or wooden things may jump from one brown or wooden thing to another. This principle exhibits a sense in which *a's* identity might be said to depend on *a's* being an instance of "tree" rather than on *a's* being an instance of either "brown" or "wooden" [which are not sortal terms]' (in Kim and Sosa 1995, p. 231). Moreover, different sortal terms often have a different criterion of identity associated with them. What is to count as one, or the same, tree, may not be the same as what is to count as one, or the same, mountain. What is to count as one person is not the same as what is to count as one bundle of psycho-physical characteristics. In addition, since to be capable of counting unambiguously instances falling under a general term requires a single principle of identity, if we can count such instances in that manner it seems that the term is going to be a sortal term. Since we can count persons (and selves as subjects of experiences, those who use the indexical 'I'), 'person' and 'self' are sortal terms'. For some critical comments on sortals see Hirsch, pp. 231 –2.

53. Cf. Gillett 1987, p. 86: 'Birth, growth, maturation, mortality, emotional sensitivities, human abilities, social interactions, culture, beliefs and so on are part of his experience. As a person's identity becomes defined, so the kind of story he tells about himself takes on a richness and depth which draw on his cumulative experience of life. That he *can* tell such a story suggests that his life and identity is more like a painting or a novel than a heap of sand [a caste-row, a rosary, a forest, an army] or a string of contingently connected events.' I suppose someone could say that the tight unity, the holistic whole, of science and experience is simply false, an illusion created by beginningless ignorance. Thus it is not necessary for the Buddhist to explain how on his or her premisses we could

'reconstruct', as it were, the human being or person of unenlightened experience. This is how it is, and the gaps can be filled with the cement of *avidyā*. But this answer seems to me very implausible. Even if one could not conclusively refute someone who maintained this (although as we shall see, it is not just a contingent matter that my pains are mine and yours are yours), one could show that it seems very counter-intuitive, does not correspond to experience and our actual behaviour, appears to lack systematic explanation, and it is difficult to see what possible grounds (apart from faith) could be given for its acceptance. These would all seem to be good reasons for thinking it false. In actual fact it seems to me that such an appeal to beginningless ignorance as an explanation of the experienced unity of persons must surely beg the question, for ignorance is a mental occurrence and *requires* the person – a person much as we think its is – in order to occur. As John Passmore has said, with reference to Hume's theory of personal identity: 'For if all that happens is that a series of very similar (or causally linked) perceptions succeed one another, there is no possible way in which this series of itself could generate the fiction of personal identity. Nor, the fiction once generated, could this series ever reveal its fictional character. Both the original fiction and the discovery that it is a fiction are possible only if there is something which is first misled by, and then, after reconsideration, can discover that it was misled by, a series of similar perceptions' (quoted in Stroud 1977, p. 262). Put bluntly, if the person thus understood is largely the result of significant falsification through primeval ignorance, *whose* ignorance is that supposed to be? Ignorance requires persons (as the subject of mental attributions), and cannot be the cause of them. Moreover we require a much clearer analysis of this ignorance before we can judge its explanatory value. As it stands, take the following problem: Consider (as we shall more fully in a moment) the series $MT(i) \rightarrow MT(ii) \rightarrow MT(iii) \rightarrow n$, where 'MT(i)' refers to the mental moment at time (i) and so on, the arrow indicates the causal relationship, and 'n' n-further moments. If it is the case that this mental series is understood to be the series of one person then if we are to understand 'ignorance' in anything like its normal meaning and if it is to offer any help in explaining the ongoing attribution of mental events to the same person it must be the case *inter alia* that alongside each of these mental moments is another mental event of ignorance (I). Thus we have:

$MT(i) \rightarrow MT(ii)(MT(iii) \rightarrow n$; and
$IT(i) \rightarrow IT(ii)(IT \rightarrow iii) \rightarrow n$ L

But there can be no *causal* relationship between the ignorance event IT(i) and the other mental event MT(i), since they are simultaneous and (at least for Madhyamaka) there can be no simultaneous causation. And it is difficult to find an explanation of *exactly* what the relationship is supposed to be between them or, indeed, how this duplication of mental events will contribute to explaining the generation of the series as a *personal* series at all.

54. We need to remember also the Buddhist causal framework, characteristically explained on the model of 'This being, that occurs; with the

non-occurrence of this there is the non-occurrence of that'. This is going to be a very loose framework to carry the burden of constructing the unity which is the experienced human being. It is also worth noting that the Buddhist contention that mental events are linked by causal relations anyway requires considerable explication and defence. In the course of a very helpful critical analysis of Parfit's views, John Campbell has observed that '[t]here seems in fact to be no causal relation, or set of causal relations, that characteristically holds among the psychological states of a single person. No such explicit reductive description has ever been given' (1994, p. 175). See also Galen Strawson 1994, p. 134: 'The human stream of consciousness has very little natural phenomenological continuity or experiential flow, if mine is anything to go by.' If this is the case, then the reductive model of Parfit and our Buddhist will be unable to get started. Even in individual cases it can be difficult to see exactly what the Buddhist means by referring to mental events essentially succeeding each other in a stream as cause and effect. That certainly is not always the way it appears to be. Take the case (from Stroud 1977, p. 126) where I first have an experience of seeing a tree, turn my head, and then have an experience of seeing a building. Let us suppose that the experience of seeing the tree is followed immediately (as immediately as possible) by the experience of seeing the building. None of this seems far-fetched. Yet we would not normally called the experience of seeing the tree the *cause* of that of seeing the building, and the latter the effect. Of course, I know perfectly well that the actual analysis would be in terms of one *dharma* succeeding another in a cause/effect relationship with considerable rapidity. Why we should think that this is how it is, how there can be causation between momentary events, and why it should be argued that this is always how it is with the mind, and particular in the present context that the relationship is always a causal one, is unclear to me. What we actually want from the Buddhist is a detailed explanation of why we should think that our mental events are linked causally, and a plausible account of how this works which does not beg the question and require the *prior* existence of a unified continuum, unified indeed as a *person*. The Abhidharma provides sources for an attempt at such an explanation. It is fascinating, but it seems to me ultimately unsuccessful. And there is another point. In the case of the mental series it seems that even if there is a linear sequence of causally related mental events this is not going to give you a person. In actual fact there can only be causal relationships 'of the right sort' between mental events precisely *because* they are indeed the experiences of the same person!

55. Of course it is possible to argue that this way of experiencing our minds is simply false. In reality there is here only one mental event at a time, but because they succeed each other with such rapidity it seems as if there are many events going on. This would appear to be an empirical position which ought to be capable of being tested. As far as I know there is no evidence for it. The other device sometimes brought in here is *avidyā*, beginningless ignorance. It is beginningless ignorance which makes us think that things are otherwise. This is scarcely very adequate,

and apart from empirical evidence that the mind actually works in a linear series of mental moments *avidyā* is not going to be very helpful in papering over the gaps. Anyway, as we saw above, it is difficult to see how we can make sense of *avidyā* without presupposing the concept of one who is ignorant, and thus begging the question. On the complexity of the actual causal system in Theravāda thought see the famous discussion of Buddhaghosa in the *Visuddhimagga*: 'Nor from a single cause arise One fruit or many, nor one fruit from many; 'Tis helpful, though to utilize One cause and fruit as representative. Here there is no single or multiple fruit of any kind from a single cause, nor a single fruit from multiple causes, but only multiple fruit from multiple causes' (*Vsm* XVII, 105–6, trans. Ñāṇamoli). Thus the actual causal situation is confused even more when it is compared with the one-to-one relationship of the caste or ant-row, or a rosary. On the many-many relationship the problem of explaining the experienced unity of the human being on the basis of causal links – links 'of the right sort' – without begging the question would seem to me to be insuperable.

56. In their eagerness to identify the continuant with the mental series and the collective with the spatially-extended body this point is rather overlooked by the commentators of *Bodhicaryāvatāra* 8:101. But of course the body for the Buddhist is also a causal continuant extended in time, and it is arguable (in spite of Locke) that the bodily continuant is crucial for the concept of personal identity.
57. It might be thought that particularly important here, and omitted from these considerations, is some mention of *karmic* causation as a central factor in moulding a causal series into a personal series. This would be an excellent example of begging the question. The process of karmic causation precisely *requires* the concept of the person, and cannot therefore be explanatory of it. One could scarcely specify volition, karmically determinative deeds and their results without reference directly or through implication to any *person* (remembering the wide sense in which I am using 'person', which would include any sentient being).
58. See also Hamlyn 1984, p. 196: 'Other people's experiences may be causally connected with the state of my body. . . if I am to distinguish from among the experiences that are causally dependent on the state of my body those which are mine, there is no way of doing so which does not beg the question as to whose they are. That is what we should expect if experiences cannot be neutral as far as their ownership is concerned. The "no ownership" theory remains incoherent.'
59. Incidentally, it is rather difficult to see what sense we can make of the *M* too, since I am not sure I can make sense of mental events without persons. This is certainly the case with pain as a mental event. I shall return to this point subsequently.
60. If this seems paradoxical consider with suitable substitutions the case of the relationship of mind to body: 'But it is simply mistaken to dissolve away the mind into a series of brain events linked by non-specific causal connections. If we observed and listed exhaustively all our brain events and their causal connections this would not give us the mind, since it

would not follow that the mind could be adequately reduced to brain events and their causal connections, or fully explained in their terms. This would be the case even if the mind supervened upon brain events and their causes and there was no mind in any sense apart from brain events and their causes.' See here Searle 1992.

61. Of course, not all unity of purpose implies (at least directly) life. Hume (1969, p. 309) held that the soul is more like a commonwealth, and a commonwealth while requiring living beings is not itself alive. But the living body is alive, and precisely to that extent is not itself like a commonwealth!
62. To repeat again, my argument does not imply that only the alternative to the Buddhist model is a Cartesian or perhaps a Sāṃkhya Self. In fact I am not really concerned with *what* the self, the person, is here at all, only the inadequacy of the Buddhist/Śāntideva's model to explain it.
63. See Sack's book for interesting details of how this particular patient, unlike Mr Thompson, was saved from the '"Humean" froth' (Sacks). He also refers to another patient (this time without Korsakov's) for whom everything had become completely equal, and meant nothing to her, 'Nothing any longer felt "real" (or "unreal"). Everything now was "equivalent" or "equal" – the whole world reduced to facetious insignificance' (p. 112). This is another patient who he felt, like Mr Thompson, had somehow become 'de-souled' as a person.
64. Cf. another Korsakov's patient treated by Sacks, 'He is a man without a past (or a future), stuck in a constantly changing, meaningless moment' (p. 28). Note, of course, that as Locke realised so clearly, this would also make it quite wrong to punish someone for having committed a crime. The one who did the crime was indeed a different person. For the Buddhist on this basis it must follow that karma and its results are completely confused. A different person gets the results from the one who did the deed even if there is just a moment between doing the deed and receiving its karmic recompense. Cf also Jonathan Bennett, *Kant's Analytic* p. 117, quoted in Wiggins 1980, p. 151n.3: 'the notion of oneself is necessarily that of the possessor of a history: I can judge that this is how it is with me now, only if I can also judge that is how it was with me then. Self-consciousness can coexist with amnesia – but there could not be a self-conscious person suffering from perpetually renewed amnesia such that he could at no time make judgements about how he was at any earlier time.'; and cf. also Hamlyn 1984, p. 190: 'When, however, one thinks back over one's own past (and . . . similar considerations arise from the contemplation of one's possible future) one inevitably thinks of all the changes that have taken place as changes *in relation to oneself*. Self-consciousness presupposes an identical self, *however that is to be analysed*' (first italics in original, second PW). Peter van Inwagen (1990, pp. 209–10) refers to the imaginary case of Alice, a 'staccato being'. Every thousandth of a second or so Alice is annihilated and a hundred-millionth of a second later a perfect duplicate of her appears. This continues for an indefinite period. No one notices any difference. This appears to me very much like certain Buddhist views of impermanence. Van Inwagen argues – I think correctly – that since there

is actually no continuous being here there could be no continuous conscious being. Since there is no continuous conscious being we cannot speak of consciousness at all [a consciousness which lasted only a split second and belonged to no continuous conscious being could not be consciousness] – 'a world of "Alices" would be a world without consciousness'.

65. Cf. Luis Buñuel, as quoted in Sacks p. 22: 'Life without memory is no life at all . . . Our memory is our coherence,our reason, our feeling, even our action. Without it, we are nothing.' To distinguish memory from fantasy we must be able to *know and truly state* that we are the same person; there has to be some sense in which we are *genuinely* the same self or person. See also Searle 1992, pp. 129–30, where he speaks of the way in which *nonpathological* mental states come to us in a unity which he refers to as 'horizontal' and 'vertical': 'Horizontal unity is the organisation of conscious experiences through short stretches of time. . . vertical unity is a matter of the simultaneous awareness of all the diverse features of any conscious state . . . We have little understanding of how the brain achieves this unity.' This just is how it is, and any attempt to reduce this given unity – which is intimately bound up with the issue of a unitary self – is going to have problems. These problems are philosophical, conceptual, as well a psychological, but also – as we see in the case of Korsakov's syndrome (also mentioned in this connection by Searle) – there are the pathological problems of what happens when it breaks down.

66. Cf. the Scottish philosopher Thomas Reid: 'The conviction which every man has of his identity, as far back as his memory reaches, needs no aid of philosophy to strengthen it; and no philosophy can weaken it, without first producing some degree of insanity' (quoted in Hamlyn 1984, p. 204). In a subject with Korsakov's syndrome, 'presented with an object he has been shown a few minutes before, he tends to respond to it as not identical or as in some manner changed' (Gregory, ed. 1987, p. 413). On the Buddhist model of constant change (one thinks of Dharmakīrti, for example), the Korsakov subject is actually right. Since enlightenment involves seeing things the way they really are, the Korsakov subject is *in this respect* nearer to enlightenment than the rest of us. Because of an awareness of constant impermanence, he or she ought also on Buddhist grounds to be less subject to attachment (more altruistic?). (Incidentally, symptoms characteristic of Korsakov's syndrome can also be produced by mercury poisoning. Since mercury was used in the manufacture of felt, this is possibly where the expression 'mad as a hatter' comes from (see Gregory, ed. 1987, p. 445). Since mercury is also used a great deal in the so-called 'precious pills' (*rin chen ril bu*) of Tibetan medicine, maybe here is a little-known and perhaps scientifically demonstrable dimension of the spiritual efficacy of Tibetan medicine!) We might grant that the Korsakov subject will be less-able to operate in the pragmatic transactional world, but he or she nevertheless is nearer to seeing things the way they really are. Of course actually this will not do! One does not need to hold to a pragmatic theory of truth to suggest nevertheless that the fact that one *is* less able to operate

effectively in the pragmatic 'transactional world' is precisely an indication that one is *not* seeing things the way they actually are. As I understand it, there are evolutionary reasons why our perception must broadly speaking be correct. If it was significantly awry the species would not have survived and we would have no grounds for even beginning the discussion. If one way something works and the other it does not, then the first way when compared with the second is at least going to be a good candidate for being correct. The Korsakov subject's perception of constant change, his or her inability to identify an item as the same over a period of time, is in general simply wrong (it is wrong to think that this is not Archibald just because he has lost a fingernail), and that explains his or her inability to operate effectively. This is clear when we remember that this perception of constant change itself is in the case of the Korsakov subject part of a whole situation where the subject is very severely impaired, and it is accompanied by significant lesions, atrophy and other damage to the brain structure (Gregory ed., 1987, pp. 413–4).

67. See here Glover 1991, p. 50: 'To speak of experiences which no one has may be to wrench words out of the context that makes then intelligible.... There is a danger in talking of "experiences" as if they were things, separable from their owners in the way that hats are. Once an experience stops being a state of a person (me feeling hot, or you thinking about your holiday) and becomes free-floating we may loose grip on what it is meant to be.' See also Campbell 1994, pp. 160 ff. who points out the problem that the incoherence of free-floating experiences causes for reductionists like Parfit. On the model of the adverbial theory analysis of pains which I shall elaborate subsequently, we might say that while there are feathers, there are no such *things* as doubts which would be capable of floating around. Sentient beings doubt, this is something they *do* – I doubt, you doubt, Archibald doubts, Descartes doubts – and of course doing requires a doer. See also Searle 1992, p. 20: 'Because mental phenomena are essentially connected with consciousness, and because consciousness is essentially subjective, it follows that the ontology of the mental is essentially a first-person ontology. Mental states are always somebody's mental states. There is always a "first person," an "I," that has these mental states.'

68. On 'Descartes' mistake' see Kant's *Critique of Pure Reason* B421: 'The unity of consciousness which underlies the categories is . . . mistaken for an intuition of the subject as object, and the category of substance is then applied to it.' Quoted in Scruton 1982, p. 56.

69. For more on Frege's own use of his 'thesis' see Kenny 1995, p. 192: 'If there is no owner of ideas, there are no ideas either; dependence on an owner was one of the features by which the notion of "idea" was introduced. There cannot be an experience without someone to experience, or a pain without someone who has it. Pain is necessarily *felt*, and what is felt must have someone feeling it' (italics original). Of course, someone (a Parfit?) could object that to have a pain *is* to feel it. If there is a pain what additional need is there for a subject of the pain? This would be to miss the point. To have a pain is indeed the feeling of it

(Searle 1992 pp. 164–7 argues for the possibility of unconscious pains, although I remain quite unconvinced), but the pain can only be felt – there can only be a pain – because there is a subject who has feelings. Frege's point is that there cannot be a pain without subjectivity. The alternative must involve the objector in free-floating pains, which seems to me to be quite absurd. Strawson himself points out (p. 132) that this perhaps explains some of the resistance to reductionist accounts of the person like that of Parfit. It is worth noting that Parfit's account, which in so many ways appears similar to that of the Buddhist, has problems with the essential subjectivity of pain, the very problem which I shall argue besets Śāntideva's version but which is so much more acute for Śāntideva's attempt to encourage altruism and particularly the removal of pain. On the need for a subject for mental events see also Chisholm 1969, p. 18: '[I]n being aware of ourselves as experiencing, we are, *ipso facto*, aware of the self or person – of the self or person affected in a certain way'; and cf. van Inwagen 1990, p. 6: '[The] grammatically singular subject and grammatically singular predicate get the ontology of thought and sensation right. When I say to my students, "Descartes" invented analytical geometry, what I have told them cannot be true unless "Descartes" denotes an object (the same object that Descartes called "moi" and "ego") and that object had the property of having invented analytical geometry. What I have told them, moreover, *is* true, is as strictly and literally true as any assertion that has ever been made' (italics original).

70. Glover relies on a discussion by Bernard Williams (see Williams 1978, pp. 95–101). Williams points out that we need to 'relativize' our thoughts to *where* they are thought, and this inevitably involves employing the indexical 'I' or its equivalent (such as 'here' or 'now').
71. Take another example. From the true thought 'I am English', and the true thought 'I live in Bristol', both thought by me, I can infer as true the thought 'I am English and I live in Bristol'. But using Lichtenberg's reduction I cannot infer from the simple occurrence (without reference to a subject) of the true thought 'I am English' and the occurrence of the true thought 'I live in Bristol', the true thought 'I am English and I live in Bristol'. This is because the *occurrence* of the true thought is not the same as *my* thinking that thought. The two thoughts may have taken place in quite different minds, and the conjunction may not be thought by anyone. It may as a matter of fact be the case that there are no English people living in Bristol. That is incompatible with my thinking the thoughts and drawing the inference, but not with Lichtenberg's reduction.
72. On *BCA* 8:101: upāttapañcaskandhamātram abhisaṃdhāya dṛṣṭānte dīyamāne na kācit kṣatiḥ = Tib. zin pa'i phung po nyid la dgongs nas dpe mdzad pa la nyams cung zad kyang med pas. Note incidentally that Prajñākaramati does not refer to the conventional self as 'the mere-I which is conceptually imputed in dependence upon the five [psycho-physical] aggregates which form its own basis for imputation', making a clear *distinction* in the way it is made in dGe lugs Madhyamaka between the conventional person itself and the psycho-physical aggregates which

are its *bases of imputation* (the principle being that what is imputed cannot be the same as its bases of imputation). It looks as if for Prajñākaramati the conventional self is simply designated as a term for the whole where the aggregates are its parts. The 'self' is a practical conventional unity given to the bundle of aggregates. Compare this with the dGe lugs pa Thub bstan chos kyi grags pa on *BCA* 8:102 (p. 533): 'it is taught that there exists self and other conventionally, as conceptualised in dependence on the aggregates, even though there does not exist an independent self and other. . . it is taught that there is the mere postulation in mutual dependence, without being established by nature, of both self and other which are the enjoyers of pleasure and pain' (rang dbang ba'i bdag dang gzhan med kyang tha snyad du phung po la brten nas btags pa'i bdag dang gzhan yod par bstan pas so // . . . bde sdug la longs spyod pa po'i bdag gzhan gnyis ngo bos grub pa med par phan tshun ltos nas bzhag pa tsam yin par bstan la). Chos kyi grags pa's lengthy comments on this verse show an distinct attempt to affirm the conventional existence of self and other, and the ways in which it is legitimate to do so (in mutual dependence), and at the same time a practical religious worry that if someone responds quite consistently that therefore there is no need to remove the pains of others, this would become the very destruction of the mind training involving equalising self and others (de nas bdag gzhan dag la brten pa'i bde sdug la'ang 'di ni nga'i bde sdug yin pas bsgrub pa'am bsal bar bya la 'di ni gzhan gyi bde sdug yin pas bsgrub pa'am bsal par mi bya'o snyam nas yal bar 'dor ba ni bdag gzhan mnyam brje'i blo sbyong ba'i gegs yin pas). See also Thub bstan chos kyi grags pa's comments on *BCA* 8:103: '[Opponent] "If there does not exist the Self, which is independent (*rang dbang*) which is the experiencer of pain . . ." [Reply] Even though there does not exist a Self which is independent still, merely in conventional transaction, there exists a 'self' which is postulated in mutual dependence, and an 'other', and the pain of those (sdug bsngal myong mkhan gyi rang dbang ba'i bdag med na . . . rang dbang ba'i bdag med kyang tha snyad tsam du phan tshun ltos nas bzhag pa'i bdag dang gzhan dang de dag gi sdug bsngal yang yod pa'i phyir). But this strategy, appealing to the conventional/ultimate distinction, is not going to work.

73. I have tended to speak of 'the Buddhist position' on these issues as if, at least for our purposes, it is fairly homogeneous. But the diversity of Buddhism in history should not be forgotten. The view that there is does indeed exist a 'person' (*pudgala/gang zag*) which is not identifiable with any of the psycho-physical aggregates, and therefore any 'person-stage', is not simply a set of person-stages or a bundle of psycho-physical parts, and yet is not another thing alongside the psycho-physical aggregates (cf. of course, the whole compared with the parts), and is also certainly not a Cartesian or Sāṃkhya Self, was in fact the view of a Buddhist school known as Vātsīputrīya-Sammatīya, usually known after its characteristic doctrine as 'Pudgalavāda'. We know little of this school (or these schools), since most of their texts are lost and we know of their doctrine mainly from their opponents, who ridiculed it (by and large the same contempt or lack of concern seems to have been the case among modern

scholars as well). It seems however that the Pudgalavāda doctrine may have been philosophically acute. At least, they may have been truer to what P.F. Strawson (1959) would call a 'descriptive metaphysics', rather than the 'revisionary metaphysics' of their fellow Buddhists. Note, incidentally, that the Pudgalavādins seemed to consider that their characteristic doctrine was perfectly in accordance with the teaching of the Buddha. We have some evidence from Chinese sources that they were actually quite numerous among the Buddhist *saṃgha* in Ancient India. They are perhaps due for a philosophical reassessment, although paucity of sources – particularly their own – would make this difficult.

74. In this, and a great deal of what follows on the bundle theory, I have been very influenced by the article by James van Cleve in Kim and Sosa, ed. 1995, pp. 65–7.
75. On the irreducibility of *all* indexicals see Glover 1991, p. 67. This is one of the characteristic features of indexicals, along with their adhesiveness ('I' is always used for me) and elusiveness ('I' does not refer to one fixed thing). It is a characteristic of indexicals that they vary in what they refer to depending on context. This is something to do with the semantics of these terms (although some people – such as Buddhists meditating on the 'nonfindability of the Self' seem to rather overdo its significance). For a version of the bundle theory which might avoid the problems we have seen so far, and which could be taken as having some similarity with theories of the conventional person like that of the dGe lugs (and unlike, I have argued, Śāntideva and Prajñākaramati), as not identical with the psycho-physical properties, see van Cleve p. 67. This theory apparently would not avoid the next objection. Van Cleve also suggests another theory which might avoid all these objections, with individuals as 'ontological emergents', 'they emerge from bundles of properties but are not identical with them' which appears also to have some similarities with the dGe lugs approach, although whether its implications would be acceptable in dGe lugs Madhyamaka remains to be seen.
76. The point can be applied to sentences concerning experiences other than pains. The source for van Cleve's criticism of Hume here is probably Chisholm 1969, pp. 10–11. Chisholm introduces the point with reference to his statement that when Hume said 'I never can catch myself at any time without a perception, and never can observe anything but the perception' (*Treatise* I:IV:VI, quoted in Chisholm p. 10), in fact Hume clearly already had a self, the 'I' which he refers to in the statement above. The opponent objects that surely Hume's point is that statements using the first-person indexical can be restated in equivalent terms but omitting the indexical. But take Hume's 'I find nothing but impressions or perceptions'. This is not equivalent to saying 'Nothing but impressions or perceptions are found' (reversal in original), just as 'I do not see any cats and dogs' cannot be expressed as 'No cats or dogs are seen'.
77. Cf. Campbell 1994, p. 162: 'I may want simultaneously to say "There is pain" and "There is no pain" without falling into contradiction. If I can use the subjectless construction to report what are in fact the states of different people, I need to be able to relativize it in some way or other.

Moreover, I have to relativize in such a way that suitable pairs of psychological ascriptions are relativized to the *same* thing' (italics original). See Campbell Ch. 5 especially pp. 162 ff. for a splendid critique of Parfit's version of the 'no-ownership' theory. Campbell points out that faced with the need to relativise psychological states in the way we normally do to persons ('*I* am not now feeling pain') but without mentioning persons, selves, or first-person indexicals, Parfit himself has recourse to the 'life' (he also sometimes has recourse to the body): 'A "life" is apparently a series of mental and physical events; he speaks of "the interrelations between all the mental and physical events that together constitute a person's life" (Parfit 1984, 226). But plainly, not just any series of mental and physical events can be taken to constitute a "life" if the coherence constraint on the ascription of psychological states are to be applied to the ascriptions made relative to a single life. We need some explanation of when a series of mental and physical events constitute *one* life' (p. 162; italics PW). See also Hodgson 1991, pp. 418 ff., and Gillett in Peacocke and Gillett 1987, pp. 75 ff., and cf. also Shoemaker's review of Parfit, 1985, pp. 446–7. Shoemaker argues that in order for a particular mental state or event to be of the kind it is (such as an experience or belief with a particular content) then it must be related to the larger context within which it occurs (see Putnam on pain as 'a functional state of the whole organism', handily summarised in Priest 1991, pp. 137–45). But that larger context will be [or include] a person. Thus there is 'a necessary ontological dependence' of mental events upon some sort of subject. Shoemaker speculates that a reduction of the personhood and personal identity of the sort Parfit has in mind would appear to involve also a reduction of mentality as well. What this amounts to for Śāntideva is that in order to be able to dispose with subjectivity and therefore the subjects for mental ascriptions like 'pain' he is going to have to dispose altogether with the mental as a *sui generic* category, explaining it, as Shoemaker points out, in physical or functional terms. This reduction of Buddhism to Cārvāka is unlikely to be very welcome to Śāntideva! Note that for Searle 1992 his opposition to (at least straightforward) physical and functionalist accounts of mind, and the 'rediscovery of the mind', is precisely based on this necessary first-person subjective quality of mental events. Thus, if there are genuine mental events then there is subjectivity. If there is subjectivity then there are subjects. If there are subjects even conventionally then Śāntideva's conclusion is not going to follow. Therefore if Śāntideva's argument is not to fall at this point there cannot exist even conventionally subjects. Thus there will not be subjectivity. And if there is no subjectivity then there are not genuine mental events. *Ergo* the Buddhism of Śāntideva (certainly within in its own Indian framework) must embark on some project of reducing the mental to the physical. What that will do for *inter alia* rebirth does not bear thinking of!

78. See also Campbell p. 167: '[T]here is certainly a unity in all of one's judgements about what are in fact one's own mental states, judgements made otherwise than on the basis of observation. They must all be

relativized to just the same thing. But this unity is secured by the fact that these judgements are, as we might say, implicitly in the first person. [We do not observe our mental states and then unite them together, perhaps by inference! As Kant states, they are *given* as united, they are necessarily all given as *mine*]. These judgements unite all the psychological states that one ascribes in this way as the states of a single person. . . . The unity of the states reported otherwise than on the basis of observation is a personal unity. This destroys the reductionist's hope of finding a way of ascribing psychological states that does not involve any appeal to the notion of a person and is more primitive than our ordinary ascriptions of psychological states.' Campbell continues by making a point also stressed by Galen Strawson (p. 169) that there is simply no such thing as a level of primitive experience where the concept of pain has not yet been ascribed to oneself simply through being in pain. That putative level would indeed be a level on which one simply observes pain, and then applies it to oneself. It would be possible then to drive a wedge between the pain and the subject experiencing pain. There is pain without subjectivity, without its being e.g. *my* pain. For Śāntideva, who must subscribe to such a level inasmuch as he subscribes to free-floating pains, there must be some level of experience in which unenlightened beings like you and me, through beginningless ignorance, observe pains and *then* apply them to themselves. But, Campbell and Strawson want to say, that is simply false. There is no such level and pains are intrinsically subjective. I think they are surely right. Note that it is not relevant to this debate to point out that it is indeed possible to observe, as it were objectively (perhaps in meditation), one's pains and thus loose some of the unpleasant quality of the pain (for mention of this phenomenon in the context of a philosophical discussion see Dennett 1978, pp. 206 ff.; cf. Damasio 1995, pp. 264–7). This possibility occurs just *because* pains are given as pains for a subject. It is not a case of observing a free-floating pain and refusing to ascribe it to me. I can observe 'objectively' in that way only *my* pains. Otherwise, since hypothetically pains are free-floating and we are talking of a level where they have not yet been ascribed to a subject, it would be equally possible for me to observe 'objectively' your pains (or rather, the pains which you are going to ascribe to yourself) as my pains (those which I am going to ascribe to myself). But I can make no sense whatsoever of someone in meditation who does not have a pain observing in this objective manner the headache of his or her neighbour. I cannot even imagine what that would be like. I cannot have another person's pain even at this non-subjective level. Our inability even to make sense of that shows, surely, the essential subjectivity of pain.

79. For these objections I have been particularly influenced by Gillett, in Peacocke and Gillett, ed. 1987, especially pp. 82ff, and Hodgson 1991, pp. 418–22.
80. It may be worth emphasising this point about how we actually experience being a person, since certainly Hume and, I think, the Buddhists seem to stress (with almost the fervour of demythologisers) that their account(s) correspond rather well with what we find if we take

a look at what is actually there, rather than drifting with conventional superstitions and fictions.

81. Supposing on this model that from moment to moment my wife perishes and is replaced by another one exactly identical except appearing a moment older. I do not notice any difference, and she does not notice any difference. But what does this mean? How could *either* of us actually notice any difference? Neither of us lasts for more than one moment and therefore cannot notice *differences* at all! Putting all that to one side for a moment, at least in my own case – this is all getting rather bizarre, I agree – is it really simply irrational of me to prefer to have my own wife than an exact replacement from moment to moment? Is it simply *irrational* of me to object to the replacement, even though as far as my experience of her – apart from any irrational objection I might make – there appears to be no difference? Is it the case with my wife, as it might be for some people with an exactly identical cat to the one that has died, that a replacement really is just as good?
82. It is indeed paradoxical that the Buddhist position, which is frequently thought of (at least by Westerners) as stressing holistic interrelationship, should in fact reduce to a form of quite loose atomistic dependence. Just as the ideal landscape shows a perfect interrelationship of diachronic and synchronic, actually the now is intimately related in a manner unimaginatively complicated but holistically to the before and after both in space and time. Yet in its reduction to atomistic moments the Buddhist perspective as an atomism is in fact a form of isolationism, reducing reality to a series of independent moments related solely by weak causation where only the present actually exists – the weak atomism of the Indian renunciate who has renounced the strongly determined social time and place of his or her village for the weakly determined individualism of the Buddhist monastic.
83. How short could a momentary person-stage be? It has been calculated that the minimum duration for a conscious experience is something like 50 milliseconds, a twentieth of a second. As Hodgson points out, in that case there must be an enduring subject at least during that time (remember, as we have seen, that there cannot be an experience without a subject at all). But it seems also that more than one conscious experience occurs at the same time. Thus there must also be a unifying subject during at least that time, the 'specious present'. Moreover we also sometimes have one experience which is a succession of events that takes longer than 50 milliseconds, such as one person hearing a succession of notes as a tune (or words as a sentence) which can only occur if the same subject hearing remains until the end of the tune or sentence. Thus it is certain that at least sometimes subjects endure. Why not always, as accords with our experience (on all of this see Hodgson 1991, p. 419)?
84. Note that I do *not* employ here the argument that pains are physiological occurrences in the brain involved in physical processes and with evolutionary and biological functions which can only be understood in terms of physical bodies. This happens to be true, and indeed so obviously true that it is difficult to know quite how to make biological

sense of Śāntideva's free-floating pains cut adrift from the subjects in pain. But my concern here is not with biology but with conceptual coherence. I think one can make sense of replacing each of the biological factors in the biological account with another factor, say as it pertained to a robot. Supposing we replaced the physiological processes of the firing of various fibres and so on with some mechanical analogues, and supposing nevertheless we granted that the robot had consciousness (whatever that might be, at least as much consciousness as I might grant to a cat). And supposing the evolutionary process of the robot species was nothing like the evolution of humans or other animals, and yet nevertheless the robot convinced us in the normal way that we might be convinced by any being that it was indeed feeling something which we would normally be quite willing to call pain. Supposing the robot jumped up and down and writhed. None of this seems *impossible*, even if we were not convinced that the robot's feeling of pain had anything to do with its survival, or protection of its mechanical body or whatever. I want to leave it open that I could still be persuaded that the robot was indeed in pain, real pain. Thus being in pain is not as such something to do with the human, or the animal, biological structure and evolution. That is just a contingent fact about pain. Nevertheless there *is* a necessary connection between being in pain and the subject who is in pain, and this necessary connection is conceptual. That is what interests me here. Because there is a necessary relationship between pain and the subject in pain, there could be no possible world in which Śāntideva's argument would work. This is not just a contingent fact about our world. But on pain, physiology and the self see also Damasio 1995, Ch. 10 and pp. 263 ff.: We could not locate a pain, and therefore there would be no pain, without a body-map. Pains *essentially* happen at a place, and that place is bodily and its identification and integration involves the unity provided by the self. In fact we might think of a pain as a particular sort of unpleasant irruption into the background feelings As such, it necessarily occurs within the context of self (consciousness).

85. This is not intended as a definition of an hallucination, but rather as a reasonable characterisation.
86. In Prāsaṅgika Madhyamaka, at least as systematised in dGe lugs writings, objects are investigated with critical thought using such models as 'Are they the same or different from their parts? All things must be either the same or different . . .' or 'Does it come from itself, from another, from both, or from no cause at all? All things which come into existence must occur in one of these ways. . . . ' etc. The idea is that if it is not found under such ultimate analysis, i.e. an analysis which aims to discover whether it has ultimate existence or not, then even if an object is given in everyday transactional contexts it still has only a conventional status (*saṃvṛti*) and is not an ultimate reality (*paramārthasat*). If the object were to be found under ultimate analysis, on the other hand, it would have the fullest sort of existence (this approach derives, of course, from the Abhidharma framework for the two 'truths' we examined earlier). The object would thus really, inherently (for Madhyamaka; *sasvabhāva*) exist. Since to exist inherently is contrary to coming into

existence due to causes and conditions, if anything comes into existence due to causes and conditions it cannot inherently exist. Thus whatever comes into existence due to causes and conditions can have only *saṃvṛti* status and, therefore, cannot be found when examined through ultimate analysis. And, the Madhyamaka claims, all things one way or another come into existence due to causes and conditions. Thus nothing exists with *paramārtha* status. All existents have only *saṃvṛti* status, and this can be shown by searching for *x* through ultimate analysis to find if *x* is or is not resistant to analysis. This characterisation of the Madhyamaka approach is probably familiar to most readers. However something here has gone rather awry. I have argued above that pain must exist in the fullest possible sense that pain could exist. It is common in Madhyamaka sources to find the claim that all dharmas (and hence all things) are illusions, or castles in the air and so on (see *Madhyamaka-kārikā* 7:34 for example). This is taken as equivalent to saying that they are empty. But there is no sense whatsoever in claiming that pain is an illusion. There is no gap between appearance and reality in the case of pain such that an illusion claim can apply. There cannot be an hallucinatory pain. Thus any critical analysis which showed that pain did not exist would be *wrong*, and any Mādhyamika analysis which looses pain is mistaken, for no such reasoning could be more certain or convincing than the certainty of the genuine existence of pain. (The same might apply with other sensation statements, but I am not concerned with them here.) Therefore it follows that pain is not empty. But if that were true, then on Mādhyamika premisses pain must be found under ultimate analysis. This would then make pain something which is inherently existent, i.e. it is not the result of causes and conditions, and thus pain becomes permanent. This is clearly absurd, and would be for pain to exist precisely in a way in which pain *could not* exist. We are thus faced with two contradictory absurdities. (i) We cannot say that at some level even under ultimate analysis pain is not found (this is not the same as saying that there is some level at which pain is not *felt*). I cannot see as coherent *any* analysis which would fail to find pain, and find pain existing just as it is *qua* pain experienced, i.e. as hurting. I agree once more with Galen Strawson when he says (in a passage which should perhaps be read by all those working on Madhyamaka thought): 'I find the suggestion that common sense makes any error about the qualitative or experiential or lived nature of pain inexplicable except as an extreme case of theory-driven Procrusteanism. If there is any sense in which these philosophers [those who deny or appear to deny the existence of subjectively experienced sensations] are rejecting the ordinary view of the nature of the experience of things like pain, their view seems intellectually and morally surd. If there is no sense in which they are rejecting it, they have not made themselves clear. As it stands, their view seems to be one of the most amazing manifestations of human irrationality on record. (It is much less irrational to postulate the existence of a divine being whom we cannot perceive than to deny the truth of the commonsense view of experience . . .)' (1994, p. 53). (ii) Nevertheless, it would be absurd for a pain to have *inherent* existence since it is the result of causes and conditions. Therefore apparently a pain cannot be found under ultimate analysis. In fact it seems to me that the Mādhyamika has conflated not being found under ultimate analysis in the sense of not existing inherently (i.e. actually being found to be the result of causes and conditions), and not being found under ultimate analysis in the sense of disintegrating into some sort of absurdity, irrationality, paradox or at least impossibility under close critical examination. *Pace* the dGe lugs tradition, for example, these do not appear to be the same thing. For example, a quick solution to our problem here might be to say that, of course, pain does not have inherent existence, and therefore it lacks *that* sort of existence, but pain still exists as a conventional reality, (indeed *qua* pain as it is experienced). Thus nothing of conventional experience is actually lost. In terms of a common strategy found in dGe lugs thought, when the Mādhyamika claims that something is illusory the term 'illusory' is being used in a very specific technical sense. It has the same meaning as 'fictional' (*mṛṣā*), and as we saw when discussing the Self and the conventional person above, to be a fiction in this sense is to exist in one way (non-inherently), and to be experienced in another (as inherently existent). Unfortunately, however, while all this may be true the problem is rather more acute for the Mādhyamika because the Mādhyamika appears also to want to claim that a *saṃvṛti* thing has a lesser sort of reality inasmuch as it is in some deep sense irrational, since it is not found when subjected to ultimate analysis. Thus actually it is merely *saṃvṛti* (*saṃvṛtimātra*). The problem can be seen as follows: Take the case of a pain P. We have seen that there can be no question of P being an illusion, in the normal sense of 'illusion', involving appearing but not *really* being the case. If P occurs, it is real. In the technical Mādhyamika sense of 'illusion', however, the claim is that the pain is still an illusion since it appears one way (as inherently existing) and actually exists in another (non-inherently). I confess I find it rather difficult to make any sense of this. What exactly could P 'appearing as inherently existent' actually *mean*? A pain appears as a pain. It hurts. The hurting is the pain. There is nothing more to the appearance of a pain than the pain itself. The only way I can begin to understand the claim is that there has to be something else alongside pain, at least in the case of unenlightened beings, called 'appearing as inherently existent'. But I find it difficult to see that this actually is the case, or at least that it needs to be the case or is always (in unenlightened beings) the case. I have difficulty making sense of it. Is it a psychological statement, a conceptual statement, a religious statement, or perhaps a therapeutic or psychoanalytical statement? How would I go about trying to find out if it is true or not. What would I look for to find out if the pain that you and I experience is always accompanied by something else called 'appearing as inherently existent'? Why should I think this is *true*? Perhaps I am told that 'appearing as inherently existent' means 'appearing to exist from its own side', and that means existing independently of the mind. But of course *no* pains exist from their own side, in the sense of existing independently of the mind (although inasmuch as the mind is an integral part of the person, perhaps Śāntideva himself is committed to this, given that pains for Śāntideva can exist apart from persons, the subjects of pains!). A pain is necessarily mental. In a pain's being a pain it necessarily exists in dependence upon the mind. But there is nothing in that which means that a pain is illusory in that it appears one way and exists another. No one *could* make any sense of a claim that a pain appears to exist independently of the mind. But perhaps the Mādhyamika claim is that the mind as a creative force somehow *imputes* the existence of the pain. I can make no sense of this either. The pain is a pain. It hurts. Its existence is its hurting not its imputing. So perhaps 'appearing as inherently existing' simply means 'appearing to exist independently of causes and conditions'. P actually exists due to causes and conditions, and not only do we not realise this but due to beginningless ignorance we positively think otherwise. We positively think the pain exists quite independently of causes and conditions. Thus alongside our experiences of pain there is some other additional mental event, a belief perhaps, that the pain exists independently of causes and conditions (a belief is a more convincing option than an additional *appearance* alongside the pain). Let us call this additional mental factor (or all of them if there is more than one of this type) F. Thus in beings like you and me (i.e. unenlightened), when we have a pain P we also have this additional factor F. Take the case of a pain, then, which now is represented as PF. *That* pain, the Mādhyamika wants to claim, is illusory since in reality there is only P. Those who have seen the truth do not have the additional factor F, which is utterly wrong. But clearly, whether or not there is this additional factor F accompanying all my unenlightened pains is irrelevant to the pain itself. F is not only not an essential part of P, but F – if it occurs at all, and that needs to be shown (I can quite plausibly claim that I simply do not have any belief that my pains are independent of causes and conditions) – is quite a different mental event from P. Indeed, not only is it a different mental event, but it appears to be quite a different *type* of mental event. P is a sensation. F would appear to be a propositional attitude. A pain is one thing. Any belief accompanying it is another. Let me repeat: a pain just is a pain, and it appears as a pain. It hurts. Therefore since F is not part of P, the appearance of P is not in itself affected by F. Or, in other words, if a pain occurs it appears (that just is its occurrence) in just the way it exists, regardless of additional strange beliefs we might now or later have about it. Therefore it makes no sense to speak of P existing one way and appearing in another. This interpretation of 'illusory' simply will not work in the case of pains. (Actually, I doubt that *any* sensation can *in itself* involve a propositional attitude. If this is right, then it would make no sense to say that any sensation in itself involved views or beliefs concerning the inherent existence of what is experienced. Perception of a tree, as an experience of a tree, would not involve any belief that the tree inherently exists. Thus nothing could as such be experienced one way and exist another. But I agree this requires some thought.) Anyway, for a pain to occur is for it to be found, and no analysis could dissolve that away. Let me here in passing apply this preceding analysis to another issue of contemporary debate in the study of Buddhist thought. There is a view that the *cittamātra* thought of Yogācāra-Vijñānavāda in fact is not setting out to contradict the ontology of Madhyamaka. Deep down they both hold that all things without exception are lacking in *svabhāva*. No thing, not even the 'mind' (*citta*) from which this approach gains its name, actually, finally, has any greater reality than any other, and all are *niḥsvabhāva*. I have long held that textually, historically and philosophically this is quite wrong. I once found a scholar working in Buddhist Studies express satisfaction that Yogācāra and Madhyamaka turned out to be holding the same ontology, since it brought Yogācāra into line with 'the eminently sensible Madhyamaka'. I have argued elsewhere that Madhyamaka should be seen as a stage in Abhidharma debate, and from an Abhidharma (Vaibhāṣika) perspective the Mādhyamika claim that all things are *niḥsvabhāva* equates with claiming that all things are conceptual constructs (*prajñaptisat*). It seems to me this would not have been seen to be sensible at all by the great majority of other Buddhist scholars, not to mention followers of other traditions, since it is a straightforward contradiction to claim that *all* things without exception are constructs. There has to be something which is not a construct in order for other things to be constructed out of it/them. Otherwise we in fact have no constructs at all, and this would have to be an ontological nihilism. This is precisely the accusation widely levelled at Madhyamaka in India. Within 'mainstream' Abhidharma those unconstructed things are called *dharmas*. Yogācāra tried another tactic with its recourse to a mentalistic factor (*citta*) which it saw as alone being that out of which other things are constructed. For all apart from the Mādhyamika these primary existents (*dravyas*) must exist in the fullest *possible* sense, in order for there to be anything at all. Thus they are indeed found under analysis. As primary existents they must have an ontologically more fundamental status than those things which are constructed out of them. This more fundamental status is also to exist *sasvabhava* ('with its own-being/own-nature'), and *for e.g. the Vaibhāṣika Abhidharma and Yogācāra this sasvabhāva status is enjoyed by the primary existents because they are primary existents, not because they are causally independent. It is the Mādhyamika who equates existing sasvabhāva with existing independently of causes and conditions. It is the Mādhyamika for whom sasvabhāva means 'with its own inherent existence'*. This is part of their 'absurd' reduction of everything to the status of conceptual constructs. Other traditions simply do not accept this absurdity, nor its absurd conclusions. Thus, for example, to point out that the Yogācāra *citta* is a causal flow does not entail that there is no ontological dispute with Madhyamaka. The issue is whether *citta* has the fullest possible sort of existence (i.e. is a *dravya*), or whether it has only conceptual existence (is *prajñaptisat*). In Madhyamaka, to be dependently originated is to be lacking in inherent existence (i.e. to be *niḥsvabhāva*), and therefore only conceptually existent (= not a *dravya*). But to be part of a causal flow is not in Yogācāra (*pace* Madhyamaka) to be *niḥsvabhāva*. Nor should it be, or we shall have nihilism. *Citta* in Yogācāra is a *dravya*, it exists *sasvabhāva*. Its existence is not simply *prajñaptisat*. These points are largely historical. Even as historical points, it does not seem obvious to me that on these ontological issues it is the Mādhyamika approach which is the sensible option. In terms of philosophical analysis, I have argued that pain – which is of course a mentalistic factor – *must* be found under analysis. Thus a mentalistic factor truly exists. To be found under analysis in Madhyamaka itself is to exist *sasvabhāva*. Thus I am arguing that *in this respect* it is incontrovertibly the case that Yogācāra was correct. There is at least one mental factor (pain) which has really real existence. In Buddhist terms it exists *sasvabhāva*. But no one wants to say that pain exists independently of causes and conditions. Thus we have to agree with the Abhidharma/Yogācāra denial of the Mādhyamika equation of existing *sasvabhāva* with existing independently of causes and conditions. The conflation of the two is simply confused. Now, to return to the Mādhyamika context. If 'not being found under ultimate analysis' *means* simply being found not to have uncaused (i.e. inherent) existence, then it becomes pretty trivial. Things are still left just as they are, and all things exist just in the ways in which it is possible for them to exist. The mountain is a mountain is a mountain, and no one actually claimed that it ever did exist independently of causes and conditions. If this is all that is meant, then no wonder that the Mādhyamika claims that all things are not found under ultimate analysis. The only analysis that is permitted to count as 'ultimate analysis' is that which enquires into whether or not *x* is the result in some way of causes and conditions. But there are nevertheless other ways of being found under analysis quite incontrovertibly to exist. The Mādhyamika has loaded the dice by defining 'being found under ultimate analysis' in terms of existing *inherently*, i.e. independently. (Nevertheless if 'not being found under ultimate analysis' actually means being found to be the result of causes and conditions then note that for *x* not to be found under analysis in this sense requires precisely that *x* does indeed exist, since if *x* does not exist it could not be the result of causes and conditions.) But on the other hand if 'not being found under analysis' means instead in some sense (as it appears to) something rather different, that the object of analysis is incoherent when subjected to the most rigorous form of critical probing, that 'it is lost' when examined closely, then *pain – a mentalistic factor – is and must be found under such ultimate analysis*. No matter how much pain is probed it is not lost. But pain does not exist inherently. It seems to me that it is up to the Mādhyamika to abandon any equation of being found under genuine critical analysis with existing inherently as being unhelpful and quite possibly intellectually incoherent.

87. In what follows I am indebted to the adverbial analysis of sensation statements particularly as crystallised by Chisholm (1957, Ch. 8, esp. p. 123) and developed with especial reference to pain statements by Tye (1984, 1989, 1995).
88. Note, there is nothing wrong with the grammar as such. Language, as Wittgenstein would say, is entirely in place. It is not paying sufficient attention to the way language works which can produce philosophical problems.

89. Of course, we could hold the view that pains are identical with brain processes, and at least in principle if the brain were opened it would be found that there is a distinctive brain process which *is* each pain. Thus a pain becomes a physical *event*. On pains as events see the next section. This brain-process analysis may turn out to be the case, although it is proving philosophically difficult to defend. Even if this were to show that *some* of these questions could be answered, it still would not make a pain a free-floating thing, and it thus would certainly not help Śāntideva, since a brain process is a process of a particular brain and is therefore necessarily a modification of a brain. As we shall see, *events* necessarily require subjects. Brains are different from each other, and are part of what constitutes a person. Thus a brain process is a modification of a person, and is just as parasitic on the person as is the adverbial analysis treated here.
90. To repeat, these are not actual recommendations for linguistic revision, but rather translations which bring out the *logical* grammar of the sentences involved. No one is saying that we ought actually to say 'I hurt knee-ly'. But if this is an adequate translation then we no longer *need* to ask what sort of thing a pain is since there is a perfectly meaningful way of saying *exactly* the same thing which does not require reference to pains at all. Actually, for my present purposes 'I hurt in my knee' will do just as well and does not require some strange English barbarism. Tye 1984, pp. 321–2 accepts the introduction of spatial regions like 'in my knee' within the framework of an adverbial analysis, and shows how nevertheless this does not fall foul of the 'pain in the trousers' paradox.
91. There is of course a noun 'hurt' which might be taken as an equivalent of 'pain'. But to think that because I hurt in my knee my knee should contain some occult thing called 'a hurt' is patently absurd – about as absurd as thinking that because I hurt in my knee (= I have a pain in my knee), my knee should contain something called 'a pain'!
92. Perhaps 'in general'? It seems clear to me that pains must be events if they are to be anything at all, and events are involved in the concept of change. But what of someone who claimed to have the very same pain throughout the whole of her life? Could one then say that the pain is a *change*? But on the other hand could one identify the pain if awareness of it were literally constant from birth to death and the awareness of it were completely unvarying? And what do we mean by talking about 'the same pain' here? It seems to me that to identify a pain at all must involve some *change* in some respect, even if only from directing attention to something else (awareness of pain *is* the pain). It must be capable of being distinguished from awareness of other sensations, and varying in degree. I doubt that a pain literally from birth to death and absolutely unwavering could be identified as a pain at all. Anyway, that is not how it is in most cases of pain. And note that our putative unwavering pain would not help Śāntideva. It is certainly meaningless to talk of an unwavering pain from birth to death without explicitly or implicitly involving the subject. Otherwise *whose* birth and death are we talking about? And unwavering for whom? We cannot say that the pain is unwavering from birth to death, but the concepts of birth and death

cannot be applied! There is also incidentally a more liberal view which would see a something's having or retaining a property as an event. This would not in itself be a change. But it seems to me that even if we take a state as an event (and I am not sure I would), a permanent state could not be an event. Thus the concept of an event is still bound-up with that of change, and correspondingly requires a subject. The 'non-relational change' referred to in the main text, incidentally, means a change which is not simply the result of something's changing relationships. Thus if Archibald started shorter than Freda, but Freda remains the same height and Archibald becomes taller than her, there is no event called 'becoming shorter than Archibald', which would have to be a change in Freda.

93. If that is the case then, of course, cause and effect are changes. Since changes, as we have seen, require subjects which persist for more than one moment (i.e. '*x* causes'; '*x* is an effect', require that *x* endures for longer than the moment of its causing or being an effect), it follows that a literally momentary entity simply could not be a cause or an effect. It becomes meaningless to talk of an entity which literally endures for only an instantaneous moment (whatever that may be) as a cause or an effect. If this is true, then it must provide problems for an ontology like that of Dharmakīrti which apparently would see reality as composed of a cause-effect series of absolutely instantaneous entities.

94. 'changes', 'is changing' are again Fregean functions requiring completion. If someone says to me 'changes' or 'is changing' I can make no sense whatsoever of what they are saying unless something tells me *what* changes, *what* is changing. The same applies to 'pains' or 'hurts'. If Śāntideva or anyone else thinks otherwise it is up to them to explain how they can make sense of 'is changing' without explicitly or implicitly involving a subject. Even for his meditation Śāntideva *must* do so, I am afraid! See Lombard 1986, pp. 240–2 for a discussion of whether there can be subjectless events. Lombard leaves open the hypothetical possibility, but he says that he cannot get a grip on the concept of an event which is not bound up with change, or a change which is not a change in a subject. Nor me, I think.

95. Remember also that we have seen already that there could not anyway be an instantaneous act of consciousness, and therefore an instantaneous pain sensation. A pain that lasted for just an instant, i.e. no time at all, could not be a pain. If we deny a temporal continuant then anyway there could be no pains.

96. Compare Galen Strawson's comment that 'if, per impossibile, there could be pain experience without an experiencer, there would be no point in stopping it, because no one would be suffering' (1994, p. 133) with Prajñākaramati's opponent in introducing *Bodhicaryāvatāra* 8:103: 'Someone might conceive an objection as follows: "So, if there does not exist anyone of whom there is pain in saṃsāra, that being the case pain would become something which is not to be destroyed. This is because there would not exist anyone of whom there is pain who could act as a receptacle for compassion".' (nanu yadi duḥkhī nāma na kaś cit saṃsāre saṃbhavati, tarhi duḥkham anivāryam eva syāt, kṛpāpātrasya duḥkhinaḥ kasya cid abhāvād ity āśaṅkamāna āha – [=Tib.] ci ste sdug bsngal

can 'ga' zhig kyang 'khor ba na gal te yod pa ma yin na / de lta na sdug bsngal bzlog par bya ba ma yin pa nyid du 'gyur te / snying rje'i zhing sdug bsngal can 'gal yang yod pa ma yin pa'i phyir zhes dogs nas /). Strawson and the opponent are quite right, and the reply in *Bodhicaryāvatāra* 8:103 will not work. The fact that we all do as a matter of fact engage in removing our own pains (even the materialist followers of Cārvāka, as Prajñākaramati points out) simply does not entail that, to be consistent, since there is no person we should also remove the pains of others. Quite the reverse. The fact that we all do engage in removing our own pains shows that there is indeed a person, and that persons are different. See also the comment by Vibhūticandra on *BCA* 8:103, which indicates the absurdity exactly: 'Being one in pain is not wanted by anyone. Saying that "I am in pain" is simply confusion.' (sdug bsngal can su'ang mi 'dod do // bdag sdug bsngal pa yin no zhes 'khrul pa kho na yod de). Unfortunately the confusion is that of Vibhūticandra. This is perhaps about as near to a contradiction as one can get!

97. I am influenced in all of this by the comment (I find completely convincing) by P.F. Strawson (1959, pp. 97–8): '[I]f we think . . . of the requirements of identifying reference in speech to *particular* states of consciousness, or private experiences, we see that such particulars cannot be thus identifyingly referred to except as the states or experiences *of* some identified *person*. States, or experiences, one might say, *owe* their identity as particulars to the identity of the person whose states or experiences they are. From this it follows immediately that if they can be identified as particular states or experiences at all, they must be possessed or ascribable in just that way which the no-ownership theorist ridicules; i.e. in such a way that it is logically impossible that a particular state or experience in fact possessed by someone should have been possessed by anyone else. The requirements of identity [*pace* Śāntideva] rule out logical transferability of ownership. So the theorist could maintain his position only by denying that we could ever refer to particular states or experiences at all; and *this* position is ridiculous' (italics original). What Strawson is saying *inter alia* is that if an experience lacks a *necessary* connection to the person who has that experience, then the experience cannot be referringly identified as being experience *x* at all. It thus could not be an experience. Strawson continues by noting that I cannot ascribe an experience to myself if I am unable also to ascribe it to others (p. 99). That is, only can I have the concept of pain if I can identify and reidentify cases of pain, and can distinguish cases of pain from other cases. But I can acquire an ability to identify pains, and indeed *my own* pains, only by ascribing cases of pain to others (apart from the conceptual point itself, how otherwise could we *learn* the use of pain-concepts?). Thus if I cannot ascribe pains to others then I cannot ascribe them to myself. But clearly I can ascribe pains to myself. Therefore I can also ascribe them to others. On Śāntideva's premisses it makes no sense to talk of self and others. Therefore absurdly we can make no sense of *our own* pains, and no sense of the pains of others.

98. See Priest 1991, Ch. 5, esp. pp. 134–5; pp. 141–5. On another popular contemporary view of mental states and therefore pains as supervening on brain-processes see Guttenplan 1994, p. 94. Under such circumstances it would make no sense to speak of pains apart from brains and therefore embodied individuals. It is also relevant to note the definition(s) of pain given by the pain-specialists Field and Price in Guttenplan 1994, pp. 452–3; 'Pain is an unpleasant sensory experience that is typically associated with bodily injury and/or is described by people using terms that imply bodily injury or damage. . . . "Pain" refers to a *subjective* experience, an unpleasant sensation, that is felt in a particular location within the body' (italics PW). And as another authority on pain, R. Melzack, has pointed out, pain is characteristically described using subjective expressions like 'throbbing, burning, or sharp', and it can be 'exhausting, wretched and punishing. Pain becomes overwhelming, demands immediate attention, and disrupts ongoing behaviour and thought. It motivates or drives the organism into activity aimed at stopping the pain as quickly as possible' (in Gregory 1987, p. 574). A pain is *essentially, by definition*, an occurrence in the history of a subject. A pain which, because it is free-floating, is divorced from its subjective basis simply cannot be a pain. Thus, again, we find that there is a *necessary* connection between a pain and the subject who is in pain. I take it that it is this necessary connection that Guttenplan means when he states that it is a conceptual point that we cannot conceive of an unowned pain, a subjectless belief, or an action without an agent (Guttenplan 1994, p. 15), and the same point that Galen Strawson (1994, p. 129) makes when he speaks of Frege's statement, that there cannot be an experience without an experiencer, as a necessary truth. This necessary connection between pain and the subject which is in pain means that in cases of pain we do not have to observe, and infer, who is actually undergoing the pain (see Campbell 1994, p. 169 and p. 197). When I am in pain I do not come to know that it is *me* by taking a look. I know that *I* am in pain simply by being in pain. Since there is this necessary connection, it would also be the same for Buddhas supposing that they underwent pains (it must be the case for their bliss-consciousnesses). Śāntideva cannot seriously think that the only reason we automatically ascribe a pain which is occurring to *ourselves* ('*my* pain') is because of beginningless ignorance (manifesting in karmic dispositions and so on) which, at some subliminal level taking a look, makes us ignorantly ascribe the pain to ourselves – and that very, very quickly indeed – although actually there is no such thing as *ourselves*. He cannot really think that we almost uncontrollably 'catch' a free-floating pain! Free-floating (subjectless) pains cannot exist in any possible world. And since pains really, really exist, any Buddhist thesis which denies the 'conventional self', the 'person' as their subject must be very, very mistaken. Here, at least, the dGe lugs tradition is absolutely right in its stress (under strong criticism from other Tibetan traditions) on the actual undeniable existence (albeit conventionally) of persons.
99. Incidentally, it then becomes very difficult to know what sense is to be made of claims found in the Diṅnāga-Dharmakīrti tradition that we

perceive the *svalakṣaṇa* in the very first moment of a perceptual act. How could one be said to *perceive* something which *itself in principle* could not be identified? This sounds like a contradiction.

100. Animals are not relevant here. I do not know what it is like to be a bat although I strongly suspect that bats do indeed experience something like pain. What it is to experience pain as a bat does, and whether this involves identification of it as 'pain', the subjection of it to a concept, I have no idea. Nor, I suspect, do you.

101. Note that, as we saw earlier, without an enduring person to do it, it is difficult to see what sense we can make of the application of a concept or indeed *reidentification* of pain.

102. See Lowe 1995, p. 116 on Locke. The identity of a pain depends upon the identity of the substance which has it. For our purposes here, the 'substance' which has pains is what I have called the person. In terms of the way in which pains are dependent on the subjects which possess them, unlike substances, we can note (using an expression derived from Husserl) that pains are 'strongly' dependent on their subjects: 'An object *a* is strongly dependent on an object *b* if necessarily, if *a* exists, so does *b*, and *b* is neither *a* nor part of *a*' (Simons, in Kim and Sosa 1995, p. 482). This contrasts with a weaker form of dependence. Note the necessary connection here again. If we can refer once more to pains as events, there has been one important attempt to identify events without reference to subjects or suchlike which might be thought to be of some use to the Buddhist. Donald Davidson (1980) has suggested that events can be identified in terms of their causes and effects, and said to be identical if they have the same causes and the same effects. This is a complex issue, but suffice to say that Davidson has now abandoned his cause/effect criterion and replaced it with one where events can be identified with reference to place and time, and are identical if they occupy exactly the same places at exactly the same time. Unfortunately this is not going to help with pains, since if we are to identify pains with reference to their places and times this can only be with reference to their subjects – persons or bodies or whatever. Moreover even if Davidson had not abandoned his previous explanation, he would have had to include references to persons, bodies and so on in explaining pains, since clearly it is impossible to identify the causes and effects of pains without reference to persons, bodies etc. (see Lowe 1989, p. 131).

103. Clearly, there simply *is* a difference between me being in pain *now* and others in pain now. Indeed it is because I experience my own pains as unpleasant that I know that others find pains unpleasant too. If I want to remove the pains of others it is because there are others who experience them as pains. If I want to remove future pains it is not because future pains will be pain, but because future pains will be pains for someone. See Madell 1981, p. 113.

104. For a straightforward introduction to 'no entity without identity' and so on, together with its Fregean context, see Benardete 1989, Ch. 21 esp. pp. 155–6. For criticisms of Quine's slogan see Hamlyn 1984, pp. 57–9.

105. That without self (indeed Self) and other there can be no sensations like pain appears to be accepted by dPa' bo gTsug lag phreng ba in his

commentary to *BCA* 8:102: 'Therefore, because no 'self' is apprehended really (or 'as real'), there is not apprehended also an 'other' in mutual correlation. That being the case, having calmed by nature verbal differentiations and characteristics, all dharmas being without distinction, there is not apprehended self and other which are the basis for distinction, and indeed pleasure and pain which are the distinguished qualities' (des na yang dag par na bdag mi dmigs pas ltos zla gzhan yang mi dmigs cing spros mtshan ngo bo nyid gyis zhi bar chos *thams cad bye brag med pa*s khyad gzhi bdag gzhan dang khyad chos bde sdug nyid kyang dmigs su med la).

106. There are other contexts where it might be argued that a bodhisattva would be at a disadvantage in not being able to administer pain. One thinks of cases like killing Hitler, or the commander and guards of a concentration camp in a context where all the inmates could successfully escape, or the use of pain as punishment. Note that the bodhisattva would also actively intervene to *remove* the pain inflicted with laudable intentions by others in these contexts. But it is at least arguable that there are cases and contexts where pain is appropriate for beneficial ends. This would seem to fit rather well with the notion of skill-in-means (*upāyakauśalya*), which is of course central to the Mahāyāna path. Unfortunately, on Śāntideva's premisses it would seem that the bodhisattva precisely cannot take into consideration the individual cases in this way, at least where the individual cases require reference (as they usually do) to the persons involved. But the example of morphine poisoning is particularly unanswerable since it would appear difficult for even a fully-enlightened Buddha to help a person with morphine poisoning without actually *giving* pain. It is the actual pain which is the cure. And I doubt it could be argued that the situation would not arise for a Buddha could prevent morphine poisoning occurring (or soak up the excess morphine by other means) since, apart from the question of free-will, it is difficult to see how one can prevent morphine poisoning without any reference to persons. On morphine poisoning see Dennett 1978, p. 196.

107. Note that the same follows here even on the traditional Buddhist view of momentariness and no Self, without Śāntideva's extreme no-subject perspective. The fact that a future person will bear, and even bear uniquely, a particular causal relationship to me does not in itself give any reason why I should care for the welfare of that person, or make plans which will involve the activities of that person. It certainly makes no sense whatsoever for me to attempt to bind that person into a series of moral commitments. On this basis when I take the bodhisattva vow to work for the welfare of all sentient beings through three incalculable aeons I am doing something which is not only irrational but incoherent. Since it will not be *me* (I shall not be the same person) in even the next lifetime, it can make no sense for me to make a vow which will bind that future person, and I can have no allegiance to vows made by previous persons even if they are uniquely related to me by some impersonal causal process. Cf. here the much less extreme case given in Stone 1988, p. 529 (italics original): 'Suppose someone says to me, "Several people

will be shot at dawn and some of them will resemble you." I feel sadness, nothing more. He adds, "One of these people will resemble you because there is a causal connection between you and him which causes him to resemble you." This is interesting but still no cause for alarm. He says, "Further, no other person will stand in this relation to you." Still, no cause for terror. But *this* is all that the fact that identity comes to, on the Reductionist account. So the fact that I will be shot at dawn no longer makes it rational to fear or even anticipate the execution.' For Stone, who is in favour of an extreme form of no-subject reductionism which he calls 'eliminativism' into which he thinks reductionism will collapse under the pressure of rationality, this conclusion is indeed appropriate. We have to accept that such fear, as indeed pride and remorse, commitments, obligations, and rights through time (see p. 530), are indeed irrational. Cf. also Campbell 1994, p. 170 – without persons there could be no appeal to pride, shame or autobiographical memory. But note that all this would be fatal *inter alia* to the bodhisattva project or even to concern for future lives. It would also have some rather dramatic implications for ordinary morality. Stone agrees with Locke that it is persons (which do not exist) which are morally interesting. Thus 'if Reductionism is true there are no persons. Either persons are extra, or there aren't any persons and deontological ethics and prudence lacks a subject matter. Reductionism, which affirms the existence of persons while denying they are something extra, is incoherent. . . . If Reductionism is true, . . . it is never rational for me to anticipate an experience I know a future person will have. . . it is never rational for me to regret performing an act I know a past being performed.' Stone accepts all these implications, and advocates 'eliminativism': 'we need to face the fact that we don't exist.' But later he adds: 'Probably we are very transient: If we exist at all we come and go in a moment. . . . I suspect this is the truth about us and that it is the inevitable consequence of science and empiricism, but how one lives with the truth I don't know.' (p. 532). Stone himself sees this as the position of the Buddha (as well as Hume). Whether it is or not, unfortunately it would be quite incompatible with the bodhisattva path. One way one could *not* live with this truth is to advocate the Buddhist path. That would be deeply incoherent. (No amount of appeal to two truths would help, since it is the persons of the conventional truth which we are trying to explain, and we have just learnt that persons are simply irrational. It is conventional persons which do not exist.) Thus one could not actually *become* a Buddha if this were true. One suspects Śāntideva would be horrified. Thub bstan chos kyi grags pa (p. 535) gives a lengthy quote from Sa skya paṇḍita in which he points out that since we are changing all the time, it should be unreasonable to concern ourselves with 'our own' futures. They are actually the futures of another. Yet we do so concern ourselves. Thus, on the same basis, we should concern ourselves with contemporary others. But even if true all this entails is that in everyday life we behave absurdly, irrationally. We should *not* concern ourselves with 'our' futures. If we are to be properly rational, as the bodhisattva is exhorted to be, we should train ourselves in 'disregard for the morrow', or even for the next hour. If this seems absurd and itself irrational, perhaps there is something wrong with the analysis which holds that we are changing all the time and therefore we are constantly becoming different persons. Otherwise, the fact that we are absurd and irrational in concerning ourselves with the future does not entail that we should also be *further* absurd and irrational in concerning ourselves with contemporary others. If the former irrationality is difficult to overcome, that is no reason for adding a further irrationality to our problems. Sa skya paṇḍita's conclusions simply do not follow.

108. Of course, I agree that it is difficult to pin down an exact sense to speaking of the quality, and particularly the quantity, of a pain. But that difficulty is not relevant here. Perhaps a Buddha can do it!

109. Well, the bodhisattva should not kill. But why not, if killing leads to the removal of some pain? (There are stories in Mahāyāna Buddhist literature (such as the *Upāyakauśalya Sūtra*) of bodhisattvas killing, employing skill-in-means, out of their selfless and compassionate motivation and for the benefit of others. See Williams 1989b.) How can the wrongness of killing the babies in order to remove pain be specified without reference directly or indirectly to persons?

110. It could be argued that in these conditions the pains would continue in some after-death state, until the full 'quota' of pain due to karmic causes has been experienced. Thus nothing would be gained in terms of pain-reduction through the bodhisattva killing the person. But this would not occur if the drug is taken when it becomes available. I am not sure I can make much sense on the Buddhist premisses of *physical* pains occurring to the very same person x after the death of that person, but anyway, some explanation has to be given nevertheless as to why in that case the same argument could not equally be applied to taking the drug. Arguably it too will only block pains which are one's due, and which will reoccur later (I have heard a Tibetan use this very argument against taking Western painkillers, although that same Tibetan seemed quite happy to use Tibetan medicine). Some explanation has to be given as to why being killed is intrinsically different from taking a drug as a means of pain reduction. Anyway, even if it is true that one could on Buddhist premisses continue to suffer in an after-death state, to take this into consideration involves the bodhisattva taking into consideration the person and his or her circumstances, rather than simply removing free-floating pains. And as an alternative, consider the case where the person could be put into a state of complete and irreversible unconsciousness, suspended animation, but not actual death, with no significant brain activity. Thus pains due in the after-death state would not occur, since death has not yet occurred. This state is irreversible, so it will end only at death. Presumably it is at that time that the after-death state will start. Since this state of complete unconsciousness will involve no pain, on Śāntideva's argument it would be preferable for the bodhisattva to place the person in pain into that state rather than wait six months for the cure. Knocking out the patient in this manner would definitely remove all pain immediately. (Presumably also Śāntideva's bodhisattva would

favour any drug which we could all take which permanently removed pain, regardless of any consequences which stemmed from 'person-implicating' factors. Readers could perhaps think up some of their own examples.)

Bibliography

Unless otherwise noted, all Tibetan bsTan 'gyur texts are from the microfiche edition produced by The Institute for Advanced Studies of World Religions, New York.

Anonymous. *Bodhisattvacaryāvatāravivṛti*, Cone mDo 27, folio 177b ff. Commentary to chapters 9 and 10.

Aristotle 1995. *Selections*, translated with introduction, notes and glossary by Terence Irwin and Gail Fine, Indianapolis/Cambridge (Hackett).

Ayers, M. 1991. *Locke: Volume II: Ontology*, London/New York (Routledge).

Barnes, J. 1979. *The Presocratic Philosophers: Volume 1 – Thales to Zeno*, London, Henley and Boston (Routledge and Kegan Paul).

Batchelor, S. 1979. *A Guide to the Bodhisattva's Way of Life*, Dharamsala (Library of Tibetan Works and Archives).

Benardete, J.A. 1989. *Metaphysics: The Logical Approach*, Oxford/New York (Oxford University Press).

Blackmore, S. 1991. 'Beyond the self: the escape from reincarnation in Buddhism and psychology', in Arthur and Joyce Berger, ed., *Reincarnation: Fact or Fable*, London (The Aquarian Press).

Buddhaghosa 1964. *Visuddhimagga*, trans. by Ñāṇamoli in *Path of Purification*, Colombo (Semage). Also reprinted in 2 vols., 1976, Berkeley, Cal. (Shambhala).

Burnyeat, M. 1990. *The Theaetetus of Plato*, Indianapolis (Hackett).

Bu ston 1971. *Byang chub sems dpa'i spyod pa la 'jug pa'i 'grel pa Byang chub kyi sems gsal bar byed pa zla ba'i 'od zer*, included in Lokesh Chandra ed., *The Collected Works of Bu-ston*, part 19 (Dza), Sata-Pitaka Series vol. 59, New Delhi (International Academy of Indian Culture).

Cabezón, J. 1992. *A Dose of Emptiness: An annotated translaton of the sTong thun chen mo of mKhas grub dGe legs dpal bzang*, Albany, N.Y. (SUNY Press).

Campbell, J. 1994. *Past, Space, and Self*, Cambridge, Mass./London (MIT Press).

Candrakīrti 1978. *Madhyamakāvatārakārikā*, in *mNgon rtogs rgyan dang dBu ma 'jug pa mDzod rtsa ba bcas bzhugs so*, Sarnath (Legs bshad gter mdzod par khang).

Candrakīrti. *Madhyamakāvatārabhāṣya,* Cone mDo 23, folio 217a ff. For the *Prasannapadā* see Nāgārjuna.
Chisholm, R.M. 1957. *Perceiving: A Philosophical Study*, Ithaca/London (Cornell University Press).
Chisholm, R.M. 1969. 'On the observability of the self', *Philosophy and Phenomenological Research* 30: 7–21.
Chisholm, R.M. 1976. *Person and Object: A Metaphysical Study*, London (George Allen and Unwin).
Collins, S. 1982. *Selfless Persons*, Cambridge (Cambridge University Press).
Dalai Lama, First 1987. *dBu ma rtsa shes rtsa 'grel*, Sarnath (Central Institute of Higher Tibetan Studies).
Dalai Lama, Fifth 1976. *Practice of Emptiness,* trans. Jeffrey Hopkins, Dharamsala (Library of Tibetan Works and Archives).
Dalai Lama, Fourteenth 1988. *Transcendent Wisdom*, Ithaca, N.Y. (Snow Lion).
Damasio, A.R. 1995. *Descartes' Error: Emotion, Reason and the Human Brain*, London (Picador).
Davidson, D. 1980. *Essays on Actions and Events*, Oxford (Oxford University Press).
Dennett, D.C. 1978. *Brainstorms: Philosophical Essays on Mind and Psychology*, Montgomery, VT (Bradford).
Doboom Tulku 1985. 'Tathāgatagarbha', *Dreloma* 14: 24–8.
Gillett, G. 1987. 'Reasoning about persons', in Peacocke and Gillett pp. 75–88.
Glover, J. 1991 reprint. *I: The Philosophy and Psychology of Personal Identity*, London, New York, Ringwood, Toronto, and Auckland (Penguin Books).
Gregory, R.L., ed. 1987. *The Oxford Companion to the Mind*, Oxford/New York (Oxford University Press).
Guttenplan, S., ed. 1994. *A Companion to the Philosophy of Mind*, Oxford/Cambridge, Mass. (Blackwell).
rGyal tshab rje 1973. *Byang chub sems dpa'i spyod pa la 'jug pa'i rnam bshad rGyal sras 'jug ngogs*, Sarnath (Pleasure of Elegant Sayings Printing Press).
Gyatso, Geshe Kelsang 1980. *Meaningful to Behold*, Ulverston (Wisdom Publications).
Hamlyn, D.W. 1984. *Metaphysics*, Cambridge (Cambridge University Press).
Hankinson, R.J. 1995. *The Sceptics*, London/New York (Routledge).
Harré, R. 1987. 'Persons and selves', in Peacocke and Gillett pp. 99–115.
Hodgson, D. 1991. *The Mind Matters: Consciousness and Choice in a Quantum World*, Oxford/New York (Oxford University Press).
Honderich, T., ed. 1995. *The Oxford Companion to Philosophy*, Oxford/New York (Oxford University Press).
Hookham, S.K. 1990. *The Buddha Within: Tathāgatagarbha Doctrine according to the Shen-tong interpretation of the Ratnagotravibhāga*, New York (SUNY Press).
Hopkins, J. 1983. *Meditation on Emptiness*, London (Wisdom).
Hopkins, J. 1987. *Emptiness Yoga*, Ithaca, N.Y. (Snow Lion).
Hume, D. 1969. *A Treatise of Human Nature*, edited with an introduction by Ernest G. Mossner, Harmondsworth (Penguin Books).

Jackson, D. 1985. 'Madhyamaka studies among the early Sa-skya-pas', *The Tibet Journal* X:2: 20–34.
Kalyāṇadeva. *Bodhisattvacaryāvatārasaṃskāra*, Cone mDo 27, folio 1 ff.
Kamalaśīla 1968. *Tattvasaṃgrahapañjikā*, in the *Tattvasaṅgraha of Ācārya Shāntarakṣita with the commentary 'Pañjikā' of Shri Kamalashīla*, critically edited by Swami Dwarikadas Shastri, 2 Volumes, Varanasi (Bauddha Bharati).
Kant, I. 1968. *Immanuel Kant's Critique of Pure Reason*, trans. Norman Kemp Smith, London/Melbourne/Toronto (Macmillan).
Kenny, A. 1995. *Frege*, London, New York, Ringwood, Toronto and Auckland (Penguin Books).
Kim, J., and Sosa, E., ed. 1995. *A Companion to Metaphysics*, Oxford/Cambridge, Mass. (Blackwell).
Klein, A. 1986. *Knowledge and Liberation*, Ithaca, N.Y. (Snow Lion).
dKon mchog 'jigs med dbang po 1971. *Grub pa'i mtha''i rnam par bzhag pa rin po che'i phreng ba* in *The Collected Works of dKon mchog 'jigs med dbang po*, Gedan Sungrab Minyam Gyunphel Series 26, Volume 6, Delhi (Ngawang Gelek Demo).
Kun bzang dpal ldan 1989. *Byang chub sems dpa'i spyod pa la 'jug pa'i tshig 'grel 'Jam dbyangs bla ma'i zhal lung bdud rtsi'i thig pa*, Delhi (Konchhog Lhadrepa).
Lindtner, Chr. 1982. *Nagarjuniana: Studies in the writings and philosophy of Nāgārjuna*, Copenhagen (Akademisk Forlag).
Locke, J. 1977. *An Essay Converning Human Understanding*, abridged and edited with an introduction by John W. Yolton, London, Melbourne and Toronto (Dent).
Lombard, L.B. 1986. *Events: A Metaphysical Study*, London, Boston and Henley (Routledge and Kegan Paul).
Lowe, E.J. 1989. *Kinds of Being: A Study of Individuation, Identity, and the Logic of Sortal Terms*, Aristotelian Society Series, Volume 10, Oxford/New York (Basil Blackwell).
Lowe, E.J. 1991. 'Real selves: Persons as a substantial kind', in D. Cockburn, ed. *Human Beings*, Royal Institute of Philosophy Supplement: 29 – Supplement to *Philosophy* 1991, Cambridge (Cambridge University Press).
Lowe, E.J. 1995. *Locke: On Human Understanding*, London/New York (Routledge).
Madell, G. 1981. *The Identity of the Self*, Edinburgh (Edinburgh University Press).
Manusmṛti 1990. *Manusmṛti, with the Sanskrit commentary Manvarthamuktāvalī of Kullūka Bhaṭṭa*, edited by J.L. Shastri, with English introduction by S.C. Banerji, Delhi (Motilal Banarsidass).
May, J. 1959. *Candrakīrti Prasannapadā Madhyamakavṛtti*, Paris (Adrien-Maisonneuve).
Mi bskyod rdo rje, Eighth Karma pa. *dBu ma gzhan stong smra ba'i srol legs par phye ba'i sgron me*, Delhi, no date or publisher.
Mi pham 1975. *Spyod 'jug shes rab kyi le'u'i tshig don go sla bar rnam par bshad pa Nor bu ke ta ka*, contained in the *Collected Writings of 'Jam mgon 'ju Mi pham rgya mtsho*, vol. 13, Gangtog (Ngagyur Nyingmay Sungrab Series).

Nāgārjuna 1960. *Madhyamakaśāstra of Nāgārjuna with the commentary: Prasannapadā by Candrakīrti*, ed. P.L. Vaidya, Darbhanga (Mithila Institute). Also includes the text of Nāgārjuna's *Vigrahavyāvartanī*.

Nāgārjuna 1977. *Mūladhyamakakārikāḥ*, ed. J.W. de Jong, Madras (Adyar Library and Research Centre).

Napper, E. 1989. *Dependent Arising and Emptiness*, Boston (Wisdom).

Newland, G. 1992. *The Two Truths*. Ithaca, N.Y. (Snow Lion).

dPa' bo gTsug lag phreng ba 1975. *Byang chub sems dpa'i spyod 'jug rnam bshad Theg chen chos kyi rgya mtsho zab rgyas mtha' yas snying po*, apparently published in Delhi by the rGyal ba Karma pa's Rumtek monastery.

Padma dkar po 1982. *Spyod 'jug 'bru 'grel dBu ma'i lam gyi sgron ma*, Sarnath (Central Institute of Higher Tibetan Studies).

Parfit, D. 1971. 'Personal identity', *Philosophical Review* 80:1.

Parfit, D. 1984. *Reasons and Persons*, Oxford/New York (Oxford University Press).

Peacocke, A.R., and Gillett, G., ed. 1987. *Persons and Personality*, Oxford/ New York (Blackwell).

Penelhum, T. 1968. 'Hume on personal identity', in V.C. Chappell, ed. *Hume: A Collection of Critical Essays*, London/Melbourne (Macmillan).

Perdue, D. 1992. *Debate in Tibetan Buddhism*, Ithaca, N.Y. (Snow Lion).

Prajñākaramati. *Bodhicaryāvatārapañjikā*, ed. P.L. Vaidya. See under Śāntideva. Tibetan Cone mDo vol. 26, folio 39a ff.

Priest, S. 1991. *Theories of the Mind*, London, New York, Ringwood, Toronto and Auckland (Penguin Books).

Quine, W.V.O. 1963. *From a Logical Point of View*, Second edition, New York (Harper and Row).

Rabten, Geshe, 1978. *The Mind and its Functions*, Mt Pelerin (Tharpa Choeling).

Radhakrishnan, S., and Moore, C.A. 1967 reprint. *A Sourcebook in Indian Philosophy*, Princeton N.J. (Princeton University Press).

Rong ston 1979. *Chos dang chos nyid rnam par 'byed pa'i rnam bshad Legs par 'doms pa lha'i rnga bo che*, published together with Rong ston pa's *dBus dang mtha' rnam par 'byed pa'i rnam bshad Mi pham dgongs rgyan*, Delhi (T.G. Dhongthog Rinpoche).

Ruegg, D.S. 1963. 'The Jo naṅ pas: A school of Buddhist ontologists according to the *Grub mtha' shel gyi me loṅ*', *Journal of the American Oriental Society* 83: 73–91.

Ruegg, D.S. 1969. *La Théorie du Tathāgatagarbha et du Gotra*, Paris (École Française d 'Extrême-Orient).

Ruegg, D.S. 1981a. 'On the thesis and assertion in the Madhyamaka/dBu ma' in Ernst Steinkellner and Helmut Tauscher ed., *Contributions on Tibetan and Buddhist Religion and Philosophy: Proceedings of the Csoma de Körös Symposium 1981*, Volume 2, Wien (Arbeitskreis für Tibetische und Buddhistische Studien Universität Wien).

Ruegg, D.S. 1981b. *The Literature of the Madhyamaka School of Philosophy in India*, Wiesbaden (Otto Harrassowitz). This is vol.VII, fasc.1 of Jan Gonda ed., *A History of Indian Literature*.

Ruegg, D.S. 1991. 'On *pramāṇa* theory in Tsoṅ kha pa's Madhyamaka philosophy', Ernst Steinkellner, ed., *Studies in the Buddhist Epistemologi-*

cal Tradition, Wien (Verlag der Österreichischen Akademie der Wissenschaften).
Sa bzang mati paṇchen 1975. *Byang chub sems dpa'i spyod pa la 'jug pa'i rnam bshad gZhung don rab gsal snang ba*, New Delhi (Distributed by the Tibetan Bonpo Monastic Centre, Dolanji, H.P.).
Sacks, O. 1986. *The Man Who Mistook His Wife for a Hat*, London (Picador).
Saito, A. 1993. *A Study of Akṣayamati (= Śāntideva)'s Bodhisattvacaryāvatāra as found in the Tibetan Manuscripts from Tun-huang*. A Report of the Grant-in-Aid for Scientific Research. Miye University: Faculty of Humanities.
Samādhirājasūtra 1961. Ed. P.L. Vaidya, Darbhanga (Mithila Institute).
Śāntideva 1960. *Bodhicaryāvatāra of Śāntideva with the commentary Pañjikā of Prajñākaramati*, ed. P.L. Vaidya, Darbhanga (Mithila Institute).
Śāntideva 1982. *Byang chub sems dpa'i spyod pa la 'jug pa'i rtsa ba dang 'grel pa Legs par bshad pa'i rgya mtsho*, Sarnath (Sakya Students' Union).
Śāntideva 1996. *Śāntideva: The Bodhicaryāvatāra*, translated with introduction and notes by Kate Crosby and Andrew Skilton, with a general introduction by Paul Williams, Oxford/New York (Oxford University Press).
Scruton, R. 1982. *Kant*, Oxford/New York (Oxford University Press).
Searle, J.R. 1992. *The Rediscovery of the Mind*, Cambridge, Mass./London (MIT Press).
Searle, J.R. 1995. *The Construction of Social Reality*, London, New York, Ringwood, Toronto and Auckland (Allen Lane: The Penguin Press).
Shākya mchog ldan 1975. *dBu ma'i byung tshul*, in the *Collected Works (gsung-'bum) of Gser mdog Paṇ chen Śākya mchog ldan*, vol. 4, Thimphu (Kunzang Tobgey).
Shoemaker, S. 1985. 'Critical notice: *Reasons and Persons* by Derek Parfit', *Mind* n.s. 94: 443–53.
bSod nams rtse mo 1968. *Byang chub sems dpa'i spyod pa la 'jug pa'i 'grel pa* contained in the *Sa skya pa'i bka' 'bum*, vol. 2, Tokyo (Toyo Bunko).
Stone, J. 1988. 'Parfit and the Buddha – why there are no people', *Philosophy and Phenomenological Research* 48, 3: 519–32.
Strawson, G. 1994. *Mental Reality*, Cambridge, Mass./London (MIT Press).
Strawson, P.F. 1959. *Individuals: An Essay in Descriptive Metaphysics*, London (Methuen).
Stroud, B. 1977. *Hume*, London, Henley and Boston (Routledge and Kegan Paul).
Tāranātha 1970. *Tāranātha's History of Buddhism in India*, trans. Lama Chimpa and Alaka Chattopadhyaya, edited by Debiprasad Chattopadhyaya, Simla (Indian Institute of Advanced Study).
Tauscher, H. 1990/91. 'Saṃvṛti bei Tsoṅ kha pa', *Wiener Zeitschrift für die Kunde Südasiens und Archiv für Indische Philosophie*, Band 34: 227–54 and Band 35: 169–202.
Tetley, N. 1990. *The Doctrine of Rebirth in Theravāda Buddhism: Arguments for and Against*, unpublished PhD thesis, University of Bristol.
Thogs med, rGyal sras dNgul chu 1982. *Byang chub sems dpa'i spyod pa la 'jug pa'i 'grel pa Legs par bshad pa'i rgya mtsho*, Sarnath (Sakya Students Union).

Thub bstan chos kyi grags pa (= Mi nyag Kun bzang bsod nams). 1990. *Spyod 'jug gi 'grel bshad rGyal sras yon tan bum bzang*. Beijing: Krung go'i bod kyi shes rig dpe skrun khang.

Thurman, R.A.F. 1984. *Tsong Khapa's Speech of Gold in the* Essence of True Eloquence, Princeton, N. J. (Princeton University Press).

Tsong kha pa 1972. *Lam rim chen mo of the incomparable Tsong kha pa, with the interlineal notes of Ba so Chos kyi rgyal mtshan, Sde drug Mkhan chen Ngag dbang rab brtan, 'Jam dbyangs bzhad pa'i rdo rje, and Bra sti Dge bshes Rin chen don grub*, New Delhi (Chos 'phel legs ldan).

Tsong kha pa 1973. *Drang nges legs bshad snying po,* Sarnath (Pleasure of Elegant Sayings Printing Press).

Tsong kha pa 1990. *mNyam med Tsong kha pa chen pos mdzad pa'i Byang chub lam rim che ba*, originally published in China by the mTsho sngon mi rigs dpe skrun khang, reprinted New Delhi (Sherab Gyaltsen).

Tsong kha pa 1991. *Drang nges legs bshad snying po: The Essence of Eloquent Speech on the Definitive and Interpretable*, edited by Geshes Palden Drakpa and Damdul Namgyal, Mundgod (SOKU Publications).

Tsong kha pa. *sDe bdun la 'jug pa'i sgo Don gnyer yid kyi mun sel*, contained in the microfiche *Yab sras gsung 'bum,* vol. 18 (Tsha), New York (The Institute for Advanced Studies of World Religions).

Tsong kha pa. *Legs bshad gser phreng*, contained in the microfiche *Yab sras gsung 'bum,* vol.44 (Tsa), New York (The Institute for Advanced Studies of World Religions).

Tsong kha pa. *sPyod 'jug shes rab le'u'i ṭikkā bLo gsal ba*, contained in the *bTsong kha pa bKa' 'bum* published with the Japanese reprint of the Peking edition of the Tibetan Tripitaka, Tokyo-Kyoto, vol. 153.

Tsong kha pa. *Shes rab le'u'i zin bris*, contained in the microfiche *Yab sras gsung 'bum,* vol. Pha, New York (The Institute for Advanced Studies of World Religions).

Tye, M. 1984. 'Pain and the adverbial theory', *American Philosophical Quarterly* 21, 4: 319–27.

Tye, M. 1989. *The Metaphysics of Mind*, Cambridge, New York, New Rochelle, Melbourne and Sydney (Cambridge University Press).

Tye, M. 1995. 'Adverbial theory', in Kim and Sosa, ed. pp. 7–8.

Vairocanarakṣita. *Bodhisattvacaryāvatārapañjikā*, Cone mDo 27, folio 95b ff.

van der Kuijp, L. 1983. *Contributions to the Development of Tibetan Buddhist Epistemology*, Alt- und Neu-Indische Studien herausgegeben vom Seminar für Kultur und Geschichte Indiens an der Universität Hamburg 26, Wiesbaden (Franz Steiner Verlag).

van Inwagen, P. 1990. *Material Beings*, Ithaca/London (Cornell University Press).

Vibhūticandra. *Bodhicaryāvatāratātparyapañjikā Viśeṣadyotanī*, Cone mDo 27, folio 192b ff.

Wiggins, D. 1980. *Sameness and Substance*, Oxford (Basil Blackwell).

Wiggins, D. 1987. 'The person as object of science, as subject of experience, and as locus of value', in Peacocke and Gillett pp. 56–74.

Wiggins, D. 1995. 'Substance', in A.C. Grayling, ed. *Philosophy: A Guide through the Subject*, Oxford/New York (Oxford University Press), 214–49.

Williams, B. 1978. *Descartes: The Project of Pure Enquiry*, Harmondsworth (Penguin Books).

Williams, P. 1980a. 'Tsong-kha-pa on *kun-rdzob bden-pa*' in Michael Aris and Aung San Suu Kyi ed., *Tibetan Studies in Honour of Hugh Richardson*, Warminster (Aris and Phillips), 325–34.

Williams, P. 1980b. 'Some aspects of language and construction in the Madhyamaka', *Journal of Indian Philosophy* 8: 1–45.

Williams, P. 1981. 'On the Abhidharma ontology', *Journal of Indian Philosophy* 9: 227–257.

Williams, P. 1982. 'Silence and truth – some aspects of the Madhyamaka philosophy in Tibet', *The Tibet Journal*, VII:1/2: 67–80.

Williams, P. 1983a. 'A note on some aspects of Mi bskyod rdo rje's critique of dGe lugs pa Madhyamaka', *Journal of Indian Philosophy* 11: 125–45.

Williams, P. 1983b. 'On rang rig', in Ernst Steinkellner and Helmut Tauscher ed., *Contributions on Tibetan and Buddhist Religion and Philosophy*, Wien: Arbeitskreis für Tibetische and Buddistische Studien Universität Wien, Wiener Studien zur Tibetologie und Buddhismuskunde Heft 11: 321–32.

Williams, P. 1985. 'rMa bya pa Byang chub brtson 'grus on Madhyamaka method', *Journal of Indian Philosophy* 13: 205–25.

Williams, P. 1989a. 'Introduction some random reflections on the study of Tibetan Madhyamaka', *The Tibet Journal*, X1V:1: 1–9.

Williams, P. 1989b. *Mahāyāna Buddhism: The doctrinal foundations*, London (Routledge).

Williams, P. 1992a. 'Non-conceptuality, critical reasoning and religious experience. Some Tibetan Buddhist discussions', in Michael McGhee ed., *Philosophy, Religion and the Spiritual Life*, Cambridge, Philosophy Supplement 32 (Cambridge University Press).

Williams, P. 1992b. 'On *prakṛtinirvāṇa/prakṛtinirvṛta* in the *Bodhicaryāvatāra*: A study in the Indo-Tibetan commentarial tradition', *Asiatische Studien/Études Asiatiques* XLVI:I: 516–550 (reprinted in the present volume).

Williams, P. 1996. *A Tibetan Madhyamaka Defence of the Reflexive Nature of Awareness* (rang rig)*: Mi pham's* Nor bu ke ta ka *commentary on* Bodhicaryāvatāra *9:26 (Tib. 25) in context and controversy*, Taipei (Jin Luen Publishing). To be reissued 1997 with Curzon Press, London as *The Reflexive Nature of Awareness* (*Rang Rig*).

Williams, P. forthcoming. 'Mahāyāna Buddhism in India: a doctrinal overview', in P. Williams *et al.*, *Buddhist Thought in India: An Introduction.*

Wilson, J. 1980. *Chandrakīrti's Sevenfold Reasoning: Meditation on the Selflessness of Persons*, Dharamsala (Library of Tibetan Works and Archives).

Yaśomitra, 1977. *Abhisamayālaṅkāravṛttiḥ Sphuṭārthā*, ed. Samdong Rinpoche and Ramaśaṅkara Tripāṭhi, Bibliotheca Indo-Tibetica 2, Sarnath/Varanasi (Kendriya-Tibbatī-Ucca-Śikṣā-Saṃsthānam).

Yoshimizu, C. 1993. 'The Madhyamaka theories regarded as false by the dGe lugs pas', *Wiener Zeitschrift für die Kunde Südasiens und Archiv für Indische Philosophie* 37: 201–27.

gZhan phan Chos kyi snang ba, mKhan po 1989. *Byang chub sems dpa'i spyod pa la 'jug pa zhes bya ba'i mchan 'grel*, Delhi (Konchhog Lhadrepa).

Index